John Elias

LIFE, LETTERS AND ESSAYS

£1-95

John Elias

John Elias

LIFE, LETTERS AND ESSAYS

Edward Morgan

THE BANNER OF
TRUTH TRUST

THE BANNER OF TRUTH TRUST
3 Murrayfield Road, Edinburgh EH 12 6EL
78b Chiltern Street, London WIM IPS
P.O. Box 652, Carlisle, Penna 17013, U.S.A.

© 1973 The Banner of Truth Trust
Memoir of John Elias first published 1844
Letters Essays and Other Papers first published 1847
This revised edition of the above published
in one volume 1973

ISBN 0 85151 174 0

Set in 11 on 13 point Monotype Plantin 110
and printed in Great Britain by
Billing & Sons Limited, Guildford and London

Contents

ESSAYS

OTHER PAPERS

OBSERVATIONS ON ELIAS'S WRITINGS

Illustrations appear between pages 210 and 211

Introduction

The record of the influence of the gospel in Wales in the century between 1735 and 1835 provides one of the most remarkable chapters in the whole of Church history. Not only did the work of preaching revive dramatically at the beginning of that hundred years, but it continued in the decades which followed and at length brought into almost every corner of the land a Christianity which was at once fervent, doctrinal and practical. Beginning and continuing for a time as it did in the Church of England the leading features of the revival were too strongly in contrast with the prevailing conditions in that Church to prevent a new label being given to the leaders and to the multiplied converts. Thus they were dubbed 'Methodists' – a phrase first coined in England to decry the seriousness and discipline of true godliness – and 'Calvinistic'; but, comparatively indifferent to these titles, the participators in the Welsh awakening regarded themselves simply as the receivers of a glorious blessing. God had turned again the captivity of Zion; their mouths were filled with laughter and their tongues with singing. 'O! highly favoured country!' wrote a minister from England to a colleague in North Wales in 1788. 'I believe that you have more of the spirit and simplicity of the primitive Christians, among the rocks of Wales, than there is anywhere else in this day throughout the whole world.'

The hundred years of which we have spoken may be subdivided into three periods. The first covers the ministries of the pioneer awakeners, Daniel Rowland and Howell Harris, who were foremost in spreading the light of the gospel in mid, south and west Wales – the former the ordained curate of Llangeitho, Cardiganshire, where he preached Christ for more than fifty years

(1735–1790) and the latter a lay 'exhorter' whose itineraries from his home in Trevecka, Breconshire, blazed, ceased, then burned again before his death in 1773.

The second, or middle period, of the hundred years saw the powerful spread of revivals across the hitherto largely barren area of North Wales (commencing at Bala in 1791) and it also witnessed the final separation of the Calvinistic Methodists from the Church of England. While several eminent preachers were continuing and consolidating the work begun by the previous generation, the ablest leader at the turn of the century was undoubtedly Thomas Charles. Trained at Oxford, then dismissed by the Church of England, Charles lived and worked at Bala from the 1780s until his death in 1814, being best remembered outside Wales for the part he played in founding the British and Foreign Bible Society.

A younger contemporary of Thomas Charles, John Elias, the subject of this volume, came to his full maturity after Charles' death and his forty-six years of apostolic ministry stretched down to 1841. By the time of Elias' death the third and last epoch of a great century was about its end. Crowded chapels, 'great' preaching-services, and a society profoundly influenced by the gospel – these were all to continue in Wales for many years to come, yet, in Elias' judgment, the 'light, power and heavenly authority' of earlier days was disappearing. The 'heavenly dew' which had long rested upon the land could not be retained by mere human gifts and it was in the true spirit of Welsh Calvinistic Methodism that Elias at his death, though regarded by many as the most popular preacher that ever arose in Wales, gave this testimony: 'If any good has been done by my imperfect labour, God in his grace performed it. To him belongs the glory; I was as nothing'.

Had it not been for Edward Morgan a great deal of what took place between 1735 and Elias' death might have remained unknown or indeed lost to the English-speaking world. Not only was Wales isolated by comparative inaccessibility and by a language no Englishman understood, but those ministers best able to record the amazing events through which they lived had generally neither inclination nor time to write. They lived to *preach* and the only commendation they sought to inherit was the one contained in the scriptural pronouncement, 'He that winneth souls is wise'.

Though Morgan entered fully into the spirit of the Calvinistic Methodist fathers his own gifts and circumstances called him to devote much of his time to writing. Born at Pyle, Glamorgan, in 1783 (ten years after Elias) he was received into a local Methodist society shortly before the end of the century and, after a local education, proceeded to Jesus College, Oxford, where he graduated in 1806.[1] About this period he took orders in the Church of England and commenced a correspondence with Thomas Charles of Bala who wrote to him in March 1808: 'I sincerely hope you will be a faithful and diligent labourer wherever you are stationed. Our time is short and sinners are perishing all around us; an idle clergyman acts a very sinful and a very cruel part, and his responsibility is awful indeed! As to a *quiet* Bishop, which you wish for, if *he* is quiet, and you are active and useful, somebody will be unquiet, wherever you are, be assured of it.'

As the last sentence implies, Morgan had been experiencing some difficulty in finding a suitable charge in the Church of England. A consciousness of an absence of those popular talents which distinguished the preachers of Calvinistic Methodism (who in almost all cases were itinerants), apparently deterred him from joining their Connexion, and by this date Anglican parishes in Wales were not open to evangelicals. Morgan was thus destined to remain in England. He was appointed to the vicarage of Syston, Leicester, in 1814, to which was added the nearby vicariate of Ratcliffe-on-the-Wreake in 1818, and in these rural charges he remained till his death in June 1869.

Edward Morgan's published works amounted to nineteen volumes and the most important of these concerned the work of God in his native land. Though well able to write in Welsh he saw the need to publicize in English for posterity the labours of the leaders of Welsh Calvinistic Methodism and in some respects, even to this day, his writings are the chief reference books available to English readers. His biography of Thomas Charles appeared in

[1] For information on Edward Morgan we are indebted to a biographical article on him by Gomer M. Roberts in the *Journal of the Calvinistic Methodist Society*, March 1962.

1828. According to a letter published in a Welsh periodical in May 1835, Morgan was engaged in research into the lives of the 'famous Divines of past ages, *viz.* Rowland of Llangeitho, Charles of Bala, Jones of Llan-gan, and Williams of Pantycelyn'. Biographies of all these men, and of others, appeared in due course.

His *Memoir of the Reverend John Elias* was published in 1844 and to this was added Elias' *Letters, Essays and other Papers* in 1847. In the present volume these two books are now printed together for the first time.

The reprint of the Memoir has been considerably enhanced by the editorial research of the Rev Gomer M. Roberts. Mr Roberts is Editor of the *Journal of the Calvinistic Methodist Historical Society* and was responsible for The Trevecka Records Series published by the same society in the 1950s and '60s. A careful examination of Morgan's text was required on several counts. Morgan's second edition of Elias' *Memoir*, 1863, needed to be compared with the first of 1844; in some cases Mr Roberts has given preference to the text of the first edition though broadly speaking it is the 1863 revised edition which has been followed. John Elias' autobiography, the original manuscript of which is kept in the Calvinistic Methodist Archives, in the National Library of Wales, was re-examined and has been retranslated in parts where it was considered that Morgan had embellished the bare simplicity of the original Welsh. Furthermore, Mr Roberts has inserted material from sources unavailable to Morgan, such as details culled from Welsh biographies of John Elias, *viz.* J. Roberts and J. Jones, *Cofiant John Elias* (1850); Dr Owen Thomas's account of Elias in his monumental *Cofiant John Jones Talsarn* (1874); R. Parry, *Adgofion am John Elias* (1859); the chapter on Elias in J. Morgan Jones, *Y Tadau Methodistaidd* (Vol. 1, 1897, and W. Pritchard, *John Elias a'i Oes* (1911).

For this important help the publishers express their gratitude to Gomer Roberts and also to S. M. Houghton of Charlbury, who has undertaken the editorial work necessary to the reprint of the Letters and Essays which are contained in the second half of this volume.

Without doubt the following pages contain much information

which has long been inaccessible and practically unknown. It is not, however, a concern merely for the recovery of historical knowledge which is responsible for this reprint. Speaking once of how the Welsh fathers of the eighteenth century had prevailed with God in prayer, and been remarkable for their spiritual usefulness, Elias said, 'It is a consolation to us that the sword and arms they so skilfully used, are in our hands: may the Lord enable us to handle them!' The supreme value of this volume we judge to be the way in which it reminds us what are the 'sword and arms' of the Church. May God use these pages to further a recovery of the light and power of the gospel at a time when contentment with small things has blighted us all!

The Publishers

June, 1973

Life

1 Elias's origin, education and early serious impressions

Great and remarkable men have appeared in every period of the Christian Church, filling important situations, and becoming eminently useful. The Lord is sovereign in thus placing and endowing his servants, as well as in every other work. Very few men have been so greatly gifted by him as John Elias of Anglesey. He was indeed a rare monument of the Lord's providential care; he was favoured with extraordinary qualifications for the ministry, and made very useful in his day and generation. The memory of the wise, the pious, and the useful, especially such a man as Elias, is truly blessed, and ought to be preserved and made known for the benefit of the present and future generations.

Elias, being so much engaged in the ministry, had but little time for writing; yet he wrote some valuable papers and letters, which together with his autobiography form the principal ground-work of this memoir. He was, in his last days, induced by the persuasions of his friends to give a short outline of the most important events of his life; which he, no doubt, intended to be filled up by some other hand. He generally wrote in Welsh, as it was more easy for him. It seems he was unwilling at first to undertake his own biography, being so humble a man, and feeling so seriously his many deficiencies. His words on the subject are the following:

Inasmuch as many of my brethren and friends have desired of me to write a few particulars respecting my life, my mind is in a dilemma. On the one hand I view my life as so unprofitably and uselessly spent, with such imperfections and failings in my best performances, that I can take to myself only grief and shame, when I remember how I have spent my life. But on the other hand, when I think of the wonderful goodness of the Lord towards me from my youth until now, and of his unparalleled and astonishing compassion, I am inclined to think that I ought to let the generation to come know this. I intend therefore, if I be spared a little longer, to write a brief account of my life.

27 February 1841   *John Elias*

He then proceeds to give a short account of his birth and parentage as follows:

I was born 6 May 1774, in a small tenement called *Brynllwyn-bach*, in the parish of Aber-erch, about four miles from Pwllheli, Caernarvonshire. My parents were in humble circumstances, but lived comfortably and respectfully in the midst of their neighbours. My grandfather, on my father's side, lived many years in the tenement where I was born, working at the trade of a weaver: by means of this employment and the smallholding under his care, he lived in comfort, and was enabled to bring up his three children respectably in their stations. My father was the youngest. When he married Jane, the daughter of Joseph Roberts of Maes-y-cwm, in Llanaelhaearn parish, my grandfather allowed them to live with him, giving him a share of the land, letting him work at the trade: a small cottage was prepared for him, it was there I was born.

Elias Jones, John Elias's father, was the son of John Cadwaladr and Ann Humphreys, his wife. Cadwaladr was descended from Elias Prichard of Plas-hen, Llanystumdwy. According to tradition he was the parish clerk. A record of Elias Jones's baptism on 30 August 1752 may be seen in the Aber-erch parish register. Jane Joseph, Elias Jones's wife, followed the Welsh custom of adopting her father's Christian name as her surname. The register also records the baptism of 'John, son of Elias Jones, Crymllwyn, & Jane Joseph' on 6 May 1774 by Robert Owen, the curate. Was Elias baptized on the day of his birth? This may be possible, but it is doubtful. Elias himself recorded his birthday in his Family Bible, and he changed '6' to '2'. It seems likely that he was born on 2 May and baptized on the 6th. The 'tenement' where Elias was born is called *Crymllwyn* in the register; it has retained that form to the present day. Elias erected a monument to his parents and grandparents in Aber-erch churchyard. 'Elias Jones of Crymllwyn Bach' died 5 December 1822 aged 70, and 'Jane Joseph, his Wife died 3 June 1833 aged 84. 'John Cadwaladr (Elias Jones's father)' died 10 March 1789 aged 79, and 'Ann Humphreys, his Wife' died 21 April 1789 aged 78. The autobiography proceeds:

My grandfather took great delight in me from my infancy. As soon as I had begun to walk and talk, I liked him very much. The goodness of the Lord was remarkable in this circumstance. My grandfather was a very moral man, excelling in this respect all his neighbours, and also my parents. He took it upon himself to teach me, and train me, as far as he could, in the paths of virtue. He begun to inform me, when I began to talk, of the danger of using bad words, – lying and swearing, taking God's name in vain, and defiling the Sabbath. He tried to teach me to respect the worship of God.

As soon as I was able to walk with him to the parish church, I was obliged to go with him there every Sabbath. My grandfather was a Churchman; to the best of my knowledge there were no Methodists in that neighbourhood. There was however one small chapel attended by a few people in a place called *Pentre Uchaf*,[1] about two miles away. My grandfather used to hold family worship in his house morning and evening. He would read a chapter of the Bible, with Mr Peter Williams's exposition on it;[2] and then he would read one of Mr Griffith Jones of Llanddowror's prayers,[3] in a very devout and serious manner. He endeavoured to teach me to read the Welsh language, when I was very young – about four or five years old. I soon took great pleasure in reading. I was able to read the Bible when I was six years old; when I was seven I had already gone through the Bible from the beginning to the middle of Jeremiah.

We cannot but perceive that there was something remarkable and promising in such a child as this. We are reminded of young Timothy, by his love of the Scriptures and diligence in perusing them. Not many have read the Bible so far as he had, even at a more

[1] Pentre Uchaf, near Pwllheli; one of the oldest Calvinistic Methodist churches in the Lleyn peninsula.
[2] Rev Peter Williams (1722–96), of Carmarthen, one of the early leaders of Welsh Calvinistic Methodism, who in 1770 published a Welsh Family Bible, containing expository notes on every chapter; it became very popular in Wales; thirty-eight editions were published between 1770 and 1900.
[3] Rev Griffith Jones (1682–1761), rector of Llanddowror, Carmarthenshire, the founder of the Welsh Circulating Schools; his manuals of prayers were extensively used in Wales during the eighteenth century.

advanced age. We find by the account Elias has given of himself, that his grandfather's pious attention towards him, particularly in training him up in the ways of the Lord, was not in vain. The early religious instruction bestowed upon him in such a kind manner had the desired effect: the Lord honoured it with his peculiar blessing, as the following account will testify.

I was deeply impressed, from my childhood, with serious thoughts respecting God, judgment, and the world to come. I used to be terrified in my dreams with apprehensions about the day of judgment, and fears of going into hell, though I was very ignorant.

When I was seven years old, I had the small-pox. I was greatly afflicted with the disease: it was very heavy. Indeed there was a doubt for weeks about my recovery. I lost my memory for some days: my eyes were closed, and I was blind for a fortnight. But the Lord was pleased to restore me. I remember when I began to recover, and to open my eyes, that my grandfather came to my bedside, weeping, and addressing me thus: 'My dear boy, do you remember what your lesson is?' I answered, 'Yes', and mentioned some chapter in the book of Jeremiah. The old man rejoiced greatly when he saw that I could remember in spite of my affliction the portion of Scripture I was reading when I was taken ill, and that there were hopes that I should have the use of my eyes again to read the Bible. I was long in a low state, and often afflicted for three or four years.

When I began to walk after my affliction, I went as usual with my grandfather to the parish church every Sabbath. He used to lift me up to some elevated place to read the responses after the minister, according to the accustomed order. The old man in every way would teach me to avoid immoral practices, such as lying, swearing, dishonesty and Sabbath-breaking. The Lord blessed his counsels to keep me from those things.

Sometimes I was enticed by children of my own age, and some older, to follow them on Sabbath evenings as we came out of church, and to engage in what they called innocent play, that is, without making any noise. Sometimes, on such occasions, I was unable to say the Lord's Prayer, and could not sleep by reason of guilt and terror. Once I heard a lad swearing (I was not allowed to keep company with such boys). I thought it was splendid of the boy to say such words. I went far from all people to the middle of a field to attempt uttering the swear-word. Alas, I said it! Upon which such fear and terror seized me that I thought the earth would open and swallow me to Hell on the spot.

How remarkably tender was Elias's conscience, and how carefully he must have been brought up in the fear of God and his holy ways!

He wrote: 'My mind was very much distressed on acount of this abominable sin for some time; I was, when trying to pray, unable to proceed, being overcome by guilt. I never attempted afterwards to utter such an awful word.'

The Spirit of the Lord was doubtless working early on his mind, producing such holy feelings and such dread of sin. Let the young who are the subjects of similar operations of the Spirit perceive by such statements as these, whose hand is on them, and whose voice speaks to them, and let them gratefully attend to the influences of the Spirit.

Elias observes next the workings of corruption within, struggling to break out into action, and leading him to an open rebellion against God. The point of contention at that time was the fourth commandment; and sin and temptation urged him to the breach of it, but the Lord preserved him. His words are these:

There used to be great strivings within me respecting the Sabbath; my conscience would insist upon keeping it holy, but my sinful bias would crave for a little amusement with my companions. But I could not silence conscience; I had no liberty to follow the multitude. My parents were not at that time careful about the Sabbath. Sometimes neighbours likeminded with themselves would come to them on the Sabbath, and would converse with them on improper subjects for God's day. I wept much on this account. Sometimes I would remonstrate with them, but they would not hear me! One Sabbath my parents sent me on an errand to the house of my mother's father, about four miles away. I was seized with great trouble of mind; on my way I saw one of the mountains before me black and smoky, after the heath had been set ablaze on it on Saturday night. I thought the day of judgment had come, that the earth was beginning to burn, and that I was going to judgment by breaking the Sabbath. Such was my distress and great terror that I was obliged to cry out; I endeavoured to pray that I might be spared from going to judgment in my sins. Notwithstanding this I was ignorant of God, and the way of salvation.

The Lord's intentions and ways as to his servants are remark-

able and full of mercy. It is gratifying to observe how he makes all
things subservient to his plans and operations. The mind of this
youth being more awakened to his eternal concerns, he became
immediately diligent in seeking the Lord, and opposing evil. He at
length succeeded in convincing his mother and others in the neighbourhood of the sin of Sabbath breaking, in having tea-parties and
conversing on improper subjects on that day. He would affectionately show they must one day give an account of these things.

Elias proceeds in his autobiography to notice other means the
Lord in infinite compassion used towards carrying on the work in
his mind for his final conversion and his great usefulness in the
world.

I heard, when I was very young, that some celebrated preachers from
South Wales, and other places, used to preach at Pwllheli, Pentre Uchaf
and other places. I greatly desired that my grandfather would take me
to hear them. Accordingly by reason of his great affection for me, he
accompanied me often, after attending the Church in the morning, to
hear some Methodist preachers in one of the places above-mentioned,
in the afternoon or evening. He was distressed by observing the people
loitering and gossiping near the places of worship whilst waiting for the
preacher to turn up. He would urge me to read by the roadside where
the people had congregated. To hear a small boy reading well, was a
remarkable thing in those days. One Sabbath, in Pentre Uchaf, we had
a long wait for the preacher to appear. My grandfather approached me,
saying, 'It is a pity that the people should lose their time in this manner;
go to the pulpit and read a chapter to them out of the Bible'. Then he
opened the door and pushed me in and shut the door upon me. I read a
part of Christ's sermon on the mount, the people listening attentively.
At length I looked over my shoulder and saw the preacher standing at
the door of the pulpit; I was greatly alarmed, I closed the Bible and
came down as fast as I could. I do not recollect what was my age then –
it might have been from nine to twelve years. This was the first time I
entered the pulpit. And neither did I nor any other person think I
should have the privilege of occupying it so often afterwards.

Elias even at this age was disposed to be useful. It is said that
some children in the neighbourhood used to go to him on Sundays
to be instructed in reading; both master and scholars were faithful

and regular in the work. Perhaps this was the first Sunday school
in the county of Caernarvon. A person that stands high in the
Lords' vineyard acknowledges that he was taught the rudiments of
learning in that place.

We shall next proceed to give Elias's observations on the state of
his mind under the preaching of the gospel. It seems he became
more anxious for the truth after the loss of his old counsellor, his
grandfather, which occurred about this time. He writes:

I was a long time hearing without understanding but a little of what the
preachers were saying. However I had a great delight in the sound of the
preaching, especially when some powerful effects attended the ministry.
Yet my feelings were not affected to the same degree as those of others.
I lost my grandfather as my guide to the sermons when I was very
young. He failed to attend through feebleness some years before his
death, so that I had neither a guide nor a friend to accompany me to
hear the sermons. Yet, mercifully, I continued – yea, the desire of hearing the gospel increased in me. I used to go to and fro on my own to
attend the means of grace. I considered myself too unworthy to draw
near to the professors of religion; yet I could not bear the conversation
of young people who did not profess at all.

What fine traits of a pious mind are displayed before us in the
above statement! We shall next see what he says of his diligence in
hearing sermons, and the light that shone on his mind under the
gospel and by means of books.

I frequently heard three sermons on the Sabbath; but I was obliged to
travel a great deal for that purpose in those days. When a popular
preacher from South Wales was expected on his rounds in this locality,
I would sometimes walk over ten miles on a Sabbath morning in order
to hear the first sermon. I would then follow him until nightfall, taking
but little food all day. I had great pleasure in hearing, though but little
spiritual evangelical light had as yet shone upon my mind. I felt at this
time a great desire to read religious books; but there were but few such
in the Welsh language at that time. I used to go very far to borrow some
book: I had a few books that were, under the Lord's blessing, the means
of enlightening my mind in the doctrines of the Gospel respecting God's
gracious method of saving sinners. The books I derived the most benefit
from, were the works of the Rev Griffith Jones, Llanddowror, his

Catechism,[1] etc., the works of Eliseus Coles,[2] and *The Marrow of Divinity*.[3]

I had a hard struggle when I was between fourteen and sixteen years old. I felt the corruption of my heart greatly stirred up. I was inclined to strong passions, like my contemporaries, as religious impressions were weakening in my mind; but the Lord spared me, so that the depravity of my heart did not gain the victory, nor did it break out openly in the sight of men.

In the next paragraph we shall see how the Lord extricated his servant out of this dangerous state, and how he brought him into greater concern about his soul. He longed greatly for the Christian communion and fellowship carried on in meetings of members in the Welsh Calvinistic Methodist Connexion: it is for spiritual experiences. This means has a great tendency under God to preserve the feeble and tempted: the solitary and mourning Christian, as soon as he enters among and is incorporated with these excellent people of God, feels and considers himself as joined to a spiritual army, and is much encouraged and strengthened. Yet Elias was a long time anxiously looking for an opportunity to enter the Society. He was doubtless kept alive to the concerns of his soul by these longings after and approaches to the communion of saints, as well as by other means. His words are these:

After this, the Lord in his infinite mercy deeply impressed the words of the Bible on my thoughts. Whilst going to the services I began to draw near to some professors of religion, and conversed with them about the sermons on the way, which proved beneficial to me. By hearing their edifying communications, and observing their godly conduct, I felt a great desire to enter into their church fellowship – the Society.[4] But I considered myself as very unsuitable for membership;

[1] Griffith Jones's *Exposition of the Church Catechism*, published in 1752, second edition, 1778.

[2] Elisha Coles' *God's Sovereignty* had been translated into Welsh 1711, and republished in 1760.

[3] Edward Fisher's *Marrow of Modern Divinity*, translated into Welsh 1651; second edition 1754, and a third edition 1782.

[4] The Calvinistic Methodist Society Meeting is held under the superintendence of elders possessing suitable qualifications, chosen by the Society, and approved by the County Monthly Meeting. Ministers, if at home, take the lead. This plan was adopted by almost all denominations in Wales, and also by the

and I was afraid that I was not pious; and if I had not the truth, that I should backslide and bring reproach upon religion. I would rather die than do that. I was under the influence of strong reasonings in this respect for over three years. Sometimes, on the Society day, I would go out into the fields to pray and to lament. But I always failed to form the resolution of seeking admission: I feared that I had not undergone a real conviction, though I saw myself a lost sinner; I did not feel brokenness of heart, self-loathing and godly sorrow, corresponding with that view. So I was retarded for years.

The next subject in Elias's diary is family prayer. It is remarkable that though he was so young and made no profession, and in an ungodly family, he should be strongly disposed to adopt that holy and exalted exercise of godliness. Alas! how many families, though professing christians, are quite strangers to it! Elias proceeds thus on this important subject:

I was in those days under great trouble of mind, because I did not keep family worship. One evening, hearing a minister preach in allusion to this, that word from *Mark* 8.38 came strongly upon my mind: 'Whosover shall be ashamed of me and of my words in this adulterous and sinful generation, of him also shall the Son of Man be ashamed, when he cometh in the glory of his Father with the holy angels', etc., I went home with a troubled heart, in tears, trying to pray. I asked the Lord to pardon me, and to give me strength to avow Christ from thenceforth. When I came home my father and mother were up. I told them my distress of mind, and I asked their permission to attempt to read and pray in the family. They allowed me, and I began that hour. I continued, every opportunity, though I had not much encouragement from my family at that time.

What a delightful picture is this of so young a person erecting a family altar, and there, in so devotional and earnest a manner, calling upon the God of Israel! What an encouragement to serve the Lord is such an example! And there is an especial promise of God's favourable attention to such: it is said, 'those that seek me early

<hr>

evangelical clergymen in the nineteenth century, especially in the Diocese of St Davids. The Methodist leaders in Wales adopted the rules of the Religious Societies laid down by Dr Woodward.

shall find me'. Then he mentions in his biography a strong desire
he had of hearing that eminent servant of God, Rowland of
Llangeitho: this wish was produced in his mind by the remarkable
account he had received respecting that great man's ministry.

When I was about seventeen years old, I had a very strong desire to go
to Llangeitho to hear the Rev Daniel Rowland; after hearing so much of
him I expected to receive something wonderful under his ministry. I
went one Sabbath to Pwllheli to hear a certain preacher, but I found I
was too early for the service at the Methodist chapel there. I went to hear
the Rev Benjamin Jones.[1] He read for his text those words, 'Know ye
not that a prince and a great man hath fallen today in Israel?' (2 *Samuel*
3.38). He said that the reason why he took that text was that he had
heard the mournful news of the death of the Rev Daniel Rowland, who
was a prince and a great man in the church of God in Wales.[2] I still
remember my feelings when I heard that news – I wept unceasingly.
My disappointment was so great, after my strong intent to see and to
hear that famous man, and my expectation to receive something wonderful in my soul through his ministry.

Elias, as we see, was most anxiously engaged about the concerns
of his soul. This was the one thing needful in his mind. Thinking
of going to Llangeitho, though upwards of seventy miles, in search
of the pearl of great price, was more interesting to him than gaining the whole world. I heard of this intended visit of Elias before.
He very kindly, when I was collecting some materials for my
"Ministerial Records of some Eminent Welsh Ministers", favoured
me with a letter respecting Rowland, and his great desire of hearing him as above stated. He also gave in that epistle some information as to the way he commenced hearing ministers that
itinerated, and how he at length became more anxious for enjoying
that ministry. He makes honourable mention in it of his grandfather,
as the means under divine providence of much good to him, and
of his enjoying many of those great privileges already stated in his
autobiography. There are other excellent points in that letter;

---

[1] Rev Benjamin Jones (1756–1823), a Dissenting minister, pastor of Penlan
Independent Church, Pwllheli, from 1789 until his death. He was the author
of a useful treatise on the Doctrine of the Trinity.
[2] Rev Daniel Rowland of Llangeitho died 16 October, 1790, a Saturday;
Elias heard the news of his death, it is likely, on Sunday, 24 October.

which, as they have not been noticed, and as they are suitable to my present purpose, I shall introduce.

Fron 21 September 1837

You asked me to give some account of the Rev Daniel Rowland; I am sorry I cannot, for I was not born in time and circumstances to make such observations; I was only seventeen years of age when he died. But though so young, yet I still recollect in a degree the effect the news of his death produced on my mind.

My grandfather used to say a great deal to me of the Bible, and also of what he knew of the great men that lived at that time, but especially of Mr Rowland. Though he was a strong Churchman, yet he respected good ministers that preached out of its pale. I began at length to feel a very strong inclination to go to Llangeitho, to hear Mr Rowland, for some persons were in the habit of going to hear him, even from my country though so far: and I frequently heard a great deal of him. It was reported that he was an incomparable preacher, that some wonderful light and power from on high attended his ministry – that some hundreds of people used to travel from all parts of Wales to hear him at Llangeitho, and that they received wonderful impressions under his gospel sermons; so that great multitudes after hearing him publishing the glad tidings of great joy, went different ways homewards rejoicing greatly. The truths he preached were a rich, delightful feast to them on their long and tedious journeys to their several habitations; and they were so supported thereby, that they never complained of weariness or fatigue, though they were so long on the road.

Mr Rowland was so aged in my time, that there was no likelihood of his coming any more to North Wales; and I was so young that I could not think of travelling so far as Llangeitho then, being about 80 miles distant; so that my mind laboured under great difficulty and distress in that respect. But I purposed when I became a little older and stronger, I would go to Llangeitho, believing and expecting I should receive some wonderful things by hearing him.

But at the time I was indulging the thoughts that I should soon be strong enough for the journey, the mournful tidings of Mr Rowland's death reached my ears; it was particularly announced in a sermon at Pwllheli. This unexpected news affected my mind exceedingly, and that to such a degree, that I knew not what the good man said further about his subject. I wept a great deal, thinking that I should never see nor hear the celebrated minister. My expectation of receiving some great blessing under him, was ardent indeed. But it is well for me that the Lord could communicate grace and blessings through other instruments.

You perceive then, that I have not sufficient ground to say anything particular of this celebrated servant of Christ, and this most useful instrument for good in Wales. I have, however, conversed with many old people that often heard him, and by hearing them relate his wonderful sayings, and their own experience occasioned by his preaching, and the remarkable serious attention of multitudes under his sermons, I conclude that he must have been an extraordinary messenger in the hand of God, most suitable for that dark and ungodly age. There were many things above the capability of human nature, visible in his ministry: very extraordinary life and power attended his preaching, such as we of this age cannot comprehend. Indeed the Lord performed great and marvellous things by him in Wales. O that he would be pleased to bestow the gifts and qualifications of this great man, as well as his lively and evangelical spirit, on this degenerate race!

It has been observed that Elias was naturally formed for the high office of the ministry, and separated like St Paul for it from his birth : and we may conclude this chapter with a few more ideas on this important subject. We have no hesitation in saying that this brother was, as the apostle, marked and appointed very early for the work of the ministry. By this I mean that the hand of the Lord in forming him, prepared and fashioned him as to body and soul, to be a vessel meet for the work which he designed him to perform. God in his infinite wisdom provided, when the body of this brother was curiously wrought in the lowest parts of the earth, that every faculty should be strong in him, and that the whole body should be properly adapted for the powers of his great soul, to work through its instrumentality. 'The silver cord, the golden bowl, the pitcher, and the wheel of this machine, were', as one observed, 'formed in wonderful adaptation to the work of grace, alloted to it by its Creator to perform. Strong lungs, a fine voice, and eloquent tongue, were given him. And in him was placed a soul adapted to entertain ideas more expansive than even his skilful tongue could, without difficulty at times, set forth. He, in whose hands are the deep places of the earth, did this. And the hand which covered him in his mother's womb, proved a shadow to hide him through the whole course of his journey from his birth to the grave.'

A part of the Rev D. Jones of Caernarvon's letter to me respecting the unimpaired nature of Elias's wonderful powers at the close of his life, confirms what has been said:

Caernarvon 4 December 1840

As far as I know, Mr Elias is as well in health as when you saw him. However, he preaches as powerful and energetically as ever. His heavenly Master knew well what kind of body he should form for him in order to bear under the strong and fiery animation of his soul in preaching, for I think that such mental energies would be enough to wear out at length nine or ten bodies of the sons of Adam in general. I hope that his tabernacle will continue strong for some time yet.

Elias, no doubt, was fore-ordained for the work of the Lord, as his ministry and life manifestly showed. In speaking of him as a chosen vessel, I know I am approaching a mysterious subject, a subject which none of us would ever have known, had not the great God revealed it by the works of his hands; for it is through his works that he unveils to our mind the secrets of the eternal counsel; he does everything according to that, as it is written, 'to do *whatsoever* thy hand and thy counsel determined before to be done'. As his operations are manifestations of his eternal purposes, then his work and influences seen in our departed brother afford us a good ground to affirm that he was indeed *chosen* by him in eternity to proclaim the gospel throughout his native land. How good and excellent was the ministry in saving sinners, and so must its plan have been! Then of course all the glory should be given to God, who plans and executes every thing as he pleases. And we may add, that *whatever* proves that our departed brother is in glory, shews at the same time that he was predestinated by the Lord in his eternal counsel. How remarkable are those words of our Saviour, and how applicable to the above subject, 'I thank thee, O Father, Lord of heaven and earth, because thou hast hid these things from the wise and prudent, and hast revealed them unto babes. Even so, Father, for so it seemed good in thy sight!'

2 Elias becomes more decided, enters the Welsh Methodist Connexion, his public engagements

We now follow John Elias into a more decided state of mind. It is a great pleasure thus to contemplate the servant of God, step by step, as he makes his progress in the divine life. Thus he writes, after recording his disappointment as to going to Llangeitho:

Sometime after this, when I was about eighteen years old, a strong desire arose in my mind to go to Bala Association,[1] thinking I should be favoured there with something wonderful. I conversed with some religious young men in my neighbourhood on the subject, and asked them if they would allow me to go with them to Bala. They answered, I might: and it was agreed for us to meet at Pwllheli, and to start together from thence. A great number of religious young people from many places in Lleyn met: they knew of the places where we could hear sermons on the way, and we started on the journey, talking about the the Bible and sermons. Occasionally we sang psalms and hymns, and sometimes we rested, and one or two would engage in prayer. Then we would proceed again on our journey, singing on the way. Very few words were uttered by any one among us all the way, except respecting the Bible, sermons, and religious subjects. Though there were many young men and women in the company, yet I do not recollect seeing any wanton looks, nor did I hear an idle word from any person all the journey. They seemed as if they well understood that they were going to the Assembly, expecting to meet God there. O that all young people who make a profession of religion in this age were like them! Thus, from strength to strength, we arrived at Bala. When we came there we saw parties from many places coming together, and the whole multitude appeared as persons of one mind, and engaged in the same business. Great sobriety

[1] The quarterly meeting of the Welsh Calvinistic Methodists; the summer meeting was held annually at Bala, as a rule in June.

and decorum were observable every where in all the streets. It was
customary with the Devil in those days to bring together his crowds of
reckless fools to such places. The ministry was so full of fire, and attended
with such power, that the Devil dreaded to let his choice ones frequent
such a place. This Association occurred in 1792, and was remarkable.
The brightness of flaming fire fell upon the Assembly, life and power
was in the ministry, and heavenly dew descended on the people. After
the Assembly we went to our several homes rejoicing, talking about the
sermons, and singing and praying. The journey, though forty miles
long, seemed to end much too soon – we all walked on foot all the way.
I had such enjoyment in the fellowship of these godly people on this
journey, that I determined to join them.

Dr Owen Thomas once met an elder who had travelled with
Elias on that journey. The old man informed him that he had never
seen such seriousness of aspect in any man as appeared in John Elias
on that occasion. At Ffestiniog, on the way to Bala, they held a
prayer meeting. A request was made for a copy of the Bible, but
apparently nobody had one. At length, the quiet, serious young
man who was a stranger to most of the company said that he had a
copy, and he produced it from his pocket. He was asked to read a
chapter. 'He did so', said the old man, 'in such a manner as to make
the chapter seem new to us all.' He was then urged to offer a
prayer. 'And if the reading was wonderful,' he said, 'the prayer was
far more wondrous. I never heard such praying in all my life!'

What amazing powers attended the Word of God in those days!
Where can we meet with such uncommon instances of the influences of the Holy Ghost on the minds of people now, as were
experienced then? The relating of such extraordinary out-pouring
of the Spirit fills us with amazement and an anxious desire that we
may witness the same. Soon after this the Lord was pleased to
visit his servant with peculiar manifestations of his love towards
him, in enabling him to venture on Christ as a lost sinner, to see
his interest in him, and enjoy the liberty of the children of God.
This joy was very great.

About this time [writes Elias] the Lord was pleased to send stronger
illuminations to my mind respecting the doctrines of the Gospel, and
the method of grace in saving sinners. One day – I remember it well, in

a certain place on the way to Pwllheli – the words 'the ministry of reconciliation', etc. (2 *Corinthians* 5.18,19) came to my mind with some light which was quite strange to me. My soul had such a feast in the words, that 'God was in Christ reconciling the world unto himself, not imputing their trespasses unto them'! I saw that the way to accomplish this was by imputing our sins to Christ, and imputing his righteousness unto us (verse 21) .The doctrine of imputation has been, since that time, of infinite importance in my estimation. I felt from the pleasure I experienced then in that word, that I could preach it to my countrymen everywhere. But I saw that this desire of preaching the reconciliation was unreasonable, because I myself had not been received as a member of the Church.

It was another strong intimation that the Lord was about to employ him soon in the glorious work of the ministry, by giving him a desire to preach the gospel at the very time its grand plan of saving and justifying a sinner came in all its brightness and power into his mind. The subject of Elias's interest in Christ is notable and has been observed by those that preached in Welsh on his departure. Mr Humphrey Gwalchmai, in his excellent sermon on that subject, alludes to the point of his deliverance from a state of bondage into that of liberty. He observes that a sermon of that most popular and extraordinary preacher, Robert Roberts of Clynnog, was made very useful to him in giving him, as in himself a poor lost sinner, most lively pleasure and interest in the righteousness of Christ. The manifestation of his safety in Christ was doubtless made to his mind on the way to Pwllheli, but it became more clear and delightful to him under Roberts' sermon which he heard soon afterwards. It was after that sermon that friends perceived a manifest change in Elias, and doubtless to it, under God, they would attribute the wonderful alteration in his experience. It had, as Gwalchmai states, a most powerful effect on Elias. He represents Roberts as preaching in the first part of his sermon on the law, in a very terrifying manner as to its curses and condemning power. It was, he says, as if old Sinai was present in its awful darkness and commotion. The lightnings of conviction flashed awfully, the thunders of condemnation sounded alarmingly, and the darkness of death enclosed poor lost sinners. Elias no doubt felt all this exceedingly. He also perceived most clearly that no confidence could be placed in our own righteousness, and indeed that there is nothing out of Christ but ruin and a certain fearful looking for of judgment. Roberts was enabled, soon afterwards in his discourse, to preach most sweetly on the enchanting strains of the gospel to poor lost sinners. It was as powerful and irresistible as if he had been favoured with a commission from heaven, which no doubt he had, to use the gospel trump of jubilee, and to proclaim most illustriously pardon and peace through the sacrifice of the cross, to all ruined penitent sinners. Elias, as might be expected, was greatly elated; seeing again that the snares of sin and Satan were broken, and the fetters of guilt and condemnation loosed, he praised God with all his might for the atoning blood of Christ.

We shall see in the next statement the steps Elias took in order to join the people of God, which privilege he had so anxiously desired for a long time.

My mind [he says] became more distressed and burdened, because a had no fellowship with religious people. I thought that if I could find a situation in a pious family somewhere, where I could follow my trade, it would be a great advantage to me. I understood that there was a Methodist preacher of the same craft as my father, and that he employed some workmen. His name was Griffith Jones, of Ynysypandy, near Penmorfa.[1] I earnestly entreated my parents to allow me to go to him for a while, if there should be an opening. Reluctantly, they gave me their permission. I went there, about fourteen miles away. Though I was a stranger, and not a church-member, I obtained the situation. The man and his wife were very kind to me. I have cause to be thankful to the Lord for their kindness towards me, and for ordering in his Providence a place for me with this godly family. I was very happy there, but I was not able to attend the Society. They would often converse with me about religion, and ask me why I stayed out; but they never pressed me to enter. The wife requested me one time, when her husband was from home, to read a chapter and pray in the family. It was soon much talked of in the neighbourhood, that a lad who was not in the Society,

[1] Griffith Jones, afterwards of Sarnau, near Bala, had no preaching gifts; but he was a godly man, of a meek and gentle disposition, yet of great force of character. It is said that he was the means of conversion of a greater number of people than any other preacher in his day in North Wales.

prayed in the family. My mind continued very uneasy about going into the Society.

One day Griffith Jones and his wife were going to the Society in a place called *Hendre Howel*.[1] The husband, as they were starting, said to me, 'We are going to the Society, do you according to your mind'. That saying affected me much: I ventured, weeping and fearing, to follow them there. When I arrived there, there were three preachers, namely Griffith Jones, John Edwards, Ereiniog (afterwards of Caerwys Mansion),[2] and John Griffith Ellis.[3] I was afraid the preachers would examine me very strictly, and that upon finding my experience so unsatisfactory, they would refuse to accept me: but they, to my great astonishment, were very kind to me. I was accepted, and had what I had longed for many years, and had often feared I should never obtain, a place in the house of God! As far as I remember, this took place about the end of September 1793. The small Society at Hendre Howel was made up of very godly people; they were quiet, kind, brotherly, of a tender conscience and brokenness of heart. I found succour there, and splendid nourishment. I marvelled, and often thanked God that I had a place among his people. The enemy opposed me bitterly, assuring me that I would soon backslide, and that I would bring reproach upon religion. I was in this state for many weeks, wondering and thankful when the Society day came, that I was permitted to have one more meeting before backsliding; and I tried to pray earnestly that 'I might dwell in the house of the Lord all the days of my life'. The enemy was vanquished, and soon I had more quietness of mind. I was often surprised, and wondered that God should have placed me with his children, and preserved me there nearly fifty years.

What an interesting account is this of Elias's entering the Society, the church of God! How humble and unaffected in all the circumstances of it! and how valuable is a fearful watchful spirit in

[1] A farm-house, near Penmorfa, where the local Methodist Society met, before the chapels were built in the district; it was the home of John Jones, famous in his day as a man of prayer.

[2] John Edwards (1755-1823); he commenced preaching with the Methodists in 1787, and in consequence he was forced to give up the tenancy of Ereiniog, where his ancestors had farmed from time immemorial. He was a pioneer evangelist in many districts of North Wales. He ended his days at Plas-yng-Nghaerwys, Flintshire.

[3] John Griffith Ellis (1723-1805), one of Howell Harris's first converts in Caernarvonshire. He exhorted with the Methodists for many years, and was regarded in his day as 'the chief exhorter of Lleyn'.

commencing profession! This account becomes still more pleasing, when we consider that it related to a person, who afterwards became the greatest minister in Wales, if not in the Kingdom, and that he himself wrote it on his dying bed.

Humphrey Gwalchmai, in his funeral sermon, relates a few things respecting Elias's joining the Society at Hendre Howel that we have not noticed, especially his great anxiety to enter it. It appears that Elias and the servant-maid were employed on the above day in the corn harvest, in a field belonging to their master, Griffith Jones. Elias, on account of his great uneasiness about going to the church meeting, was very strange in his movements and work. The concern of his soul, and the solemnity of the world to come, filled his mind so much that he was not disposed to go home for dinner, and sleep had forsaken him for some nights. The girl, not knowing what was the matter with him, told her master that the lad's conduct was very strange: that sometimes he would work with all his might, then would stand as if in deep thought; at other times he would weep much or go to the other side of the hedge with deep groans as if about to die. The master, knowing the cause, said to the girl, 'Good will come of all this'. It seems that he and his wife, in going in the afternoon of that day to the Society, passed through the field where Elias was at work, and that he then spoke to him as has been related already. It appears that as Elias gave an account of his experience in the Society, the members were greatly affected, and were perfectly satisfied that the Lord had begun the good work in him (1 *Kings* 18.46).

Elias's manner in going after Griffith Jones and his wife, was noticed by the maid-servant; sometimes he would walk near them, then he would stop under the hedge; it was, according to her idea, like the manner of one in great fear. Doubtless the fear of backsliding and being like the foolish virgins, and also a sense of his own vileness, had thus humbled him, and disposed him to fall down on his knees in prayer, that he might be sure as to the root of the matter. He was also impressed with great reverence for the house of the Lord, the Church of the living God. It might be something like the awe on Moses' mind before the burning bush. David says 'Holiness becometh thy house for ever.'

Griffith Jones gave the following account of Elias's entering the
Society to the Rev William Roberts, of Amlwch (Elias's kinsman),
in 1819:

A sermon was preached in my house one morning: we that belonged to
the Society stopped behind after the service was over, for church
communion; and as he was not a member then, I told him, 'John, you
will go to make hay in the field'. When I went to the field after the
Society was over, I found him much distressed; I asked him what was
the matter. He answered, 'Oh my dear uncle, that word broke my
heart, *And those that were ready went in, and the door was shut;* you shut
the door today and I was out'. I then advised him tenderly and told him
that the door of mercy was not closed against any miserable troubled
sinner. His painful thoughts became more quiet, yet he was uncomfortable until he entered the Society at Hendre Howel, which was soon
afterwards.

Elias, after this, was requested by Griffith Jones to engage alter-
nately with him in family prayer, and he appeared to excel in it,
wrestling with God as Jacob of old. There was something in his
spirit when praying that caused all that heard to forget everything
but praying. His prayer was also very comprehensive, presenting
every needful petition before the Lord. Soon afterwards he was
requested to go to prayer in the Society; this was at a time when the
Lord was pouring the dew of his blessing upon his inheritance and
refreshing the land that was weary, so that the graces of the saints
revived and blossomed. A heavenly gale was also sent down upon
the church at the same period; it blew upon this garden so that the
spices thereof did flow, and filled all with gladness and joy
(*Canticles* 4.16). Elias had great pleasure in examining the Scriptures, and a great desire for acquiring scriptural knowledge.
Griffith Jones found in some holes in the walls of the workshop
many of his manuscripts, containing good observations on certain
verses that came powerfully into his mind, and some of them
before he entered the Society.

We shall now notice the commencement of Elias's ministry.
The step in the course of God's providence that led to his exhorting and addressing poor sinners was his engaging in religious

exercises at Hendre Howel. He was much pleased with the people there, whose character he is again disposed to describe. Thus he commences his statements:

There were very godly people in the little Society at Hendre Howel, where I had been received. They were humble-minded, self-denying, and broken-hearted. They revered the Lord Jesus greatly, and they were very fond of talking about him. I enjoyed great benefit, and had much pleasure among them.

The Sunday Schools had not commenced then in that neighbourhood. We had a night-school, held in various houses, in the winter; and as I could read Welsh well, I had to undertake much of the public services, such as engaging often in prayer, catechising, and I was encouraged by them to exhort my fellow-members. In my simplicity, I endeavoured to do whatever they requested me. I was very fond of my religious friends, especially the old people. I was nourished in their society, and had great delight in hearing them relate their experiences, and give accounts of their religious progress.

Providence, as we have seen, opened the way in an easy and remarkable manner for the exercise of Elias's talents in speaking; and his religious friends acted properly in encouraging him to use them. It would be advantageous if persons in the Church of England paid more attention to this most important subject. It is our duty to seek out and to help such young men as promise, by their piety and talents, to be useful in preaching the gospel. By prevailing upon such a man to enter the ministry, we adopt the way God has appointed to call the ungodly. Let us train our young people in the ways of usefulness, enlist them in Sabbath School engagements, and gather them into Bible classes, exercising them in giving their opinion on the different subjects that occur. Let us invite them to speak in religious social meetings, or experimental societies, like those in Wales. Those of them who show signs of decided promise, should be kindly noticed by the brethen, and taken by the hand. In neglecting this point we may have lost men of great piety, good talents, and strong sense, who, timid from a feeling of unworthiness, have kept in the shade. It is very painful to observe such a number of improper characters, men that are not truly changed, obtrude themselves into the awful work of the ministry. Let us then remember that, whilst we pray for more labourers for the harvest, we must use prudent means in order to obtain them.

Elias was encouraged, as his talent increased, to take a more enlarged part in the public service and to assume a more prominent character. He informs us in the next paragraph that he was at length employed in praying and speaking in a public manner. The following are his words:

There were frequent prayer meetings in the neighbourhood; and the friends persuaded me to accompany them, and encouraged me to commence the meeting by reading a chapter in the Bible. Some old disciple in his simplicity urged me to speak a few words as an exhortation to them, whilst reading the chapter. Soon afterwards, I felt a desire to do so. Some verses would come to my mind, and some words of exhortation or admonition from the verses. When preachers failed to fulfil their engagements, the people urged me to give an exhortation. It was soon noised abroad that the lad with Griffith Jones had begun to preach! This caused a general talk and commotion in the county, and no wonder! I was a complete stranger to all the preachers in the county up to a few months previously.

Similar is the account his kinsman, the Rev William Roberts, of Amlwch, gives of him at this particular juncture.

His spirit [he says] was so zealous, as if in a flame of fire, like Jeremiah of old: he would avail himself of every opportunity to warn his fellow creatures. He would go many miles on the Sabbath to hear sermons; and would if the congregation was waiting anywhere for the preacher some time, read a portion of the Scriptures, and set forth some inferences from those grand truths to the people, till they were experienced in the conscience, like salt on raw flesh. And the consequence was, that he was admired by some, and disliked by others. But notwithstanding all things his bow remained strong: so that he continued his rather irregular habits, until by the encouragement of a preacher, William Dafydd, of Llanllyfni,[1] he was more fully and regularly employed as a preacher, and had the privilege of being an instrument in the hand of the Lord of conveying the truth as a live coal or flaming fire, which his own soul felt, to congregations in Wales.

[1] William Dafydd, who began to preach in 1764. He was a gifted man and highly esteemed by his brethren. His sermons were short and sweet. He deeply sympathized with young preachers, such as Elias. He died in 1802.

Elias was thus led on gradually in the work, though almost unperceived by himself. According to Humphrey Gwalchmai's statements, prayer-meetings were established following the stirring occasioned by Elias's instrumentality. Such was his humility that he took no notice of it in his autobiography. Indeed there was no appearance of pride or conceit in him: there were, however, great sobriety and gravity in his spirit and words. He lived as on the borders of eternity. Amazing effects, as might be expected, were produced. Gwalchmai says that the word of reconciliation committed to him, burned within him like fire, as he viewed the state of a lost world and the worth and suitableness of Christ to such creatures. He could not help speaking to his family, his relations, and his neighbours, about these most important concerns. Salvation to the lost he would continually proclaim wherever he was, in a house or by the sea-side. Great numbers of his friends and neighbours would accompany him to and from the means of grace: they used to hang on his lips, while their hearts burned within them, and tears rolled down from their eyes as he conversed with them. It was with fear and trembling he proceeded in this great work, lest he should rush into it in a presumptuous manner. It was indeed a matter of much prayer.

Though this is but a short account of his commencement in calling sinners to repentance, yet it is pleasing and satisfactory. We perceive that his intentions were sincere and that his soul was filled with longings after the salvation of the lost. Less than this would not satisfy him; admiration and applause were nothing; compassion for souls stirred him up. His great aim and desire was for the conversion of souls. His feelings were in some degree like the apostle's when he went about warning and entreating sinners, night and day, with many tears. He, as observed before, had a very remarkable manifestation of God's reconciling love and his interest in it. And he seemed to have an immediate desire to preach the doctrine of reconciliation to a lost world. Elias, after he began the ministry, was encouraged to go on by the kindness and prayers of friends. His autobiography relates their tenderness towards him, and the steps which the Lord in his kind providence used in helping and guiding him in this most important business. He was at the same time kept very humble and low, having a sense of his nothingness and unworthiness. The following are his words:

Soon afterwards some of the elder brethren consulted with me, asking me if preaching dwelt much on my mind. I answered that there were some compulsions on my mind to say a word of exhortation to the people; but that I knew I was not fit for the task by reason of my youth, and lack of knowledge and experience. They encouraged me to pray and foster that which was on my mind. There was an old preacher at Llanllyfni, named William Dafydd, I soon became acquainted with him; he often encouraged me to think of making an attempt to preach to the people according to my ability, assuring me that I would be taught of the Lord. I was frequently obliged to commence the services before him. He was very kind to me.

It appeared then that the life-giving Spirit that formerly moved the wheels that Ezekiel saw, had begun giving such impulses in Elias as could not be hidden: much good was done, and the name of the Lord was magnified. He went on for some time in this useful career. However, he had not as yet undergone any particular examination or scrutiny by men of great knowledge and experience in the ministry. It was not the plan of the Connexion to which he belonged to allow any one to exhort or to preach before he had been examined first at the Monthly Meeting and then at the Quarterly Association. Having gone on for a considerable length of time in the work of preaching, he was advised by the brethren to attend the next Monthly Meeting. The ordeal of examination appeared alarming to him. This no doubt arose from his sense of great insufficiency and unworthiness. His account of the approaching meeting, his appearance there, and appointment to labour in the ministry, is as follows:

The regulations now in force in reference to persons entertaining thoughts of preaching, were not established that time. I was encouraged by the brethren at Hendre Howel, and by the elders of the neighbouring societies, particularly by one John Richards, Garndolbenmaen, to attend the next Monthly Meeting, which was to be held at Brynyrodyn, near Caernarvon, on Christmas Day. John Richards would have me go to his house on Christmas Eve, on my way to the meeting. He published that I would preach at Garn Chapel in the early Christmas morning service, which was not in accordance with the rules. Afterwards I went with him, together with several friends, to the Monthly Meeting, much troubled in mind and heavy-hearted by fear that I should be condemned for my presumption. My friends tried to support me by saying that a young man, Richard Jones, Coedcae (afterwards of Wern),[1] had been accepted with great tenderness in the previous Monthly Meeting; and another young man the Monthly Meeting before that, named Evan Evans, of Waun-fawr.[2] But that was of no great comfort to me; I knew that those young men were known to all the preachers in the county, and that they had far greater knowledge and gifts than myself. There were preachers of great renown in Caernarvonshire in those days; they appeared to be angels in my estimation – Robert Jones of Tybwlcyn,[3] John and Robert Roberts of Llanllyfni,[4] Mr Evan Richardson of Caernarvon,[5] and Mr John Jones of Edern.[6] I was obliged to stand before them, in awe and great fear. They examined me, in a very serious manner, respecting my convictions and my apprehensions as to my lost state, and my dying to the law: and also my views on the scheme of salvation, my experience of Christ, and his grace. Surely I was a babe in my answers! They told me a great deal about the magnitude and great importance of the work. But to my surprise they treated me with much kindness, and though they were perfect strangers to me, yet on the testimony of Griffith Jones, John Edwards, and John Richards of Garn, they gave me permission to exhort the people on Sabbath days in those places where my services were called for.

[1] Richard Jones (1772–1833), was born at Coedcae-du, Llanystumdwy, but moved to Wern, Llanfrothen. He began to preach in 1794, and was ordained in 1816. He was an able man. In 1836 John Elias edited and published a collection of his hymns.

[2] Evan Evans, of Waun-fawr, Caernarvonshire, a young preacher of great gifts; he was accepted as a preacher in 1794, but he died prematurely in 1797. His brother was John Evans, the explorer.

[3] Robert Jones (1745–1829), usually known as R. J. of Rhos-lan, a teacher in Griffith Jones's circulating schools who began to exhort with the Methodists in 1768. His book, Drych yr Amseroedd (1820), is still read on account of its style, and its interesting narrative of the early years of Welsh Methodism.

[4] John Roberts (1753–1834), kept a school at Llanllyfni, Caernarvonshire, but he lived for many years at Llangwm, Merionethshire. He began to preach with the Methodists c 1780. His brother, Robert Roberts (1762–1802), was a hunchback, but he was a preacher of extraordinary power and vivid imagination.

[5] See below, p. 38.

[6] John Jones (1761–1822), of Edern, Caernarvonshire, who began to preach with the Methodists in 1784. He was a convincing preacher, and on one occasion was the means of awakening 180 persons.

Then Elias proceeds to make these suitable, simple and pious observations on the important business of setting himself apart for the preaching of the Gospel. He acknowledges in particular the hand of God working in a mysterious way in that matter. He thus goes on, with his eye on his heavenly Father's care over him that day and henceforth:

Christmas Day, 1794, was a day to be remembered by me. I was received a member of the Monthly Meeting, and was allowed to preach the Gospel. I was but twenty years and six months old, and had been only two years and a half a professor of religion, very deficient in knowledge and experience of spiritual things. So I commenced in my simplicity a work, the nature, importance and excellency of which, I very imperfectly understood. However, from the very beginning, I was not left to view the work as a human art, undertaken capriciously, nor to talk in a trifling manner about it. I was sensible that I knew too little of God in Christ to be able to speak in a clear manner of him; little of the evil of sin, and the wretched state of sinners; to address the people in a rousing manner. I saw myself very deficient in my views of the glory of Christ and experience of his love, so as to speak clearly and fervently of him to the people. But God bore with me, and supported me in a wonderful manner.

An interesting story is related in connection with this Monthly Meeting at Brynyrodyn. John Jones, of Edern, was a strong character of an original turn of mind. He enquired what was the young man's name, and he was informed, 'John Jones'. He then enquired what was his father's name, and he was told, 'Elias Jones'. 'Good gracious!' he exclaimed, 'call the boy John *Elias*, or else we shall be all John Joneses before long!' Consequently, he was ever afterwards known as John Elias. The story is probably true, but in using this style, Elias simply conformed with the old Welsh usage of adopting his father's Christian name as his own surname.

It may not be improper here to observe that Rowland, and the other serious clergymen that commenced the Welsh Methodist Connexion, were on account of the awfully dark and immoral state of Wales, most glad to avail themselves of the help of such pious and promising laymen as Elias, in the great work of enlightening the country and saving souls from eternal ruin. They were distressed at seeing the dreadful state of lost sinners; and were impelled to do everything in their power for rescuing them out of that situation. Their plan in this respect was much like that of the Wesleys. Apostolical succession, so much spoken of now, never entered their minds; all they cared about was the salvation of souls, and for that end they exerted every nerve, adopted every plan, that might be subservient to that end. They established a monthly meeting in every county, to receive such men as were thought proper to exhort and to preach: they transacted other important affairs belonging to the Connexion in that meeting. They had also a quarterly meeting, called the 'Association'.

Those eminent clergymen, however, who commenced such an important revival in Wales, had no thought of ordaining; but accepting of the aid of such as were useful and talented, to spread the knowledge of the truth with them, through a benighted country, acting as missionaries; and such indeed they were, traversing the Principality as men commissioned from above, to turn many from darkness to light, and from the power of satan to serve the living God. And the subject of these memoirs proved at length to be one of the most useful and successful ministers that ever appeared in Wales.

3 Elias at the commencement of his ministry, his desire for learning and knowledge

Though Elias had commenced preaching before, yet he must not be considered as moving in a regular manner in the Connexion till after he was set apart in the Monthly Meeting at Brynyrodyn. Indeed, he felt more satisfied after that important dedication to the work of the ministry. No doubt he prayed most earnestly to the Lord to accept him as his minister, and looked unto him for every qualification suitable for such a high office. Elias, being so solemnly and devoutly dedicated to the Lord's service, doubtless felt deeply impressed. His feelings on common occasions were generally excited and animated, but how much more so, when he was publicly devoted, as then, before heaven and earth, God and man, to the most important of all offices! How much must such words as those addressed by St Paul on a similar occasion, have thrilled through his very soul: 'I give thee charge in the sight of God, who quickeneth all things, and before Jesus Christ, who before Pontius Pilate witnessed a good confession, that thou keep this commandment without spot, unrebukeable, until the appearing of our Lord Jesus Christ.'

We may think that fresh courage was infused into his soul on such an important occasion. And he having received the wise direction and kind approbation of his brethren in the ministry and the elders of the churches, and being animated by their warm and earnest prayers and good wishes, went forth no doubt from their presence in a more hearty and decided manner; indeed he might be considered as flying on eagle's wings to do his heavenly Father's will, in declaring the glad tidings of salvation to a perishing world. His whole dependence for all qualifications and everything requisite for the great work was at the same time most entirely upon his divine Master, who had engaged him in his vineyard. Never did he take so much pleasure in anything as in surrendering himself body and soul and spirit, and all that he had, to the Lord. No one ever, especially in our days, lived more in the spirit of self-dedication to his heavenly Master. He always considered himself and all his talents as his. Under this feeling, he generally concluded his letters to his friends, saying, 'Your servant *for* Christ.

It is most evident that the Lord accepted him as his servant, qualified him with rare and peculiar talents for his sacred office, and gave him a spirit and a heart suitable to the grand message he was to convey. Indeed, his heavenly Father favoured him with ministerial gifts and blessings in every respect. He, above all things, poured upon him from on high, 'the spirit of wisdom and understanding, the spirit of counsel and ghostly strength, the spirit of knowledge and true godliness'. We may say, 'he was filled with the spirit of holy fear, and the manifold gifts of grace'. The Lord indeed gave him 'boldness, with fervent zeal, to preach the gospel to all people'. He certainly was an extraordinary character, highly favoured by heaven. It is probable that those who set Elias apart for the work of the ministry little expected, when they looked on him then, that he was destined by the Lord to be such an extraordinary instrument for the glory of his name and the good of souls. A casket may contain most precious articles, though the outward appearance of it may be mean.

It is not improbable but that many, at the commencement of Elias's preaching, did not think very highly of him, by reason of his low origin and employment. And perhaps some may, on the same ground, be unwilling, in reading his life, to entertain a very high opinion of his character. His divine Master, the Lord Jesus Christ himself, though the King of Glory, was not well received, by reason of his humble appearance. Many of the Jews were astonished at the power and wisdom with which Jesus spoke, yet they remained cavilling and captious. 'How knoweth this man letters', they scornfully asked, 'having never learned?' So with regard to Elias, though prejudice and ignorance could never form any objection to his doctrine and his remarkable manner of delivering it, nor an evil eye discern any inconsistencies in his life, yet some have been and others may be disposed to disparage his excellencies, by consideration of the humbleness of his origin and calling. Have such persons forgotten that many of our Lord's servants were originally in very low circumstances, as well as himself? Some were fishermen and tent-makers. We should therefore be always ready to trace spiritual gifts to their right source, and to receive what we know to be the words of wisdom, though it were from one who had no learning. Is not the finger of God manifested by such an instance as that of Elias, so remarkable a preacher though unacquainted with human learning? Does it not demonstrate that God acts as a Sovereign, humbling human pride, and glorifying himself? Those preachers that were engaged in setting Elias apart for the work of the ministry were not mean persons; but pious, useful, and some of them endowed with very rare and extraordinary talents, especially Robert Roberts of Clynnog. Well might Elias look upon them, as it is stated, as angels of God; and such indeed they were in the churches.

It may be proper to state here that Elias was appointed to no particular place or people as his charge, but to go and preach everywhere. A most suitable person for this important work he was, not only on account of the endowments just mentioned, but also by reason of experimental qualifications. Having life and peace in his own soul by believing, he felt anxious to preach them to every child of man: having tasted of the Lord's saving goodness, he would proclaim its riches abroad: being himself reconciled through the blood of the Lamb, he besought men everywhere to be reconciled to God. This was the ministry of reconciliation indeed; the embassy, the office of life and peace; 'the olive branch that shewed abated waters; the silver trump that proclaimed the year of Jubilee'. The effect was wonderful; the Spirit of the Lord attending his preaching; it was like a strong wind bending and carrying all before it; it was like a hammer breaking the hard rocks, the hearts of men; evil habits and customs were given up for the paths of peace and holiness.

Itinerant preaching was the peculiar plan of the Welsh Calvinistic Methodist Connexion. No method can be more suitable for

arousing and awakening a country dead in trespasses and sins.
It is the way the disciples and apostles of our Lord pursued, and
that which the reformers of ancient and modern times adopted.
And it is the mode which missionaries in foreign parts constantly
use. Itinerant preaching is that kind of ministry that the Lord has
peculiarly blessed in every age for the conversion of immortal souls.
It was wise also in the Welsh Methodist preachers to follow the
plan of itinerating, manifesting thereby their regard for the
Established Church; for they did not wish to interfere with it as a
settled and stated ministry. Many of these itinerant preachers
were themselves lay members and ministers of the Church of
England.

It is time now to let John Elias speak for himself on the important subject of going forth to proclaim the everlasting gospel.
'After I was received to preach,' he says, 'I was called every
Sabbath to various places in the county. The people were filled
with curiosity, being avid to hear such a young man preaching, so
that I had no rest. Some times I would go far on the Sabbaths, as
to the confines of Merionethshire, and to Llanrwst, etc., without
being aware that it was irregular for such a young man to go so far
away from home. Some of the old preachers called me to account,
and kindly reproved me for my irregularity. But in a short time
they consented that I should give publications for preaching
through many North Wales counties, and also in Liverpool and
Manchester. By this time I knew the rules, and would not go
without the brethren's consent.'

Dr Owen Thomas heard that the leaders of the Monthly Meeting
treated young Elias harshly for his irregularity. But the demands
for his services were such that the people could not be restrained.
He provided himself with a small pony and a saddle, to equip
himself for his itinerant ministry.

We here perceive how zealous and active Elias was in the first
steps of his ministry: the Lord blessed him exceedingly in that
great work, which was his delight. Though so popular even then,
yet how humble! He attributes the reason of his popularity to the
novelty of his appearance; but there was something besides
novelty: it was the Spirit's influence. Indeed Elias was peculiarly

distinguished and owned by his heavenly Master everywhere, and at the most public opportunities. He went when about twenty years old to an Association in Llanfair Caereinion, in Montgomeryshire, and he was appointed to commence the meeting with prayer. Humphrey Gwalchmai says that, though he himself was but a boy then, he perfectly recollects Elias's very serious and sober appearance, and his very importunate intreaties in prayer for a blessing on the Association.[1] Though the inhabitants of that place were in general revilers and persecutors of religion, and preaching then might be attended with the loss of property and life, yet the prayer of Elias was accompanied with such power from above, and so much owned, that 'all around me', says Gwalchmai, 'were in tears as well as myself; indeed we trembled as if we were going to appear before the judgment seat of Christ'. There was more conversation for some days after the Association concerning young Elias's prayer, than respecting all the sermons that had been heard. The importunate solicitations and calls for his ministry in different counties in the Principality were then increasing and pressing upon him; and wherever he went preaching the Word, there were evident proofs that the Lord was working in a remarkable manner through him. The small churches of different denominations were roused and increased; false religion and hypocrisy were exposed to contempt and trodden down; old sinful customs and superstitions of the Welsh were made to appear odious and disgusting; and the strongholds of sin and Satan were broken up. The country which seemed like the valley of dry bones formerly, was now full of noise and commotion; multitudes were coming together; the breath from the four winds was breathing on them, and the dead were receiving life!

About the same time Elias met with another trial. One Sunday, after travelling all the way from Penmorfa to Bala, he was astonished to find Mr John Roberts of Llangwm there before him; he was making arrangements with the elders, and took upon himself to conduct the services for the day on his own. Indeed, Elias was

---

[1] This Association was held in April 1796, when Elias was in his twenty-first year; Gwalchmai was then a lad eight years old.

not allowed to preach at all at Bala on that Sunday, so that John Roberts had no opportunity of hearing him. But Elias had an enagagement on Monday evening in a chapel in the vicinity, and Roberts went there surreptitiously to hear him preach. During the service he became convinced that the young preacher – like John the Baptist of old – had been sent from God. The only possible explanation for Roberts' conduct was that he was a stickler for rules, and that Elias (as usual) was breaking them!

The piety and talents of the young preacher had become very conspicuous and public by this time. The desire of the people for hearing him preach wherever he might be had become very importunate and pressing, so that they would have him hold forth even in the Monthly and Quarterly Meetings, the most important and responsible opportunities in the church, and their request was granted. The Lord stood by his servant from the beginning. He clothed him with grace and beauty, and endowed him with strength from above, and caused the mighty expressions of his servant to stick fast in the hearts of the numerous hearers, like sharp arrows, until the vast congregation was overwhelmed, their eyes and faces being suffused with tears, and many crying out 'What shall we do to be saved?' and others praising and magnifying God for such a wonderful method of salvation. Thus was the prejudice of the opposers of the gospel overcome and done away. The sober and grave appearance of the people in returning home, and when there, testified to all that saw them that they had been at some very notable and uncommon means of grace. Many every- where turned from darkness to light, and from the power of Satan to God, under his ministry. The tents of Zion were much increased thereby, and the aspect of the country was much changed for the better; so that the talk of the people was in general respecting him as a great prophet, even from Holyhead to Cardiff. Many of the old people were also greatly surprised at hearing him, and exclaimed with gladness that the great reformer Howell Harris had appeared again! But others affirmed, 'He is a greater preacher than Harris ever was!'

The Rev E. Williams, of Radnorshire, favoured me with the following anecdote respecting Elias's increasing renown from the commencement: 'I heard my father, one of the heavenly pilgrims in those days, who went to glory about the same time as Elias, say, that when the report of his popularity first reached South Wales, the church sent him and another leader to the Bala Association, under strict orders to prevail on him to visit them in that country. My father, arriving there, met with one of the first preachers, Mr John Roberts, of Llangwm, and asking him, "Will it be agreeable that we should solicit Elias this year to preach in South Wales?" he answered, "Pray, don't attempt that now; leave him alone that we may see what the Lord means to do with him. It is probable that he will be raised up very high, or permitted to come down greatly. Our opinion of him is, that he will be a great minister, if he should not be spoiled as he is reared up." Such was their fear lest young preachers should be injured, by being puffed by popularity.'

The next subject in Elias's life is also very important; it is that of learning and knowledge. A man of his mind and penetration must have seen that education and instruction are very necessary for such an office as that in which he was now engaged. Having never enjoyed these advantages, he must at the time have felt very much the need of them. He never was at school prior to this time; he knew no more than what his grandfather had taught him when a little boy, which was reading the Scriptures in Welsh, as we have before observed: and very pleasing was the account. From that circumstance, however, we might gather that he was apt to learn and fond of instruction. No wonder then he should now be so desirous of improving himself, and of becoming acquainted with such learning as might be useful to him in his new and most important occupation. The following are the sensible words of this young, popular preacher in reference to learning:

The great importance and weight of the work soon pressed heavily on my mind, and I perceived my deficiency as to knowledge and experience to teach people. I had a great desire of going to school to learn a little of the English language. A few Welsh people at Manchester were anxious I should go there to school, and promised to support me whilst I should be there, in order that I might preach to them on the Sabbaths. They were then very destitute of the means of grace. In the Monthly Meeting of Caernarvon, I enquired if they would allow me to go to

Manchester for half a year's schooling. I was sharply rebuked by them for making such a request. They said it was the pride of my heart, a desire to be a great preacher, that made me think of going to school. I know that it was their care for me, and for the cause of religion, that made them act thus towards me. They were afraid that I should be puffed up, and consequently made wholly useless for the work. Their reproof proved beneficial to me.

It was delightful to see a young preacher, though so popular and careful, yet so anxious to retire for a while for the attainment of learning, though it was not thought much of in those days, but oftentimes decried. It was a sign of a great mind labouring under great difficulties and struggling for freedom. Yet he manifested great humility in quietly submitting to the judgment of his brethren. They did not act properly in this respect, though their motive was right. Many a young person would have been quite discouraged by such repulsive treatment, and would have no more thought of education. But nothing could impede such a mind as that of Elias in attaining every kind of knowledge necessary for him. We find him therefore again soliciting the favour of going to another place in search of learning: and as the situation was near, and under the superintendence of one of the Welsh Methodist preachers, his request was this time granted. His statement on the subject is the following:

A short while after this, I enquired in a Monthly Meeting if I could have permission to go for a while to the Rev Evan Richardson's school at Caernarvon: my request was granted. I was with Mr Richardson for a few months: he treated me with great kindness, and it was a great blessing to be with him. I soon learned enough English to enable me to understand the substance of what I read in a book in that language. I did not learn anything to perfection, for I was but a short time there; but I was set on the way to learn many things through my own application. I was given help to work diligently day and night until I acquired in some degree a general knowledge of the things that were most necessary for me. But I am still learning, even in my sixty-seventh year, and see a greater need of knowledge. This weighed heavily on my mind, namely, that the churches and congregations should not be losers on account of my disadvantages in not having learning when young. I

determined, if the Lord would help me, that I should make up this
deficiency by study.

Evan Richardson was a very respectable minister, and a sweet
preacher; there was generally much unction attending his sermons.
He was a native of Llanfihangel Genau'r Glyn, Cardiganshire,
born in that parish in 1759, and brought up at Ystrad Meurig
Grammar School, with a view of taking orders in the Church of
England. But he came under the influence of the seraphic Daniel
Rowland of Llangeitho, and was induced to enter upon the
itinerant plan of preaching among the Calvinistic Methodists.
He settled at Caernarvon in 1787, and established a very useful
school there, giving instruction not only in Greek and Latin, but
also in French and Hebrew, and in commercial literature. He
employed a good usher, in order to relieve him when he went out
to preach. Elias was very fortunate in being placed under such a
teacher, who was very fond of him, and desirous of improving him
in every kind of knowledge necessary for him as a minister of the
gospel. Richardson had a great facility in conveying instruction to
his pupils. He used to pass great encomiums on Elias as a scholar:
'I never had', he used to say, 'any one like him, so desirous of
learning, and so apt in acquiring languages. Not only was he
enabled to understand the English language in a short time, but
also its grammatical parts.' He became in time tolerably conversant
with the Greek and Hebrew Scriptures, especially by means of
Lexicons. He was so well acquainted with the chief subjects in
every chapter of the Bible from beginning to end, that he could
easily make use of them on any occasion: he was also in possession
of the thoughts of our most eminent divines on those points.

Richardson also, it seems, took pains with his pupil to correct
certain unseemly bodily contortions whilst preaching; and especially he cured him of a peculiar grunt in his throat, which occurred
as soon as he became heated up in preaching. He lost all these
peculiarities under Richardson's discipline. He became, in his style
and deportment, one of the most seemly persons who ever
addressed a congregation; his control over his voice was perfect.
Michael Roberts used to say that the first English book he read was

Brown's *Compendious View of Natural and Revealed Religion*. He digested the work from cover to cover, after consulting every verse quoted by its author; he mastered it so thoroughly that he had memorised it almost completely.

Such were Elias's incessant and unwearied exertions for the attainment of knowledge needful for a minister that he at length became acquainted with ancient history and eastern customs. His hearers could not but be struck with instances of such attainments in his sermons. He also made considerable advances in the sciences that were suitable for him as a teacher: his mind being of so penetrating a nature, would soon perceive and enter into their meaning and utility; exploring the precious mines of literature, and expatiating on their excellencies. The following instance shows how well versed he was in astronomy: a conversation took place, some years ago, at his own house, about the eclipse of the sun that was expected to occur; he observed that Moore's Almanac was wrong as to the exact time; he had worked the problems of calculation with such care, skill and minuteness, so as to state precisely the exact time, manner, and termination of the eclipse, which the fact corroborated shortly afterwards. It amazed his friends and confirmed their opinion of his great knowledge of the solar system.

His knowledge of the human constitution and its different diseases and their symptoms, had become considerable. He had also studied the various remedies suitable to these disorders, and had made considerable progress in the science of medicine, especially in the botanical department, connected with the properties of herbs, as marked out by chemical processes. It is also stated that his skill in giving medical advice was not inferior in some cases to that of physicians, and that in general it had its desired effect. It also appears that by diligent study, the reading of excellent authors, and the observations of his own penetrating mind on natural philosophy and divine revelation, he made large and extensive attainments in knowledge, knowledge sanctified for the service of the ministry. Elias's thirst for attainments must have been great. The more he became acquainted with subjects, the more he saw their beauty, and longed after a complete knowledge of them. But he was blessed above all with that knowledge which flesh and blood cannot attain to, spiritual knowledge: and he was pre-eminently the minister of the mysteries of God. This knowledge had the chief place in his soul; it kept him humble, and prevented him from being puffed up. The love of Christ was like a torrent carrying him on, compelling him to persuade men to be reconciled to God.

Mr William Parry, an elder in the Welsh Calvinistic Methodist Connexion at Bangor, favoured me with the following lines respecting Elias at Richardson's Academy at Caernarvon:

Bangor 3 January 1844

I enjoyed the friendship of the late Mr Elias from my boyhood, having become acquainted with him at the Rev E. Richardson's school in Caernarvon. Mr Elias was then about the age of twenty-two, and I was not above seven or eight years old. I could notice but little of his superior qualities. He was viewed as being above us all. His general demeanour was such as to command respect and admiration, being always solemn, yet not without a becoming degree of complacency. The pupils were generally glad in attending his lectures, which were always very good and energetic. A school-fellow about my own age, in returning home with me one evening from chapel, asked me, 'Why does John Elias accompany his words with such motions, and why does he stretch forth his arm?' 'O!' said I in my simplicity, 'it is to point out the way to heaven.' 'Does he know the road there?' asked he. 'Yes,' I replied, 'and all the people say he does *uncommonly well.*' This shews the light in which he was even then viewed by the public. His emphatic expressions were perhaps accompanied then with too much motion, but which under the instructions of our revered and excellent teacher, were brought to a most decorous and graceful manner in the delivery. His silent motions preached, and his dumb smile created ideas.

According to all the accounts which have survived, Elias appeared like a comet, in full blaze, at the beginning of his ministry. He made progress in the course of time with regard to the richness of his resources, such as elegance of speech, appropriateness of style, and all the ornaments pertaining to the craft of oratory. But in force and vigour, warmth and originality, he never surpassed the opening years of his ministry. That is why the Rev William Roberts, of Amlwch, once remarked to Dr Owen Thomas, 'You have never heard John Elias'. 'Of course', Dr Thomas replied, 'I have heard him preaching hundreds of times.' 'No, never,' Roberts countered, 'you heard *Mr* Elias – you never heard *John* Elias!'

4 Elias's removal to Anglesey, the state of religion there, and the great alteration therein at his departure

We are to notice in this chapter Elias's removal from Caernarvon-shire into Anglesey, and the remarkable consequences attending it. Changes to many are difficult and disastrous, though to a man like Elias, travelling about so much, a removal like this might not be deemed painful, yet he felt it greatly. Not only was Caernarvon-shire his native county, but there he was born again, and received in a remarkable manner his spiritual liberty, and was united with brethren of various orders and offices in very friendly and inti-mate bonds. No doubt the separation from them was keenly felt by this warm-hearted young Christian: and none can tell what is felt on these occasions of separation between believers, especially between ministers and people, but those who have experienced such a trial. But his presence in Anglesey, as a resident minister, was felt exceedingly, and no one can tell the good that resulted from his diligent and energetic ministry, in connection with others, under God's blessing. This will be known only in the last day, in its full and all-important extent. And doubtless when he entered on this new field of labour, he was greatly roused by a view of the awfully wicked state of the island. His holy soul was stirred, like St Paul's, by observing the depraved and dreadful practices of the people. We might think his zeal was enkindled to the highest degree; and he, we might suppose, got all his weapons of warfare well prepared to attack satan's kingdom; and we may imagine we perceive him going forth in the name and strength of the Lord, well equipped for the support of the cause of God, and the kingdom of his dear Son, in that benighted county.

He was known to Anglesey before; his tutor, Richardson, had

sent him there to preach in his stead at a Monthly Meeting. However, when he arrived there, they looked upon him with a degree of contempt, by reason of his youth and humble appearance. They were disappointed when they saw the tall, lank, pale young man, scarcely twenty-two years of age. But they whispered to one another that he was the strange young man from Caernarvonshire of whom they had heard such wonderful reports. The leaders of the Monthly Meeting could hardly refuse to accept him, because he had been sent by Mr Richardson, who commanded their respect. But many were hesitant, and looked askance at the unassuming young preacher, then quite unknown to them. When he ascended the pulpit steps, he did so in a manner which drew their attention. He read a chapter of Scripture in such a way as to convince his hearers that they had never heard that chapter before! His prayer was humble yet striking, quiet yet fervent; the worshippers ascended with him even to the very portals of heaven. His sermon on the occasion is not remembered, but the Anglesey-ites changed their minds before he had finished his discourse, and treated him with much respect. They even asked him to come again, and he promised to pay them another visit soon.

Elias records his removal to Anglesey in the following words: 'In the beginning of the year 1799, Providence ordered my removal from Caernarvonshire to Anglesey. It was a sorrowful experience to part with my friends, but we separated in love – to God be the praise!'

There is no doubt but that the Lord, in mercy to Anglesey, brought Elias there: for it was sunk into the lowest state of corruption and immorality. The sins and iniquities of the people were like those of Sodom and Gomorrah, crying up to heaven for vengeance. But the Lord, instead of dealing with them according to their abominations and rebellions, showed the most tender compassion towards them, brought one of his choice ministers there, and commissioned him to publish to them peace and reconciliation through the blood of the Lamb! And great and astonishing were the effects which attended that ministry.

That the improved condition of Anglesey might be seen to advantage, we must more minutely review its awful state of sin and misery, when Elias went to reside there. I believe there are no less than seventy-four parishes in the island, which is twenty-nine miles long and about twenty-two broad. It is lamentable to observe, that the regular watchmen in Israel were then sleeping at their posts; and worse still, they even partook of the follies and corruptions of the age, and went so far as to oppose the messengers of peace and salvation to the island in those days. The Rev Daniel Rowland and the Rev William Williams were prevented by them from preaching the words of everlasting life at Llangefni. Besides, Howell Harris and other preachers of the gospel were in danger of losing their lives there. It is a cause of great thankfulness that the revival of religion which has taken place in the island since Elias went there has extended also to the Church of England, and that the Clergy appear far more respectable there now than formerly. As to the nature of the abominations in Anglesey, much may be known from a small pamphlet published by Elias some years afterwards, with a view to reform the place. It was written in the form of a dialogue, and alludes chiefly to the sins that arose from the corrupt intercourse between the young people of both sexes, in the lowest class of society. The sin of fornication was countenanced to a very great extent. The manner of intercourse of young people before marriage was most corrupt! Those painful abominations are exposed to our indignation in the Word of God. *Job* 24. 15, 16. *Proverbs* 7.15—18. The many illegitimate children in that county were proofs of the awfully depraved state of the young.

Great were Elias's exertions with the parents of children and teachers of Sunday Schools, as he was catechising, to put a stop to those most corrupt and depraved habits. He would teach parents and children principles of the greatest abhorrence of those depraved practices, yea, as much as theft and murder; and assured heads of families that if they tolerated their servants and domestics in such evil ways, their blood would be required at their hands. How awfully would he represent the account they should give of themselves in this and every sinful connivance, in the day of judgment. He would urge most forcibly the attention of Sunday School teachers to guard the rising generation as much as possible against such corruptions; and he would show ministers the necessity of crying down with all their might such abominations; saying, 'that except they took such a decided and zealous step, their account would be awful in the last day.' 'O! let ministers, teachers of Sunday Schools, and heads of families,' he would say, 'speak as kindly as possible to the young people, and assure them that nothing but their eternal benefit urges you thus to speak to them.' Thus he endeavoured by all means to put a stop to the current of iniquity that seemed to deluge the whole country. There were a few like Elias, whose souls were grieved by reason of the iniquity of the place, as Lot's was on account of the abominations of Sodom. Drunkenness was also most prevalent among the common people in the island; than which nothing can be more hurtful to health and morals, as it leads to all other evils. Another crying evil there, was the plundering of vessels that were wrecked on the Welsh shore. They used to go there like hungry dogs or beasts of prey, in search of the property of those who were in the greatest distress and suffering. Even the heathen of Melita showed a very different spirit towards Paul and his companions in distress (*Acts* 28). Sabbath breaking was very common! Quarrelling and fighting were practised then in a terrible manner in the county. By the account Elias gives of the state of religion in Anglesey, it must have been very low. The following statements relate to periods later than 1799, when he went thither:

'When I went to Anglesey in 1799', he says, 'there were very few chapels in the county, and some of them small and very inconvenient. The hearers were not numerous, but when popular preachers from South Wales, or an occasional one from North Wales, came to Amlwch and a few other places, the hearers increased. The religious societies were in general very small.' Elias met with great encouragement from the societies: 'There were some godly members in them', he says, 'shining like luminaries, though their gifts were not great; but their consciences were tender, and their spirits broken, and their hearts blazing in love to God, Christ, his cause and his people. God's gracious presence was often evident in these small societies! There were here a few laborious and faithful preachers and elders, such as John Jones, of Bodynolwyn, who was the chief elder of the Monthly Meetings,[1] and many others, who were faithful and diligent. Also, Mr Richard Lloyd, Cae'r-glaw (afterwards of Beaumaris),[2] who was at that time a diligent young man, and very acceptable. He had the honour of being faithful unto death; "he kept the faith, and received the crown". He was beloved by all the brethren. He was a humble man and very peaceable. The Church in Anglesey suffered such a loss in his death, that it has not yet been made up.'

Elias highly valued Richard Lloyd, and was much attached to him. The union and friendship between them shall be noticed hereafter. Though Anglesey was in a most distressing state as to religion and morals, when he commenced his labours there, yet the aid he had to proceed with in that all-important engagement was very promising and very congenial to his taste, and suitable to his hand. He soon appeared here also under the blessing of God to be a very uncommon minister: his gigantic and vigorous mind, and holy zeal, soon enlivened and animated those fellow-labourers whose hearts were right with the Lord. He was indeed a burning and a shining light among them, and they rejoiced greatly in his light. His energetic and active soul aroused and quickened all that was dormant and ready to die. He soon gained an ascendancy among them in consequence of his illustrious talents, as well as the spirituality of his mind and devotedness of his heart. Perhaps he was in no degree inferior to Daniel Rowland or Howell Harris for zealous energetic activity in awakening a dead sleeping country. Like them he was most eminently qualified for the arduous office of prophesying to a valley of dry bones. He was filled by the Holy Ghost with amazing vigour and readiness for the work. He went forth as a giant to run his course, and the Lord was with him and

---

[1] John Jones (1747–1814), a native of Cardiganshire, where he began to preach. He came to Caernarvonshire as a schoolmaster, and moved to Anglesey in 1780. He used to preside in the Monthly Meetings in Anglesey. He was much persecuted on account of his religious beliefs.

[2] Richard Lloyd (1771–1834), a grandson of William Prichard, of Clwchder-nog, a pioneer of Nonconformity. He joined the Methodist Society at Gwalchmai in 1789, and began to preach in 1794. He moved to Beaumaris in 1800. He was ordained in 1811, and until his death a respected minister in the island. John Elias's remains were laid to rest alongside his in the quiet churchyard of Llanfaes.

prospered him exceedingly in this new part of the vineyard. He having the help of such instruments ready for his hand, entered upon his arduous labours in Anglesey with great intrepidity and zeal. The Monthly Meetings soon found that the Lord had raised up a great prophet among them: they soon experienced the uncommon spiritual heat and light that were diffused among them from above through his means. The leaders of societies went home from those meetings to their several charges with uncommon joy, communicating under the Spirit's blessing the light, warmth, and life they had received, to those spiritual children that were awaiting their return at the different societies. The consequence was, that those small churches were soon strengthened, and also enlarged; for they had the benefit of his personal visits, and experienced the power, sweetness, and unction of those great doctrines from his own lips.

His preaching became at length the most attractive in the island, his fame going forth everywhere, so that he was attended by the whole population of the neighbourhood wherever he went; and places of worship that were before despised and shunned as most contemptible, were frequented when he occupied them, by even the respectable people. So the poor degraded cause began to lift up its head everywhere. Moreover, wherever the Associations were held, they were exceedingly crowded by reason of this uncommon preacher, and there he shone as brightly as he did on his itinerant journeys. When he came forward on the platform, the greatest attention was paid to him, and he by the blessing of God brought forth such truths as edified and astonished all. The Spirit of the Lord owned him exceedingly on these occasions, so that the Divine presence crowned the Association, that was before so low. There was no doubt that the Associations and itinerant sermons of Elias and his friends had the most happy and reciprocal good effect upon each other, and unitedly tended to arouse a country dead in trespasses and sins. No man could be more suitable for these most important public opportunities, as well as itinerant preaching, than Elias.

Soon Anglesey appeared a very different country; a great thirst for the Word of God was apparent everywhere. The people were greatly impressed with regard to their souls and eternal concerns. The works of darkness, in which they had been so deeply engaged, began to subside gradually. When the Sun of Righteousness did arise upon that benighted country in its glorious light and benign warmth, superstition, immorality and vice could not be so bold, but were obliged to retire, and in a great measure to give up the place. Religion, truth and righteousness appeared in the land and gained ground. It is delightful to state that those evils for which Anglesey was so peculiar soon sustained a great check, and were viewed as odious and shameful. The success his sermons met with is wonderful. The gentlemen of Anglesey intended having horse-races once: Elias heard of it, then itinerated through the country, and preached so powerfully and alarmingly, till the people were so terrified, that all ideas of having horse races were given up. He also drove the players entirely out of the island by means of his sermons, though they tried to make him an object of ridicule on the stage. He was most determined and resolute in all he took in hand. The Gospel is the instrument intended and employed by God for the pulling down of the strong holds of sin and satan. And he has declared that 'his word shall not return to him void', when commissioned to execute his will, but that it shall prosper in doing all his mind.

The plan of the Welsh Calvinistic Methodists is peculiarly adapted for seeking the lost sheep; the shepherd goes *after* it until he finds it. The spiritual ambassador enters the very camp of the enemy, in search of the captives of satan, and there proclaims salvation to them by the death of Immanuel. There seems to be no plan so well calculated for missionary exertions as that of the Methodists. Anglesey and Wales itself was at that time more like a heathen country than anything else. It is evident that the great cause of its present much altered condition, was itinerant preaching, and attacking, under God's blessing, the enemy on his own ground. One of the chief leaders in those powerful and successful inroads upon the kingdom of Satan was John Elias. It is a mark of Divine wisdom to have introduced him into this wilderness country. God had appointed and qualified him in an extraordinary manner as a minister of the gospel, and now in his wise providential care leads him where he had much work for him. It is not probable, humanly speaking, that he would have been so useful in his own county, especially as he was of a low origin: we know that no prophet has any honour in his own country, however well qualified and gifted he may be. Not that he had left Caernarvonshire entirely, for on the itinerant plan, ministers were allowed a wide sphere of exertion. Elias went occasionally there, as it is an adjoining county, and there his popularity and usefulness were more extensive.

The cause of God in the Connexion was greatly revived under the influence of Elias's ministry and that of kindred men. No doubt many persons went to hear him everywhere over that county as well as Anglesey that would not otherwise enter the chapels; I mean more particularly those in the higher and middle classes of society. There was a necessity soon of enlarging the chapels in most places, and of building new ones in others. What a proof of the success of his ministry is such a chapel as that of Caernarvon, capable of holding about 3000 persons!

But it was not only in Anglesey and Caernarvonshire that the wonderful influence of Elias's extraordinary sermons was felt, but in every part of Wales. Wherever he went, he was exceedingly well attended: thousands went to hear him every where. The Word of God was exceedingly blessed from his lips, and many persons were convinced and converted; and such as should, it is hoped, be everlastingly saved, were added to the church in every part and district.

Though most usefully engaged in travelling through different counties in preaching the everlasting gospel, he was not free from liability to various dangers and temptations. But the Lord took peculiar care of his servant, and he felt truly grateful to his heavenly Father. There is a passage in his autobiography containing a remarkable observation on his preservation from the spirit and manners of the world, which we shall introduce here as it is worthy of great attention. He was indeed liable, very liable to these evils, especially in commencing his itinerant labours. He relates with great simplicity his fears and apprehensions of such evils in travelling through a country so full of danger. His eye was directed

to the Lord for help. His words on this remarkable occasion are the
following: 'I had much fear, as I was a young, unmarried man,
lest I should be permitted to become frivolous and jocular,
following youthful inclinations, and thus bringing a disgrace on
God's cause; but the Lord preserved me for his great name's sake.'

This is very valuable and pleasing information. We trace everything to the source of all goodness, the grace of God. A young
preacher like Elias, having the range of the whole country, and
being exceedingly popular and beloved must have been very much
exposed to temptations, especially those of vanity, levity, and
folly, so incident to youth at all times, even to those that are converted. But Elias was on his guard like young Joseph and Josiah,
both in spirit and conduct, fleeing youthful lusts, and walking in
the fear of the Lord. His life indeed, and prudential manner of
proceeding, are bright examples to young men similarly circumstanced.

The conduct of Elias's brethren and fellow-labourers in
Anglesey towards him, when he came among them, was highly
creditable and praiseworthy. Instead of manifesting any unpleasant feeling towards him on account of his great popularity,
they showed every kindness and respect, and encouraged him to
take an active part among them, and to abound in the ministry
and in labours of love. His own account of the happy union is the
following: 'The brethren in the Anglesey Monthly Meeting
were very kind to me. Though I was a young man, coming from
another county among them, yet they received me in a brotherly
spirit, and called me forward to work with them, and to pull
under the same yoke with them. Through grace we continued
to work together peaceably until many of them finished their
course.'

Then Elias goes on to give an account in his usual simple,
affectionate manner, of the frequent and urgent calls on him from
the beginning, to preach the gospel every where in the island. The
labour would have overwhelmed him, had he not been young and
very strong. But the Lord was with him in supporting and blessing
his ministry most abundantly, as we have already observed. Thus
he proceeds in his narrative:

There was a great call on me to preach not only on the Sabbath, but also on week-nights in many houses of the people. In this way, the Lord stirred the minds of the people to attend the places of worship more regularly. Some of these were saved by God through his infinite grace. I used to preach often in solitary places – on a mountain side, by the sea shore, on the wayside. I was at times greatly supported by the Lord when engaged in those exercises in such places. The Lord blessed these means to bring many to hear; perhaps some persons received eternal benefit; but that will be seen on the Great Day.

Wonderful must have been the attraction of his ministry, since such a vast body of people used to attend it even in a wilderness. And with what diffidence do we observe him speaking of their conversions! However, he notices what was perceptible to all: and he observes in his autobiography the great success that attended these efforts in conjunction with his brethren, for the good of souls and the glory of God in the island. Thus he speaks on the subject:

A great increase in outward things has attended the cause of religion among the Methodists in Anglesey during the last forty years. Great multitudes flocked to hear the Word; the number of professors has greatly multiplied: many large and convenient places of worship have been built. About forty-four chapels have been built within the last forty years; some of them very spacious. The Sunday Schools are numerous.

Such is the retrospect he took on the state of things in the religious world among his people, on his departure. It must be a cause of thankfulness. The Lord had done wonderful things for his great name in the island, by humble instruments.

I will here subjoin a few more of the rules that were intended by Elias and his friends to govern the members of the Connexion, that we may see how much society must improve by following them.

6.   That every member be careful and attentive in faithfully discharging the several duties enjoined him in the Word of God, according to his respective relation and situation in life:
   Husbands to love their wives, and honour them as the weaker vessels, and not to be bitter against them. *Ephesians* 5.25-31. *Colossians* 13.9. I *Peter* 3.7.

Wives to love their husbands; to submit themselves to them in the Lord, and to obey them. I *Corinthians* 7.34. *Ephesians* 5.22. *Colossians* 3.18. *Titus* 2.5. I *Peter* 3.1.

Parents to love their children, and not to provoke them to anger; but to govern them, and to bring them up in the nurture and admonition of the Lord. *Deuteronomy* 6.7. *Proverbs* 1.10; 13.24; 22.6, 15. *Ephesians* 6.4. I *Timothy* 3.4. 2 *Timothy* 3. 15.

Children to love, honour, and obey their parents in all things in the Lord. *Genesis* 47.12. *Exodus* 20.12. *Numbers* 30.5. *Proverbs* 10.1. *Colossians* 3.20.

Masters to be just and kind towards their servants, and to forbear threatening. *Genesis* 18.19. *Deuteronomy* 24.14. *Matthew* 8.6. *Ephesians* 6.9. *Colossians* 4.1.

Servants to obey their masters, in singleness of heart as unto Christ; not with eye-service as men-pleasers, but as the servants of Christ, doing the will of God from the heart – not answering again, not purloining. *Ephesians* 6.5, 6, 7. I *Timothy* 6.1, 2. I *Peter* 2.18, 19, 20.

7. That they be not unequally yoked in the marriage state with unbelievers; and also, that in their previous intercourse, as well as in their manner of entering into that state, they would conduct themselves with all decency, sobriety, and godliness. 2 *Timothy* 2.22. 2 *Corinthians* 6.14. *Deuteronomy* 7.3.

13. That they be people of pure speech—avoiding all corrupt communications, foolish talking and jesting; not double-tongued, nor given to detraction. *Matthew* 12.37. *Ephesians* 4.29; 5.3, 4.

14. That they ask and give to all what is just and equitable—according to the rate of the market. *Deuteronomy* 2.6. *Proverbs* 20.10.

16. That they speak no evil of dignities, but that they conscientiously honour and obey the Queen, and all that are put in authority under her; showing all fidelity in word and deed to the Government we happily live under; acknowledging, with gratitude, the protection, the liberty, and the great privileges, both of a temporal and of a religious nature, which we so abundantly enjoy. *Exodus* 22.28. *Romans* 13. 1, 7. I *Timothy* 2.2. 2 *Peter* 2.10. *Jude* 8–10.

I will here introduce a few Rules of this Connexion, that strongly oppose some of the vices mentioned in this chapter.

That they be willing and determined, in the strength of the Lord, to forsake every evil way; to dissolve association with sinful companions; to renounce the pomps and vanities of this wicked world; to abstain from all corrupt practices, such as card-playing, going to plays, and assemblies for dancing; from intemperate feasting, rioting, and drunkenness. *Romans* 12.2. 1 *Corinthians* 10.31. *Ephesians* 5.4. *Titus* 2.12. 1 *Peter* 4.3. *Isaiah* 5.22.

That they do not trade or deal in smuggled goods. *Romans* 13.7. *Luke* 20.22, 25.

That no one is to continue a member, who is implacable and unforgiving towards his brethren, who may have offended him; nor such as is contentious and quarrelsome among his neighbours. *Titus* 3.2. *Colossians* 3.12, 13. *Ephesians* 5.2.

That they and their families keep holy the Sabbath-day, abstaining not only from all worldly transactions, but also all unnecessary words about worldly employments and recreations; idle talk and visits; all vain and foolish conversation. *Isaiah* 58.13, 14.

It is delightful to observe that a cause so spiritual, beneficial and glorious did arise in such a wilderness as Anglesey: a proof of Elias's amazing usefulness. His influence under God's blessing was productive of great good: and his superintendence over Christ's household was very extensive and beneficial. The nature of his stewardship will be seen in the following letter, which was written to the leaders of one of the societies in that county, when he was in London, preaching to his countrymen.

London 21 April 1817

I take this opportunity of saluting you, dear brethren, though I am absent from you in body, yet I am present with you in spirit. Everything is very quiet now in this great City, though thousands of the poor are much distressed. When Cobbett, Hunt and others, were silenced, the people became calm immediately. Things in the church are also better: we are enabled to proceed with every part of the great work in peace and harmony. A great concourse of people attend the public means; many of them cannot get into the chapel. Blessed be God, I am not left to myself in preaching to them. It is an unspeakable mercy that the Lord should favour me, one so vile and unworthy, with a degree of his presence and support. Alas! many of the people that attend the preaching of the Word now, are generally very negligent of that ordinance: yea, many of them are very erroneous, being deists and socinians. O! that I might be a faithful witness for God and the truth to them! I am very unsuitable and insufficient in myself to be profitable to any of them in a spiritual manner. O! brethren, pray for me.

The Lord's work is also very great in your country; you will therefore look up for his guidance and support. It is most desirable that you should take heed to yourselves, and all the flock of Christ under your care; nothing can be more important than to feed the church of God, whom he hath purchased with his precious blood, and to watch willingly over souls, as they that must give an account. *Acts* 20.28; 1 *Peter* 5.2; *Hebrews* 13.17. O! brethren, pray for grace to be faithful; so that you may be useful in the church, and be able to give up your account with joy. It is of little signification what talents you have, and what office and situation you occupy in the church, but it is of the utmost importance to be faithful. We have talents enough, when we consider the account we are to give of them in the last day. We have sufficient ground to occupy, when we think of the strict examination we shall then undergo, as to the cultivation of it. The hand will not complain in that awful day that it had not the office of the eye, nor the foot that it had not that of the hand. Every one will have to give an account of his own occupation and employment: let us therefore pray that we may be faithful.

Let us endeavour to act in every thing for God's glory, not seeking our own interest in any respect or manner whatever. We should aim not only to appear before men as sincere in the Lord's work, that they may have no room to imagine we are selfish, but we should also take care that our principles and motives are pure *before* God. If self-denial is absolutely necessary for all the followers of Christ, how much more so it must be for the officers of his church. We shall not be acceptable with God without this grace, though we had the talents of men and angels! It would be very easy for us to deny ourselves, if we knew ourselves that we are such sinful and miserable creatures, so vile, weak, and imperfect christians, so unlike Christ, that our graces are so poor, feeble and obscure. It is when we are humble we are likely to be useful.

Let us also be careful, brethren, that the cause of religion be very near our hearts. Let us be particular, yea, excel in all our endeavours, for the building up of the church of God. Let us mind also, that the disposition and tendency of our spirits, words, and conduct, be not the means of injuring the great cause in any way. Let us be sure to observe the little foxes that injure the vineyard, and by the grace of God to extirpate them. *Canticles* 2.15. And let us pray much that we may be spiritual persons in the Lord's work, and that we do not appear unfeeling, dry, and selfish in any part of our employment therein.

Let us persevere in our endeavours to keep the unity of the Spirit in the bond of peace. Love to God is primary and influential: when our love to Him gets cold, brotherly love will do the same. Love and union are great things in a country, neighbourhood, and family; how much more so in the church, which is the house of the God of peace, the kingdom of the Prince of peace, and the dwelling-place of the sons of peace, the heavenly Jerusalem. In order to preserve this holy fire, we must be watchful, self-denying, meek, kind, forbearing, forgiving, courteous, avoiding evil speaking. The tongue of the slanderer, and the ear of the receiver of evil communications, are Satan's great instruments.

Dear brethren, labour much for growth in unfeigned love of the brethren, that you may 'love one another with a pure heart fervently'. I *Peter* 1.22. May you be of a humble, meek and evangelical spirit in the great work of the Lord, that you may strive with one mind, heart, and expression, for the faith of the gospel! Submit yourselves one to another in the fear of God; and so you will help each other in the work the gates of hell are opposed to. *Ephesians* 5.21. Union is the strength and the glory of the church. There is union and concord in hell against us; may we withstand them by a stronger and better union, yea, union in the Lord. Again I say, may you all be obedient to each other: be inwardly adorned with the grace of humility, and 'in honour preferring each other', considering the humblest place in the church too good for you, and wondering that God and his people should give us the least employment in his house, and that he has not deprived us of the talent, and cast us away as unfaithful and unfruitful! O! that we may be examples to the flock in every grace and virtue, in spirit, in word, and conduct; let us all follow the great Shepherd. As in accounts, all the cyphers stand for nothing, if not put after some figure; so all the under shepherds are nothing, except as they are united to Christ, the chief shepherd, and following his example. May we be also the light of the world, the salt of the earth, that neither his Word, name, doctrine, cause, or people, should be blasphemed on our account!

Dear brethren, I am myself sensible of the need of these things continually, therefore I recommend them to others. The way I came to possess a few of them, was by going, as a poor sinner, to the throne of grace, seeking them out of the fulness that is in the great Mediator. A view of him impresses some measure of his image on the soul; he is the delight of my poor soul. O that I may enjoy more of his fellowship. O that I may see him more clearly

Over the momentous subject of marriage Elias had exercised many
an anxious thought, and offered many prayers, seeking in the
formation of this relationship, in an especial manner, the Lord's
guidance and providential care. No doubt he favoured his servant
greatly in this as well as in every other respect. The person that he
had appointed for him, was truly pious and conscientious, and in
every way suitable for him, as we shall presently see.

The lady of his choice lived in the small village of Llanfechell in
the northern part of the island. Miss Elizabeth Broadhead kept a
shop in the village. Her parents lived at Tre'r Gof, Llanbadrig,
about a mile to the north-west. She was the eldest of six sisters.
Her father, Richard Broadhead, was descended from a craftsman
who had been sent from England to repair Caernarvon Castle; he
was a wealthy man, and possessed a small estate in the district.
Elizabeth had been brought up by her uncle, a clergyman who
lived with his sisters at Neuadd Cemlyn. She was well educated
according to the standards of her day, and had been brought up
befitting her station in society. It appears that she had sinned
against the proprieties of her family by consorting with one
Edward Jones, one of her father's tenants, who was also an elder
with the Methodists. A Methodist preacher from South Wales
noticed her, and laying his hands on her head he remarked,
prophetically, 'Perhaps she will *see* one day'. Her family was
scandalised by this impropriety, and utterly cast down when she
was converted under the ministry of a Methodist preacher. Life
became unbearable for her at Neuadd Cemlyn, and she was compelled to seek shelter in the home of Shadrach Williams, her
maternal uncle. The doors of Neuadd Cemlyn were shut against

her, and she could not regard Tre'r Gof as her home any longer. But through her uncle's influence and help, she commenced a small business on her own responsibility in a house owned by him at Llanfechell. She soon joined the Methodist Society at Llanrhuddlad, a village situated about four miles from Llanfechell.

Elias met Miss Broadhead during one of his journeys in Anglesey, and very soon they became attached one to another and arranged to be married. But Richard Broadhead objected to his daughter's marriage. It was unthinkable, in his opinion, for a landowner's daughter to be married to an impoverished Methodist preacher. But love had its way, and John Elias and Elizabeth Broadhead were joined together in the holy estate of matrimony. The bridegroom's friend, on the occasion, was Richard Jones, of Coedcae-du (afterwards of Wern), who delivered a sermon by the house at Llanfechell in the evening after the marriage service, on the text, 'And Adam called his wife's name Eve; because she was the mother of all living'.

Elias's account of this interesting occurrence in his life, is as follows:

On 22 February 1799, I married Elizabeth, the eldest daughter of Richard Broadhead, of Tre'r Gof, Llanbadrig, Anglesey; she was then living at Llanfechell. Four children were born to us. The two eldest are still alive; they were nurtured in the church, and have been preserved there until the present day (1841). They are both over forty years of age, and have families. My son John lives at Llanfechell in the house where he was born. My daughter Phoebe lives now in London. The greatest thing in my mind respecting them was bringing them up in the Lord, that they might dwell in the house of the Lord all the days of their lives, living in godliness to his glory in the world. Blessed be God who did not reject my prayer for them. Our two youngest children did not survive in this world but for a few hours. I gave them, before they were born, to him who promised to be a God to me and my children. I am persuaded that they were allowed to flee from the womb, in a few hours, from the afflictions of this life to everlasting happiness, through the sovereign grace of God, being purified through the blood of the Cross.

What strong consolation it is for parents, under such bereavements, to have firm ground to believe that their departed children are gone to a world of perfect bliss and happiness. It was this prospect that made David change his appearance and conduct, rejoicing that he should go to his child in the land of glory. Elias having seen the wisdom and goodness of the Lord in all his ways, was disposed to acquiesce in his holy will in this bereavement; and under all trials and afflictions he doubtless learned much of the Lord's ways; namely, that man is a dependent creature, and that God is the fountain of all goodness, from whence different blessings flow to us, which he has a right to recall whenever he pleases.

After his daughter's marriage, Richard Broadhead soon relented; he withdrew his opposition and they became reconciled. He knew that his son-in-law had but a precarious living as a Welsh Methodist preacher. His resources were very slender, even according to the standards of that age. Mr Broadhead, however, was soon won over by the gentlemanly conduct of his son-in-law, and in time he even became proud of his connection with a preacher of such fame and popularity.

The manner in which the surviving children of Elias were brought up was very good and promising, affording a strong ground to hope that it would be under the blessing and sanction of him who has said, 'Train up a child in the way he should go, and when he is old he shall not depart from it.' To be brought up in the church of God has a greater meaning than many are aware of; it is to enjoy all its privileges. To these they have a right, as members of the church, into which they were admitted in baptism. These Christian privileges are very considerable in Wales: there, Christians of orthodox principles, meet once a week as a church, to hold the communion of saints by conversing on religious subjects and divine things belonging to the kingdom of heaven. Surely it is an unspeakable privilege for the rising generation, the children of believers: hearing the most godly persons speaking of the love and goodness of that God to whom they were dedicated in baptism, and hearing such a conversation, and the various experiences of such humble, penitent, simple-hearted Christians, weekly, must excite their attention, and draw their minds to the consideration of those divine truths. And at length they are likely, under the blessing of God, to become acquainted with religion in its beauty and excellency, and by degrees take pleasure in it, finding its ways to be ways of pleasantness, and its paths, paths of peace. In course of time, that particular promise is also often verified in the experience of these highly privileged young ones: 'He that walketh with wise men, shall be wise.' *Proverbs* 13.20. Who therefore that is entitled to such an invaluable privilege, but would most joyfully avail himself of it for his children? It is, as we may well suppose, greatly prized by parents in the Principality; and they take their children with joy weekly to the church of God. I here subjoin an article of religion belonging to the Welsh Calvinistic Methodists.

Every member who has children, is enjoined to bring them at the earliest dawn of reason, to the private society, or meetings of the church, into which they are initiated by the ordinance of baptism; where, unless they manifest any immorality of conduct, they are allowed to remain with their parents, entitled to the instructions, admonitions, and watchful care of the society, and subject to its discipline. But they are, nevertheless, withheld from the Lord's supper, until they arrive at years of maturity; until they, by their conduct, evidence a change of heart, and until they express a desire to commemorate the Saviour's dying love.

Elias had a great regard for home discipline, as well as for the great advantage of church membership, for his children. His corrections and discipline at home were built on gospel principles, and conducted according to the Word of God. It is a very great point in training up children rightly, to maintain proper authority over them. It is by no means unimportant that parents should obtain the victory over their children in the very first affair, where their wills clash. Elias would at times vary his mode of discipline; it was of course according to the nature of the crime, and the circumstances of the transgressions. He would not in a general way, the main principles being established, chastise for the first offence, but would rebuke, giving the most serious, impressive, and suitable instructions and advice. If the same act of disobedience should ever be repeated, he would treat it in a different manner: it was necessary to have a surety for the child's good behaviour then, as if the matter were of the greatest importance, in which one's property or life might be concerned. But if the same offence was committed again at any time, he would make use of the rod to chastise, and that sharply. But he and his wife would, however, first of all engage in prayer on this painful occasion, laying their case before the Lord, intreating him to have mercy on the child and bless the intended chastisement. But both were not present when the rod was used.

Elias endeavoured to put his children out of the way of temptation, especially at times when enticements were presented. Fairs are kept three times in the year at Llanfechell: he would be sure to send the children out of the way from home to some friends during that time. And after they were grown up a little, and become useful in the shop, he would put some articles of the shop goods under their care to sell, and give a considerable reward for what they disposed of, during the fair: they took such delight in the business, as it afforded them constant profits, that they forgot to look at crowds of young people.

Elias's conversation with his family was cheerful and instructive. If he had been reading something particular and suitable for the children, he would write it down and give it them. It was Mr Thomas Charles's Catechism he recommended. But he would sometimes, when at home, also catechise the children out of the Scriptures which they had committed to memory.

Dear father [says Phoebe] would always, if absent on the Lord's day, inquire on his return how we had spent the Sunday, and where the texts were, and what we had heard. He was very particular as to the company we kept: and so was my dear mother: she often used to tell us to be very cautious as to our deportment, and to conduct ourselves as became those that professed godliness. 'Remember also', she would say, 'the great cause, and your father's name; how can he stand up to teach others, if his own children do not walk in the way in which they should go?' Family prayers were kept up very regularly, which was a great advantage to us. Nothing was suffered to prevent them. In the summer time, we were obliged to open the shop very early, long before breakfast; but the doors were always closed at family prayers. My mother, in my father's absence, prayed with us, and never omitted this good practice whoever might be in the house. He often reminded us of our duty to our mother, to do every thing in our power to make her comfortable when he was from home. He always governed with authority, yet love dwelt on his lips.

Elias was most earnest, urgent, and solicitous before the throne of grace, for the divine blessing on his exertions with his children. He knew that all was in vain, except the Lord would favour his attempts in the important work of correcting, and maintaining discipline. When the time came to put the children to school from home, he was very particular in placing them under the care of those that feared the Lord. His son once wrote to me on this subject as follows:

Our beloved father was very careful as to the company we kept. I well remember when he took me to the Rev Mr Lloyd of Abergele's school, how he began, as we drew near the village, to advise me in the most serious manner to make the best use of my time, and to avoid all evil companions; and although I was rather high-minded then, yet his words made such an impression on my mind, that I could never forget them. Some time afterwards, he removed me to a school at Chester; and as I become older, and more liable to temptations and dangers, he warned me on the way in such a solemn manner against evil companions, and spoke in such terms, urging me to avoid their company, that it affected me so much, that I was afraid of every stranger I met, thinking he was the messenger of Satan to entice me out of the Church of God, tempting me to sell the Son of God for thirty pieces of silver.

No one can imagine how seriously, solemnly, and impressively he would speak, and communicate his ideas on subjects which he deemed important. It is not therefore wonderful that his son was so alarmed at seeing strangers, fearing his being drawn aside, after such particular warnings. The son, in the same letter, mentions another circumstance that occurred to him, in consequence of a conversation his father had with a friend at Mold one evening when he was preaching there. He thus relates it:

Understanding that my father was to preach at Mold, I went from Chester to meet him there, at the house of Mr Mathews, a friend of my father, who had a family. The two parents soon conversed upon useful and religious subjects. My father asked Mr Mathews if his children were in the society; he answered that they were. Then he asked another question, whether the young disciples had been fully received and admitted to the Lord's supper? He answered that they had not gone so far. And my father also observed very seriously that his children had not been favoured with that privilege. Their conversation had a great effect upon me: it laid hold like fire on my heart, so that I had no quietness in my mind until I was fully received as a member of Christ's church, receiving the holy sacrament. I wrote a letter to him afterwards, stating my case and uneasiness. I received a very kind and excellent letter from him in return, when far from home, which led me more into the subject, and made me more decided for taking the Lord's supper. If conversation of parents was ever blessed to their children, that was undoubtedly made very useful to me, though they said not a word to me personally on the sacrament.

The letter is the following:

London 29 April 1817

I send thee a few lines from this far distant city, hoping that thou art well, contented, serious, and comfortable. I think much of thee, my dear child: thy temporal and eternal welfare lies near my heart. I frequently remember thee before the throne of grace, and am at times rather confident that God will hear me on thy behalf. I have had much pleasure hundreds of times, since thou wast born, in endeavouring to give thee up unto the Lord, and to bring thee up in his house. When, my dear son, wilt thou give thyself unto the Lord with full purpose of heart to be his for ever? When wilt thou see the value of Christ and salvation in his blood, so as to induce thee to flee unto him and rest upon him, in order to be rescued into life everlasting? When wilt thou feel pleasure in making a personal profession of the Lord Jesus, and taking hold of the covenant? Thou didst receive one of the seals of the covenant in thine infancy, namely, baptism. But that privilege thou didst receive in the right of thy parents, under the idea of accepting the other in addition at some future time; and thou wast consequently brought up in the church of God. O what a privilege! When, my dear son, wilt thou come to take hold of the covenant for thyself, and to receive the other seal appertaining to it, namely, the Lord's supper? That is the time thou wilt show thy consent to what thy parents did for thee, in presenting thee to the Lord and bringing thee up in the church of God. O my beloved son! dost thou begin to see and to take hold of thy privilege? Unless thou seest its value thyself, it will not be much longer ere the world, the flesh, and the devil, will deprive thee of it! I hope such a dreadful event will never be the case. Must thy father, before he goes to the grave, endure the great affliction of seeing thee alienated from the church of Christ? God forbid. Now, therefore, my beloved son, 'hold thou fast that which thou hast, that no man take thy crown'. Pray much, that the Lord be pleased to enable thee to believe in his son Jesus Christ; then thou shalt never be lost, all thy sins shall be forgiven, and thy nature sanctified; thou shalt have the will and ability to 'live soberly, righteously, and godly, in this present world'.

Avoid more carefully the things that injure thy soul: abhor those things as the most bloody murderers, yea the murderers of thy soul: thou knowest thyself what they are; levity and jesting, hastiness and passion, impatience and sullenness under correction. Each of these things leads to very bad and dreadful consequences. Thou art aware of them, my dear son: therefore thou wilt not be offended at thy father, who loveth thee as his own soul, for pointing out what tend to thy eternal ruin. Therefore 'hear counsel and receive instruction, that thou mayest be wise in thy latter end'.

Think of the great God, who is everywhere present with thee, and seeth thee at all times – think of thy soul, which is immortal, and to endure everlastingly – think of the shortness of thy time, it is but little; what a pity to spend it in vanity: when a day has passed, there is no possibility of recalling it in order to be spent over again. Think frequently of death; it is a very solemn thing to die! Think of the judgment day, when we must render a strict account, yea for every idle word! Think of eternity; we shall soon be there! Think of Jesus dying, and be amazed and happy.

How suitable and sensible is the preceding letter, to one circumstanced as Elias's son was at that time, about sixteen years old, and seriously disposed. How few professors and ministers pay so much attention to the spiritual interest of their children as Elias did! Youths, consequently, instead of taking the yoke of Christ on them, rush into all the follies and vanities of the age!

A letter was written by Elias to his son at school on education ; it shows his mind on that important subject fully and distinctly, especially as to its value. It is the following:

Llanfechell 14 August 1819

I hope that thou now beginnest to take pleasure in thy learning. This is thy harvest, and if thou shouldest neglect this, thy treasure-house will be empty, as long as thou livest, of the greatest worldly wealth, that is, learning! What are gold and silver, houses and land, without knowledge? Nothing! Man is like the brute beast, without education. A person that is unlearned, cannot well enjoy the pleasures that human nature is capable of, especially under the influence of religion. Learning is very important, inasmuch as it teaches the mind to delight in true knowledge, and in making greater attainments in it; – to view the excellencies of others and to follow them, being never satisfied till we acquire them, – to observe the faults of others, and to flee from them. I have said a little respecting the value of learning, being sensible of my own deficiency in that respect. I think if I had to make a choice, whether to have all India, or Sir William Jones's learning, I should prefer the latter.

It is not in an easy, careless manner that we can get learning, understanding, and knowledge; no, it must be by labour, industry, and toil. It is necessary 'to cry after knowledge, and lift up the voice for understanding – to seek her as silver, and to search for her as for hid treasure' (*Proverbs* 2.3, 4). We are not to be disheartened and cast down, in not succeeding to obtain knowledge of things at the commencement; it is the work of time. It is not at once that flowers, animals, or mankind, arrive at full maturity; they grow *gradually*, and that by having a nourishment and support: so learning and knowledge; it is not at once and quickly they are attained, but by application, labour, and hard study. It is true that many a person wishes to be a scholar, and learned, but may not like the pains that are necessary to attain that end, and never enjoys what he desires. How true it is, 'the desire of the slothful killeth him; for his hands refuse to labour. But the hand of the diligent maketh rich' (*Proverbs* 10.4; 21.25).

Having spoken thus of the value of human learning and knowledge, I must say that there are more excellent attainments; the teachings of the Holy Ghost, and the knowledge of Christ and the Father. The Spirit has been promised, to teach us all things respecting Christ. It is the anointing of the Holy One, that is, Jesus: he teacheth us the knowledge of all things as they are, enabling us to know God, ourselves, and the Mediator; he instructs us how to live godly, to acquire every virtue and excellency, to hate the evil and to flee from it, to die happy, and to obtain eternal felicity. Every knowledge in comparison of that of Christ, is but loss and dung; to know him is everlasting life.

My dear son, be not disheartened as to the attainment of this knowledge: Christ, the great Prophet, makes the simple wise unto salvation. He is a kind teacher to those that are willing to learn of him, though slowly. It is not all at once that he instructs his disciples, but gives them line upon line, and precept upon precept; a little here and a little there, and that very patiently. So be thou diligent and constant in his school, sitting at his feet, to receive the words that drop from his lips.

Elias thus encourages his son in another letter:

Be not discouraged in finding thyself rather backward in Grammar and the English language. I know by thy letters that thou hast improved in these already. Thou shalt find it much easier to advance, as thou proceedest. Perfection is not to be had at once, but gradually, in diligent use of means. A man without learning is like an unpolished marble; there is beauty and excellency in the stone, but it will never shine, till it is polished.

The next letter we shall notice is one to his daughter on religion and education, being the first on record he wrote to her. She was then at a boarding school, about the age of fifteen, needing greatly such instructions as are conveyed in the following letter:

Llanfechell 23 August 1815

It affords me great satisfaction, my dear child, that thou art under the care of a pious lady, who feareth God, and loveth our Lord Jesus Christ; and therefore I know that she will recommend God in Christ, by her conversation and example, as the worthiest object of thy fear and love; and therefore, my dear daughter, I beg you will be careful, patiently to hear her instructions, readily to attend to her counsels, and diligently to follow her advice and example. For till thou hast more experience in the world, it will be far better for thee to trust in her than in thy own judgment.

O! consider the counsel and advice of the wisest of mankind: 'Remember now thy Creator in the days of thy youth'. The duty enjoined is expressed by the term, *remember*: the object to be remembered, is our *Creator:* the persons particularly called to remember are the *young:* and the time specified to do the duty, is now, 'in the days of thy youth'.

Read seriously, every morning and evening, a portion of the holy book of God, and acquaint thyself with the precious and heavenly matter which it contains. It is a book full of light and wisdom, it is able to make thee wise unto salvation through faith in Christ: it will furnish thee with principles and direction to guide and conduct thee safely and prudently through this vain and evil world, and to lead thee to eternal happiness.

My dear daughter, spend not the time of thy youth in vanity and sin;

thou must ere long give an account to God of every day and every hour of thy life, and for every word and action! But redeem the time, and with diligence gather some information and knowledge in the paths of piety and virtue, which shall be of use to thyself and friends for the remainder of thy days. Do not allow thyself to live in any known sin, nor in the neglect of any known duty. O! my dear child, flee to our Lord Jesus, our only Saviour; there is refuge and strength. Believe in him, then thou shalt have life; yea, thou shalt receive of his fulness, not only forgiveness of thy innumerable sins, but also every grace, and strength enough to enable thee to live godly and soberly in this present evil world. O! do not neglect secret prayer, but go to the throne of grace *as you are,* and humbly commend thyself to God through his Mediator Jesus Christ – implore his mercy to pardon you, his Spirit to direct you, his providence to protect you.

I hope the friends at *Tarvin* will have no objection to grant thee the privilege of being in the *society* with them; especially as thou hast had that great privilege ever since thou wast born: and I hope thou wilt enjoy it as long as thou livest. I think it would break my heart if I should ever see thee outside of the walls of the church of God. I trust, my dear girl, that thy conduct will be such as becometh the gospel of Christ, and thou wilt not give offence to any of the brethren, nor give any occasion to the enemies of the gospel to blaspheme, or to speak evil of the ways of God.

Elias wrote about this time another letter to his daughter, exciting in her feelings of gratitude and thankfulness to a friend, with whom she had been staying. It is the following, without date:

I wish thou wouldest gratefully acknowledge the great kindness of Mrs Jones and her family to thee. What are we, my dear child? We are not worthy of such kindness in any respect: it comes only for Christ's sake! Let me ask thee, my dear child, Dost thou know this? Is not Jesus Christ worthy of thy best thoughts? Dost thou love him? It would be a dreadful thing to appear before him at the last day, without knowing and loving him, after receiving so many privileges and mercies for his name's sake. I hope the merciful Lord will open thy eyes to know the Saviour – now in thy youthful days: this is life eternal. I hope thy conduct is humble, obedient, and becoming to every one in the house – so kind!

Do not these letters show that there is some extraordinary

pleasure and benefit in the house of God, the private society, that many are not aware of? And who could have thought that a person who had lately only three or four months' education in the English language, of which he was totally ignorant, could have written so good a letter? But, in general, he used to write letters to his children and friends in Welsh, which are translated. Elias used to go to London once in every three years, to preach the everlasting gospel to his poor countrymen there, so destitute of this means of grace. From thence he wrote the following letter to his daughter:

London 29 April 1817

I know, my dear child, that thy dangers from the world, the flesh, and Satan, increase in proportion to thy advancement in age. O! pray much for grace – for godliness. I feel a pleasure in praying for thee. Thou art in the most advantageous position to look for every blessing – in the means of grace, in the church of God. O! ever abide there. Wait patiently there for the Lord. Think often of Jesus Christ, the Saviour of sinners, and the Saviour of children. He delights in having young disciples. He took children in his arms; he was pleased to be praised by children in the temple; he raised up from the dead the daughter of Jairus, when twelve years old; he saved the woman of Canaan's daughter; who knows but that he will save my daughter also! I think the Lord heard my prayers, and those of others for thee, when thy natural life was in the greatest danger. Who knows but that thou wast saved from that danger, in order to be saved into everlasting life!

My dear Phoebe, endeavour to learn those things in thy youth, which will not be a disgrace to thee when advanced in age, if spared. Avoid every temper and habit which may be painful and disgraceful. Avoid a high proud carriage; it is abominable in the sight of God, and unbecoming before men. Beware of being impatient of instruction and correction – beware of an ungoverned dissatisfied revengeful temper – seek the meek and quiet spirit, which is in the sight of God of great price. 'The meekness of wisdom, which is gentle, easy to be entreated – the gentleness of Christ.' A lowly gentle temper is part of Christ's image; and 'after this manner the holy women of old adorned themselves'; and so the virtuous woman mentioned in *Proverbs*, has 'the law of kindness on her tongue' (31.26). The following things are accounted among the chief virtues of London ladies:

Modesty: this gives the most pleasant air to our looks, gestures, and conversation, and has obtained such an esteem among the judicious, that it will cover many defects. But without modesty, wit or learning will not shine, beauty will be ungrateful, and even quality will be contemptible; nothing can atone for the want of modesty.

The other quality of a lady, is good temper. If we give indulgence to bad temper in youth, it will be extremely difficult to govern that temper, or to reform it, when grown to years of maturity; and it is certain that more evils arise from ill temper, than from what they call ill fortunes. Therefore the government of the temper is of the greatest importance; and much of the happiness of private life, and of families too, depends upon this. Nothing can be more pleasing than good temper. Therefore, my dear daughter, pray often and earnestly for grace to govern your temper.

> *All ladies should endeavour to possess,*
> *An elegance of mind as well as dress.*

Be humble and submissive to thy dear mother – kind and agreeable to thy brother – pleasant to our servant girl. Don't tyrannize over her. My dear, do all in thy power to make thy poor mother happy, and to make our family an example of order and happiness. I hope thou wilt consider these things that thy poor father has sent in love to thy body and soul, and with a desire for thy happiness in time and eternity.

The stress Elias places, in this and other letters, on temper and conduct, as evidences of regeneration and effects of faith, plainly shows that the tendency of his ministry was far from being that of Antinomianism, with which some might charge him. Elias's daughter was now advancing into years of discretion and reflection, and showing signs of conversion; and he was in hopes, that in consequence of all the means of grace she had enjoyed, and all the attention he paid to her spiritual concern, she might under God's blessing, be disposed to come to the Lord's supper and make a full profession of Christ. He wrote a similar letter to her as the one to his son, already seen: he had the pleasure of seeing them both coming, when young, to the Lord's table, with right views and motives.

Elias's son, when at school, used to write to him for information on some difficult points of divinity. He was much pleased at perceiving in him a tendency to make inquiries of that kind, and would endeavour to encourage and satisfy him.

Llanfechell 1819

Thy letter has too great a leaning to the Antinomian doctrine, in mistaking what is said about man's inability, and thereby tending to put the blame on God. Thou dost appear to think as if thou hast nothing to do, except something wonderful should arrest thee, as happened to Saul in going to Damascus. Nothing to do but to remain in thy sins! And that the Almighty is to be blamed, that he does not call thee from them, and draw thee even against thy will! O! my dear son, beware of erring. Though man is dead in trespasses and sins, yet he is not dead as a stone or wood. Man is not without a soul and faculties, to act powerfully and quickly. But, alas! man's spiritual death and inability is his enmity against God, and his love to sin and evil! *Romans* 8.7, 8. There is no inclination in his will to forsake sin, and to turn to the Lord. *John* 5.40. Our sin is our disgrace, and our inability is our shame. We ought to be ashamed, and to blush to confess, that we are unable to love God who is so delightful and glorious, and unable to hate sin which is so odious and abominable; unable to receive Christ who is so precious and excellent, and freely offered without money and price. The Lord, in saving sinners, deals with them as rational beings. He does not draw them as stones, or drive them as brute animals; but works in them as men, showing them the evil of sin, their deserts and misery, and that their ruin is entirely at their own door; then exhibiting Christ and complete salvation by him to them as lost sinners, until the soul is brought to desire, choose, and receive Christ, to cry out from the heart for salvation, saying, 'O! to be found in Christ!' And if thou, my dear son, seest thyself in a miserable state – thy sins innumerable, and pressing heavy upon thee; flee, flee quickly to Christ. Why shouldest thou die? There is no deficiency there, but an unspeakable fulness, always free for the needy. Only believe God, who cannot lie, bearing testimony of his Son – only go to the door of mercy where none are rejected. Give over despairing words. Thou shalt never say that thou hast been at Christ's door and hast had no reception. Use all the means of grace, and wait humbly as a sinner that deserves nothing (*Habakkuk* 2.3.) Thou shalt not be lost in the act of looking at the door of mercy; seek to rest in Christ as the chief of sinners, thou shalt have strength to do so.

How well does Elias explain the doctrines of grace to his son! and how desirable is it that pious parents should thus encourage their children to open their minds to them on religious subjects! We shall introduce another letter of Elias to his son on two important subjects; namely, that a change of heart is more than an emotion of the passions; also, that Satan's devices are peculiar to young disciples. He begins this letter in reference to obedience to seniors:

Llanfechell 8 December 1819

I am not sorry that thou hast been at Liverpool, as it was to hear those eminent ministers. But I hope thou didst ask leave of thy master, and Mr Parry. It is most becoming for young persons to consult their superiors and governors. Indeed, following their own devices has been the means of ruining many a youth. I was glad thou didst hear Mr O. Jones, but was not pleased that thou didst murmur, because thou hadst some fine feeling under the preaching. My dear son, thou shouldest not presume to chalk out the way and time for the Almighty to work; and think, because thou couldest not weep under the sermon as others, thou hadst no benefit, and that if thou didst not receive the blessing soon, it would never come.

True religion does not consist in emotions. The passions of many are much excited under sermons, without a change of heart! Others may be changed; their hearts broken, conscience tender, sin hated, self loathed, but perhaps without many tears. There is a great difference in the natural temper of people, which accounts for the difference in their feelings under the Word preached. I confess that if people are easily moved under natural causes, but unmoveable and unaffected under sermons, it is a very bad sign. But the thing we should aim at in hearing the Word, is to see more of the greatness and majesty of God, the purity of the law, evil of sin, our miserable state by nature, the preciousness and excellency of Christ, the privilege of giving ourselves to him to be saved in his own way, and to serve him all the days of our life; and the feelings may be affected by those circumstances as God may see proper.

As to that expression, that except thou art soon converted, it will never take place, it is most presumptuous. Is it not rising above God? Is it not better to wait on him patiently, as it is directed in *Habakkuk* 2.3? Is it not becoming and proper for a sinner to wait at the gate of mercy even to death? None was ever lost there.

Satan has some design in filling thy heart with distracting thoughts of that kind. Perhaps his aim is this, to decoy thee to his service! Seeing some disposition in thee to come to his ground, and to be in his work, he suggests that it is hard thou art not at liberty to have thine own way – thou hast not real religion, and yet art confined in the church with professors as in a prison, and losing a great deal of pleasure thou mightest enjoy, had it been otherwise! And besides, he hints, 'Thy continuance thus in church society will be all in vain, for God never intends giving thee true religion. But if thou shouldest have such a thing, it will be by hearing such and such a preacher; and if thou shouldest not have that by hearing such ministry, it might be as well for thee to hear none. Besides, if God meant to give thee true religion, he would have granted it before now. See what pleasures and delightful things there are in the world at thy service; thou deprivest thyself of much pleasure that youths of thy age enjoy; thou shalt not be better than they at last; it answers no end to be a hypocrite'! O the depth of Satan's devices, and his awful blasphemies! O that thou mightest come to know those destructive devices and temptations, and also to withstand him firmly in the faith, and oppose him in the following manner, saying, 'Satan, I have heard of thy crafty devices and snares; now I experience and begin to know them. Thou chief enemy of God, and destroyer of men; who, by thy pride, didst rebel against God, and by that didst lose a blissful habitation thy Maker placed thee in; and through envy at our first parents in their happy state, didst succeed in bringing them into a miserable condition, by tempting them to sin against God: now thou endeavourest also to deceive me, by suggesting that I lose much pleasure by being in the church of God and with his people, and thou triest to create in me narrow and hard thoughts of God, hinting that he is not disposed to save me, and that, consequently, my lot shall be with the transgressors, and that therefore I had better enjoy carnal mirth and pleasure with the people of the world! But, Satan, I am determined, by the help of him that bruised thy head on the cross, that I will not attend to thy voice. I know that thou art the father of lies, and destroyer of men's souls. I know, Satan, that the church society is the best place on the face of the whole earth, and that I have no need to lose any proper pleasure suitable to human nature by being there. I know this is the best place to wait on the Lord in his visits, in his courts, and at the post of his gates. Whatever will become of me hereafter, this is the best place to spend my earthly days. And should I fear and doubt being happy in the other world? Who ever waited on the Lord in vain? Who was ever lost at the gate of mercy? What poor sinner under a sense of his sins was ever rejected by the merciful Saviour? Who can put limits to the Holy One of Israel? He saved some even from the time in which they were born, and some in the midst of their youthful follies, some immersed in the world, and some in their advanced age. I will wait therefore on him all the days of my life; I will pray against thee and my corruptions, for help from my God.'

I think thou makest another mistake in religion, by supposing that if thou wast a pious man, thou shouldest feel no corruption in thy heart. That is a great error; there are none who feel so much of their inward depravity as believers; they groan being burdened under that body of death; they continually mortify their members that are on earth. They have no rest day nor night from the plague of their corruptions.

I think thou dost also apprehend that every godly man knows that he is a believer, and that thou expectest as clear a conviction and conversion as that of Saul of Tarsus, and that thou shalt know thou art a child of God the day thou art made such. A natural child does not know on the day he is born, whose child he is, nor does he know it for many days afterwards. Many of God's children, after they are born again, are long ignorant whose they are, and other persons often know whose children they are before they themselves do. But there is life, there is breathing towards heaven in prayer, as soon as they are regenerated. There is a 'desire for the sincere milk of the word', and a desire for growing thereby. But *as sinners* they look towards the cross, they flee to Christ and depend on him, not as viewing themselves elect, or redeemed, or regenerated, but as lost sinners, having failed to obtain life elsewhere. And their only ground for proceeding, is God's testimony respecting his Son, that he receives and saves the chief of sinners, that he rejects none that will come, and that none shall perish that will apply and believe. My son, be still, and wait quietly for the salvation of the Lord. Value the privilege of being in the house of God. Use all means of grace, seriously and diligently: they shall not be in vain to thee. The Lord is very gracious and merciful.

In another letter to his son Elias says:

Do not murmur, because thou dost not see that God hath produced a great change in thee. But be sorry on account of thy conduct towards God; forgetting him, yea, going away from him. Grieve that thou dost not believe and receive the gospel, rejecting Christ ready to receive us, and salvation ready to relieve and comfort us. Use the means of grace, and wait on the Lord. Stretch forth thy hand, though withered; arise like the prodigal son, though in a far country, and dying for want. O! go to thy heavenly Father, who runs to meet thee. Seek, and thou shalt receive more than thou canst desire or solicit.

John Elias, junior, under his father's tutelage and spiritual care, became a faithful member of the church, an active supporter of Sunday Schools and the cause of temperance in Anglesey. In his day he was one of the leading elders of the Monthly Meeting, and was regarded by all and sundry to be a man of God, instant and fervent in prayer. He carried much influence in the church meetings, and took after his famous father in zeal and warmth of spirit. But unlike his father, he had no eloquence; he could not deliver a long address; his zeal and fervour would soon burn out and words would fail him. He wrote much to *The Treasury*, the Connexional monthly magazine. He resided at Tre'r Gof, his mother's old home, where he entertained the ministers, and succoured the cause of God; he gave plots of ground at Cemaes, and two chapels were built theron. A truly godly man, he died in the year 1875.

Elias's daughter, Phoebe, married Evan Williams, a draper who lived in Machynlleth in Montgomeryshire. When her father heard of the attachment between Phoebe and her future husband, he sent her the following letter, which speaks highly of his care for his daughter's eternal welfare:

Fron 29 September 1830

I understand, through John, that there is a friendship between you and someone in Machynlleth. The news has caused me great uneasiness, because I still care much for you. I am not in any way against a change in your condition; on the contrary I would be glad if you would do so in the fear of the Lord, and according to his Word, that this may be to your comfort, and to your temporal and spiritual benefit. But I beg of you to be careful, cautious and discreet, especially since the man is a stranger and living so far away; thus making it difficult to know something of his religion and circumstances. There is much deception in the world. I fear that the man is not a member of the visible Church – yes, I am certain he was not so quite recently. I hope that you cannot sell the privilege of being in the Church!

The best advice I can now give you is this: go some day to Mynydd y Gof, and see Mrs Roberts,[1] and share all your confidences with her. She, as you know, is a wise woman, and very religious; she has all the

---

[1] The wife of Dr David Roberts, of Mynydd y Gof, a prominent Anglesey elder; she was a lady from Machynlleth, a granddaughter of Simon and Sarah Lloyd, of Plasyndre, Bala.

advantages to give you counsel, and I know she will do so. O! my dear Phoebe, beware of doing anything rash. Pray much, that you may be taught of God. The matter is very important.

Be on your guard, and beware of casting yourself into a net by word or letter. Take time; many things will come to light. Believe me, your spiritual, eternal, and temporal welfare is very close to my heart. You will see this plainly some day. If you could find your mind free towards us, it would comfort us; we love you and wish you every success.

6 Elias's difficulties, afflictions and oppositions

Elias's difficulties, as already observed, were great from the commencement of his religious career. These did not decrease when he had entered the married state, but rather grew upon him and multiplied. Not that they arose from the matrimonial tie; for it must be concluded, from all appearances, and from the testimony of his children, that he was very happy in that state. His difficulties arose from outward circumstances: he had but slender means of support, a small shop in a humble cottage in a poor village, the times against him; and the Methodists also were a despised and persecuted people. Here are his words in the autobiography on this subject:

We were, the first years after marriage, in adverse and trying circumstances as to worldly matters. My mind was much distressed by fear that we could not pay our creditors, and thereby become guilty of injustice to men, and bring reproach on God's name and cause. It was well for me in those circumstances that I had liberty to go to the throne of grace. Many times I tried to pray earnestly that the Lord would keep me from doing an injustice to any man. I did not desire or ask for riches, but means to deal justly with every man. I can say that God, in his great mercy, heard me, and granted my desire. In a few years our business improved, and we were enabled to live comfortably, to pay our way, to bring up our children, and to give them education. This came from God's mercy and goodness. I was enabled to give up the business at last, without causing loss to any one, and leaving a little to my children to help them in carrying on the business. I would like to say to the next generation that it pays to commit our worldly affairs to the Lord; he can bring us through all difficulties. He is merciful and faithful, and he will perform it! Where he gives a principle to act justly, he generally affords the means to do so. My mind was very perplexed many times during the first years after we began having a family. My circumstances were rather dark, and my thoughts were troubled. Worldly affairs demanded my time and thoughts; I could not have leisure to read and to study, as I wished to do. My dear wife sympathized with me, taking as much as she could of my burden upon herself, endeavouring as much as possible in great difficulties to carry on the business, that I might have time to go on with the work of the Lord. This troubled me very much; I saw myself placing too heavy a burden on her, especially when she was nursing the children. But from a love for God's cause, and obtaining leisure for me, she worked cheerfully. After the children had been brought up, the Lord in his great kindness smiling on our situation, my wife took upon her shoulders most of the bother and toil of our business, in order that I might give myself up more entirely to the work of the Lord. I had the privilege of itinerating for the cause through Wales, Liverpool, Manchester, London, and Bristol.

Elias's wife proved indeed a helpmeet to him. He certainly would have sunk, if his wife had not been a woman of uncommon energy and prudence. She did, indeed, from the best motives, lay herself out in business to the utmost of her ability, in order to relieve him as much as possible for the work of the Lord. The son writes to me thus on the subject:

My mother endeavoured to take all the cares of the house and business on herself, so that father's mind should not be disturbed. She would not give way to any consideration to slacken her exertions, but would significantly wave her hand, saying 'his concerns are far more important than those of the shop'. Her labours in the world were exertions for the gospel. This was her language in the midst of her business, 'Behold, thy handmaid is a servant to wash the feet of the minister of my God.' My father was greatly affected by this remarkable conduct of my mother, and he made a memorandum of it in a very particular manner the day after her death.

Equally striking is the account the daughter gives of the mother's exertions at the time of their humble circumstances in life, in order to relieve her husband for God's service. She concludes with this remarkable observation:

Dear mother, even in her last illness, would not suffer our beloved father to stop at home and desist from going out to preach. He went to Holyhead according to his engagement: it was the last Sunday for her in this world; she then altered greatly for the worse. My brother and myself wanted to send for him home; she overheard us, and would not allow it, but said, 'No, by no means; for what is my life to the cause he is engaged in?'

Mrs Elias dealt in drapery and millinery; it was her name – 'Elizabeth Elias' – which appeared above the door of the shop. The goods for sale came from the wholesale merchants in Liverpool, and were shipped from there to the little harbour of Porth Amlwch. Elias's kinsman, William Roberts of Amlwch, and his wife were engaged in the same trade. In April 1818 the new ship, *Marchioness*, carrying goods from Liverpool to Anglesey was driven by a storm and was wrecked on Dulas beach. Pirates and thieves ran to the wreck, and completed the work of the storm, by taking away everything moveable from the ship; and numbers of small business people of the island – including Mr and Mrs Roberts, and Mrs Elias – suffered great losses.

William Roberts, who was newly married, was distracted, and in his desperation went to Llanfechell to consult with his kinsman; but Elias was not at home. The nature of Roberts' visit is made clear in the following playful yet penetrating letter which Elias wrote to his kinsman after returning home.

Llanfechell 18 April 1818

My dear brother, I am sorry that I have to make a complaint against a kinsman of mine, who lives a short distance from me to the east, who one day visited my family, who were beset by a little trial. I would have thought that my pious kinsman would have given them good counsel, cautioning them against grumbling, and exhorting them to submit to the wise vicissitudes of providence; comforting them, and showing them that all things work for good, etc. But my kinsman, too, was in a misfortune of the same nature; he had lost sight of providence in what had happened to him, and had slipped in his mind as if God had forgotten him, or that God was dead; and that no one could sustain him any more, and prosper him in his circumstances and give him a bite of bread. He had forgotten Job's example; he had forgotten the 6th of Matthew and the 12th of Luke, or else he had cast doubt on the veracity of these chapters. Thus, instead of giving my family a good example, and good counsel suitable for the occasion, he behaved as one who had no belief in God, knowing not how to trust him under his chastisement, looking up to him through clouds hid him from sight. He spoke like the Gentiles who know not God, and threw my family into a deeper despondency.

If you know my kinsman, and if you are conversant with the state of his mind these days, please endeavour to convince him; try to turn his face towards God's rule over all things; that he at all times orders matters for the best purpose; that in tribulations and crosses one must exercise trust and submission; and must avoid thinking, in the midst of the darkest night, that God cannot change it into shining daylight, causing the light to chase away the blackest darkness. Say, also, to my kinsman (if you find opportunity to meet him), to beware of killing the new kind and tender wife that he has been presented, through his dissatisfaction; and remember to quote these words to him: 'Thou therefore which teachest another, teachest not thou thyself?' Please also inform him that I have not written this as a Stoic, but with my eye fixed on God's providence, believing that he makes all things good, and that it is possible to be joyful in him though bereft of the things of this world.

Yet, in spite of all this, I would gladly welcome my kinsman here as often as he likes!

Give my kind regards to Mrs Roberts. I hope she finds support to live far more devoutly than the person mentioned above.

I am, your afflicted friend and brother and fellow-labourer.

John Elias

We cannot be but greatly struck with Elias's account of the first years after marriage, seeing the wisdom of the Lord in using such means to keep this very popular man humble in the dust, and teaching him whereon to depend and to whom to go for all help and assistance; and also in training him in the school of affliction to preach experimentally to the afflicted, tried, and tempted. No one can imagine the benefit he received as a minister, by those great and long adversities. No doubt they were the means, by God's blessing, of qualifying him in a great measure for the extensive work before him. We may observe another providential circumstance in this case; the Lord by these trying affairs, kept Elias more to the work in his own county, which was so exceedingly dark and wretched. Had he been at liberty, his zeal would have carried him far and wide over the Principality, in the commencement of his appearance in Anglesey. Ministers who have all their time at their command should be most thankful and take care how they use it.

One of Elias's earliest acquaintances was Daniel Jones, a pious preacher among the Welsh Calvinistic Methodists at Liverpool; who experienced greatly the changes of this world. We find a letter from Elias to him on that subject, about the time he was in those trials himself: the following communication may assist in exhibiting more fully the temper of Elias in such circumstances:

Llanfechell 6 February 1800

My dear friend and brother in tribulation, I am very sorry that you and your wife should be at all disappointed; but I was glad that your hearts turned to the Lord the God of Elijah, in whom none shall ever be deceived. It would be well for me also, to fix my eye more upon him in all things. I meet many a Jordan, that will not subside before any but himself. And indeed, dear brother, this is the only refuge for you to flee to in all troubles and crosses, disappointments and injuries from all, and from those that profess religion: that is their dissimilarity to him; for he never errs in any of his dispensations: 'righteousness and judgment are the habitation of his throne.' It seems we must have the bitter waters of Marah to drink sometimes in the wilderness, lest we should make our home there: some, moreover, must have great storms of tribulation from the world, and perhaps the church also, else they would stop short of coming to Christ.

As to myself, I have cause to be thankful for every storm, after it is over, though I do not always see this whilst under the waves. But the trials I experience from within are the worst and longest. My distance from God, the wickedness of my heart, the strength of my corruptions, and the want of thought and consideration, are the greatest and most constant troubles which I have to fear. Oh how difficult it is for my mind and thoughts to remain with God and the Bible! How easy it is for me to be engaged with temporal and unimportant things all the day! Oh how difficult it is for me to set my affections on things above! Yea, and how easy it is for me to wander to any place from the right and proper state. And if it had not been for the good Shepherd, I should never return home! And to my great astonishment I can say, that he does restore my soul from the distant strange land. There are, dear friend, two things in particular that give me trouble in the great work –

Being so little acquainted with the Bible, which contains the mind and will of God, and his rule and directory, by which I should live and labour:

Being not so near to God the source of all light and happiness, which occasions the mists and darkness between me and the spirituality of the Scripture. It is well for me that my help is laid on one that is mighty.

I was surprised at your kindness towards me, when I saw the book you sent me, the most unworthy of your brethren. I thought that not only God, but also man, cared more for me than I do myself. I imagine, however, you did not judge rightly, when you supposed that I should make the best use of it. I am too apt to misuse every mercy. If I had properly employed and exercised those talents and mercies I receive, there is no doubt but that I should be more useful.

Certainly, it is very humiliating that, in a Christian country, a man of such extraordinary and such wonderful success, should be so circumstanced. His poverty might prove unfavourable in more ways than one. Elias and his wife were very particular as to discipline in the church meetings. 'My father', says the son, 'was always called upon to perform that work when needed; and sometimes he was obliged to turn out of the church some respectable persons in the neighbourhood, and these greatly threatened to injure our business: as our trade was on a small scale, and dependent, it was easy for a person of property to trample upon it and to crush it. However, my mother was much composed, trusting to the Lord; smilingly she would say, "My beloved and tried head, being innocent, escaped out of the snare". She was much afraid lest any toleration or connivance at sin in the powerful should be manifested, and the church of God sustain an injury thereby.' He adds, 'Though my parents were so humble in circumstances, yet with them preachers from North and South Wales made their home, as they itinerated in preaching the Word: little was the time for sleep, as they were so delightfully engaged in spiritual and sweet conversation with my father. Though our circumstances were so low, yet the destitute and the widow, knowing the kindness of my parents, would apply to them in their distress, with tears running down their faces.' Such instances of humiliation, suffering, and benevolence, at the same time, in the lives of eminent ministers, are wonderful in the providence of God. A view of the conduct of the Almighty in this and similar respects, induces us to exclaim in the language of Scripture, 'O the depth of the riches both of the wisdom and knowledge of God! How unsearchable are his judgments, and his ways past finding out!'

Elias suffered from afflictions of a peculiar kind, which have been mentioned. An extract from his autobiography, above, mentioned the death of two children. The following letter refers helpfully to the matter:

Llanfechell 19 March 1810

The Lord has been pleased to take me through sharp trials lately. Yet, though they were unpleasant for the present, I think I had some benefit thereby. I know that it was out of great wisdom and goodness the Lord thus acted towards me; indeed he does all things well. My dear wife was in great peril and danger during her confinement for three days; yea, she was dying! But the Lord had compassion on us, and delivered her out of her great affliction. The dear infant's life was sacrificed, by means of the surgeon's instruments in the trying circumstance. To him the time to be born and the time to die, were near the same moment! I perceived in this dispensation the goodness and severity of the Lord; goodness in sparing the life of my wife, and severity in the death of my child. But, 'righteousness and judgment are the habitation of his throne'.

Elias having experienced these peculiar trying circumstances, was able to speak a word to a brother similarly situated. Some of his letters which have come into my hands, being written to persons bereaved of their offspring, contain wise and excellent counsels.

Elias was at times afflicted in his bodily health; and no wonder, considering the labours and incessant fatigues, and exposure to different kinds of weather he endured. Two of his letters in reference to his illness, as they breathe the spirit of a Christian in such circumstances, and may be useful to others, are introduced here: they were written to a beloved sister in the Lord, Mrs Jones of Wrexham, as follows:

Llandrindod 8 September 1808

I have been very indifferent in my health since I saw you at Bala. I was very low when entering upon my journey. I thought sometimes that I should never return home, and yet was not satisfied to withdraw from the engagements which have been announced. But the Lord was pleased to have compassion on me in delivering me wonderfully: I had strength in the work beyond expectation; so that though I was very low and unwell frequently, yet I did not miss one opportunity. Captain Bowen of Llwyn-gwair,[1] and many of the friends, advised and encouraged me on my return to go to Llandrindod Wells, assuring me that the waters would most likely be very beneficial to me. I have been here since Monday last; and I have, from experience, ground already to hope that God will bless these waters and make them very beneficial to me. I shall rejoice if my recovery should be to the glory of his name, and for the good of immortal souls. But if leanness of soul should attend my recovery, it will not be a blessing; I should prefer ill-health with God's favour and the light of his countenance, to health itself however great a blessing, under the hidings of God's countenance. There are wonderful waters here; I am astonished at the wisdom of God in their arrangement. There are three sorts of waters here near each other, *saline*, *sulphuriate*, and *chalybeate*! I drink three pints or two quarts of the saline in the morning; it operates very well and without pain, in less than half an hour. I drink chalybeate about mid-day and four o'clock; this warms me within, and I feel as if I had taken some strong spirits: it has a wonderful tendency to strengthen the nerves. I think the Lord will, in kindness, bless these waters to me. Forgive me in speaking so much about my bodily health; I know you are concerned for my restoration, and that causes me to make so free.

It seems he returned from Llandrindod in good health; but such were his exertions in preaching the gospel, that he soon had a relapse. And having experienced such benefit at the Wells, we find him there a second time towards the autumn of the ensuing year; from whence he writes again to the same friend.

Llandrindod 19 October 1809

I was taken very unwell after I saw you at Bala. I was poorly and dis-

---

[1] Essex Bowen, a member of the famous Bowen family of Llwyn-gwair, Pembrokeshire, who befriended Methodists and evangelical clergymen.

heartened in my way here. Through mercy I reached this place, and am already much better. Symptoms now appear that my health is likely to be considerably improved. If the Lord should think fit to grant me this favour, I humbly hope that I shall be more zealous for his glory than in time past. Indeed, I consider myself an unfruitful and worthless creature, and wonder at the goodness of God in allowing me to remain in his house till now. And certainly, if his patience had not been infinite, he would not have suffered such a one to continue in his church and vineyard. But here I am, a monument of his boundless mercy and grace. I am lukewarm as to God's glory, inclined to go astray from his paths, and to amuse myself with some vain and worthless things, and thereby lose his fellowship! Alas! to be deprived of his communion is worse than losing the whole world. Notwithstanding all, he even calls after us, saying, 'Return, O return to me!' Oh infinite grace and unspeakable favour! And I will cry with all my heart, 'Return, O my soul unto thy rest, for the Lord hath dealt bountifully with thee.' It is well for me that the Father draws the soul to Christ, and that the life and growth of faith depend as much upon God, as the communication of it at first. His mercy and goodness will support me all the days of my life; else I shall fail again, yea, perish. But in the midst of a sea of vileness and unfathomable depth of corruption, I have nothing to do but to turn my eyes to God in Christ. There is a wonderful fulness to meet all the poverty, guilt, and depravity of a helpless sinner!

It seems that you are also in the midst of storms. I think of you before a throne of grace, and call upon the Lord to support you in all your trials, and deliver you out of all temptations. The strength of our enemies is *nothing* to him who is almighty. It is an unspeakable mercy that 'our life is hid;' all the waves cannot reach it! O! lift up your head and give no encouragement nor room to your many doubts, fears and distressing thoughts. Our poor prayers may ascend up as sweet incense, and be accepted in his name. The Holy Ghost is promised as a guide in this wilderness, as a comforter in this troublesome, miserable world. What more can we desire? It is not, the glory of God that you should be fearful. Take courage, and make it manifest that you have a God worthy of your utmost confidence, able to keep you from falling, and, present you in his own good time, before the presence of his glory with exceeding joy. Say to your enemies that you will believe God's Word and promise, rather than their accusations. O! let us now and then for a few moments turn our eyes in the midst of war, and look beyond the field of battle into the land of rest and joy, where thousands of our brethren have arrived perfectly safe, though once full of doubt and fears like ourselves. The blessed world is engaged for us also, with a most sure and strong promise.

We have mentioned some of the things in which Elias seemed peculiarly affected, particularly in his worldly circumstances and health. He endured other causes of affliction, though they were little known; these were very trying, and no doubt were keenly felt. An attempt was made on one occasion to interrupt him in the commencement of divine service in a certain place. It appears that he was appointed to preach in his rounds in Brynyrodyn, Caernarvon, before Mr John Jones of Edern. There was a room adjoining the chapel, as in most places of that kind. When Elias came there, he was very much tired, having walked a long way through rain and mud, the roads being bad and the weather inclement. However, there was no welcome for him in the room; Mr Jones scarcely spoke to Elias when he came in; and no one rose up to ask him to sit down, being prejudiced against him by the behaviour of the other preacher. Elias took off his great coat, and putting it down, said he would go and commence the service. They followed him in a while, and Mr Jones went up to the pulpit after him: Elias was commencing prayer, and seemed to go on very well. His partner, however, endeavoured to disturb and put him down as much as he could. It was done in a way similar to that in which people manifest their disapprobation of a speaker in a Bible or a Missionary meeting. But Elias was not to be daunted. He was so much engaged in his supplication to God at the throne of grace, that he could not be distracted or drawn away by circumstances of that kind. He went on most sweetly and profitably in his prayer, and the blessing of God seemed to descend on him and the congregation, so that the most prejudiced were disarmed, and became friendly towards him, loving him as a brother. When he commenced his sermon, there was the same attempt to obstruct and hinder him in the pulpit! But he was quite regardless of it, and went on preaching the Word in a very delightful manner, as if not at all aware of the individual behind him. After he had finished, which was evidently under the blessing of God, the other preacher stood up and took his place, and proceeded and laboured hard, but with no success! It was a difficult work, he was nearly unable to proceed, though a talented preacher. When he came down from the pulpit, he was rather ashamed of himself, and he had the grace to confess his fault, and acknowledge himself wrong. From that moment, he entertained a very high opinion of Elias, and observed that he would become a very great and useful preacher. He always befriended him afterwards, and showed him every kindness.

Mr John Jones had the advantage of Elias as to age and experience, and was popular; he was a man of ready wit, as we have already seen (*p 28*), but rather satirical. His purpose, no doubt, was to put to the test, by the above strange treatment, the zeal of Elias, who was then commencing his ministry. But such conduct, it must be said, was highly unbecoming.

In his itinerant journeys in the Lord's service, Elias was exposed to many inconveniences and frequent dangers, in such a bleak and poor country as Wales. He was at one time very near losing his life in crossing a river, in order to preach at a particular place. The circumstance was as follows: When he was crossing over to Caernarvon from the Anglesey side, he requested the ferryman not to hoist the sail, else his horse would take fright, and put their lives in jeopardy, by leaping over into the sea. After they had gone a good way from land, they had the sail up; the spirited animal immediately took alarm: Elias perceiving it, moved towards him to take hold of his head, thinking he might be quiet by his old master; but he was unmanageable; he leaped into the sea, thrusting Elias before him into the water. One of the boatmen immediately jumped in after him, but Elias was soon up, and seen floating easily on his back, and was taken up directly into the boat. He felt the wave like a pillow under his head. He preached uncommonly well at Caernarvon in the evening. In going to preach in another place in Caernarvonshire, near Criccieth, Elias had to cross a certain river. The water being very high at the time, and his pony being small and weak, he was in considerable danger in attempting to ford it; and was soon carried away from the horse by the stream. However, he was providentially conveyed towards some willows by the water side, and taking hold of them, he came up to land!

These were wonderful providences, in delivering him from great dangers.

Persecution from the world was also at times Elias's lot, though that evil had subsided much when he had commenced preaching. His predecessors in the ministry were called to endure more of that turbulent behaviour and scandalous opposition, and they bore the heat and burden of the day valiantly. But from the specimens of his courage, wisdom, and good conduct on such occasions, we may conclude that he would, under God's blessing, have gone through those fiery trials as well as any of them. There was something in his mien, countenance, voice, and manner, that was very command-ing and calculated to overawe and subdue most persons however hard and presumptuous. Places in which he was exposed to the danger of persecution presented no obstacle to him.

There were in his days, especially in North Wales, the very strongholds of Satan, who seemed to domineer over some towns and districts, as the prince of those parts, and as if he had the exclusive right to them. The inhabitants were under his full sway, revelling and rioting in all manner of sin and ungodliness! Even the Sabbath was trampled upon, and made subservient to their sin-ful propensities! No day in the week was so devoted to the service of sin and Satan! This was not only in Anglesey, but also in all parts of North Wales in some degree; and it was dangerous for preachers to interfere with them in some places. Rhuddlan, in Flint-shire was one of these strongholds. It seems that sin here was at the full height of its strength; and no doubt the cry of their abomina-tions ascended to heaven for vengeance: but God, instead of smiting them with the sword of his justice, sent to them the sceptre of peace and reconciliation. Elias, being moved with compassion, having the same spirit as his Master, was induced to go to this wicked place, and to preach the gospel of Christ to the people. His friends would fain dissuade him from such a dangerous undertak-ing, knowing what characters were congregated there on a Sunday: and what made it still more hazardous, there was also a fair there at that season for some Sundays, to dispose of scythes and hooks, and other implements for the harvest. It was apprehended that if Elias went there to preach to the people, it would so excite their evil passions, that they would attack him, and endanger his life. However, he would go in the name of the Lord. Farmers also hired labourers at the same time. All this had been done every year from time immemorial! When Elias arrived on the ground, they were on the point of engaging in their abominable transactions: a great number had their hooks and scythes on their arms and shoulders: there was the sound and noise of harps and fiddles; the players were in liquor. There was the noise of a fair and of making bargains. There was a great concourse of all sorts of persons; some thousands of people attended the meeting from the surrounding neighbourhood and towns, to hear him preach and to see the result: he was expected there according to the announcement. Elias commenced the service in the open air, even in the camp of the enemy, and in the midst of men with sickles and scythes. He stood on the steps of the New Inn, belonging then to a Mrs Hughes. He manifested amazing boldness and intrepidity, his spirit being moved within him. He appeared also very grave and compassionate. He gave out a stanza of the 24th Psalm to be sung. 'I never', says an eye-witness, 'heard more serious and impressive singing.' He adds, 'the sobriety and awe in Elias's voice and manner, were very impressive. Such effect was produced shortly on the people, that not a hook nor a scythe was to be seen! Nothing but opposition and persecution were expected; but scarcely anything of the kind was experienced; for they all put their different implements of husbandry out of sight very soon. Elias read a chapter in the most solemn and impressive manner; then engaged in a very earnest prayer. He was most importunate with the Lord in prayer and supplication: it might remind one of Jacob's wrestling with him until he was blessed. His heart was in a very melting frame, from which his words flowed, and the tears ran profusely down his grave and serious countenance. The people by this time were seized with awe and great sobriety. He repeatedly thanked the Lord that he did not suffer the earth to open and swallow them up alive into hell. He most earnestly entreated the Almighty several times to incline the hearts of the respectable and influential men in the neighbourhood, to regard the Sabbath, and to prevent the evil practices that desecrated it so awfully: he prayed and entreated the Lord, with the greatest feelings of compassion, for the farmers, labourers, servants, publicans, and all the men of evil practices. Amazing effects followed his words in prayer.

Elias took for his text, *Exodus* 34.21: 'Six days thou shalt work, but on the seventh thou shalt rest: in earing time and in harvest time thou shalt rest.' His spirit was soon stirred up within him, and the words of the Lord came with amazing force out of his lips, carrying light and conviction home to the consciences and hearts of the wicked. He made some very pertinent and homely observations in a powerful manner, suitable to his audience. 'Should we', it was asked, 'rest on the Sabbath day if it were a fine day, the harvest being very wet and bad, and the corn much injured?' '*Yes*', he answered in a most powerful tone of voice; 'yes, you should obey the Word of God at *all* times. It is said, 'in earing and in harvest thou shalt rest''. The Lord had rather send a legion of his angels to manage thy harvest, than that thou shouldest disregard his holy day.' He exclaimed repeatedly to the people with all his might, the following words, with his arm lifted up, and tears flowing down his face: 'Oh robbers! Oh robbers! Oh thieves! Alas! stealing the day of the Lord! What! robbing my Lord of his day! Oh robbers! the most vile and abominable!'

It might be asked again, he said, 'What if one should suffer and be unable to pay his way, having not made all exertions even on the Sabbath, when it is a wet harvest?' He observed in answer to this: 'Thousands that keep the Sabbath at all times have been enabled to live far better than thou, and certainly die infinitely better than thou art likely to do.' Then he made strong allusions to London and other cities, that were set on fire, which he represented as a punishment from the Lord for the disrespect shown to his holy day. He particularly observed the threatenings in the Word of God for abusing the Sabbath; and enlarged on what is said in *Jeremiah* 17.27 as a threat to set Jerusalem on fire for disregarding the Lord's day. He also dwelt on the promises made in the Bible to those that keep the day holy.

The people soon became greatly alarmed, appearing as persons guilty and miserable. There was no idea of lifting up even a silent voice, or of giving utterance to a word against the truth: all the men of arms lost their courage, and seemed to lay down their weapons of opposition. They seemed panic struck! Indeed, great seriousness and sobriety of mind possessed the multitude! Many were heard saying that they would not on any account go again to such a place to do business on the Sabbath. They kept their word, for such misdeeds were never seen again in Flintshire. A complete stop was put to the evil so rampant and dreadful at Rhuddlan. This was done, not by any human power, authority, or force, but merely by preaching the gospel. It was seen then that 'the weapons of our warfare are not carnal, but mighty through God to the pulling down of strong holds.'

It is said that the following observations of Elias, under God's blessing, aided in producing the desired effect: 'It may be hinted by some one', he said, 'that this fair is an old custom, it will recover itself.' He replied in a very awful manner, 'If any one will give the *least* encouragement to its revival, he will be accursed before the Holy Trinity, Father, Son, and Holy Ghost. But blessed is the man that opposeth this and every other species of iniquity.'

It seems that several persons were truly converted under that extraordinary sermon. One man was so alarmed by hearing the things Elias said of Sabbath-breakers, that on his way home he imagined that his arm on which the hook rested, was really withered; consequently the instrument fell to the ground, he feared taking it up lest the other arm should be disabled. He lost the hook, and had the use of both arms; and more than that, he was born again, under Elias's sermon! During the remainder of his days, he lived a decided Christian; he walked by faith, and died a happy death. In his prayer after the sermon, Elias again entreated the Lord to put it into the heart of some of the great people, to come forward in behalf of his holy day and the cause of his dear Son; he prayed with great respect for the Bishop and Dean of St Asaph, the Magistrates and Clergy. The Dean soon afterwards heard of the circumstance, and sent a threatening letter to the place. But the nuisance had already been broken in its main strength.

Elias has himself noticed the above remarkable circumstance in his autobiography, as follows: 'The Lord strengthened me, in the face of a great tumult, to preach at Rhuddlan in a fair held there on a Sunday during the harvest season. He gave me the victory. Very soon the custom was discontinued.' This astonishing event occurred in the summer of 1802. It seems that Elias was in bodily danger in consequence of preaching the gospel at other places; for instance in the town of Flint. 'When I was preaching on the road in Flint', he says, 'in a parish wake, the persecutors intended to let loose a wild bull into the midst of the congregation; but they were disappointed, for the beast fell down and broke its leg!'

Elias was at times disturbed, I am sorry to say, by men in authority! Persecution, however, was subsiding at this time, else he would have been more molested. But he was so wise, and meek, as well as bold and courageous, that he was able, under God, to overrule these oppositions; besides, his eloquence overwhelmed them. 'Two magistrates molested me', he says, 'when I was preaching on the road; one at Llanidloes, and the other at Llanfair Caereinion; but I was not hurt. The gentlemen set me free kindly and without imprisonment or fine.'

Elias notices this singular affair in another place, namely, in his letter to his son, 29 October, 1819, in the following manner: 'In answer to the query in thy letter about the little disturbance at Llanidloes, I have not much to say. There was nothing scarcely worth mentioning, only a gentleman who was a magistrate, came up to the waggon where I was preaching, and took hold of my arm, and requested me to leave off preaching, and to go with him. I asked him for his authority. When I understood that he was a magistrate, I told him that I would obey him, but asked the favour to conclude the service by praying and singing, which he readily granted. He was very kind when the service was over; and he told me that he was sorry that he had prevented me, but that he was instigated by others to do so.' It is not unlikely but that the Lord touched the heart of this man under Elias's prayer, and that he was consequently softened. [This took place, as in Flint, during the local parish wake; and it is said that about five thousand people had gathered together. His text on the occasion was, 'And I, if I be lifted up from the earth, will draw all men unto me' (*John* 12.32).]

Elias was at this time in the zenith of his strength. But no manly power or courage could have been sufficient to face and suppress such a host of enemies; it would all have been in vain, except God had been with him: then indeed the gates of hell could not prevail against him. There was a great deal of that evil spirit manifesting itself in his own country, notwithstanding the light spreading far and wide, and the gospel making great inroads on the kingdom of Satan. The attack was made in a different manner from any of the previous ones. It appears that it was about the time Elias entered upon his labours in Anglesey; it is thus related in his autobiography: 'Some of the respectable men of this country were much disposed to persecute in those days. One dignitary wrote a book, contending that we were against the church and state. The Rev Thomas Charles wrote an excellent defence of the Connexion, entitled *The Welsh Methodists Vindicated*. We sent a copy of the book to every gentleman in the country; the storm subsided.' [The scurrilous pamphlet referred to, *Hints to Heads of Families*, was written by the Rev T. E. Owen, Rector of Llandyfrydog, Anglesey, and published in 1801; Charles's masterly and devastating reply to it, *The Welsh Methodists Vindicated*, appeared in 1802, 'by order of the (Welsh Methodist) Association.]'

Latterly, a much better feeling subsisted between Elias and the clergy at large. His excellences and principles being more known, asperities and animosities that formerly existed were removed. And if opposition seemed to arise in any quarter, Elias knew how to prevent or overcome it. An instance of his tact is as follows: he was preaching in a village out-of-doors, not far from the parish church; a great many of his audience, viz. the junior part, sat on the wall of the churchyard opposite him: the clergyman of the parish came that way, and observing the men sitting on the wall, he desired them to come down; they seemed obstinate and refused. Elias, perceiving that, spoke immediately to them, and begged of them to obey their minister; which they did directly without the least hesitation. The gentleman was so pleased with this act of Elias, that he called upon him after the service was over, thanking him for his kindness, observing that his mind was changed towards him, not expecting such civility. Thus Elias always conducted himself in such ways as won much upon the feelings and hearts of the clergy, and others of every class.

However, the malignant spirit of persecution lingered a long time in Anglesey. Mr Parry of Bangor, before mentioned, in giving an account of Beaumaris Association in 1809, states the following painful instance of opposition to the great cause of religion, which alarmed Elias and his friends greatly:

I now proceed to give a few particulars of Beaumaris Association in June 1809. The public meetings were held in the open street, close to the Bull Hotel: at five o'clock in the evening, the Rev T. Charles of Bala, preached from *Acts* 26.18, and the Rev J. Roberts of Llangwm, from *Psalm* 5.11. It is customary for Methodists on those occasions to hold family worship in every house in which they are stationed, punctually at nine o'clock in the evening. Mr Elias was then entertained at the Bull Hotel, and at the above hour was performing devotional duties in the large front parlour, which was crowded: while he was engaged in prayer, a gun was discharged near the window, which was open! Those being days of persecution, the firing of a gun so near, and under such circumstances, considerably alarmed the worshippers; each, whilst thankful for his own preservation, was concerned and anxious for the safety of his friends. Elias himself was greatly alarmed by the report of the gun: I was close to his elbow; he looked towards the window through which the smoke was coming into the room, and uttered the following words· very feelingly: 'O Lord have mercy upon thine enemies! Save thine enemies!' Having concluded, a hymn was given out to be sung, during which the host entered, requesting that that part of the worship should be dispensed with to oblige him, as it appeared to irritate the passions of a gentleman in the hall. This request was immediately complied with. This gentleman was the same that fired at the window. Having just returned from field sports in company with others and discovering what was going on in the parlour, he discharged his fowling-piece at the window; its muzzle, however, was directed upwards. Elias had an interview with the party in the course of the evening.

What a kind, merciful, benignant spirit influenced Elias on all occasions! And the more the opposition and hostility the enemy manifested, the more did this spirit of the gospel appear in him, as on the above occasion. How different are worldly men! When they meet with provocations and insults, they are full of rage, fury, and revenge. This is quite contrary to the mind and command of Christ, who says, 'Love your enemies, bless them that curse you, do good to them that hate you, and pray for them who despitefully use you and persecute you.' *Matthew 5.44.*

We shall now allude to another heavy stroke of affliction that Elias met with, and which he sustained with great fortitude; it was the removal of his beloved wife, endeared to him by many considerations. He takes notice of this very trying circumstance in his autobiography, in a feeling and affectionate manner, as might be expected. 'In the year 1828, April 2nd, God was pleased to call unto himself the soul of my dear wife, after we had lived together, and enjoyed together much of God's goodness, kindness, and mercy, for over twenty-nine years. I shall never forget her love to God's cause, and her labour on behalf of his cause and work. She rests now from her labour.' These separations are most trying; and none but those who have experienced them, can know what they are: there is, however, sufficient support to sustain us under them. And we see in Elias and others, striking instances of the Lord's goodness in consoling the mind so helpless and feeble in itself. The following letter was written by him to a clerical friend on this painful subject, as an apology for his silence:

Llanfechell 5 March 1829

I received your kind letter last February. I am sorry I have delayed answering it till now. My dear friend, my case is such, that you cannot properly sympathize with me. It pleased God about twelve months ago to take from me my dear partner; and my spirits were so low for many weeks, that I was scarcely fit for anything. My friends and doctor advised me to go from home on an excursion. I accordingly took my departure, and went to Llanidloes, Aberystwyth, Liverpool, Manchester, and Bala, preaching. Indeed, I travelled most of the year, and found much benefit thereby. But it was very painful to my feelings, on my return home, to see, though I had kind children, my own house so strange, destitute of my dear partner! I had much to do when I was at home for a few days; and besides, my mind was so confused. I feel much obliged to you for Mr Charles's Memoir: I approve of it very much: I have recommended it to many of my friends, and particularly in one or two of our Associations.

I cannot write much more now, having just returned from a journey, and being rather poorly. Perhaps I shall have the pleasure of seeing you in London next May, if the Lord pleases. I am much alarmed concerning the state of the nation, and afraid that our dear rulers are blind: they don't see the intention of the Roman Catholics. All my comfort is, that 'the Lord reigneth'. Yet I am afraid of his rod on account of our formality, lukewarmness, and unfruitfulness. May he forgive, and reform us!

Elias had another affliction, the loss of health, in consequence of a fall from a carriage, on his way to Bala Association, in 1832. It shall be more fully noticed hereafter.

No doubt the Lord had a wise and good end in view in these afflictions of his servant. He became a more matured and experimental preacher, and he was a more devotional and studious man. He was then intimately acquainted with those three qualifications Luther mentions as necessary for a minister – prayer, study, and affliction.

There is another advantage Elias had at this time as a preacher; his children were now of that age, that they could take the concern of the shop off his hands, and he was consequently more at liberty to devote himself to the service of the Lord. He notices this circumstance in his autobiography thus: 'After this, I determined to give up my worldly business to my children, which I did. Then I was free to a great degree from the weight of worldly cares. I resolved, through God's grace, to consecrate the remainder of my life entirely to the service of the Lord.'

7 Elias's ministerial character, his intellectual and delineating powers in preaching

Elias shone pre-eminently as a minister of the Lord Jesus Christ; he possessed extraordinary talents for that office; and became a most popular and notable character. Illustrious in the pulpit, he was likewise splendid in all his exercises; the glory shone on him in every place and employment. In the ministry he came forth as one of the most valiant men of Israel; nor was he inferior to any of them in greatness of mind, in fervency of zeal, and in impressively awful appeals. Even Whitefield and Rowland were not, perhaps, endowed with greater skill in attacking, overawing, and overwhelming a congregation. It is true there was at that time more physical agitation; but the minds of the people had not perhaps been more seriously impressed than they were under Elias. He was argumentative, as well as zealous and powerful. He might perhaps be considered more like a philosopher in his eloquence, than the above-named celebrated ministers. Anyone might perceive, even by his external appearance, that he was a man of amazing powers: indeed many were at once struck with his commanding and penetrating mien, as well as with the gravity of his countenance and simplicity of his manners; and were prepossessed with great awe and reverence for him. Though he was perhaps more philosophical in his discourses than his predecessors, yet he possessed the art of spiritual painting, and representing things in new and vivid colours, as much as any of them. All these great talents combined, made him, under divine blessing, an extraordinary, and popular preacher. Elias's hearers were more intelligent than those of the great men before him had been. Having in general had the advantages of a religious education and gospel ministry, they were enabled to attend better to argumentative eloquence and strong reasoning.

Howell Harris's ministry was particularly adapted to occupy and strike the attention of people in an ignorant and heathenish state, as the bulk of the Welsh peasants were in his days; at that he aimed, and in that way, under God's blessing, he wonderfully succeeded, denouncing divine wrath against a sinful, rebellious, lost world, as a messenger sent from God. He seldom took a text, never went on like Elias, explaining and elucidating divine truths as a master in Israel. He could not therefore bear upon his hearers as Elias did, with flashes of conviction, strong appeals, and overwhelming inferences from those lucid statements. Each was eminently qualified by God with gifts suited to the time in which he lived. Having thus given some outlines of Elias's preaching talents, especially his lofty intellect and brilliant imagination, we shall now enter upon a more minute exhibition of those most important qualifications.

First, let us particularly notice Elias's great intellectual powers as a minister. He was a man of very acute, as well as vigorous and sublime genius. His mind was most penetrating, piercing, like his eye. We never heard a preacher who seemed to have such an insight into the Word of God: this was manifested by the manner in which he handled it. He exercised his great powers with much delight, in the field of the Scriptures. His strong intellect and solid judgment were clearly developed in his compositions, speeches, and sermons. Perhaps no mathematician could arrange his ideas better, no logician could draw forth more correct and proper inferences from them, and no orator could bring them to bear on the people in a more commanding and influential manner, by the instrumentality of voice, manner, and eloquence. One might think by his eloquent manner of speaking that he was well acquainted with these arts and sciences. His discourses possessed amazing depth, solidity, and power. There was no lightness and superficiality in them.

His excellent judgment was apparent in preparing his sermons. His manner of choosing his text, for instance, showed much discretion and caution. He would not choose a word or two, breaking up a sentence and mangling the sense and meaning of the Scriptures; but he would prefer a full sentence, containing a clear reference to some object, either historical or doctrinal, that he might have a fair and sound foundation for his sermon. He would also avoid long texts, except occasionally, as when a text contained a parable. He was also careful to select texts the most adapted to oppose the evils prevailing in the world and the Church, or the texts best calculated to promote and exhibit the virtue of practical religion, or to set forth the principles of Christianity, defending the true doctrines and opposing the false. In this he was never remiss, but always diligent, declaring the whole counsel of God, keeping back nothing that was profitable; but as a faithful servant, 'bringing forth things new and old', and 'giving meat to all the household in due season'. He would never look out for a text, but with a view to carry it as a message from God to the people, and such as he considered them in need of.

The following observations on the subject are taken from *Yr Haul*, a Welsh Church Magazine:

Elias took deliberate care in the introduction to his sermon, to explain well his text in the relation it bore to the circumstances and character of the times when spoken or written, as well as the reference it might contain to the popular and well-known customs of particular countries. He would even notice the peculiar wording, its adaptation to the subject in hand, and the doctrine it involved. Elias's introduction was a natural entrance to his sermon: that was the key to it; if that was lost, the substance of what followed was less clear and intelligible. After concentrating the scattered rays of information and doctrine contained in the introduction, into a point or focus, he would then grasp his subject with masterly ability, exhibiting it in all its richness of thought, propriety of doctrines, and applicability to his hearers. He would exhibit it in its various beautiful views, until it burst with divine glory upon the audience. Elias never spent a long time in breaking the husk, but he would with great dexterity and rapidity extricate the kernel of his text; that is, its appropriate and natural doctrine, without anything far fetched, and without doing the least violence to the plain and necessary meaning of the subject. He never forced the text to support any particular doctrine; but he simplified it in such a manner as to exhibit the doctrine in bold relief. Thus the genius, dexterity, and excellency of this un-

rivalled preacher became more and more conspicuous. After explaining
his text, he would classify it into several sub-divisions, without any
confusion: his thoughts were in the text, though not previously dis-
cernible to the hearers; when he pointed them out they were plainly
recognized; for they were indigenous to the truth in question and not
exotics unnaturally transplanted into a climate inimical to their proper
growth and native beauty.

No doubt Elias's judgment was under the direction and influence of the Lord. He would always endeavour, by close study,
to be perfectly satisfied as to the context of the Scripture of which
his text was a part, before he would divide and arrange his discourse, and make remarks and draw inferences. His criticisms on
difficult passages were very satisfactory. His judgment was also
very conspicuous in the composition of his sermons. He was in
general very systematic, setting forth the exposition, the connection, the reasoning, and the application, in a regular way. There
was a remarkable *union* in all the parts of his discourse; the grand
subject was always conspicuous; all the work was most compact
and complete. His sermon was like a wheel, one piece of beautiful
work, every spoke being in its proper place. His manner of composing his sermons was the following: he would first, after prayer,
look into Scott's Bible for references; then he would write down
some of the most remarkable words in the text, with some suitable
explanations; he would afterwards look into different commenta-
tors for their expositions; he would then put his own ideas down.
Presently he would look into the contents of different books.
Having found the subject in question, and satisfied his mind, he
would then fill up the sermon. Elias had admirable tact in the
arrangement of his thoughts. This will appear still more remarkable, when it is remembered that his sermons were streams of
thoughts, and each in its proper place. He would, moreover, show
the relation they bore to one another, and the corresponding
joints which made them adhere together in one compact whole.
He was a complete master of his subject, having sounded it to the
bottom, and having made himself acquainted with its length,
breadth, and height, as it were, so that he was in no danger of
puzzling and bewildering his hearers. Their feelings were perfectly

comfortable and at ease in hearing him, for they apprehended no weakness or insufficiency in the preacher.

Elias would clothe the deepest points in divinity in such a way that the weakest understanding might comprehend him. He had talents sufficiently dignified to address kings, and yet humble enough to teach rustics, causing both to rejoice at the same moment. The learned philosopher would be struck at the ingenuity of his ideas, while the rude peasant would deeply feel the force of his oratory. His reasons would bear to be tried at the bar of the most subtle logician, when he would, at the same moment, convince the ignorant of the truth of what he advanced. The established divine would admire his eloquence, while he administered the sincere milk of the word to babes in Christ. Indeed his sermons in general were proofs of the exercise of a powerful, penetrating, and methodical mind. They contained, as we have observed, deep and striking thoughts, well-digested and organized ideas. And no doubt, the remarkable arrangement which he gave to his powerful thoughts assisted under the blessing of God in producing the amazing effect that attended his ministry. Nothing was dry and conceited in his discourses, all was most strong and powerful. There was as much impassioned eloquence as strong reasoning: there was the influence and combination of both! His sermons and speeches possessed an elevation of tone and character, deeply impressive and permanently useful. His soul, through the divine influence, was always engaged in the blessed work, and his meditation being in the doctrines of grace, day and night, the savour of them was evidently on his mind. He was never observed destitute of the spirit of preaching. He was a scribe well instructed unto the kingdom of heaven; and he would always have something new in his sermons. Those who knew him best testified that they cost him many a tear, many an earnest prayer, yea many a sleepless night! He was 'a good soldier of Jesus Christ', not entangling himself with the affairs of this life, his chief delight being in his study.

As it was his great aim to edify the people in all things, he would of course endeavour to convey his mind to them in a plain intelligible manner: and in this also he manifested much wisdom. He would avoid words that were not easily understood, or that were unsuitable to the truths delivered. His style being so simple, his preaching was plain, clear, and yet animated and searching. He did not aim at high turgid words, though from his knowledge of the Welsh language, he might have employed them readily. Neither did he employ words too low for the pulpit and the glorious gospel he preached, but proper and scriptural words, according to *Ecclesiastes* 12.10, 1 *Corinthians* 2.4, and *Titus* 2.8. Each of his sermons was in general quite complete in every respect. It is a great cause of thankfulness that some hundreds of his skeleton sermons, prepared for the pulpit, were preserved, and are intended for the press.[1]

A clergyman, with whom Elias was well acquainted, favoured me with the following anecdote respecting his preparation for the pulpit:

I observed that on one occasion, when he was staying at my house, he was reading over, with great attention, the sermon which he was going to deliver at the Calvinistic chapel in the village that evening; and upon my expressing my surprise that with his talents, and after preaching such numbers of sermons, he should prepare such copious notes, and devote so much attention to them, previous to his going to the pulpit, he replied that he had done this through life, and that the cause of it arose from the following circumstances. Soon after he had begun his ministerial career, he went into that populous part of South Wales, the neighbourhood of Merthyr Tydfil. Whilst there, he preached upon one occasion to a very large congregation at two o'clock in the day; and his matter and his manner were so acceptable to the people that his friends begged of him to afford them the privilege of hearing him preach another sermon at six o'clock in the evening of the same day, and that in a still more populous district, at the distance of a mile from the place where he had preached at two o'clock. He yielded to their entreaties, and instead of taking a sermon which he had prepared, he took quite a new text, 'It is good for us to be here', and ventured to trust to his extemporizing powers, so as to preach without giving the subject any further consideration than he was able to do during the time occupied by the person who prayed before the sermon. When he began to preach, he

---

[1] A collection of Elias's sermons was published in 1846; and a second collection was published in 1849.

soon discovered his own deficiency, and felt that he had been guilty of a great sin before his God, in presuming to preach his Word to an immense assembly of perishing sinners without bestowing sufficient reflection upon the subject, and invoking a blessing. His self-sufficiency and presumption met with their reward; he was unable to manage the subject; his powers seemed to fail him; and he was obliged to curtail his discourse; and when he finished it, such as it was, he fell down upon his knees in the bottom of the pulpit, suffused with tears, and prayed to God to give him grace that he might never again be guilty of the like presumption.

Elias alludes in his autobiography to the subject of composing his discourse, and the large notes he prepared for the pulpit.

It was often a great trouble on my mind, [he says] to have suitable subjects to set before the people, things likely to be of benefit, things that God would be pleased to work through them. My time to read and meditate was limited and my spirit was often too far from the Lord. But I wish to say, to the praise of God's mercy and grace, that he was very good to me in many a trying circumstance; giving me sometimes more in an hour, from the midst of business cares, than I would get all day many times after obtaining more leisure. In the year 1800, I received wonderful things from John chapter seventeen. I was given wonderful and delightful views respecting God's plan of salvation in his sovereign grace, the graciousness and stability of the plan of salvation! I now long for some of those manifestations. For more than a year I preached only from the 17th of John, except in a funeral or some special occasion. The Lord was very good to me; he gave me an open door to speak on the great subjects of the gospel and the wonders of grace. I am amazed to this day at the goodness of God in this; he gave such amplitude to one of such limited knowledge and talents and advantages! I had neither time nor opportunity to write regular notes on what I was speaking: thus nothing has been preserved. A few years afterwards, when I had more leisure, I used to write copious notes containing my meditations on some verse, thinking of preaching them to the people. I never tried to compose words for a sermon, but I would expect light and support whilst speaking. I expected to receive suitable words. I endeavoured to search, meditate, and pray that I might comprehend the doctrine in the text, and the proper inferences from it. I also strove to pray as I went into the pulpit, for light, and for suitable words to speak to the people. Sometimes the Lord would think it proper to hide himself, quite justly, from me, leaving me in the pulpit in great darkness, without words to speak to the people. These occasions were very bitter, yet they proved to be profitable to me. I would see more clearly after such occasions, from whence my aid must come. At other times the Lord would afford me such light and assistance in preaching that I was humbled to the dust, and made very thankful.

Elias's knowledge, as we have observed before, was extensive; it was of great use to him as a minister, it expanded his views and aided his judgment; and he was thereby greatly helped in his preparations for the pulpit, and in the delivery of his sermons. His great talents, by due and proper exercise, became more energetic as well as more matured. His knowledge and acquaintance with things were truly surprising. When, for instance, we heard him expounding so readily the numbers of the followers of the beast, we might have imagined that he had been studying calculations for a long time. When he dwelt on the success of the gospel in foreign parts, describing so easily places little known to his hearers, we might have thought that he had paid great attention to geography in his lifetime. In hearing him at other times so familiar in ecclesiastical and civil history, we might suppose it had been his exclusive study. He would expound the Word of God, and set forth the deep things in it, so strikingly, that we were obliged to think it was not a smattering, but much knowledge that he possessed of everything. His great abilities were manifest in all his communications, either at religious or social meetings. When he had anything to state at one of the private meetings of an Association, he would explain it and make such remarks on it, as surprised every one. What he said was so full and satisfactory, that it was never known that any person could cast further light on the subject, or in any way improve the statement.

Elias's judgment was also remarkable in introducing and managing his several important subjects in the pulpit, so as, under God's blessing, to answer the end in view. He always endeavoured, by the Spirit's aid, to enlighten the conscience of the people as to their awful situation, before he would bring before them gospel truths. He trembled lest his work in publishing the gospel in its amazing freeness should have a tendency to ease the minds of the impenitent, and indirectly make them sin more boldly against God; and and he would therefore endeavour to guard against such evil consequences.

I may conclude this head by saying that his discourses were so methodical, striking and impressive, and so easily retained, that they were long remembered afterwards. I have frequently heard clergymen from Wales relate parts of them with great accuracy and delight.

Having dwelt at some length on Elias as very intellectual in the ministry, we shall now in the second place particularly notice his brilliant imagination, and the influence of it in his sermons, blended with his other great talents. I shall make use of the observations of others on this subject, as well as my own, and these will confirm my remarks. Elias preached with remarkable clearness and judgment, as we have observed; having calmly, soberly, and seriously laboured in the work of dispelling the darkness, rectifying the judgment, enlightening the mind, and convincing the conscience of his hearers, he would bring in to his aid the force of his imagination, using all manner of figures. Great was his skill in personifying things. One might imagine that the scenes represented in the Scriptures were really acted over again before his eyes: for instance, our Saviour in his various intercourses with mankind, such as the lepers, the woman of Canaan, Mary Magdalene; and especially in the last tragical events of his life. This power of representing things was most striking.

But it was the power of the Spirit, which we have intimated, that produced the saving influence, and made his preaching so strong. It was the divine influence pervading his discourses that gave them the power which overawed the people, and that induced them to flee from the wrath to come. What lustre was consequently added to his natural talents and acquirements, and what dignity to his person! And O! what an expression of devotion in all his manner! What simplicity and power of speech did he exercise in the pulpit! What life and spirit in the subject he treated on! It is almost impossible to meet with a preacher who could rivet the attention of his hearers so strongly. How amazing were his delineations of things!

An eminent minister speaks in the following way of Elias's remarkable pictorial powers in setting forth alarming and consoling truths, and the effects made thereby on the minds of the people:

He would preach of the fall of man in such a way, that we felt ourselves as if going into the depths of misery below, and as if before the everlasting prison: while we cried out, 'What shall we do to be saved? Save Lord, we perish!' After having placed us before the judgment seat, naked and destitute of all righteousness, he would then change his subject, and in a most captivating manner would show us the plan of salvation by Jesus Christ, till we felt ourselves raised up, as it were, from the depths of the fall, and fixed upon the Rock of Ages, with songs of thanksgiving in our mouths, forgetting our poverty, and thinking no more of our calamity and distress! How powerfully were the law and the gospel brought to bear on each other! Elias's whole soul was engaged in the work, and there was everything correct in him. He had great self-possession when most animated and using the strongest figurative expressions; and could modulate his voice with perfect ease. It would not be too much to say of him, taking all things together, that he was the first preacher in the world.

Another friend, speaking of Elias's manner of describing scriptural subjects, says:

Once I recollect, when he was preparing the minds of the people to receive the glad tidings, he was led to speak awfully of the day of judgment, representing it in such lively colours that the people were very deeply and awfully impressed, apprehending that it was near at hand, and opening before them: in consequence of which, Mr Richardson of Caernarvon, a most evangelical preacher, cried out loudly, as if he saw the judgment coming.

Elias was preaching in another place in such a descriptive and terrific manner on hell torments that the people were panic-struck, and thought that they were on the point of going there; one man cried out in his distress, 'O that I could hear Richardson of Caernarvon but for five minutes!'

It is related that Elias preached a remarkable sermon at Pall Mall Chapel, Liverpool, in 1809. His text was: 'That at that time ye were without Christ', etc. (*Ephesians* 2.12). There was a feeling of tremendous awe in the hearers' hearts as he described to them man's wretched condition without Christ. Many were terrified and pale with fear. Elias himself was under the most intense feelings, and could not forbear from tears.

Oh! Oh! [he cried] the wretchedness of those without Christ! They are naked without clothing! sick without a Physician! famishing without the bread of life! guilty without righteousness! unclean without a fountain! lost without a Saviour! damned without atonement!

He bent over the Bible on the pulpit before him, his tears wetting the pages of the sacred Book. A strange, oppressive silence, and a sense of terrible solemnity brooded over the packed congregation. The people were overwhelmed by a sense of deep sadness, and many of them were on the verge of utter despondency. But suddenly, the preacher raised his head, and the people saw that his face was now transfigured. He was supremely happy, and his face glowed with heavenly joy. 'Blessed be God!' he cried, 'Christ can be found tonight for those who have been without him!' Light and divine power attended this statement with its message of hope, and scores of men and women leaped unconsciously to their feet, glorifying God for his mercy. Joy without measure filled the hearts of the people. How can we explain this divine power and unction? In the first place, it was the power of the Spirit; and secondly, the preacher himself had entered into the spirit of his sermon.

Elias's method of making an impression on the mind of his hearers, was peculiarly figurative [says another minister] especially when he was handling some weighty subject. He would at times suddenly say, 'Stop! Silence! What are they saying in heaven on the subject?' It seemed to bring them within the very precincts of glory! The effect was often thrilling. When the subject was of an alarming nature, he would, at times, make use of the same extraordinary mode, and the effect was equally remarkable. Then he would exclaim, 'Stop! Silence! What do they say in hell on this awful subject?' The awe and solemnity that seized the multitude for a moment, was most affecting; they were nearly all breathless, and the preacher would expatiate on the most likely and natural things to be uttered in heaven or hell on the theme under consideration. Oh the effect of his preaching – it was unutterable! It is more easy to be conceived than described. Had the people heard those terrific things from the invisible world they could scarcely have been more alarmed.

I remember to have heard Elias preaching in a most awful and terrific manner on the subject of the last day, representing the wicked as tares made into different bundles, according to their degrees in sin and iniquity, and then cast into the everlasting burnings. A certain flaxdresser was, in a daring manner, going on with his work, in an open room opposite to where Elias was thus preaching on the platform; but the flashes of divine fire increased more and more, till the man was obliged to leave his work, and run into a yard behind his premises, to get out of the reach of the awful peals, more dreadful to his agitated and trembling soul than the loudest claps of thunder: but 'the awful language of Elias followed me there also', said the panic-struck sinner!

Another minister speaks as follows of Elias's talent in setting forth those great truths:

He would portray his matter to his hearers by his words, his voice, his motions, in so suitable and effectual a way, till his matter and manner were so deeply impressed on the minds of the people, that they became their own ideas and feelings. His motions were very becoming, and attended with the greatest solemnity. He would represent the judgment day, under such awful, impressive figures, as to make the people tremble. He would speak of sin and transgression in such a way, that he would, under the blessing of God, create a hatred to it in the heart: he would describe grace and virtue in such glowing terms, till they were loved and admired. He would penetrate into the depths of divine truth in such a manner, that even the wise and learned were amazed. He would some-times lose the order he had previously formed, and confess it; but then in an instant he would recover himself, and pour forth such unexpected torrents of eloquence as overcame all. A peculiar talent and originality appeared in him: he would preach the deep things of the cross intel-ligibly, by means of striking figures: he would unfold the mysterious work of the Spirit in the soul, the depths of Satan's temptations and the manifold effects of grace. He would also explain the various doubtful cases of conscience that harass and perplex the believer, till the poor soul was relieved, strengthened, and comforted. At another time he would penetrate far into the wonders of the gospel, till he was obliged to restrain himself: but then he would, with a peculiar motion of the hand and the expression of the countenance in silence, let the mind of the hearer run into depths of meditation, till he was filled with floods of overwhelming ideas.

Elias's manner and power of delineating subjects of a mild nature were equally astonishing and effective; such as the death of Christ for instance. He preached once at an Association on those words, 'Christ died for our sins, according to the Scriptures'. The representation of Christ's death was so graphic, vivid, and powerful, that many of the people were so affected as if they had seen him crucified. This extraordinary sermon was delivered in the morning. Mr Ebenezer Richard was to preach at two o'clock. When he appeared on the tented platform, he thus began, 'My dear friends, I think I shall not be able to preach, as my mind is so overwhelmed by the morning sermon. I thought when hearing our beloved brother describe the crucifixion, that I saw it before my eyes in the field where we were assembled! The effect and the impression of the *astonished view*, is still on my mind in a most lively and vivid manner!'

Elias's power of describing things was indeed most striking. I well remember him, though many years ago, representing Christ as triumphing over the evil spirits on the cross, in a very interesting and novel manner. He seemed to give a clear idea of the conversation between Christ and those malignant spirits, at the time of the crucifixion, by personifying them, knowing how they tried him in the wilderness, and supposing they would not now in the last struggle relax in their opposition; but Christ triumphed over them on the cross.

In nothing did Elias's power appear so much as in representing things, and setting them before the people in their proper colours. The Rev W. Morgan, Incumbent of Christ Church, Bradford, Yorkshire, favoured me with the following brilliant idea he once heard in a sermon of Elias's. Every sermon abounded with such ideas.

I was always much pleased with Elias [says he]. I heard him once preach a very striking sermon, the subject of which was our Saviour's miracles. He referred in a beautiful manner to the Panorama then in London: 'But', said he, 'suppose we were all viewing a Panorama of those miracles of the Son of God. Then look on one side, and you will see the blind gazing on him who gave them sight, the deaf listening to him that had unstopped their ears; and, on the other side, you will perceive the lepers that had been cleansed by him, telling what he had done, the lame who had been cured by him, walking, leaping, and praising God. Then see yonder the dumb, whose tongue had been unloosened by him, proclaiming his praises; the dead he had raised up, so animated in his service, and setting forth his glory; and those once possessed of devils, calm, and in their right mind, magnifying God for being set at liberty. But O! what shall we say of the spiritual cures of Jesus – these are but faint representations of them! In the Church of God you have the Panorama of them full to the very life; there they are in reality.' Here his talents shone exceedingly, in setting forth the Saviour's excellencies in performing the most astonishing miracles on the souls of lost sinners, referring to many there present, as living monuments of those divine operations, and that such a Panorama of these wonderful cures might be exhibited there. I was at the time very ill, but I was animated with the description, and I have often rapped the comparative cold English, with the account.

Elias in the course of his sermon at the close of an Association, made use of the following striking and bold delineations of characters on the subject of man's spiritual deliverance. His text was 'Shall the prey be taken from the mighty, or the lawful captive be delivered' (*Isaiah* 49.24).

'Satan,' exclaimed he in a very peculiar manner, 'what do you say, "Shall the prey be taken from the mighty?" ' 'No, *never, never*; I will increase the darkness of their minds, the hardness of their hearts, the lusts of their souls, the strength of their chains; and my holds shall be made stronger. The captives shall *never* be delivered. I utterly despise the puny efforts of ministers.'

'Gabriel, messenger of the Most High God', exclaimed Elias again in a different tone of voice, looking upwards, ' "Shall the prey be taken from the mighty"? what dost thou say?' 'Ah! I apprehend not; I have been hovering these two days over this vast assembly hearing the Word of God, expecting to see some chains broken, some prisoners liberated; but now the opportunity is near over, and the multitudes are on the point of separating. Ah! there is no sign of one being converted: and I shall not have to convey the glad-tidings of one sinner repenting for his sins, to the heavenly world.'

Then Elias, turning to the preachers, asked, 'What think you, ministers of the living God? "Shall the prey be taken from the mighty?" ' 'Alas! "Who hath believed our report? and to whom is the arm of the Lord revealed?" "We have laboured in vain, and have spent our strength for nought." The Lord seemeth to hide his face from us; his arm is not stretched out. Oh! we fear there is but little hope of the captives being delivered.'

'Zion, "Shall the prey be taken from the mighty?" What do you say?' Ah! the Lord hath forsaken me, and my Lord hath forgotten me. I am left alone, and am childless: so that my enemies say, "This is Zion, whom no man seeketh after!" Oh I am afraid none shall be delivered.'

'Praying Christians, what do you think, "Shall the prey be taken from the mighty?" ' 'Lord God, *thou* knowest, "High is thy hand and strong is thy right hand". O that thou wouldest put forth thy strength and overcome! "Let the sighing of the prisoner come before thee: according to the greatness of thy power, preserve thou those that are appointed to die." Though I am nearly weary in crying, yet I have a slender hope that the year of Jubilee is at hand.'

Then Elias looked up in a very serious manner, as if going to speak to the Almighty, and asked, 'And what is the mind of the Lord respecting these captives?' 'Thus saith the Lord, even the captives of the mighty shall be taken away, and the prey of the terrible shall be delivered.' 'O! delightful,' he exclaimed; 'there is now *no* doubt or hesitation respecting the liberty of the captives, it is *positively* declared, they shall be delivered, they shall be saved. Yea, "The ransomed of the Lord shall return, and come to Zion, with songs and everlasting joy upon their heads." '

The eloquence of the preacher was wonderful, and the effects that followed were amazing and indescribable. The above is merely an outline of a small part of the excellent discourse. Indeed, brilliant but chastened imagination, rich but simple eloquence pervaded the whole of his discourse. Every sermon of his always appeared to his friends as a complete masterpiece of elocution, a most suitable and well-fitted oration.

Let ministers expend all their intellectual powers, like Elias, in the exposition of divine truth, and the consequence, under God, will be surprising. Shall natural men bestow upon their favourite studies most intense application, striking sketches of touching pathos and of thrilling power? Shall the appeals made thus to the passions and interests of men, move and electrify assemblies? Surely the intellect that has been consecrated to the grandest of all pursuits, that of saving the souls of men, should be urged beyond mere common-place exertions. The gospel themes, if not shorn of their glory by unskilful preaching, would be sufficient to eclipse the orations of natural men, and would, as in the instance before us, command the notice and admiration, even of a depraved world. If discourses in general were the results of sufficiently industrious and consecrated studies, the glowing, powerful, and attractive exhibitions of divine truth would surely be heard, and deeply felt. Permanent impressions would be made by such appeals. While the substance of preaching would remain the same, the modes of illustration and enforcement would be greatly diversified, as Elias's were; the minister, animated by the subject, sometimes thundering with all the warmth of holy indignation, sometimes expostulating with the earnestness of brotherly anxiety, sometimes seeming to be transfixed in wonder and silent astonishment.

8 Illustrations of Elias's great powers, testimonies to his success

Other great qualifications of Elias as a minister may be here mentioned; and, in the first place, the principles by which he was influenced, and the end at which he aimed. Without right principles and motives, a man is far from having the essentials of a minister. St Paul said, 'Though I speak with the tongues of men and angels, and have not charity, I am become as sounding brass, or a tinkling cymbal.' But the love of Christ and of souls was predominant in Elias. It appeared at times that he was, as it were, filled with that love which is so essential to the being of a Christian, and of a good minister of Christ. He had likewise a consciousness of possessing the gospel treasure himself, and this gave liberty of heart and utterance; this gave boldness and fidelity. Elias was not one of those who have no concern whether few or many are saved under the Word preached; for it was for this end he prayed and laboured. And O what pleasure it afforded him to exhibit to the lost, Christ and him crucified! That character given in Revelation, to a loving minister, 'the face of a man', well suited Elias. He had most tender compassion towards the miserable, as well as the understanding and wisdom of a man. To man was his message directed, and it was the benefit and salvation of man that were always in his view.

The other great excellency of Elias's ministerial character that made him so notable, was his aiming at God's glory. He often used to admire and adore that infinite love and almighty power, which rendered his ministry useful and beneficial. He knew he was only the medium of communication, and that all good and perfect gifts came from above, and that nothing originated with him. Elias, regarding not his own but his Master's work, which appeared to him infinitely glorious, was truly devoted to it; and his attention to it was undivided. This right frame of mind made all labour light and pleasant to him, even that which might be considered by some very irksome and difficult. We shall not enlarge on these subjects as we have before touched upon them.

Elias's *delivery* was extraordinary. His manner of speaking was truly lively and powerful. His voice was strong and clear, and his articulation easy to understand. The most numerous congregation that attended him, could hear the first word he uttered. His voice was, at the same time, pleasant and agreeable to the nearest person. His elocution was superior to that of most men. There was a peculiar impressiveness in his preaching that strongly arrested the attention of the people.

I remember meeting the Rev Christmas Evans, after hearing Elias at the Caernarvon Association in 1836, and joining with him in praising Elias as a preacher, delivering his great ideas so well, though so old and nearly toothless. Evans observed: 'He has acquired the art of regulating his voice.' I asked Elias some time afterwards, if this was true; he answered, 'Yes, Mr Charles taught it me'. The late excellent Mr Simeon of Cambridge, would thrill an audience by his weak voice! The plan he recommended is the following: 'Always speak in a natural voice. If you speak to 2,000 people, you should not rise to a different key, but still preserve your customary pitch. You know that on a violoncello, you may sound scarcely to be heard; or that you may strike it (on the same string) with such force, that it shall twang again. So it is with your voice; it is by the strength, and not by the (undue) elevation of it, that you are to be heard. You will remember that a whole discourse is to be delivered, and if you get into an unnatural key, you will both injure yourself, and weary your audience.' *Christian Observer*, 1835. It is likely Charles gave Elias similar directions. He always spoke in a natural voice – when he spoke to thousands he did not raise it to a different key. His speaking was free and easy, and quite agreeable to the listener: though at times the torrent of his oratory was overwhelming, still every letter, syllable, and word had their proper sounds and accents! Elias's eloquence was not art, but nature decked in her best ornaments.

His preaching, especially at the commencement of his ministry, was of a very awful cast, but also consoling. He did not deal deceitfully with the Word of God, but 'commended himself to every man's conscience in the sight of God'. I conceive of him in the habit of preaching as like one who must give an account of his work. He prayed much in composing his sermons: he delivered them also feeling the importance of the work, the value of the souls of his hearers, and the strictness of the reckoning which he should give of his ministry. And yet he did not always deal in terrors; for after preaching the most awful menaces, he would, as we have seen, bring forth the promises in their unsearchable riches, until scores and hundreds in the vast assemblies would 'draw water with joy out of the wells of salvation'. And what gave great effect to such heart-rending and then joyful expressions, was this, they proceeded out of a most feeling heart. The tears were running down his solemn countenance at the time of addressing sinners, while the Holy Spirit was blessing the whole.

His appearance in the pulpit was very remarkable, especially for seriousness, command, and authority. One might think that a most extraordinary man was going to speak. As soon as he took the Bible into his hands, he appeared as a person that had some great business or message. His looks were full of significant expression. He seemed to be full of thought and great concern, as one engaged in a work of vast importance. He generally appeared in preaching, like some grave philosopher, speaking with great authority and effect. There was also such lowly modesty and such holy boldness in his appearance, that drew the attention of every eye, and prepared every ear to listen. The people felt that a man of extraordinary mind, a *man* sent from God, was about to speak. He was very judicious in reading and expounding his text. He read it as one who had received it as a message given him of the Lord to the people, with much seriousness, soberness and emphasis setting forth the sense, so that new wonders opened upon the mind of every one who heard it.

The attention of his hearers was rivetted from the very commencement of his discourse, and it grew more as he went along, and became more intense: the dropping of a pin might be heard. The people were occupied in the most important business possible: if engaged in the most serious concern before an earthly tribunal, they could not pay greater attention. Indeed, the attention of the congregation was so arrested under his preaching that they could not think of anything else. The grandeur of his subjects, and the manner of setting them forth, so impressed the minds of the people that they became exceedingly solemn and serious, and could not be disturbed for a moment. They had no time to give vent to their feelings in any way, though so warm. Robert Jones of Rhos-lan, a notable minister, asked a person who had just heard Elias preach, how he liked him; he himself had never heard him. 'Oh,' said the man, 'I never heard such a preacher in my life.' He asked him further, in rather an ironical manner, whether there were any *Amens*, or any heavenly, spiritual dew descending with the Word, for he had an idea that he was a dry preacher, having only 'great, swelling words', making no impression. The man replied, 'Indeed Mr Jones, there was *no time* to say Amen!'

In short, there was something so engaging in Elias's manner of speaking, that it is difficult to describe it. He was indeed a complete orator. His language was simple and beautiful. According to a correspondent in a Welsh periodical, 'He twisted the most elegant terms into sentences wholly original, which at the conclusion of his sermon, appeared one large consistent chain.' His every gesture was co-operating to give effect to his words. He could even express his matter with bodily motions, so that people who understood but little Welsh, might perceive his meaning; at least they were greatly assisted thereby to understand him, and were prepossessed in his favour. There was something more remarkable in him, in this respect, than we ever observed in any other preacher. When he was preaching once in Brecon, some of the French prisoners in that town were led to the ground where he was holding forth, and were greatly struck by the serious manner, and commanding, impressive, and powerful delivery and appearance of the preacher. Though, of course, they understood not a word that was uttered, yet they imagined that something interesting must have been spoken by him. They testified that there was a peculiarity in him that they had not seen in any one before. The amazing attention of the people must have struck them also.

The same observation respecting Elias's preaching powers was made by some Englishmen who happened to hear him: they confessed that their attention had never been more drawn by any preaching, even in their own language, than by his, since they found delight in seeing and hearing him. There was something in his person, attitude and manner of delivery that attracted their attention. What then must have been the force of his preaching on those that understood his language? Once, in his sermon at Liverpool, he was induced to speak a few words in English; and the effect on some English persons present was very strong and even saving. The words were so delivered, in his usual grave and impressive manner, respecting eternity, that they carried conviction home into the heart, never to be eradicated. There was no rest until application was made to the great Saviour.

Occasionally, the full spate of his eloquence would come to a sudden stop. It appeared as if his tongue, under the stress of deep emotion, was refusing to function. It was not a stutter, but a complete muteness which – as the Welsh poet Eben Fardd states in his elegy – was far more effective than the most fervid eloquence. It was not induced by art; it just happened. He had a habit, on these occasions, of sucking in his cheeks into his mouth, and with lips tightly clenched, in a silence which could be felt, he would cast his eyes over the congregation as if he was seeking someone. Then, with arm outstretched, his long forefinger would begin to move as if it possessed a life independent of his arm and the rest of his body. Suddenly, words would come forth once again from his lips, and the tension was relieved.

Elias's preaching was of a very *authoritative* nature, when his subject required it. He spoke like a man that was commissioned from above to address perishing sinners. Such was his holy boldness in the gospel that the commanding character given to some ministers in the Revelation of St John suited him well, 'the face of a lion'. He really taught as one having authority. His ministry frequently produced a terror and alarm not only among open transgressors, but also on hypocrites, and withstood and subdued the corruption of the age. His holy undaunted boldness, courage and dignity, combined with gentleness and love and other great qualities, had a most happy influence on his delivery.

The testimony of a few ministers will corroborate what has been stated respecting Elias's delivery. The Rev G. Hughes, the Wesleyan minister at Aberystwyth, spoke of him thus:

The late Rev John Elias of Anglesey was like the Phœnix. They say of this bird, that there is but one of the kind at a time in the world. Such was our brother Elias. When he preached, it was in a way superior to others. And when he harangued at a Bible or an abstinence meeting, or on any other occasion, he went beyond us all. Doubtless he who formed the lip of man, gave him a tongue 'as the pen of a ready writer', and furnished him, in this respect, with talents above the ordinary standard. The clearness of his utterance, the power of his voice, and the motions of his body, were in harmonious co-operation. And his practice of giving the consonants their proper sound, and not drowning his words in drawling out the vowels, caused his words to be penetrating, and his manner of delivery delightful to the ear: and when divine light accompanied, and the hand of the Lord co-operated, the sternest tempers were often overcome. I do not recollect any one who could make so fair a distinction between preaching and haranguing. He would not preach as one haranguing, nor harangue as one preaching. It might be thought that his soul was a storehouse of the sciences, and composed of logic; and that his tongue was a well-mounted instrument of oratory and eloquence.

The Rev. D. R. Stephens, of Newport (Mon), said:

There is something peculiar in the great orator of Anglesey, a something in the motion of his right hand, and the manner of his delivery, which made an abiding impression on the mind. The wave of his hand was eloquence; the pauses in his discourse were eloquence; all was eloquence. It might be sometimes thought, in hearing him, that his mind was overfilled with ideas. He would pause for half a minute, to allow his soul to survey the wonders before him. While he paused, his countenance would be deeply serious; his eyes would, as it were, sparkle; and his face and arms would be in serious emotion, as one who had some *new* discovery, and wanted language to set it forth. But when he began to speak, the wonders of divine truth would break forth as a flood upon the assembly, and the hearers would often be drowned in tears.

The following is a striking account of Elias as a minister, though but little more than the substance of what has been stated in this and the former chapter. It is taken from *The Christian Reformer:*

Elias's chief characteristics were a clear and masculine understanding, great tenderness of feeling, a discriminating judgment, strong reasoning faculties, and a spirit of genuine unpretending piety. His preaching was always in Welsh; and in compass and vigour of language, he had no rival. He could exhibit such extensive views of what he regarded as 'the deep things of God', and of the requirements of the gospel—its awful denunciations, its precious promises—and could connect them with *pictures* of the *human character* so vivid and often so true to nature, and to our experience, that he seldom failed to touch, and even thrill our heart. It was impossible not to be struck with the luminous order in which his ideas were arranged. He had a quick perception of what belonged, and what did not belong, to any question that came before him. He knew how to reject all that was extraneous; hence no one could mistake him. Without the appearance of any effort, he always left a strong and well-defined impression upon the minds of his hearers. He had no turns of thought remarkable for nothing but their strangeness; no smart sparkling witticisms, no false transports. It was not his practice to deal in satirical, sarcastic remarks; and he was entirely free both from coarseness and from flippancy. For the most part, his sentences were simple; but they were never cast in a rugged or careless mould. When he adopted a colloquial style, he took the utmost pains to avoid everything like vulgarity.

He preached not to amuse, but to convince: there was an earnest solicitude about him, which gave an elevation and persuasiveness to his discourses, far more capable of awakening a deep and lasting interest than the most adorned specimens of artificial eloquence. The expression of his countenance, the tones of his voice, and his gestures, strikingly corresponded with what was passing in his mind. His whole manner was artless, dignified and graceful; and if we take all these circumstances into consideration, we shall be at no loss to account for the extraordinary attraction of his public addresses, or for the almost magical dominion which he had over his auditors, whatever might be their age or their attainments. The sorcery arose not more from the strength than the versatility of his genius.

Having considered Elias's ministerial powers in a general way, or as used in his common course of preaching, we shall now view them when exerted on particular occasions. The talents of great men appear more conspicuously and illustriously at some great and remarkable opportunities. And so did Elias's gifts. The grand field of labour where he was seen to the greatest advantage was that of the great Association, where many thousands of people congregated, and where ministers, not only of his own, but of every other denomination met. The Lord highly owned and exalted his servant on these, as well as other occasions; and all acknowledged his superiority. Mr Ebenezer Thomas, a friend of mine, who distinguished himself greatly in writing Welsh poetry (under the name of *Eben Fardd*), lately favoured me with a letter respecting the preaching talents of Elias, particularly on such occasions. The description is excellent; and as it is satisfactory and conclusive on this point, I introduce it here. He had a considerable advantage in writing this account of Elias, as he was well acquainted with him, and had before composed the Welsh elegy on his departure already noticed. The letter is the following:

Clynog 17 November 1841

It is difficult to form an estimate of Elias's preaching talents, and brilliant eloquence: however, we are not in danger of over-rating his wonderful abilities. He stood forward so pre-eminently among his fellow-labourers as to be easily distinguished, as well for his sterling merit and usefulness as for his superiority in the exercise of those qualities and powers, which we imagine to constitute a pre-eminent character in the Presbytery of the church. He was formed by nature and by grace for the ministry; 'he had been anointed by God with the oil of grace and eloquence above his fellows'. Nature, though at times endowed with uncommon talents, is still rude and uncouth, without the auxiliary graces, and adventitious aids of learning and art to polish it. In the present instance, nature, under God, supplied the powers and faculties, while grace and sanctified learning taught the right use and exercise of them, to the glory of God and the edification of the church. Thus was Elias enabled to discharge his public duties, at all times, with the most astonishing and agreeable effect.

We shall pass by his in-door, or chapel preaching, and just take a view of his addressing an open-air congregation, at an Association, in one of the Welsh towns. And, first, just take a glance at the whole concern and proceedings. A large tent-stage is erected at one end of an extensive field in the vicinity, and many thousands of attentive and devoted hearers stand in the front of it. Then take a slight survey of the congregated multitudes previous to his appearance. We shall find, on the covered platform, a clever, lively preacher, addressing the vast audience: he seems to be a very highly gifted man too, and elicits considerable marks of approbation. Professors in general appear to be edified through his discourse; still, business is alive in the town. The streets are paraded by thoughtless crowds of young people; the lawyers' offices are crammed with litigating parties, and others who have some stake in the land and money and things of this world. The inns and public houses are filled with reckless and dissipated parties, the shops with customers from the country; and those who have remained in the town can hardly miss the thousands in the field. Again, the main body of the assembly is flanked with some scores of vehicles, thronged with people; and on the adjacent fences and eminences, some hundreds of saunterers are to be seen, listlessly estimating the extent of ground covered by the multitude, or feasting their idle curiosity on the motley appearance of the almost countless throng of town and country people. But just as the fluent precursor of Elias concludes his address, there is a perceptible change in the scene. A general stir ensues, the town pours forth some additional multitudes, consisting not only of tradesmen and common people, but also of a considerable number of ladies and gentlemen. The occupants of the several vehicles begin to gaze towards a certain spot, and to place themselves in the most favourable position. The loungers, from the heights and hedges, eagerly approach the main body; and now the whole irregular groups are consolidated into one common mass of rational beings. The grand focus, where the innumerable angles of vision all concentrate, is the stage; and just now the looked-for individual makes his appearance at the stage-desk. In stature he was somewhat tall, slender, and of a dark complexion; having high cheek bones, discoloured teeth, considerably exposed when his mouth was opened – his eyes animated and expressive, his posture erect, bold and commanding. He had naturally a serene and placid countenance, indicating true christian meekness and humility, and illuminated with a faint smile when he appeared on the stage. Then, contracting his lips, he would exhibit a solemn and serious aspect, as he surveyed the immense multitude; and as he pointed out the text, and read it in his sweet, clear, penetrating voice, the anxiety of the assembly was relieved. There was a deep silence, and the most devoted attention pervaded through the whole audience, even to the outskirts of the grand assembly! All were on the tip-toe to catch a glimpse of the favourite preacher, devouring with avidity the minutest words that dropped from his mouth. Most resigned themselves to the influence of his extraordinary eloquence. By this time he finds himself in his usual good frame, and proceeds in a masterly style, under the divine blessing, emitting such brilliant flashes of holy eloquence as to charm his numerous hearers with his sweet and superior oratory. He was chiefly remarkable for his originality, and his magnifying and simplifying talents. Whatever subject he handled, he could never be anticipated. None could guess the course he would pursue; but, as soon as he marked it out, it was impossible, in the opinion of all, to think of any better plan. It appeared so natural, striking and consistent, that all wondered that they did not think of it before.[1] Those mooted points of doctrinal and practical religion, which the ears of the audience were perpetually accustomed to, and which in common hands, possessed no peculiar interest, he laid hold of, and began to dress with such novelty, and magnify to such a degree of vital importance, as to make the hearers almost fancy themselves for the *first* time listening to a minister of Christ's gospel.[2] He took, at other times, an abstruse point of doctrine or duty, and held it as it were between his fingers, divesting it of all its difficulties, and supposed incongruities, and exhibiting it in its bare and simple essence and reality, thereby rendering it so definite and intelligible to the dullest understanding, that all were astonished why they ever entertained any doubts respecting it. His manner too was truly oratorical; his eyes, mouth, arms, hands, fingers, and even his head and body, all spoke at once, heightening the effect with indescribable form and beauty, charming the audience to the most devoted attention and admiration.

If he had a sorrowful theme to dwell upon, as the infatuation of sinners, perishing in their evil courses and rejecting salvation, he would weep and sigh, and modulate his voice to the subdued notes and tones of lamentation and pity, wiping off his tears with a handkerchief,

---

[1] 'We never heard any preach more forcibly than Elias, but in hearing him it might have been thought that preaching was the easiest thing possible, for it was as natural, and attended with as little effort, as the swallow in its evolutions through the air'.

[2] 'He was in his glory in the middle of an argument. Never did his oratorical powers shine more brilliantly than when the burden of the argument rested on his shoulders. His ideas were, at times, like the waves of the sea swelling successively, yea accumulating and expanding to such a degree, as to make him appear superior to man.' – *Yr Haul.*

till the whole audience felt themselves buried at once in the greatest distress. When, at another time, he felt a sanctified jealousy for the honour and glory of his divine Master, seeing, like Moses formerly, the people rashly embracing an idol, and disregarding the worship and the injunctions of the one Jehovah, and adhering to their corrupt and evil ways, he warned them with a beautiful vehemence. He assumed a threatening attitude, wore on his countenance such an awful frown, and stretched forward his arms with such a manly courage, as to make the scoffer grave and crest-fallen, the obdurate to tremble, and the thoughtless votaries of levity and pleasure to hang down their heads in dismay, and for once at least to reflect on their headlong course of depravity.

When he again began to display the inexhaustible riches of free grace, and expatiate on the infinite love and unbounded mercy of a Saviour, and his all-sufficiency to meet the most desperate case, he assumed a gladsome and triumphant aspect, and smiled with such full confidence, and lifted his hands unto heaven with such indescribable joy, and with such force and beauty of diction and delivery, that the reiterated ejaculations, amens, and hallelujahs which rang through the audience, made one almost think he was really in the abode of the blessed, beholding the ineffable glory of the Saviour, and listening to the never-ending praises of the glorified saints.

This beautiful poetical painter, favoured me with a postscript to the above excellent letter, containing remarks on what he had written of Elias.

The 'smile' alluded to, was slight, or something approaching to it; indicating the inward joy he felt at seeing such vast multitudes of lost sinners in so favourable a situation to hear the good news of salvation through Jesus Christ. The slight contortion of the lips indicated some thrilling sensation that crept over him, excited by the lively sympathy felt for the congregated thousands before him, who, he knew, would soon be summoned to account for such meetings, at the awful tribunal of heaven. His simplifying talents added much to his popularity. He could lay hold on some stupendous mystery of the divine counsel, and simplify and explain it, so as to edify babes in Christ; and on the other hand, silence the idle cavils and objections of the disputer of his word. His daring originality, too, rendered him an object of popular admiration. He could not drudge on along the beaten path, but he struck out a course for himself, and started forward with such taste and ability, as rendered him the wonder and delight of all who heard him.

Such a description of preaching I never read before. Even in Philips's *Life of Whitefield*, no such instance of amazing eloquence is to be found. A comparison between him and that celebrated man, has already been made; yet here we may say, that, as a divine, he was his superior. President Edwards, of America, did not enter more deeply into divine truths, and unravel difficulties with greater success than Elias did. It was asked the venerable Newton once, who he thought was the greatest preacher he ever heard? 'Whitefield,' he replied. And who was the greatest divine? 'Edwards,' was the answer; 'there is as much in his little finger, as in Whitefield altogether.'

Wales has, within the last fifty years, been favoured with preachers of uncommon talents; but Elias possessed greater preaching abilities than any of them. In looking to Beaumaris, Bala, Denbigh, Twr-gwyn, Wern, Caernarvon, Tregaron, we think of dear departed eminent ministers of Christ with great tenderness, and respect; but not one of them was supplied with such store of excellencies as was bestowed on this brother. His popularity indeed was astonishing, not only at Associations, but wherever he preached. The multitude of his hearers, whether it were in his own neighbourhood, or in a distant quarter, was always immense. Whatever day of the week, or hour of the day, he was announced to preach, it was always the same. It mattered little at what time or season; business was laid aside and the shops closed, and multitudes would assemble to hear him; so that he was generally obliged to stand in the windows, or outside of the chapels, to preach. There would be seen, generally, in the congregation, religious professors and ministers of all the different denominations in the neighbourhood: and in South Wales, there would be, at times, no less than ten or twelve clergymen present.

The success of his ministry was more extensive, under God, than that of any of his contemporaries. The great day which is to come, can alone show the exact extent of his ministerial success. But we know as much as this, that religion was at a low ebb in Wales when the Lord raised up Elias to his work. The churches were but few and small, compared with what they are now. The chapels in Anglesey were but few when he first went to the island, and the greater part of the inhabitants were 'sitting in darkness, in the valley and the shadow of death'. It is true the Lord raised up other eminent men to his work soon after him who became fellow-workers with him, in the best cause; but he it was that appeared most eminently employed to stir up the inhabitants, and to bring them under the sound of the gospel. Elias's delight in the service of the Lord and devotedness to it, conduced to his exerting all his powers in it, and the Lord thus disposing, blessed him with great success. He experienced those operations on his mind by which he 'knew the fear of the Lord'. He was under the impression, that 'it is a fearful thing to fall into the hands of the living God'; and this stirred up his mind to *persuade men*, with extraordinary animation, 'to flee from the wrath to come'. He did not go out into the streets and lanes, and highways and hedges, to trifle with men, or to lull them to sleep in their dangerous situation; but he went to search out their spiritual hiding places, to break up their nests, to show the nakedness of their state with respect to God and the judgment to come, and to compel them, by the strongest reason, to escape and flee from the danger. His object was to induce them to come unto God in Christ, where the great supper, that is, the feast of salvation, is to be had; and as the hand of the Lord was upon him, to bless him in the great work, he succeeded in bringing multitudes to 'the banqueting house'. I am happy, in order to show Elias's success, to introduce a letter of the Rev D. Charles, tutor at Trefecca, grandson of the celebrated Thomas Charles. It is the following:

Bala 31 March 1842

As a preacher, he was powerful and persuasive. He simplified everything, and set all truths forth in their clearest light, so that a child could understand him. His sermons, I was going to say, invariably reached the heart. In all my journeys through Wales, I have not heard of any one minister whose preaching has been so universally blessed to the conversion of sinners, as that of John Elias. In almost every country place, village, or town, you can find some person who will ascribe his conversion to one of his sermons. This I have witnessed in very many cases. You know that we are accustomed to very powerful preaching in Wales: indeed I may say, with truth, there is no ministry on earth that can compete with the Welsh, in *solidity*, *warmth*, and *energy*. Yet John Elias was remarkable among the Welsh. Some of his sermons, which I heard while yet a boy, are still fresh and vivid on my mind, and will never be effaced, while thousands of other sermons have passed into oblivion. I can never forget the extraordinary effects produced upon the multitudes assembled at Bala Association, about seven years ago, when he was preaching from *Isaiah* 6.10. There was not, I believe, a dry eye in that vast assembly on the occasion. The preacher wept and prayed in the pulpit; multitudes fell down as dead, and every countenance seemed filled with terror and dismay. 'Well, well,' said a friend, at the close, 'let them say what they will of Elias, there is however none like him; he is higher by his shoulders than any of us! But he is gone!'

Once Elias was preaching in the forenoon, at another Association, on those remarkable words: 'That ye may be able to comprehend the breadth, and length, and depth, and height, and to know the love of Christ, that passeth knowledge,' in a most powerful manner. The sermon was most amazing in its effects; under God's blessing, it quite overwhelmed the whole congregation. It appeared afterwards (in English) in the *Evangelical Magazine*, January 1859. The observations made at the end of the sermon on the prolonged, uncommon effects are these:

After the sermon was over, the people were still so overwhelmed, when, in moving from the field, they appeared as if not knowing the way out. Many were of the opinion that it would have been advisable to close the Association after this sermon; every attempt made to gain the attention of the hearers in the remaining services was fruitless. 'The breadth, length, depth, and height, of God's love to a lost world', continued ringing in every ear and every heart, during the whole day. Hundreds were added to the churches in that town and neighbourhood.

The late Ebenezer Richard used to speak of him thus, when he was expected to preach in Cardiganshire:

I sometimes almost feared [said he] to hear of his coming through the country, as there was so much talk about it, and all preparing for the opportunity to weigh him, as it were, in their scales – the evil and the well disposed. I almost feared lest he should be lowered in their esteem, and that he should not answer the expectations formed of him. I was almost sorry to see him, and to observe them coming to hear him. But when they came together, I was very glad to see the two parties there. Elias was enabled to go on most triumphantly in preaching the gospel, and all were deeply, and some, it is to be hoped, savingly impressed; even such as were not convinced of sin were greatly amazed. I never saw the cause of religion so much exalted by the preaching of any other individual.

The following anecdote is an additional corroboration of his power. There had been some coolness between him and that great man, his old friend, the Rev David Griffiths, the Vicar of Nevern, Pembrokeshire. It was on account of the plan of setting apart some of the preachers to assist the clergy in the Connexion to administer the sacraments. Griffiths had been one of the chief leaders in the body; and in consequence of the above circumstance, became cool and distant towards them, and even alienated from them. Yet when Elias, some years afterwards, came in the course of his ministerial excursions to preach in Griffiths's neighbourhood, the weight of his character induced the Vicar to go and hear him. The power of the old doctrines preached by Elias affected Griffiths exceedingly. He was preaching at an Association in Cardigan. Griffiths went up to the stage where he was preaching; and after Elias had finished his sermon, went to him, and most affectionately embraced him as a brother in Christ, and said, 'My dear old friend, I greatly love you as an honoured minister of God: how sweet, delightful, and precious, are these truths of the gospel you have been preaching: they are the old and grand truths; they will uphold, satisfy, and gladden our souls for ever.' The effect of such an interview between two such eminent soldiers of Christ was most delightful and impressive. Opportunities of holy fellowship occurring here in the world, such as that between Griffiths and Elias, have a wonderful tendency to bring them to a better understanding, and make them love each other. This concord of Christ's disciples used to appear in a striking manner at Bible Society meetings in former times. The influence of such men as Elias, men of so catholic a spirit, so humble, and so greatly blessed in their ministry, tends to do away with party spirit, and to bring the Church of Christ to greater union and fellowship.

Elias, notwithstanding his great popularity and usefulness, was a very humble man. His observations on this subject, in his autobiography, are very striking and useful; they are the following:

Though large crowds used to hear me, and many appeared to receive something by hearing, the Lord kept me from conceit, although my heart was so depraved, and Satan so crafty! I frequently trembled, lest I should be tempted to pride by reason of popularity; but the Lord kept me through grace. The thought of the deficiencies and imperfections of my best sermons made me grieve when I thought of the sermons the people were praising. I was glad, many an evening, after preaching, to have the opportunity of praying that my sermons might be washed in the blood of the Lamb. Thinking of the thousands that had heard me without any profit, caused my mind to sink and lament that I was traversing the country in so useless a manner. On my return home from my journeys I had nothing to boast of, nor anything to be proud of, but cause to grieve on account of my great defects in the best things, and to praise God for supporting and strengthening one so feeble!

Few ministers being highly gifted, like Elias, have been kept so humble and low. Alas! many, with not half his popularity, have been swept off the field of usefulness by the dreadful influence of spiritual pride. To show the need of watchfulness in this respect, Elias would at times make use of the following anecdote. He said he was once in company with John Newton, of St Mary Woolnoth, London, who in speaking to several ministers present, made this observation: 'Satan hates you more than any other Christians, for you are the spiritual officers in the army of the living God; and he is more bent upon destroying you, than any other part of the army; as in the time of the French war, it was usual for the enemy to prepare some men purposely for destroying the captains and other officers; the clothes of these men were of the same colour as the grass, that they might not be discovered in places of ambush, laying in wait to shoot at the officers. Thus exactly, my brethren,' said the old gentleman, 'Satan aims at the destruction of myself, and the ministers of the gospel. The enemy has very remarkable riflemen; and they are so disguised that they are not perceptible, for he employs the very persons of my best friends. Sometimes these come to me, saying, "O dear sir, what a pity it is you are getting old; we are afraid we shall lose you very soon! Oh, what shall we do without you, sir?" I see Satan here shooting at me,' said Mr Newton, 'through my *friends*. Brethren, I know him well, I am not ignorant of his devices; I avoid being shot at, and continue in the dust, seeing that I am still nothing but an unprofitable servant.' 'Thus,' said Elias, 'it is with me; and this idea has always been useful to me, making me cautious of the enemy in the dark.'[1]

Much of Elias's mind as to the ministry may be seen in his compositions on the subject. There is a letter of his extant, written to a person desirous of entering the sacred office, in Mr Griffiths's neighbourhood. The young man seemed to be under the exercise of improper motives. Elias was then but young himself; but the letter is worthy the pen of a Dr Owen, though it was written in a hurry. It is the following:

Llanfechell 22 January 1805

With regard to the exercise of mind which you mentioned yourself as being under, I desire help from God to address a word to you upon it in much seriousness. It is needful for you, at all events, to have much discretion and sobriety from God. The exercise you speak of proceeds from either of these three different sources:

1. From the devil. We read that there are 'ministers of satan.' It is no great thing if his ministers be transformed as the ministers of righteousness. There is also mention of 'the doctrines of devils'. They are easiest known by their end and fruit. Their end is not to profit the souls of sinners, or to glorify God, or set forth the glory and comeliness of the Mediator. But the devil purposes to make use of them, either to oppose the *true* doctrine, or hinder evangelical discipline, or to make professors licentious in their lives, that the doctrines of the gospel may be evil spoken of on their account. A preacher not sent of God, is one of the devil's most faithful servants.

2. The flesh, or carnal motive, induces many in these days to enter on the ministry. The flesh again is not desirous of the salvation of man, or the glory of God, or the advancement of the kingdom of Christ in

---

[1] Elias, in showing whence our strength comes, would at times relate this anecdote; 'Once, some King sent his messenger to a great warrior in his day to see his sword, as it had done some great exploits; which was granted him. "There is the sword," said he, "but tell your King," he added, "that the sword *itself* will be of no use to him, except he has also the arm that wielded it." '

the world; but rather of selfish, carnal ends, such as honour and reputation. There is more danger of entering the ministry from these inducements, at present, than ever; because there is greater quietness in preaching the gospel, and greater respect to its ministers, than have been for ages. It was difficult for any carnal ends to succeed in bringing a man to the work of the ministry at such times, when there were so many crosses and troubles to be unavoidably encountered in it. But, at present, the flesh may lift a man into the pulpit, as a player on the stage, to show himself off, and to seek for praise.

3. From God. Notwithstanding all that has been said, God has not yet given up this work of calling ministers, neither will he give it up altogether, while the world stands. Now there is a difference between the impulses and excitements of God, and those of the devil and the flesh. They are different in their effects on the mind, the end in view, and the fruits which follow. It is not because they think themselves to be better qualified, that they enter on the ministry, but from a view of the work being done, from love to the souls of men, zeal for the glory of God, and an ardent desire to publish abroad the name of the Surety. A knowledge of the fear of the Lord moves such ministers to persuade men; that is, a knowledge of the dreadfulness of our appearing before the judgment seat of Christ in an unconverted state; and from seeing this themselves, they persuade others to flee from the wrath to come. The love of Christ also constrains them to speak of him to others; that is, their experience of his wonderful love to themselves constrains them.

Besides this, 'the word of reconciliation has been given unto them,' in their own experience; and this is as fire in their bones, burning within them for want of speaking to others. But, in opposition to all these excitements, they see their own unworthiness and unfitness; so that they are ready to faint, when thinking of this incomparable work; and they cry out, with Jeremiah, 'I am but a child'; and with Isaiah, 'I am a man of unclean lips.' The greater their solicitude of mind about proceeding to the work, the more do they see their own unworthiness. Their aim is not the attainment of such and such a place in the church; but to do something for God, in any place he may see good to choose. In general, the Holy Spirit points them out to the church, so that it may call them to the ministry, as that passage exemplifies, 'Separate me Barnabas and Saul for the work whereunto I have called them.' Consequently, the message of such as these will produce fruit. Though they go to their work fainting through discouragement, yet the Lord prospers them, 'that the excellency of the power may be of God, and not of us.'

Oh! Brother, the work is great indeed! Yet not too great for the Lord to raise up some (though mean) persons to enter upon it, and to prosper them in it. O! do not think, without trembling, of such a work; and yet do not suppress such thoughts, lest they should be from God. Betake yourself very often to the throne of grace. Ask the Lord to annihilate these thoughts in you, if they are from Satan, or from the flesh; and to cherish and strengthen them if they are from above. Our God is one who is ready to hear prayer; – he is 'very pitiful.' O! seek for godliness, in the power of it, for yourself, whatever may be the case. Otherwise, if at any time you go to speak to sinners of their lost condition, you will be preaching your own condemnation! And in speaking of the glory of the Son of God, you will condemn yourself, for want of receiving and embracing him! Oh! godliness, godliness!!

Further, it is needful that the understanding be opened largely respecting the way of reconciliation, lest we should 'darken counsel by words without knowledge'. It is an awful thing to misrepresent God and his mind in his holy Word. In endeavouring to preach we speak of God as it were to his face! It is a great thing to speak rightly of the state of a sinner, and of a free salvation through Christ, in the view of our own sinfulness. 'Who is sufficient for these things?' None but those whose 'sufficiency is of God'. Again, it is necessary to have an enlarged experience, that we may be able to say with David and Paul, 'I believe and therefore have I spoken. We also believe, and therefore speak.'

There is great need, if you think of putting your hand to any part of God's work, to be kept in the dust. The Holy Ghost speaks of the danger of being 'puffed up', – the consequence is, 'falling into the condemnation of the devil!' There is much need of self-denial in entering on the work: 'Let him deny himself.' It is needful for every Christian to have self-denial, but especially for the preachers of the Word; for it is possible they may be praised by some, and they will, on that account, be 'puffed up', except they be very self-denying. They are sure of meeting much contempt, and 'many tribulations', on account of which they will be discouraged and disheartened, unless they possess a good measure of self-denial.

I can do no more, my dear brother, than commend you to the care of the Lord, and pray that his hand may be upon you to the end. Come what will, may we be in his hand! Something will be made of us there. Be very deliberate, dear brother, about the matter which is upon your mind. I hope that nothing I have said may be any discouragement to you in the slightest degree. My aim assuredly was not to dishearten, but to direct and edify you. Grace and mercy be with you. Amen. Exercise your talents a little in the Society, in a wise, humble and cautious manner.

Your brother, and servant for Christ.

J.E.

This letter manifests an uncommon acquaintance with the ministerial character. Elias knew the experience of a man called by God into the ministry, and he had carefully examined every evidence of that call: he had himself trod all the steps in the right way to the ministry, and had a perfect recollection of them. He was not one of those who had come to the work without much prayer.

Elias, certainly, was the most remarkable preacher of his age in Wales, and when the Welsh Calvinistic Methodists decided to ordain their own ministers in 1811, he and eight other preachers were set apart and ordained to administer the sacraments. This ordination caused much heart-searching, and even controversy, among the Calvinistic Methodists. When the proposal was discussed at the Pwllheli Association in September 1809, Elias made 'a terrible speech', which (it is claimed) was one of the causes which led to Thomas Charles's consenting to lead the movement for ordination. It was decided, at the Bala Association in June 1810, to ordain suitable brethren, and this agreement was confirmed by the Association in South Wales in November. Elias's views on the whole question may be gleaned from a letter he wrote to a friend in Liverpool who had requested his advice:

Llanfechell 26 November 1810

Dear Brother,

I have received a letter from Mr Ebenezer Morris, after the Swansea Association, giving me a comfortable account that they had agreed with what had been passed at Bala with regard to extending the privileges of the churches. This was done at Swansea in a quiet manner; the whole Association agreed, without one single hand being raised in dissent. It was a strange turn of providence that this was brought to pass so peacefully; it was more than what was expected.

The Rev Rowland Hill had heard that the matter would be discussed at the Swansea Association, and his mind was so stirred that he came from Bristol to the Association at Swansea; it seems likely that the Lord had sent him, and he succeeded to a great extent. Some of the clergymen (so-called) tried to move some objections against the Connexion having an extension to the privileges which it seeks. Mr Hill replied to all their objections, and shewed the necessity of granting the Connexion that which it seeks. He said that he had been brought up with a bias in favour of the Church of England; and that he loved the ministers who preached the gospel within its pale; but that, inasmuch as the generality of its ministers deny the doctrine to which they have once pledged themselves, godly people have been obliged to leave it, and that the children of God cannot live on chaff. He also said that the renowned Mr Whitefield had lost much, because he did not do in his day what is now desired by our Connexion; had he done so, that very likely the whole Connexion would be one great Body throughout the whole kingdom; instead of that, it had split up into many branches; and he added that our own Connexion would certainly go the same way unless they were granted what they desire. So it was decided to allow the Bala Association to proceed with the matter, and they then would follow suit.

Write to Bala and ask Mr Charles or Mr [Simon] Lloyd to come and administer the ordinances to you; if they do not come, I do not think it would be a great sin if you were to ask Mr Jones of Denbigh, to come to you.

9 Of Elias's zeal in the cause of religion

Much has been said in the last chapters of Elias's intellectual powers, and other excellencies in the ministry, to represent him fully in that respect. The portrait, even now, will not be complete without a more particular description of his zeal. When he was young, his zeal carried him to some lengths of extravagance as to over-exertion; and no wonder, as it was approved in the Connexion. When Thomas Charles, about that time, opposed the wild zeal of some of the preachers, Elias, being convinced of his error, confessed it at once, before all, in a meeting of ministers at an Association.

The qualifications, which he possessed in so eminent a degree, were delightfully combined in him, and exercised a mutual influence on one another. Elias, like other great preachers, was clearest when most vehement; the understanding seemed to gain additional light even in the heat of excitement. The judgment, fancy, memory, and all seemed to receive the force of the amazing impetus of burning zeal and compassionate feelings. And when the glorious and divine subjects of the gospel were exhibited by such powers of judgment, extraordinary animation, and sanctified by the Spirit, they were most captivating and edifying. We know the mutual influence those great powers of the soul have on one another, even when engaged in studies and compositions. The hurry of composition, under the warmth of zeal and passion, strikes out new thoughts and images. It was the due exercise of holy and animating feelings, in connection with his other powers, that made Elias, in the hand of God, such an amazing preacher.

Having, in the last chapter, alluded strongly to Elias's zeal *in preaching*, we shall not have occasion to enlarge much on it here, but in connection with the cause of religion. First, then, we shall dwell a little upon this most important qualification in him as a *preacher*. He had a great share of zeal; and even Elias, without this excellence, would not have become great as he was. This zeal, however, was not blind and ignorant; it was properly directed, as well as warm. That burning zeal and vehement animation of Elias, however excellent, without his powerful and well-directed judgment, might have terminated in much wildness and enthusiasm. He would have been like a fine vessel without a rudder and ballast, sailing beautifully in fair weather, but in imminent danger in tempestuous seasons.

The following anecdote will, with what has been said before, confirm our observations on Elias's animated manner of speaking. A person asked one of the first-rate poets in Wales his opinion of the most popular preachers in the Principality. When Elias was spoken of as the most gifted, he made this pointed and valuable observation: 'It is easy to understand from Elias's manner in preaching that he is most anxious for the salvation of sinners. He does not in the least spare himself: the feeling on his mind in their behalf is apparent every time he enters the pulpit. The language of his soul to his body on that all-important subject, one would think, would run somewhat in this manner: "You must become a sacrifice now for one hour, and you must endure all my fire, animation and exertion, however powerful." ' If common Christians on account of their zeal, are compared to a company of horses in Pharaoh's chariots, what should preachers of the gospel be likened to but a flame of fire?

Two other circumstances setting forth Elias's zeal as a preacher shall be introduced. Thomas Jones of Denbigh, having to preach the annual sermon before the London Missionary Society, requested the Rev Matthew Wilks, one of the Directors, to give his opinion whether he had better deliver a written discourse, or preach as usual, extempore. 'Perhaps,' replied Wilks 'you had better, on such an occasion as this, write your sermon. At all events, let us have plenty of your Welsh fire in it.' But, observed John Elias, who was present, 'he cannot carry fire *in* paper.' 'Never mind,' rejoined Wilks, 'paper will do very well to light the fire with.' A minister whose style of speaking was *rough* and *blunt*, had the following advice from Elias, on his appointment to preach to the Welsh in English towns: 'Be sure,' said he, 'to singe the hair off your old sermons;' also 'to pare their nails and to break their teeth,' added a friend. 'Oh, no,' replied Elias, 'the nails and teeth will be useful to lay hold of the consciences of the sinners in the towns, as well as those on the mountains in Wales.'

Zeal is not only useful in the delivery of divine truths from the pulpit, but also in enabling the soldier of Christ to go through all hardships in his cause. It carries a man, under God's blessing, through all difficulties, like wings; and he is enabled thereby not only to proceed, but to perform uncommon labour. Such difficulties and labours Elias had to go through. He was always most diligently and actively engaged in the Lord's work, and his soul was most fervent and warm in constant engagements for his divine master. It might be said that he was 'a burning and a shining light'. Unceasing were his travels in the service of his God, from his youth, in every part of Wales! Scarcely does he enjoy repose in the bosom of his family, ere he again proceeds with his laborious work, and that in all sorts of weather! Besides, he was a man that might have had a place of worship for himself, with a most handsome salary, as some of his brethren in the ministry had, preferring a stationary life. But he could not sit down in one place, however excellent and desirable. There was a 'necessity laid upon him' to preach everywhere. It would have been doing violence to his feelings to cease from such a labour. It might be said of him, in a subordinate sense, as of his master, 'The zeal of thine house hath eaten me up.'

It was not a small portion of zeal that would enable a minister to face, undaunted, the bold, stiff-necked, brazen-faced sinners of those days: their very aspect was threatening, savage, audacious and brutal. Unless a minister had been endowed with strength and zeal from above, it would have been impossible for him to stand and address them on subjects so disagreeable and abhorrent to their natural disposition. But such an anxious desire as was implanted in Elias to preach salvation, out of pity to poor perishing sinners, under the blessing and support of heaven, carried him

firmly through all insults and opposition. Not only was the ruined
state of immortal souls the object of his compassion, but also the
cause and church of God. And as he exerted himself for these great
and all-important objects, so he was most anxious that his fellow-
labourers should be awake, active, and successful. His soul was
filled with the most painful feelings, if he saw, any where, the
work and vineyard of the Lord in a low and withering state. Not
only was he under great concern for the salvation of the backslider
and the ungodly, but he was very anxious that all his brethren in
the ministry should feel like him, and that they should yearn with
himself over the sad state of souls around him. He took a deep
interest in the work of the Lord, and had great zeal for its success.

Elias also, like the inspired Psalmist, mourned for Zion. Indeed
he could scarcely under any circumstance have been more alive to
its prosperity. There are several letters of his on this most important subject, manifesting his zeal, arousing the church, and warning
it of its lukewarm and dying state. One of these, showing his feelings for the decayed state of the church, and his longings for the
out-pouring of the Spirit, runs thus:

Fron 3 July 1837

I am happy to hear from my daughter, who is here now, that things are
comfortable among you. But Oh! we stand in need, both in Wales and
London, of those fresh, powerful manifestations from heaven. We are,
alas! accustomed to go on with the service of God in human strength;
praying, hearing, and preaching in that way! We are so lukewarm,
without the light and the power of the Spirit! We neither feel nor see
others experiencing his powerful operations! It is very seldom you
hear a sermon that is fully and evidently different from a speech that is
of man's own production! You scarcely ever perceive stronger effects
produced on the hearers of a sermon than on persons that listen to any
other speaking. It is not often that unbelievers may, when they come to
our congregations, cry out, 'God is of a truth among you'. It is but
seldom that we have clear proofs of men being converted and saved.
And, alas! there is but little lamentation on that account. Moreover, the
children of God are great strangers to much comfort, and strong
assurance. What shall we do? At Bala we appointed the 8th of August a
day of humiliation and prayer on that account. O! that it may please
the Lord to bestow upon us the Spirit of grace and of supplications!

'Ministers', says Elias in another letter, 'seem often satisfied with having freedom to speak, and seeing many hearing them with attention and delight; but alas, without experiencing the effects of the power promised to attend the ministry of the gospel, the power necessary to produce a saving change in the sinner! The people too are content with an eloquent discourse, sweet voice, and melodious accents, or the gifts of the preacher; without experiencing, or seeking to experience, greater things than such as are human through the ministry.'

It is thought that the influences of the Spirit are not so powerful, and that piety is not so deep in the church now as in former days, though its members are more numerous. It is feared that professors are more light and worldly. Elias, even in his last illness, when writing the outlines of his own life, espied in the Connexion he so much loved, some evils of this nature, and felt most anxious that they should be removed. Comparing the spiritual state of the Connexion at present, with what it was in former times, he thus expresses the sympathizing emotions of his mind:

The cause does not appear to be so flourishing as it used to be, in spiritual matters, which is the very life of religion. The light, power and authority formerly experienced under the ministry of the Word, are not known these days. The ministry neither alarms, terrifies, nor disturbs the thousands of ungodly persons who sit under it. A great many of those who attend the religious societies are personally unacquainted with their state before God; nor do the churches know what they are. And what is worse, they are willing to be without knowledge. It is difficult to judge by the fruits of hundreds of professors that they are godly! There are signs of worldly-mindedness in many of the aged. In others there is a lack of principle in doing righteousness. The young people conform to this world, following its ways and foolish fashions. Others delight in wrangling disputes, and foolish and unprofitable questions. Servant-men are high-minded and disobedient, with few 'doing service as to the Lord'. There is a multitude of mixed people in the army, lusting after the things of Egypt – hankering after the expressions and the baser things of other denominations and religious parties. They delight in swimming in the stream of the spirit of the age in things political and religious. They are unlike our fathers of old. Rowland, Harris, and other renowned fathers, and the late Rev

T. Charles, would not know or acknowledge them as belonging to their family, nor to the congregations gathered by the Lord through their indefatigable labours in Wales, and in some of the towns in England. No experimental, thoughtful Christian can deny that God has withdrawn himself from us, as to the particular operations of his Spirit and the especial manifestation of his grace. Is not this a proof of it, that thousands of the ungodly hear the Word unconcerned and without trembling? Another proof is that so few that profess godliness have any assurance of hope, and have no experience of the joy of salvation. There is but little thirst for the gracious and powerful visitations of God; and also, the prayers for these blessings are weak and cold! There are many who, in their attitudes, cannot have communion with God whilst they continue in them. If people want God's presence as the early fathers of the Connexion were blessed with it, let them take care that they be of the same principle, under the guidance of the same Spirit, and walking in the same pathways, 'seeking not their own things, but the things of Jesus Christ'. *Philippians* 2.21. My day in this world is near ending; I am almost at my journey's end. I have been for months confined to my room, under 'light affliction'.

30 April 1841

It is not yet clear what is my heavenly Father's purpose respecting me; whether he means to remove me out of the world by this affliction, or spare me a little longer; but let him do what seemeth him good. One of the most grievous things to me, when I think of leaving this world, is seeing the decay in the cause of religion in our midst. Good things I once saw in the Connexion are now lost! Renowned preachers and elders have died, but there are none so excellent rising up to take their places; though it is said by some that there is an increase in order, and in many good things; that preachers are more gifted, and that the people have more knowledge. If that is so, greater things have been lost. If some preachers are better orators, yet they are not equal to their predecessors in speaking to the conscience; their addresses do not terrify and alarm the ungodly, neither do they give comfort and sustenance to experienced Christians. As to knowledge, their spiritual and experimental knowledge in things relating to their peace is but little. Few among the thousands of hearers who know the only true God, and he whom he sent, Jesus Christ, have peace with God, or assurance that Christ is in them, that they have been born of God, and have passed from death unto life. It is rare among professors to find those who know that their state is good. They are satisfied to be without this knowledge. They walk in darkness, without knowing whither they go; and the ministry leaves them in that condition. O how sad! God, no doubt, is hiding himself! There is strength, light, and warmth wherever his gracious presence is found. O! that he would return to us, for his name's sake! O! that he would turn to revive us! We have deserved this on account of our great iniquities, but he can visit us in his grace. O! that I might see one gracious and powerful divine visitation, in Anglesey, before I sleep in death. O! to see God raising up spiritual, evangelical, holy men to be pastors of his people in this country! The working day of many who are now on the field is nearly finished. I desire to see elders – spiritual, experiential and faithful men – in all the societies; and that the churches may be filled with godly, regenerate men, 'living stones in his spiritual house'. And every one in his place, adorning the doctrine of God in all things; and the glory of the Lord returning to its place, until thousands fall on their faces by the power of its brightness! Then Zion will sing as in the days of her youth. May the godly among us be awakened to cry out until this come to pass!

Elias was acquainted with wonderful outpourings of the Spirit after a long dark spiritual night. He had to preach at an Association at Pwllheli, in 1832, when the state of religion was low and discouraging. A great spiritual darkness and lethargy had prevailed in the Connexion for upwards of ten years. Elias was greatly moved when he rose to preach, and took these words for his text: 'Let God arise, let his enemies be scattered' (*Psalm* 68.1). The truths delivered by him then had, under God's blessing, the most happy and astonishing effects; many of the people fell down to the ground in great terror, crying for mercy. It is said that no less than 2,500 persons were added to the church in Caernarvonshire that year, in consequence of the powerful impetus which was given, under the blessing of heaven, by that extraordinary sermon.

Most *feelingly* did Elias expostulate in letters, previous to this time, with sleepy, starving professors. One of those is the following; may it be blessed still!

Fron 28 June 1831

Is there not reason to fear that the prayers of many of us are merely customary and formal, asking many things without feeling the need of them? We seldom inquire whether our prayers are answered; and if not, what hinders them? Do we avoid indulging in those thoughts or practices that hinder and mar our prayers? Are we in a state of reconciliation with God? Do we live in the exercise of faith in Christ? Are we indifferent as to the aid of the Spirit in prayer? O seek his face – his face; seek him with *all* your heart! There are many in the church, I believe, who have seen better days, and have felt something greater and stronger; but they sleep so heavily now, that they scarcely recollect the days they once saw, and the divine impressions they once experienced! Alas, what a state! Love is growing cold, because, perhaps, some iniquity has abounded. O that I could lift up my voice, and cry to those that sleep – 'Alas, it is a great pity that you live so poor, and that your sustenance is so wretched! *You*, children of the King! *You*, the spouse of Christ! You, that saw better days, how is it that your support is so poor, and your appearance so miserable now, while the riches of your Father are so great, his house so full, and his table so loaded, and the love of God not changed, and the great salvation as full as ever? Oh! why will you live in poor prisons, and on empty husks? Homeward, homeward, prodigal sons! Our day in the world is nearly coming to a close! Believers, you draw near the heavenly world. Should you not then be more holy and heavenly, as you approach that world? Oh! children of God, be not satisfied to live in such a lethargy, and at such a distance from your God.

'Hypocrites are not aware of the spiritual food that some have tasted. They draw their joys out of other wells, lusting after forbidden things, desiring the enjoyments of the world, delighting in the company of worldlings, and following their customs! There are many in the church that never had a kid – that never had a small portion of spiritual food to make merry – that know nothing of the spiritual feasts that are enjoyed on the return of prodigals! These have but a poor religion to meet death and judgment with! O my dear friends, let each of us examine, and see what he has. Let us not sleep, and let us not be indifferent about knowing whether our religion is sound; and if not, let us strive to obtain that which is so. The most worthless of all things is false religion. Oh! the truth, the truth! O! brethren, let us not be discouraged; but, like the watchmen, look for the morning. Say, in faith, 'I shall see it yet again.' I know that some souls are like the thirsty land, longing for God, and crying out, 'When shall I come to thee?' Believers, if we must live in some degree of darkness till we arrive at Jordan, it is a consolation that it is day light, without any clouds, on the other side. You shall be there soon. I long in these days to fly higher than the tumultuous atmosphere of this world. If we fly high enough, we shall not meet with clouds, thunders, and the stormy wind and tempest, but with a bright, delightful day! I am obliged to finish – I am very poorly. Oh, brethren, pray for me!'

We shall now notice another object of Elias's concern – *the Word of God in its purity*. There being a mixed company in the church, and many of them unsound professors, the difficulty of introducing erroneous views, and contaminating the body, would not be so great. He was truly jealous for the truth, and much afraid lest the doctrines of grace which had been held so strenuously in the church, and preached with so much pleasure and success by himself, should be obscured and marred. He had been very careful in preventing the Connexion from being injured with false views. 'The Lord,' he used to say, 'hath favoured us, poor Methodists, with the glorious truths of the gospel in their perfection. Alas! errors surround us, and Satan, changing himself into an angel of light, sets these pernicious evils before us, as great truths! I have been endeavouring to put thorns, as it were, in the gap, to keep them out, and prevent my friends from going astray. I hope the Lord will, in mercy, raise up some one to do this act of kindness after I am gone. I mean, to keep the Connexion from false views and doctrines; and may he, in tender compassion, make the preachers most efficient, so as to preach the Word, not as the scribes and Pharisees, but with power.' The following quotation from his Diary gives his thoughts on the subject of maintaining sound doctrines:

The Connexion was not called Calvinistic Methodists at first, but simply Methodists, as there were not yet any Arminian Methodists in the country. When the Wesleyans came it was necessary to add the word *Calvinistic*, to show the difference. Before this, there was union and concord in the great things of the gospel among the various denominations in Wales. The Independents agreed fully with the Methodists in doctrine; they acknowledged the Westminster Catechism as containing the whole of their doctrine. There was union, love, concord, and 'speaking the same thing' among the brethren. There was no dispute respecting any branch of doctrine; there was no doubt as to any preacher deviating in doctrine. Some time before this, a few in South Wales inclined to Antinomianism, and some to Sabellianism. After this, the most delightful concord in doctrine prevailed among all the ministers and preachers; there was no dispute, nor preaching of controversial matters, nor any abstruse and curious points. They saw, judged, and said the same things. All, from the least to the greatest, preached plainly and very clearly; and the most learned of them excelled in this. The fall of man, and his total corruption, the great misery of his state under the curse of God's righteous indignation, his complete inability to save himself; free salvation, by the sovereign grace and love of God; Christ the righteous Saviour, willing to save the chief of sinners; inviting the lost to believe; and exhorting believers to excel in good works. That was the sum and substance of their preaching; 'the hand of the Lord was with them', so that a great multitude believed. They often preached in the 'manifestation of the Spirit, and with power'. They prayed earnestly for the Spirit to teach and strengthen them; they were waiting for him, knowing that they could do nothing of themselves. That was the method of preaching that subdued Wales.

The arrival of a number of itinerant Wesleyan preachers in Wales in the opening decade of the nineteenth century, sent by the English Methodist conference, resulted in renewed controversy over Arminianism, especially concerning the extent of the atonement. All the leading Welsh preachers and theologians of the time held that the atonement was limited in its purpose, i.e. to obtain the salvation of the church. Numbers of sermons and books on this subject appeared and Elias was especially outspoken in his opposition to a general redemption. In one sermon his zeal for the efficacy of the blood of Christ caused him to state that the propitiation of Christ was enough and no more than to make the scales of justice even, that it was a full 'equivalent' for the sins of all the elect. In an ensuing vigorous debate with Thomas Jones of Denbigh he was led to see the infinite intrinsic sufficiency of Christ's satisfaction and merits, but, he said, 'it is as clear to me that for the church alone it was made'.

After Thomas Jones's death in 1820, Elias, in order to guard against false views, and to prevent heresies, took a leading part in the formation of a Confession of Faith for the Connexion. At a meeting held at Aberystwyth in 1823, Elias read the Articles prepared by the brethren from North Wales, and Ebenezer Richard read the Articles prepared in South Wales. The two sets were compared, revised, and supplemented until complete unity was obtained in every Article of Faith. These were fully and finally agreed upon at two Associations of ministers and elders of the Connexion in the year 1823, and they were printed, both in Welsh and in English. The above Confession of Faith is truly excellent, much like that of the Church of England, in the main or cardinal points. How thankful should we be to God that we have such a bulwark against all heresies that surround us in these days[1]! After the adoption of this Confession, a parliamentary Act was necessary which would, in the words of Elias, 'bind the Methodists in one Connexion in the sight of the law of the land', and 'to secure all the chapels and their government to the Connexion alone'. Elias defended the doctrines set forth in the Confession of Faith with great firmness and zeal. Yet he drew a grand distinction between them, however good, and the Word of God, saying that 'they were the confession of his faith, but that the Word of God was the foundation of it; and that all saving sound faith was built upon it.' He took great care to exhibit the difference between the foundation and the superstructure.

We may safely say that Elias's ministry was full and complete, corresponding with all his propositions and observations. He preached the whole counsel of God, without 'holding any part of the truth in unrighteousness'. So one at least of the ministers of Christ has gone to judgment, pure from the blood of all the hearers of the Word in the Isle of Anglesey. He preached the duty and responsibility of man, and the sovereign grace and mercy of God, in the most energetic and lucid manner. His zeal was not only manifested in preaching and watching over the cause of

[1] It is well known that the orthodox Presbyterians in Ireland are now in danger of losing much of their church property: some say in consequence of not having a Confession of Faith in time to go by. It seems they had no test of faith but the Bible some years ago. It was at length discovered that there were Arians and Socinians in the body. Dr Cook, and other Trinitarian ministers, succeeded in having the Westminster Confession of Faith adopted; the consequence was the ejectment of the unsound part; but they retained the places of worship. Five-hundred erected by Trinitarians in England and Ireland are now occupied by Socinians.

religion, but also over every thing in the house of the Lord, taking care that there was no decay or impropriety. Though he became more indifferent to the things of this world as he was approaching eternity, yet he did not forget to watch over the cause of God, and the concerns of religion, even to the last. Great attention had been paid of late years to singing and Sunday schools. Young people, and worldly persons, had taken an active part in the *singing*; and Elias was afraid that they paid more attention to the sound than to the meaning. He therefore strongly pointed out to them the evil of such a proceeding, and urged them to regain the old pious spirit of singing.

He was the means of doing great things in Anglesey. He stirred up the inhabitants, though before rather worldly, to some very liberal acts. Among other things, he prevailed on them, by his zeal and stirring eloquence, to pay off some hundreds, if not thousands of pounds, which lay as heavy debts on the chapels in the island. He would say that it was difficult to preach Christ, who had fully paid the debt of sinners, in chapels encumbered with debt'. And he it was that first (on the occasion of nearly losing some chapels), in his zeal suggested having a deed to ensure to the Connexion the property of all places of worship belonging to it. He also zealously exerted himself for many years in behalf of establishing a college in the Connexion. This terminated at length very success-fully, so that two seminaries have been established, one at Bala and the other at Trefecca.

The Welsh Associations were much abused about the time he commenced his ministry, especially in North Wales. However, through his means, standing forth in almost all the Associations in the North, in front of the platform and exhorting the people to *decency* and *sobriety*, great changes have been effected in those meetings. In the Holyhead Association in 1824, Elias appealed for sobriety and decent behaviour during the meetings. He spoke with power against drunkenness, as a sin that degrades men more than any other evil. 'Are there any drunkards here?' he cried. 'I am afraid there are. I beg of you, will you – at least *today* – control yourselves. If you have no respect for the Almighty, no respect for the laws of your land, no respect for yourselves, will you please

– for our sakes today – behave soberly and decently. You are, by attending our meetings and by your drinking and disorderly conduct, undermining our character. Our enemies are not all dead. They are ready to use everything they can lay hold of as an occasion to destroy us. We have nothing but our character on which to fall back. We are not rich; we are not learned; we are not gifted; we have no high titles; we have no one of any high authority in our midst. But we have our character; we have a very high opinion of our character; we are unwilling to allow anybody to destroy our character. But the drunkards who are attending our Associations are undermining our character. What can we do with them, my brethren?' Someone made a remark, referring to a sermon that had been preached that day. Elias shook himself. 'I feel within myself this minute,' he cried, 'to offer them for sale, by auction, to whomsoever will take them, that they might not disturb us any more.' Then, at the top of his voice, with his arm outstretched, as if he held them in the palm of his hand, he shouted, 'Who will take them? Who will take them? Churchmen, will you take them?' 'We? We, in our baptism have professed to renounce the devil and all his works. No; *we* cannot take them.' Then, after a moment's silence, 'Independents, will *you* take them?' 'What? We? We, ages ago, left the Church of England because of her corruption. No; *we* will not take them.' Another interval of silence. 'Baptists, will *you* take them?' 'We? certainly not! We dip all our people in water as a sign that we take those who have been cleansed. No; we will not have them.' Silence again. 'Wesleyans, will *you* take them?' 'What? we? Good works is a matter of life with us. We do not want them.' Then he stretched forth his arm once again, as if holding the poor drunkards in his hand; and once again, at the top of his voice he shouted, 'Who will take them? Who will take them? Who will take them?' Then, suddenly, his whole nature became agitated. His eyes flashed as he turned his head aside, and in a low tone which could be heard by all, he said, 'Methinks I can hear the devil at my elbow saying, "Knock them down to me! I will take them."' Then, after thirty seconds of dead silence, he cried, 'I was going to say, Satan, that you could have them, but' – looking upwards, he said in a loud, clear, yet gentle voice, 'I can hear Jesus saying, "I will take them! I will take them! Unclean, to be washed; drunkards, to be sobered; in all their filth and degradation, I will take them, and cleanse them in mine own blood." ' The effects of all this can be better imagined than described. The ministers, preachers and elders were stunned; and the huge congregation was stirred with a spirit of tumultuous joy and exultation.

Horse races were to be held on the same day as the Methodist Association at Manchester in 1830. Elias's spirit was much moved within him at the thoughts of them, and he prayed to the Lord most earnestly in the morning of that day to put a stop to them. There was something so remarkable in his prayer that someone observed, 'Ahab must prepare his chariot and get away'. The sky became so dark soon afterwards that they were obliged to light the gas in most of the shops in the town. It began to rain very heavily about eleven o'clock, and continued so until five o'clock the next day. The multitudes on the race ground were dispersed in less than half an hour; and did not reassemble that year. It seems that the shower was confined to that vicinity.

Shipwrecks occurred sometimes on the sea-shore of Anglesey, and many of the inhabitants were guilty of plundering the cargoes. Elias's holy indignation rose against such disgraceful practices. His awful appeals to those people in his sermons proved so alarming that many of them conveyed some hundreds of cartloads of the plunder to the shore where they got them. On one occasion he was asked by the Monthly Meeting to visit the church at Holyhead, the most flourishing in Anglesey, to deal with accusations of plundering wreckage. When he arrived he soon found out that the guilty ones were so numerous that the only right course of action was the dissolving of the whole church. This he did in a solemn manner; at his command every member went out and Elias was left alone under the pulpit. On a suitable occasion, soon afterwards, he paid the church another visit; he readmitted the members into communion on their acknowledgement that they had sinned, and that they were now contrite and repentant.

Who ever spoke in a more spirited manner against all low, corrupt and disgraceful practices among the young people of Wales than Elias? Who ever spoke so much as Elias against those licentious meetings called 'invitation-weddings'? – those convivial parties which were productive of great evil and scandal? Their purpose was to help young couples, on marrying, to set up their homes. But they often degenerated and became occasions of drunkenness, fighting, and immorality. However, these and the like corrupt meetings came to be considered in Anglesey as contemptible. No species of corruption maintained its ground against the spirit and energy of this Elijah. Who spoke so effectually against horse-racing in Anglesey, and such follies, as he did? How much drunkenness and vileness were connected with all these practices, greatly demoralizing the people! A painful view of these abominations first induced him to give consideration to the Total Abstinence Society, and afterwards to join it.

He also exerted himself, as a good soldier of Christ, in behalf of all that is excellent. He eminently promoted experimental and practical religion by his sermons, writings, contributions and example. He did not spare his bodily frame, weakened by affliction, but exerted it more than his friends deemed prudent: he thought his time was short. The Lord had given him a spirit to labour as well as zeal in order to success. No law is more immutable and universal than the necessity of labour. Important results are nowhere to be produced by a few strokes, however mighty. No man steadily pursues that on which he has not fully set his heart; and there is nothing, under God's blessing, that gives a minister so much power and influence as laborious habits.

10 Elias's exertions for the Bible
and the London Missionary Societies –
Sunday schools – and the temperance cause

It may be seen by the previous chapters how highly Elias valued
the Holy Scriptures. His grand business even from his youth was
to read, search, examine and digest them. He seemed to have lived
for the cause of the Bible. He valued it indeed as the *Book of
God*. No wonder then that he was so zealously engaged in aiding
the Bible Society!

It is well known that the Bible Society[1] owes its origin to the
wants and cries of the Welsh people for the Word of God. Thomas
Charles of Bala, and Thomas Jones of Creaton, were led to procure Bibles for them from the Society for Promoting Christian
Knowledge. They could not, however, obtain a good supply
until Charles thought of a plan for that purpose. The subject
of obtaining Bibles for the Welsh was always much on Charles's
mind; and on a certain morning while awake in bed (in London in
1802), the idea of having a society established similar to the Tract
Society occurred to his mind; and he was so pleased with it that
he instantly arose, dressed himself, and went out to consult with
some friends on the subject. This finally led to the formation of
the Bible Society. 'I also recollect,' says Elias in a letter to me,
'that Charles related to me the *same* things respecting the origin of
the Bible Society.'

Elias was exceedingly delighted with this institution from its
commencement, and exerted himself to the uttermost in assisting
Charles in establishing Auxiliaries and Branches of the Bible
Society in Wales. After the death of that excellent man, Elias
took the lead in North Wales in the affairs of the Bible Society.
All his zeal and eloquence were exercised in the cause of this noble

[1] British and Foreign Bible Society (founded in 1804).

institution. He preached, he spoke at meetings in the most hearty and effective manner for it: his journeys in its behalf were not confined to Anglesey, but extended to the whole of North Wales. He also went to Liverpool, Manchester, Chester, and the towns on the borders of Wales, on the same errand. The whole population within his sphere of influence were moved in its behalf. And these exertions continued till his dying day.

It is with difficulty that we can procure any fragments of speeches delivered by Elias at Bible meetings. It is certain that he attended more meetings and delivered a greater number of addresses on the subject than any other man in his time, though not in official connection with the institution. But it did not occur to any one to take down his extraordinary effusions on such occasions, nor has he left anything behind in the shape of notes of addresses. But who could write while Elias was speaking? His manner spoke while his voice only was heard; and in order to enjoy his addresses, it was necessary to *look* as well as *listen*. This may account in some measure for the scarcity of materials under this head.

Great was Elias's knowledge of general history, geography, and ancient customs and manners, which he frequently employed in the cause of the Bible Society: he was happy in bringing his various stores of information to bear on this grand subject. When delivering a speech for the Bible Society at Ruthin Association, his *knowledge* of the history and geography of foreign parts destitute of the Scriptures appeared very remarkable. He spent about an hour going over a vast number of those countries, describing them and their populations as in misery and darkness, with as much minuteness as if he had seen them: so that one gentleman said to another, as they heard him, 'I never heard such a speech in behalf of the Bible Society before'. The other replied, 'Wonderful!', adding, 'that man knows the history and geography of the whole world!'

'I once remember', says the Rev R. Davies, of Liverpool, 'being with Elias at a Bible meeting, and was much struck with the conclusion of a passage, wherein he was speaking of the *value* of the Bible. "To speak of the Bible," he exclaimed, "I must speak of the God of the Bible. O! for a seraph's tongue! But I sink, I sink, in the unfathomable abyss." Such powerful strokes were frequently introduced into his addresses, and the efficacy of them was greatly increased by his animated manner and tone of voice.'

The first Bible meeting in Anglesey took place at Llannerch-y-medd on 25 February, 1813, and to give notice of it, Elias published the following:

The intentions and purposes of the Bible Society are very liberal and extensive; they know of no end or termination. It comprehends in its noble views the children of men every where, of every colour and language, purposing to furnish them with the Holy Scriptures in their own languages, that they may read therein 'the wonderful works of God'. These excellent purposes cannot be fulfilled without general, liberal, and unceasing pecuniary aid. There are very large and extensive countries, and thickly populated kingdoms, whose inhabitants live in the greatest ignorance as to the things that concern their salvation. 'They are without hope and without God in the world!' The Holy Scriptures have never been translated into the languages of most of them, and those that have been favoured with Bibles in their own tongues are in great want of more, as they have become in many parts very scarce! There are hundreds of millions, perhaps five hundred millions of the inhabitants of the earth without Bibles! And consequently they are destitute of the means of knowing the way to everlasting life! What heart is there that will not be deeply moved with compassion for their wretched situation, and excited by strong desires of assisting according to the utmost of his means an institution that aims at supplying such countless multitudes of human beings with the light of the truth? They must, without this, perish for lack of knowledge!

There is, it is evident, a necessity of endeavouring to spread or disseminate the Word of God more abundantly in every part of our own country. Minute search and inquiry were made into the state and circumstances of the county in respect of its want of Bibles; it was discovered that many poor families were in more wretched circumstances in this respect than could be imagined: there are in our own small island hundreds of families destitute of this invaluable treasure, the Word of God! And thousands of persons above ten years old are unable to read the Word of God! It is very distressing to think that such ignorance still exists in our own country. The Bible, and the Bible alone,

is able to make people wise unto salvation. And therefore, to be without
the Scriptures, or unable to read them, i sto be destitute of the means of
knowing God and Christ, and to be in the way to eternal destruction for
the lack of knowledge. The thought of immortal souls so precious being
lost for ever is too much to be endured even for a moment. Therefore
there is a loud call for the active co-operation of all to disperse the thick
destructive darkness that covers the land. Let everyone come to the
field of labour in the great cause, and do all he can, and no doubt the
success will be accordingly. And our own souls will prosper in this
blessed work, and we shall be watered ourselves as we water others;
and then our meeting together at the last day will not, through God's
mercy, be uncomfortable. Therefore let us be steadfast, unmoveable,
always abounding in the work of the Lord, forasmuch as we know that
our labour is not in vain in the Lord.

Elias felt it keenly, as may be expected, whenever the institution
so dear to him was attacked. Never did he feel it more than when
some brethren took umbrage at some imaginary causes of offence,
and when they consequently formed themselves into what is
called the 'Trinitarian Bible Society'. He always considered that
the committee and the managers of the original Society acted
prudently and uprightly in all its difficulties. He thought that
nothing less than divine wisdom could have guided them. About
this time, considerable sensation was produced in some parts of
Wales on the subject, and Elias's views, being so highly valued,
were sought; and having given the subject his serious consideration, he thought it best to remain in the old Society, and advised
all his friends consulting him to do the same. The following is one
of Elias's letters on this occasion:

Fron 24 January 1832

I am truly sorry for the separation in the Bible Society. I think that we
as a body should be quiet, and work as before. We know that, under the
blessing of God, the old Society prospered exceedingly, but we are
ignorant how the new one will go on. I do not admire its name,
'Trinitarian Bible Society'. I have great respect for many that are in it,
and their zeal for the Person of Christ and his atonement. But I think
they have been too hasty, and that many of their accusations are without
foundation. Time will reveal things.

So weighty and influential were his opinions and observations on the points, that not one corner of Wales was disposed to leave the Society in that critical moment, but remained faithfully with the former institution.

I shall here introduce a letter of the Rev T. Phillips, Agent of the Bible Society, showing Elias's exertions for the Society:

Hay 15 November 1841

The only point on which I may be expected to give any information is the service rendered by our late friend to the Bible Society. No one hailed its formation with greater delight, or stepped forward more readily to promote its interests. Being on intimate terms with the late excellent Charles, and occupying the same wide field of ministerial labours, they moved in concert in carrying out the principles and objects of the Society in the Principality. During the first year, 1804, Elias preached sermons bearing on the subject, throughout the whole island of Anglesey; and at the conclusion of the service he generally descended from the pulpit to receive the contributions of the people. Thus the large sum of £570 and upwards was collected in a very short space of time. He continued to exert himself by applying personally to individuals and by appealing to congregations for their pecuniary aid, until the Auxiliary was established, embracing the whole county. This took place in February 1813. Before the Parent Society adopted the plan of sending deputations to the various societies, Elias with many others of different denominations kept alive and extended the cause by holding meetings and making collections. And when after the formation of numerous Auxiliaries and Branches, in the towns and larger villages, it was found necessary to keep up the interest by occasional visits, it is well known that his presence and addresses rendered the meetings popular and effective. The Revds Messrs Acworth, Langley, and several others who visited North Wales as representatives of the B.S., can bear witness to the effect produced by his speeches. When he rose simply to give in Welsh the substance of an English speech just delivered by the deputation, it was generally remarked that all the facts and statements seemed to improve under his hands. I have often heard it stated that his translation frequently exceeded the originals in interest and effect. I am fully persuaded that amongst the numerous friends of the Society in Wales, there is not one individual, living or dead, whose services to the cause can be compared with his in value and duration, except Charles of Bala. His influence in his own Connexion, his extraordinary talents as a public speaker, his long career of usefulness, his own example of liberality, as well as labour, were all exceedingly beneficial to the Bible Society. It was no wonder therefore that the Parent Committee should, a few years ago, mark their sense of the value of his example and exertions by placing his name on the list of 'Honorary Governors for Life', among those who have 'rendered essential service to the Society'. But I must bring this hasty communication to a close, praying that it may please the great Head of the church to give poor Wales many an Elisha to supply the place of this Elijah; and may a double portion of his spirit rest upon all those who bear the name and sustain the office of Christian ministers, that each in his sphere may be a burning and a shining light.

The following letter, written by the Rev W. Acworth, Vicar of Rothley, Leicestershire, respecting Elias in connexion with the Bible Society, will also be read with pleasure:

Rothley Vicarage 10 July 1844

I should feel regret, had you presented a memorial of our departed friend Elias to the public, without bearing my testimony to his worth. Few persons living in England had greater and more frequent opportunities for acquainting himself with his character than I had. During several successive years we met and travelled together over a large portion of North Wales. And never can I forget how the people flocked together from remote distances to hear him advocate the claims of the Bible Society. It was enough to know that John Elias was to be present to ensure such an attendance of persons as is seldom seen at any religious meeting in England. And when I sometimes reminded him playfully that he was the object of attraction, his countenance would put on more than its usual seriousness, under the recollection that his extraordinary popularity greatly augmented his responsibility. As we usually travelled together in my gig, I had frequent opportunities of marking the depth of his humility. On one occasion, when observing the multitudes on the road who were going to the meeting which he had promised to attend, he gave me the outlines of a sermon he had recently preached on the parable of the talents, which I learned from those who heard it and were capable of judging, exhibited extraordinary comprehensiveness of mind as well as fervency of piety; that sermon strikingly manifested that his sense of personal responsibility affected him oftentimes to sadness. There was a peculiar unction in his mode of addressing the people, which was evident to myself, in the very tone of his voice, though to a great degree ignorant of the language in which his thoughts were conveyed.

He seldom attended a Bible meeting at which I was present that he did not prevail upon the Officers and Committee to retire first into some private room to unite in prayer for a blessing on the speakers and assembly, as well as the objects of the meeting. And in some instances when he doubted his influence to accomplish this purpose, he invariably retired for devotional purposes before the meeting began.

And it was his fervent piety, controlling and sweetening a temper perhaps not very amiable by nature, as well as his great talents, that won for him a name and influence which no other man in modern times has obtained in Wales. And he possessed this ascendancy not only over the members of his own denomination, but all classes of society bore ample and willing testimony to his merits as a Christian and a minister.

On one occasion, a Lord Lieutenant in Wales, and a nobleman filling one of the highest stations in the Government of the land, the Marquis of Anglesey, highly respected, promised to attend a Bible meeting at Beaumaris, and to take the chair. Many persons tried to prevent him doing so, on account of the number of Nonconformists who were expected. But the hero of Waterloo[1] refused to be influenced by them. The Rev D. Stewart of Liverpool had been invited to address the meeting in English, and John Elias in Welsh. It was expected that the presence of the Marquis would attract a number of the higher classes: but many objected to John Elias. However, neither the officers of the Society, nor the public, would listen to them. The great meeting took place; and the eye of the public was upon it. The neighbouring gentry were assembled, and all were anxiously listening for the noise of the carriage-wheels which would convey the noble Marquis, who at length arrived precisely at the time appointed, and immediately took the chair. He opened the proceedings by explaining in a few words the object of the Society, and said he fully approved of it. All went on in a pleasing manner. At length the name of John Elias was pronounced as the next speaker; this changed the aspect of many; they immediately threw out the scornful lip, turned up the nose, and cast at Elias disdainful glances; the faces of some were even directed towards the door. But all this strange conduct was not sufficient to put him down: he came forward and addressed the chairman in a polite manner, who returned the

---

[1] The Marquis lost a leg at this battle.

compliment with a smile; he evidently saw something extraordinary in him at the first glance.

When Elias took first a view of the state of the Welsh before they had the Bible, it was soon seen that he was perfectly acquainted with the history of his country; especially when he gave an account of the Welsh *translation* of the Scriptures. When they heard him mention the names of William Salesbury, Dr William Morgan, Dr Richard Davies, Thomas Huet, Cantor of St David's; Dr Whitgift, Dr Hughes, Dr Bellot, Dr Gabriel Goodman, Dr David Powell, Vicar of Rhiwbon; Archdeacon Edmund Prys, Dr Richard Parry, and others, a sound attracted their ears which they did not expect; such names seemed to stir their hearts like sweet music. As he went on giving a statement of the different *editions* of the Welsh Bible, mentioning the names of Thomas Middleton, Rowland Heylin, Walter Cradock, Vavasor Powell, Thomas Gouge, Stephen Hughes, David Jones, Bishop Humphrey Lloyd, Moses Williams, and others, he gained their feelings, attention, and approbation; the frost had melted away imperceptibly; and, as he went on with his address, his good language, powerful words and persuasive eloquence overcame every contemptuous look; all persons listened with avidity; and as he led the assembly to view the present state of the Welsh, showing the necessity of some *further attempt* more effectual than any hitherto, however excellent, they were quite struck.

Then he moved to a higher elevation; he set forth the moral state of the country, as in warfare between light and darkness, holiness and sin, Christ and Belial; that the two large armies were drawing nearer, and that the truth *must* prevail. He shewed that the happiness of the world depended on this great struggle; and that an *example* of the warfare and the victory had been seen lately at Waterloo. By this time the feelings of the people were completely at his command. He went forward to describe the late great struggle at Waterloo; showing that the happiness of nations, the progress of business, success of the arts, increase of knowledge, yea the prosperity of the gospel, turned on this important hour. But the hand of providence was seen *visibly* in it. Their captains were endowed with wisdom and power necessary for such a conquest. 'The Lord is a man of war; the Lord is his name.' Then he turned to describe *one* commander going forth to the field, the moment the scales were turned in their favour for ever! He made use of the description given in the Book of Job of the war horse, and his rider, to set him forth. 'I imagine I see him,' said he, 'coming forth to the field on his white horse: which despiseth every fear and alarm; he paweth the

valley, and rejoiceth in his strength; he mocketh at fear.' He set the
horse forth as running in the midst of the trumpets, saying, Ah! Ah!
in contempt of them. 'He smelleth the battle afar off, the thunder of
the captains and the shoutings.' But the great rider is all the time in
perfect self-possession, in the midst of smoke and fire, directing and
leading his armed men until he surrounded the enemy, who could move
neither backward nor forward – but he was too great and honourable to
kill him, though within his reach.

At this juncture the speaker was obliged to stop on account of the
outbreak of the assembly, who were overwhelmed. But he soon resumed
his address; and as he increased in warmth and power, he became more
and more effective. 'Now,' he said, 'I think I hear the shout of victory
before it is gained; yes, a conquest! – but it will be at the sacrifice of one
of the most illustrious of our nation! – no, not the sacrifice of himself,
but of one of his members! Then death advances, throwing a ball,
cutting off one of the brave captain's members – but what of that?
Divine providence comes forward the same moment, calling on death
as the angel did on Abraham formerly – "Stay thy hand, so far shalt
thou go, and no further. Touch not his life, go no further than taking
off his limb. I shall have need of his service hereafter, in a warfare of
much higher nature than this – as a leader in the chair of the Bible
Society – I shall have need of his service to dispense the Word of life
to every country, language, people, and nation over the face of the
whole world!"' He cried out at this time, with a strong but melting
voice, 'The enemy is bound, but the word of God is not bound!' By
this time the whole assembly was altogether in a state of confusion;
now silence prevailed, then whisperings and questions. The English
who did not understand Welsh were more anxious than any, on observing the general thrill which passed over the assembly; asking – 'What
was that?' – 'What did he say?' – 'What is the reason for this excitement?' Silk dresses were wetted with tears – the buckram softened, and
the starch dissolved. After a little silence and recovery of feeling, the
noble chairman turned suddenly, and with some anxiety, to the friend
on his side, and inquired what could be the cause of the great commotion? He, approaching his ear, said, 'It was an allusion to yourself,
my Lord, and to the accident at Waterloo, when the interception of
providence spared you to preside over this meeting.' The chairman was
then seen searching in haste for his pocket-handkerchief to wipe off the
tears which ran down his face in drops as large as peas. Let the reader
imagine what feelings were produced on the assembly by this time; here

is the strong military man weeping like a child! All the thunders of the cannon at Waterloo produced no more effect on his feelings than on the rock – but now the speech of a Welshman turned the strong rock into a pool of water. The ball that took off his limb made no impression on his spirit; but behold the effect produced by an address at a meeting of the Bible Society, softening one who set his face like a flint, and making him tender and feeling as a little child. (This nobleman later sent Elias an invitation to his house and table, which was respectfully declined; he did not wish to make his popularity subservient to personal renown.) Elias then concluded by making a strong appeal from the Apostle's words, 'Finally brethren, pray for us, that the word of God may have free course and be glorified.'

This speech gave fresh impulse to the Bible Society, and the funds for it were greatly increased. Anglesey has since signalized itself by its efforts for the Bible Society above every other place in the kingdom.[1]

The Committee of the Bible Society was pleased to make the following particular reference to Elias in its Report, following Elias's death, which was unanimously adopted at the Annual Meeting:

There is another subject to which, in conclusion, we would advert – a subject always interesting, and unless it be our own fault, always instructive, and that subject is *death*. After the lapse of thirty-seven years it was to be expected in the common course of nature that the departure of the founders and early friends of the Society would become more frequent. To the habitation of one of these the pale messenger has been sent in the course of the last year, and found him 'with his loins girt and his lamp burning'. To the memory of the Rev J. Elias, a more than common tribute of affection and regret is due from the friends of the British and Foreign Bible Society. After the decease of the indefatigable and lamented Charles of Bala, he was, humanly speaking, the Society's main support and its untiring advocate in North Wales; and it is believed that he delivered more addresses, and collected more money in its behalf, than *any* other individual not officially connected with the Society. The influence of his example, and the force of his appeals, were deeply and generally felt in his own country, where in the very

[1] This account is taken from Mr Acworth's *Letter,* and R. Parry's *Adgofion am John Elias* (Denbigh, 1859).

first year he collected after a series of meetings the large sum of £550. In the decease of this revered and much loved servant of Christ, the Society has lost a praying member, a liberal contributor, an eloquent and most efficient advocate. May his mantle, with a double portion of his spirit, fall upon his survivors!

The London Missionary Society was another great object of Elias's peculiar attention and regard: his exertions in its behalf were considerable and successful. Considering his remarkable character as a preacher, and even as a missionary in Wales, we may well suppose that he would be most happy to give all the support in his power to such a society as this. Indeed he exerted himself exceedingly for that as well as the Bible Society. The collections which he annually obtained from that poor country for the missionary cause were wonderfully large, when we consider what sums he collected there for the Bible Society, and for the support of the chapels and other charities. Elias and the brethren used to collect in North Wales no less than from £200 to £300 towards the London Missionary Society every year. His taking such an active part in the missionary cause had no doubt a great effect on the country at large; and his influence in this as well as every other respect was very animating, powerful, and effectual. His call on all hands to activity and labour in the vineyard of the Lord was very impressive and forcible. It was like the voice of a messenger from the world above.

Elias used to preach also in London in behalf of the Society. In a letter to his daughter from thence in May 1819, he says: 'I preached last Sabbath Day a sermon for the London Missionary Society, in *Albion Chapel*, a Scotch Church. It was full of Welsh people. The collection amounted to £30 9s 0d; a large sum for the poor Welsh. The Lord be praised for his presence, and inclining the hearts of the people.'

After Thomas Charles's days, Elias took the lead in the transactions of the Connexion with the London Missionary Society, as well as every other important affair. He consequently corresponded with that Society for the Association in North Wales. His letters manifested his usual good sense and excellent management.

Elias's addresses on behalf of the L.M.S. were always well

received and much appreciated by the people. On one occasion, in Anglesey, he reviewed the activities of the various missionary societies then in existence, observing that they were all of one aim and spirit. During the course of his address, he imagined that he and the congregation stood beside the 'angel standing in the sun' of the Book of Revelation, from that vantage looking down on the earth in its motion around the sun. He described the city of London receding from their view, and Ireland with its millions of Catholics coming into view; then the United States of America, the Pacific Ocean, the South Sea islands, the vast continent of China, the plains of India, the Himalayas, Tartary, Persia, Arabia under the dominion of the false prophet, Palestine where Abraham, David, and Solomon had lived, Calvary where Christ had been crucified, Africa, and Europe coming once again into view. 'Look', he exclaimed, 'we have returned to our old home, and we can see the dome of St Paul's, and the office of the London Missionary Society'. Then he spoke of the certainty of God's promises, and that the gospel would most surely succeed. 'The tabernacle of God will be with men', he cried, 'and all the peoples of the earth will be one family, with all men breathing love, peace, and goodness.'

Sunday Schools were greatly encouraged by Elias. He had a natural fondness for children: he conducted himself very kindly towards them in those benevolent institutions; and they looked up to him as unto a beloved father. He greatly excelled in the delightful work of catechising. I never heard any one catechise in so solemn and impressive a manner. Charles's way was of a more soft, tender, and benignant kind. Both had their peculiar and great excellencies in this most useful employment. Much of Elias's *mind* in training up the rising generation may be seen in the account we have already given of the manner in which he educated his own children. Many of the Sunday School children were seriously impressed, and eventually became members of the church of God. It was by the instrumentality of Sunday Schools in a great measure, that Elias influenced the country to abandon their corrupt practices. But preaching the gospel was his grand forte.

The cause of temperance and sobriety was always greatly encouraged and inculcated by Elias. The vice of drunkenness was most odious to his pious soul. He always endeavoured to suppress and stop it by every means. He would warn the people in a very forcible manner against intoxication, especially at Associations. Once at Llannerch-y-medd Association, urging them in the strongest terms to beware of temptation to that vice, he made use of the following strong figurative language: 'Friends and neighbours,' said he, 'let me guard you in the most kind manner against the vice of intemperance and drunkenness. You may be aware that there are two flags held out here at this time, a black and a red one (meaning two opposite interests). The black flag is in the window of the house of drunkenness and revellings; the red one is unfurled by the preachers of the gospel, proclaiming atonement for sin by the blood of Christ. Take particular care, I beseech you, that you do not go near the black flag; Satan reigns there, and you will be drawn into his snare. Each party will be known and discovered by the flags and colours they are under. Choose, O! choose the banner of the cross; and fight manfully under it against the world, the flesh, and the devil.' The warning had the most happy effect; very few persons, comparatively, went into public houses; and those that went, conducted themselves in a sober and orderly manner. It could not have been known by their behaviour that the black flag, the flag of death, was in the town, or that intemperance existed there at all!

Elias observing that drunkenness was gaining ground and spreading its dreadful influence over a vast portion of the inhabitants of Wales, notwithstanding all attempts to check it, was persuaded that some new and uncommonly powerful means must be adopted to withstand the destructive floods of the overwhelming evil. He thought that the temperance and total abstinence societies, then appearing in Wales, were very likely means, under God, to stem the torrents of the dreadful malady.

He makes the following remarks on the subject of these societies, in a letter to a friend in 1836:

I judge the principles of the temperance society are such, if implanted in the mind of the nation, as would, under the divine blessing, stop every sinful propensity to all inebriating liquors. Care must be taken that nothing be said disrespectfully of the Total Abstinence Society: those that are under temptation to drink to excess, should abstain entirely from fermented liquors. Let the temperance meetings be held in a more religious manner, let all the speeches on sobriety be founded more upon Scripture: let the preachers and elders take the lead in the meetings; and let no room be given to unwise and carnal speakers, that the work may not be injured.

Elias seemed to grow in favour to the Total Abstinence Society, no doubt by seeing its salutary effects on the population of the country everywhere; under this impression, he writes to a friend in London on the subject, in 1838:

You see that our collections are larger this year (for the Missionary Society); we must attribute the increase to the prosperity of the Abstinence Society in this Island: many enjoy the good effects of the society; many distressed wives and naked children are well and decently clothed now: there is comfort in many an habitation, that was without it before! Our towns are quiet and industrious; men engaged in markets and fairs are decent and well behaved. The multitudes in our religious Associations conduct themselves in a proper and moral manner, yea *many* from the Total Abstinence Society enter our communion. The good hand of the Lord is clearly seen in the work that is done. Many that halted between two opinions come now zealously forward, and place themselves in the ranks of the society, lest they should lose the privilege of being fellow-labourers in this great work; and having at length perceived the excellency of the institution, they express their approbation of it, and testify that they have themselves experienced great benefit from it. There is not one that complains he has received any injury by abandoning intoxicating liquors altogether. Example goes far by way of recommendation.

Elias seemed now to prefer the Total Abstinence to the Temperance Society: no doubt it was for the purpose of reclaiming drunkards. The cause of total abstinence has prospered much among the Welsh everywhere. No doubt but that Elias was one of the chief promoters of its success. The last public act of his life, was attending a meeting of this Society, in the winter of 1840, at Llangefni chapel, where he addressed the members, giving them most useful directions founded on gospel principles. In coming out of the chapel, he walked before the children, though very weak; when in the street he turned to a company of young men standing there looking on them, and exhorted them to join the cause of temperance, as the path to comfort: one of them at least was deeply impressed, and became a new creature.

11 Elias's second marriage, his private character and catholic spirit

God in his infinite wisdom and goodness had planned for his servant's welfare in every respect, and led him all the way safely and happily. Having lost his first wife, who had exerted all her energies to set him at liberty to preach the gospel, he at length meets with another helpmeet to soothe him in his bereaved state, and to aid and console him in his affliction and declining years. 'A good wife is a gift from the Lord,' to be respected and treated as such at all times. Elias felt his obligations for both these valuable gifts, and thanked the Lord for them most gratefully. The former marriage has been noticed before, and in the following pleasing manner he speaks of the latter in his autobiography:

10 February 1830, I married Lady Bulkeley, the widow of the late Sir John Bulkeley, Presaddfed. We went to Y Fron, near Llangefni, to reside, where we are to this day (22 April 1841). The tender Lord once again provided me with a helpmeet, a cheerful companion, a tender nurse, who is of much comfort to me in my troublous days, and a great help to me in the Lord's work. I can say today, at the end of a long season, after going through many kinds of weather, 'Hitherto hath the Lord helped me'. I now desire to give him the praise; but when all the journey of the wilderness is seen, having gone through it to the end, he shall have my perfect praise.

Lady Ann Bulkeley, the daughter of Griffith Williams of Aberffraw, Anglesey, had been brought up in humble circumstances. She was reputedly one of the most beautiful young girls in Anglesey, in figure, countenance, and deportment. There are two traditions respecting her marriage to Sir John Bulkeley, who was a retired officer of the Royal Navy. One relates that Ann was in service at Dronwy, a country mansion. One day she remarked to her mistress that Sir John was a fine-looking man, and her mistress passed on the remark to him; his curiosity was so aroused that he made a request to see the young girl, with the result that he fell in love with her and soon married her. The other tradition relates that Ann was in service at Presaddfed. One day she was occupied with a certain duty outside the house, opposite a window; Sir John opened the window in a merry mood. 'Ann', he said, jokingly, 'will you marry me?' 'Yes, Sir John', she answered, in the same jocular mood. They were soon married, to everybody's astonishment; and she became the mistress of the house where she had served in the past. Sir John died soon afterwards, and left his widow in comfortable circumstances.

Lady Bulkeley's second marriage was almost as romantic as her first. The good qualities of the lady, her unaffected piety, her kind disposition, and her affectionate and amiable manners, had been known to Elias for years. He wrote a letter of sympathy to her on the death of Sir John in September 1819. Lady Bulkeley was staying at Dronwy, near Llanfachreth, Anglesey, with a family named Edwards, at the end of summer, 1829. Elias had a preaching appointment at Llanfachreth, and he was entertained on the occasion at Dronwy.

'Mr Elias gave us a fine sermon tonight', remarked Mrs Edwards to Lady Bulkeley when she returned home after the service; 'it's a pity you were not there to hear him.' 'I was there,' she answered. She had gone to the service, disguised (in order not to draw attention) in her maid's Welsh costume. 'I never heard such a sermon in my life,' she continued. Her admiration for the preacher was unbounded.

The following morning, at the breakfast table, where they sat together in private, they began the courtship that eventually led to their marriage. They kept the affair as secret as possible, and Mr Edward Hughes of Henbont, the lady's brother-in-law and an elder in one of the local churches, acted as their intermediary. When he decided to change his condition, Elias had some difficulty in giving the news to his children. However, on 24 December 1829, when he was away from home, he wrote them the letter printed in the latter part of this work (*p* 196). He promised not to dispossess them of anything; indeed, he would rather suffer poverty than do anything so mean. He intended, on his return home, to give over everything to his children before changing his condition.

He fulfilled his promise, and the wedding took place at St David's Church, Liverpool. Elias acted wisely in making such a choice: and his marriage was beneficial to his children as well as to himself. Not only was he enabled thereby to give them all his property, but also to live near them, and afford them every advice and direction needful both for temporal and spiritual concerns, and to aid them in many other ways, without being in the least burdensome. His wife also, possessing an ample fortune, was very kind to Elias's children, showing a motherly and affectionate disposition towards them, and evincing a real concern for their welfare.

It is impossible to express his kindness and tenderness towards his wife. His conversation with her was generally on something of a religious nature, always edifying and profitable. He was interesting also in his communications with her when on his preaching excursions; the comparisons he used to draw on the way from temporal things to illustrate those that are spiritual, were very edifying. When a short distance from the home, upon setting out for a journey, he always used to repeat two or three times with great earnestness, these words: 'Be pleased, O heavenly Father, to go with us.' He used also in the gig, and everywhere on the journey, to pray for the same blessing. And on their return home he would almost invariably take an opportunity of retiring with his wife, to return thanks to God for preserving them during the journey – safe return and domestic comforts. He used to notice travelling as well as other mercies in a very grateful manner. He was very fond of his study, would enter it very early, and thought a great deal on what he had read. His wife used to beg of him to come down and take a walk for the benefit of his health; but she very seldom succeeded; he would gently say, 'Oh my dear, I have no time, my Master's work is great and urgent.'

As to his demeanour in the house and family, it was truly agreeable to the Word of God, always kind towards all around him in different circumstances. Towards none did he manifest any improper spirit or impatience, and of none did he think evil. Religion in all its branches was attended to with regularity, seriousness, and ardent devotion. His wife would not enter his study without knocking at the door; for having on one occasion gone in suddenly without giving that notice, she found him on his knees. In his family he was always what he would wish to be thought to be among his friends and enemies. His wife saw and felt that he was a man that walked with God.

Much of Elias's private conduct has been already described; it was so intermixed with his public life, that the one could not well be mentioned without the other. He lived in obedience to God. There was in all his domestic and other transactions, an implicit reference to the will of God, and reliance on it. His domestics never heard him murmuring and complaining. Blessings prevailed much where he presided and moved.

Elias was peculiarly a man of prayer. There was an uncommon reverence manifested towards his heavenly Father at the commencement, and a peculiar earnestness and seriousness throughout his prayers. 'I always used to imagine,' says his wife, 'that the eye of his mind in prayer saw God on his mercy-seat, and that he was in a manner conversing with him, which undoubtedly he did by faith.' However, his holy freedom and boldness were clothed with humility and solemnity. His prayer used to be very impressive. Elias walked with God continually; yea, his thoughts in general flowed in the divine fellowship. As he had tasted of the sweetness of intercourse with God, he could not bear to be absent from him. The blessed influence and support of God's continual presence afforded him a store of sufficiency and consolation. The peace and serenity he enjoyed were through the merits of Christ. Having made his requests known unto God, he left his trials with him. If they happened to come across his mind again, he would look up unto God, as conversing with him about them. Many a suitable thought and promise suggested by him by way of answer, proved to him the presence of the Lord, and the truth of those words, 'Ask and you shall receive, that your joy may be full.'

Elias used to watch earnestly for answers to his prayers. His daughter, object of his many prayers, was once very unwell and likely to depart. However, in opening the Bible, he observed those words, 'Take courage, thy daughter liveth,' which gave him great satisfaction, and enabled him to hope that she would recover; which proved to be the case.

At another time a certain woman, a neighbour's wife, was extremely ill. Her case pressed much on Elias's mind in prayer. One morning he said to his wife, 'I have somehow missed Elizabeth in my prayer today, I fear she is not alive.' Just as he finished the expression, the husband of the woman was at the door, to inform them of her departure! He used to have great satisfaction in prayer, even as to things that were very difficult and perplexing.

Other remarkable instances of answers to Elias's prayers might be mentioned; the painful case of certain players occurs to our mind. He was once very much grieved when at Caernarvon he learned that some mountebanks were corrupting the place with their sinful amusements. They obstinately continued their diabolical work, though repeatedly requested to desist. Elias being in the society at the chapel about that time, had great liberty in prayer to the Lord to put a stop to their mad proceedings: many were struck with the earnestness, fervency, and power of his prayer, as being very extraordinary. The next day, awful to relate, three of the players came to an untimely death; the waggon in which they travelled was overturned, and they were killed! Two others, in the act of dancing on the rope, fell and broke their necks! The people at large could not but view these calamitous occurrences as tokens of divine displeasure.

It may here be observed how remarkable were his prayers for his first wife when in labour. She was in general subject to great pain and danger at those periods. Being in that state on one occasion in particular, when she was considered by the surgeon to be in imminent peril, even past all hope, Elias prayed most earnestly in the next room, and the Lord was pleased to hear his prayer, in delivering his wife from the jaws of death. The medical gentleman said that the divine interposition was no less than a miracle.

Elias maintained such a delightful state of mind, as to be able

at any moment to converse with the most heavenly and spiritually
minded Christian, and make him perceive that he drank into the
very depths of his spirit, and relished his most exalted themes. He
was ready to administer words of advice and encouragement at all
times, especially to the weary and heavy laden. His warm affectionate heart would pour out its stores, when occasion required,
like streams gushing from the fountain. This was generally
witnessed and experienced by persons who consulted him, and at
the private society or church-meetings. In those meetings he
would lead on the weak and humble, and encourage them to
converse with him, by giving them his own experience, dwelling
on some portion of God's Word suitable thereto, or relating parts
of the sermons he had lately heard. He would in particular direct
them all to Christ, as the only refuge for a sinner.

Elias was easy of access, open and communicative, yet cautious
and faithful. Many consulted him on numerous difficult subjects:
his counsels were judicious and satisfactory; and 'he was faithful in
heart, concealing the matter.' If any one consulted him on the
subject of changing his situation in life, it would go no further, not
even to his wife. A young woman once consulted him, in a trying
affair of this kind. She had been engaged to a papist; but she was
in the meantime brought to the knowledge of the truth; and she
could not therefore think of living with such a man: but breaking
her engagement was equally grievous. Elias was consulted on the
subject. He advised her to ask the young man at his next visit,
concerning the state of his soul. She did so, and he left her entirely.
How excellent is the following direction he gave to another person,
however he might be circumstanced! 'In whatever situation, state,
or circumstance you may be placed, let the glory of God be your
object, the Word of God your rule, and the love of God your
principle; you will thus have God as your guide, protector, and
comforter.' Elias was thus prudent in his conversation and friendship; in his social, domestic, and church relations. He maintained
purity of principle in all his communications and transactions. Any
perversion of things was odious to his holy soul.

Elias's character was also composed of determination, perseverance, and mental energy, to a high degree. Nothing appeared to

him to be too heavy a task, however contrary to his personal feelings, when he saw the propriety of it. He would do everything required in the path of duty, resist everything contrary to it, and continue in the pursuit of his object to the end. He was punctual in all his engagements, both private and public. Consequently he never appeared hurried in a business which concerned the souls of men. The character of pious gravity was stamped on all he did. Slovenliness and hurry were not usually manifested in his actions. He was a man that cultivated and instilled peaceful principles everywhere. But when he considered any thing wrong in a person, he would not yield or compromise the matter at all, but he would strive for the truth.

If Elias had not possessed such a prudent, peaceable, loving, yet firm mind, he could never have maintained his ground for so many years at the head of the Calvinistic Methodist Connexion in North Wales. He took the lead in all the monthly and quarterly meetings, and societies. The weekly societies were filled by the revivals which took place chiefly under his ministry. The representatives of these brought the various cases to the higher courts of the above meeting, and there his judgment and prudence were much exercised to satisfy many querists and inquirers: also to elucidate doctrines, and clear up various difficult points. He used to say to a friend who had complained of the brevity of his letters, 'I have a large district to attend to, you have only a parish.' Elias might be said to have had the face of an ox, in the sense stated by the Apostle John; he was strong, firm, constant, unyielding; and that in behalf of every good society, establishment, and service.

Elias's personal piety was eminent – in his spirituality of mind, modesty of heart, long-suffering, patience, calmness and meekness, uprightness, holy conversation and godliness. How remarkable was his character in these respects even from his youth! Shall we say that he ministered before the Lord, girded like Samuel, with a linen ephod? Nay, he was endued with what is infinitely superior, the graces, gifts and influences of the Holy Ghost. These things were to him an ornamental dress; and with them he appeared with as much, if not more distinguished comeliness, taking all things together, than any other of his age. How awfully is the ministry degraded, when assumed by men of unsanctified and boisterous passions! But grace had subdued such tempers in him. He had not the surly, greedy disposition of the bear or the wolf, nor the cunning of the fox. He was free from quarrelsome, revengeful thoughts. He did not retire to rest with anger in his heart.

Elias was of a very liberal and benevolent disposition, and was always ready to assist his neighbour in temporal as well as eternal things. Having received a taste for the healing art, he would, when he had some spare time, study medicine; and at length he became so far proficient as to be able to aid the poor in their bodily afflictions. The Lord blessed his endeavours to relieve and restore many a sick person to his usual health. He was not fond of quackery, he would forbid people to take medicines from persons ignorant and unskilful. He never pretended to go beyond his knowledge in medical cases. Such aids are most valuable in many parts of Wales, where medical men are not near. This sort of practice relieved his mind from too much devotion to study.

Elias was also very remarkable for humility. Who was more watchful than he in his conduct where he lodged – more easy to be pleased, or thankful for an act of kindness? Who heard the humblest of his brethren (when preaching) with so great a pleasure, and so easily condescended to men of low estate, as he? Never was there an instance of an attempt at exalting himself in any of the religious services in which he was engaged. He was a man that knew much without appearing to do so: he knew how to conduct himself in the mansion and in the cottage. Sometimes he had poor accommodation on his journeys, but he would not allude to these circumstances on his return home. He would take care, however, to inform his friends where the Lord was working. He was free from egotism, loquacity, and dogmatism. He would always show great regard to the brethren. He was ready when at home to commence the public service before any itinerant preacher that came that way; and he would never determine upon anything in the church, without the consent of his fellow-labourers.

Elias was not only an example to believers, but he also reflected Christ's image upon the world. He was never known to cast off the livery of his noble calling upon any occasion. The seriousness of his appearance would repel any disposition in others to levity and frivolity.

More might be said of Elias's friendly disposition and benignity. We shall, however, say a few words of his *catholic* spirit: he acted at all times in an open kind manner towards every person; and he uniformly conducted himself in such a way towards the clergy in particular, as won much upon their hearts and feelings. He did not wish any unkindness to be manifested towards the Church of England. He used to say that their Connexion was a branch from it, and had been brought up under its wing. It has been observed, that the clergy have improved of late years in Anglesey, as well as in other parts of Wales. Several of them preach the gospel in its purity, and also live according to its precepts. A very good understanding existed between Elias and many of them. They took him to be a sincere friend of the church, and always treated him with kindness. The young clergy that sought his acquaintance, he encouraged to remain in the Anglican Church, thinking it to be their proper sphere of usefulness. His temper was candid and open to conviction, so that by conversation with such friends as Thomas Charles of Bala, and by reading books on the subject, he became favourably disposed towards the Church. There is an allusion to this in a letter written by one of his clerical friends:

The last time Elias was in this place he preached an admirable sermon on *Hebrews* 13.20, 21. When he came from chapel to my house, he found upon the table that interesting book, published by the S.P.C.K., *The Liturgy compared with the Bible.* He read a portion of it with great pleasure, took it with him to his bedroom when he retired: and when he came down next morning, I begged his acceptance of the book: he appeared highly pleased, and said that he would rather have that book than that I should have given him £20. He also said that he had always entertained the highest veneration for the Liturgy of the Church – that he had many discussions respecting it with dissenters – and was delighted to find his opinion of it confirmed by that book. A few months before his death he sent me a kind message by a mutual friend, expressing his fears that he should never see me again, but he had not ceased to value the book I gave him.

Several interesting anecdotes might be mentioned with regard to Elias's intercourse with clergymen, showing his attachment to the Church. The last time Elias was in Liverpool, he was invited to attend an important meeting held by the clergy. His friend, the the Rev R. Davies, took a car, went for him, and brought him to the place. Elias most cordially united with them, and took breakfast with them. Dr Wolff was on one side of Elias, and Dr Tattersall on the other. The conversation and addresses after breakfast, on various religious subjects connected with the Jewish cause, were delightful. Elias seemed to enjoy the opportunity very much; and in going home he observed to Mr Davies, that as there was so much harmony among them, and holy feeling pervading the whole meeting, he had no doubt but that the love of God was influencing them, and that they would prosper. Occasionally he was invited to visit sick clergymen: his conversation seemed to be blessed to some of them on their dying beds. One of them in particular – a Mr Hughes – seemed to come like a poor sinner to Jesus.

As Elias always encouraged the evangelical clergy in their work of serving God and preaching the gospel, he greatly lamented over that which had a tendency to mar and injure the Church. He sympathized greatly with the clergy on account of that pestilence that seemed to attack the Establishment; and it was a matter of lamentation to him on his dying bed. Thus writes a friend who visited him, as to his views and feelings at that period, on this painful subject: 'During the last interviews which I had with Mr Elias, when confined to his chamber, he sorrowfully alluded to the pernicious doctrines which threatened to invade the Protestant world. "This," observed he, "is an age of novelties; numerous and strange are the notions lately broached, and now Puseyism besets us. I dread the consequences." Then he clasped his hands together, and with signs of perturbation, continued, "Dear Parry, the Puseyites are sure to do mischief! God alone knows what will be the end of these things." ' The account concludes by describing Elias as a 'worthy man by whose death Zion lost a clear-sighted and faithful watchman, who described evil from afar, and never failed to give warning of its approach.'

It was once observed to Elias that rather than the emoluments of the Established Church in Wales should be alienated and devoted

to some secular purpose, as it was then intended with the Irish
Church, it would be far better to give them to the Methodists, as
they were nearest to it. Elias made this reply: 'No, there is a great
alteration in many of the clergy; and there may be an improve-
ment, yea, a reformation in the church; so it will recover its
strength and hold on the affections of the people.' 'Besides', said
he, 'I think it is to the advantage of religion to have a stationary
and itinerant ministry in its favour. The itinerant goes into every
corner, and reaches what the other does not. They may be compared to the regular dragoons and the light infantry; both engaged
in their own sphere and way against the grand enemy.' In a letter
in 1833, he says: 'I am very far from wishing the downfall or
destruction of the Established Church: I love her prosperity in
everything that is good. I sincerely love her pious ministers and
members. I do not envy her property nor her emoluments. As for
reforming the Church, I wish to hear of a scriptural one conducted
by some of her own learned, pious, eminent ministers. Every
denomination of Christians among us, has enough to do in
reforming itself.'

Elias was not only opposed to Puseyism in the Church of
England, but also to the Unitarianism which was gaining ground in
Nonconformist circles in certain parts of Wales, for example,
Cardiganshire. The Rev J. R. Kilsby Jones has given an account
of a remarkable sermon delivered by Elias at an Association in
Lampeter in 1819, near the district where the Unitarians flourished.
He chose as his subject, *The Godhead of Christ*. Kilsby Jones gives
the following account of the occasion:

"Within a few yards from the platform there were a number of
open carriages, and in one of them sat the staff of St David's
Church of England College, Lampeter, – the late Dr Llewelyn,
grandson of the famous David Jones of Llan-gan, the late Professor
Rice Rees, and Dr Oliphant, the Bishop of Llandaff. The first
two knew enough Welsh to understand and appreciate the words
spoken by the eloquent orator; and the Bishop had a smattering of
Welsh – enough to whet his appetite to know more of the vernacular.
In the course of his sermon, in order to confirm a proposition, Elias
offered a revised translation of a certain verse. He remarked that

he had no expert knowledge of the original scriptural tongues; 'but', he added, 'I am pleased to see with us a number of learned scholars, who are able to judge whether my revised version is in accordance with the laws of Greek grammar.' He looked in the direction of the learned professors, and bowed like a courtier. They, in their turn, bowed their heads to signify their agreement. Then he went on with his sermon, reasoning carefully every inch of the way in order to prove his thesis. . . .

"The sermon is now over; his only remaining task was to draw two conclusions. 'First', he said, 'if we, Trinitarians, as we are called, are deviating from the truth, we are guilty of idolatry'. Then, in his own inimitable manner, he recited a long list of the most terrible Old Testament threatenings against idolatry; and followed by another list of the heavy judgments administered on idolaters by the Lord God of Israel in respect of this grievous sin. 'Secondly', he said, 'on the other hand, if we are orthodox, what shall I say of our opponents?' Near me stood two or three Unitarians, and no sooner than they heard the second inference, than one of them whispered in the ear of his companion, 'Now for hell-fire! that's the place where we'll be sent to, boys!' They seemed to be quite indifferent, brazen-faced and challenging in their attitude. Yet they gave ear quite attentively, – like criminals awaiting their sentence. The preacher seemed to be in some inner turmoil, as if heavy seas were boiling within his soul. His lips were trembling like the leaves of the aspen, and an infinite tenderness appeared in the corners of his wide-opened eyes. With his arm outstretched, his long forefinger weaved back and fore like a weaver's shuttle. It looked as if he was on the point of bursting by reason of the necessity of saying something, and yet unable to utter a word – as if his organs of speech had refused to function, his whole spirit was oppressed by the burden within his soul. 'How can I declare the condition of these people – where can I find comparisons keen enough to describe their condition? – where can I find words strong enough to picture their situation? I am afraid . . . (another bout of complete inability to speak, and his long forefinger weaving back and fore quicker and yet quicker still) – I am afraid . . . (sighing and groaning as if from the very bottom of his soul) – I

am afraid that they have gone astray, in error'. I happened to look
upon the face of one of the Unitarians, and I heard him whisper to
his companions, 'Men, this is terrible!' (for, to the Unitarian,
nothing can be more dangerous than erroneous doctrine). But
where is the preacher? He has disappeared, and I never saw him
again. And what of his congregation? The people looked as they
had been stunned by astonishment and terror; and for a few
minutes they could not be set free from their bonds, and regain
their self-composure."

12 Elias's declining years and happy end

Towards the close of his life Elias was often far from well. Yet such were his zeal and desire for being useful to the end, that nothing could prevent him from preaching the everlasting gospel, if he was in the least able to leave his home. He used to say, 'I shall soon be in my grave; I must work whilst it is day.' In the summer of 1831, he caught a heavy cold whilst travelling from London to the Bala Association; yet he made a special effort to preach in the open air, which worsened his condition. He was never indeed altogether well after he had a fall from a carriage in going to preach at Bala Association, in June 1832. In fact at that time he narrowly escaped death. John Davies of Bronheulog, near Bala, one of the gentlemen that was with him in the vehicle, furnished me with the following account:

Elias, Mr Smith and myself were travelling in a two-wheeled covered cabriolet, drawn by one horse. Two lads got behind the carriage, and jumped off in descending a hill near Bodwaen, upon which the shaft gave a loud crack; then Messrs Elias and Smith leaped out. I remained a few minutes in the carriage until the horse became more restive, the top of the vehicle having fallen on his back; I then sprang out myself on the other side: I sustained no injury, and was happy to find Mr Smith also safe. But alas! I saw Mr Elias laying on the ground insensible, having fallen upon his head! He was put into an arm-chair lent by a neighbour, and conveyed to Bronheulog. Mr Williams, surgeon at Bala, speedily arrived, bled him and administered some stimulants to him: he soon recovered his senses in some degree, but was occasionally delirious for several days. The distress of the people at the Association was, on account of the calamity, most poignant and undescribable. Most of the leading ministers and elders visited him during the Association, in a feeling and sympathizing manner. The greatest affection was manifested towards him on the occasion as a brother dearly beloved. Take him all in all, we shall never, see his like again.

Through the mercy of God, Elias gradually recovered and was able to use his pen slowly. Two months after the accident he comments on his state of health in a letter to a Liverpool friend:

Fron 29 August 1832

I have often wished I was able to write a few lines to you. However, I am now mending; my arms are much better; but still the sinews are aching, and the hand is trembling and tired in writing even a line! My body gains strength, and my head gradually improves.

I know not what our gracious Lord intends doing with me hereafter. It is a wonderful thing that my life was spared; and it is equally astonishing that I am thus restored. 'Here I am, let him do with me, as seemeth him good. He has done all things well unto me; in faithfulness hath he afflicted me; and in measure hath he debated with me' (*Psalm* 119.75; *Isaiah* 27.8). I was enabled to learn many things in this affliction. I experienced the Lord in his mercy, when I was unable to attend a place of worship, as a little sanctuary. I have been enabled to read the Scriptures and to pray as a poor sinner; and had great pleasure therein. My hand is unable to write more.

Elias was at length so far recovered as to be able to preach in North Wales, his mind and faculties apparently as strong as ever. In 1833 under God's blessing, he resumed the work of the ministry, and met with his former measure of success. However, he was often afterwards troubled with a nervous complaint, and liability to giddiness in his head. He was never free altogether after that from stiffness in his hand, which was a considerable impediment to his writing. It is wonderful, under this circumstance, that he wrote so much. But as he was so delicate in health, his indisposition would speedily return in cold weather. In order to invigorate his constitution, he would at times, take excursions to the mountains and hills of Caernarvonshire, and other places.

We are now approaching the end of Elias's afflictive years. It seems that the malady that terminated his life was a cold that fixed in his foot whilst he was preaching at Llannerch-y-medd Association in 1840. It was evident to him – for he knew the symptoms – that gangrene had set in, and that he was in the greatest danger. He exercised and manifested a proper spirit under these trying dispensations. He was at length finally confined to his room, to resume the sacred office no more! Thus he wrote in his autobiography: 'My time in this world is about to come to an end. I am nearly at the end of my journey. I am now, for many months, confined to my room, under a slight affliction (30 April 1841). It is not yet evident what is my Father's will. Is it to remove me from this world by means of this affliction, or will he prolong my life a little again? Let him do that which is good in his sight.'

Elias's active and heavenly mind was much directed now to the world above, his home and everlasting rest; he thought much of the glorious inhabitants, and his fellow-labourers, who were once here below in great tribulations like himself. He made a particular allusion to them in his autobiography. The following are his words:

There were at that time many celebrated men with the Methodists in Wales, taking the lead in the work; some of them were learned, gifted, and very laborious, and the Lord worked wonderfully by them. There were in South Wales many learned, godly, and very useful men, brought up in the ministry of the Established Church. Some of them continued in the ministry of the Church all their days, and serving the Methodists throughout Wales too; but the majority of them lost their situations. The most notable of them were the Reverends Mr [David] Jones of Llan-gan; Mr [David] Griffiths, Nevern; Mr Nathanael Rowland [son of Daniel Rowland]; Mr [John] Williams of Lledrod; Mr J[ohn] Williams of Pantycelyn [son of the hymnwriter]; Mr [John] Hughes of Abermeurig; Mr [Howel] Howels [of Tre-hill], &c. And there were others that served the Connexion occasionally, but very useful men. There were also in South Wales notable men, laborious, gifted, and very useful, not brought up in the Established Church; some of them gave themselves up entirely to the work of the Lord, itinerating throughout all Wales under many difficulties, and the Lord doing great things by them. They are too numerous to name them. They have all gone home – those who were renowned in the gospel field when I had the privilege of entering into the work forty-six years ago.

But I was more conversant with the work in North Wales during my life. There were very notable men taking the lead in the work when I was young. Although not many of them were learned, the Lord gave one very learned man to North Wales, the late Reverend Thomas

Charles of Bala, who was as a Prince of God in our midst. The late Reverend Thomas Jones of Denbigh was a learned man, laborious and very useful, although not ordained a minister of the Established Church. He and Mr Charles pulled together very peaceably under the yoke. Soon after this, the Reverend Simon Lloyd of Bala joined the Connexion; he was a very learned man, and wrote many books.

Although we had no very learned men in North Wales, apart from the three already named, we had eminent elders, who were considered revered leaders in the Connexion. Some of them were with the Connexion from the beginning, such as Mr John Evans of Bala, and Mr Robert Jones, Ty Bwlcyn – godly, wise, and sensible men. There were besides them some notable preachers, such as Mr [Evan] Richardson of Caernarvon (he was a learned man); Mr John Roberts of Llanllyfni; Mr Robert Roberts, of Clynnog (who was remarkable as to the authority and effects attending his ministry); and Mr John Jones of Edern. I have mentioned these persons because they were considered the leaders of the Connexion at that time. There were others in North Wales, very useful preachers who itinerated a great deal, and the Lord doing great things by them. They loved one another very much, and they were very humble at each other's feet.

Concerning the Quarterly Associations in North Wales, the cloud of God's glory was often upon them. The trumpet-blast of the King was heard among the assemblies. There were evident signs of God's gracious presence in the private meetings as well as in the public preaching. The Reverend T. Charles was a wise Moderator in these meetings – fatherly, very tender, yea, a Moderator set by God on us. None of us coveted his place, or wished to take his chair. He was at all times ready to place profitable things before the brethren, in points of doctrine and of discipline; he used to state them in a wise and proper order. He would encourage the brethren to speak their minds on the matters under consideration: he would assist the weak, and guide the disorderly. At the end of the discussion, he would sum everything up into a systematic order; and he would exhort the brethren to take everything home to their congregations. Oh what heavenly dew descended in these meetings!

The public ministry in those meetings was generally with great unction. Light, power, and heavenly authority accompanied the ministry, so that great crowds of people were sobered, the ungodly trembled, many sinners were converted, and the saints were delightfully feasted. Great sobriety and decorum were visible in the multitudes that came to hear. The spirit of the fair or market could not raise its head, nor did the young people dare to show their empty folly there. But alas! that great power is now lost! The attitude of the crowd has changed. 'My soul longs for the first-ripe fruit.'

In connection with this, we shall now add the few remaining lines in his autobiography, showing his mind and feelings at this critical time, when on his dying bed.

I have written a brief account of my life from infancy till now (sixty-seven years of age), of the Lord's goodness towards me, and a review of his work amongst the Calvinistic Methodists. I have written this in my sick room, not knowing but that I am on the plains of Moab, on the brink of Jordan. I wrote a few lines now and then, in sorrow and through difficulty, considering myself as writing every line in the presence of God, and writing perhaps that which will be read when I shall be quiet in the grave. I have nothing to say of myself, but of my sinfulness, vileness, and great misery; but I would be happy to speak of God's goodness, mercy, and grace towards me. 'This is the poor man that was raised out of the dust, and the needy man that was lifted out of the dunghill, and set with princes, even with the princes of his people'. If any good has been done by my imperfect labour, God in his grace has performed it. To him belongs the glory; I was as nothing. This shall be seen in the day when God will reveal all secrets. If God took me to be an instrument in his hand, to bring some sinner or sinners to Christ, this is an unspeakable privilege. It will be a joy to me, 'in the day of Christ, that I have not run in vain, neither laboured in vain'. But if I had succeeded in bringing thousands to the Methodists, without coming to Christ, it would be vain and worthless before the throne of Christ! The work should be burned, and the preacher sustain the loss.

The Methodists throughout all Wales knew the value of Elias, and duly appreciated him as an ambassador from heaven, yea, as one of the greatest gifts ever bestowed by God upon the Princi-pality. Members of this Connexion, at an Association occurring then in Montgomeryshire, determined to send a letter of con-dolence to Elias in his afflictive state; the following is a part of it:

Newtown 30 April 1841

We do with one accord salute you, dear brother, sympathizing with you in the most sincere and affectionate manner, in your present affliction. It would have afforded us the greatest pleasure to enjoy your presence amongst us here, as in the many years gone by: we feel cast down and sorrowful that we have been lately deprived of you in our meetings.

We feel obliged to acknowledge gratefully the grace of God which supported you in the ministry for nearly half a century. You have occupied a conspicuous station amongst us all those years, having kept yourself unspotted and your crown untarnished. Our hope and prayer are that the Lord of the harvest, to whom nothing is impossible, may prolong your days. – At the same time we would humbly commit the cause unto him, submitting to his holy will; for we believe you are in the hands of a Father that is infinitely good and wise. He is the Lord, he knows what is best, and he will do it. We are glad to understand, dear brother, that the truths you preached during your lifetime, administer consolation to you in your affliction. Receive this as a mark of our warmest affection and remembrance of you in affliction.

In this letter they, on the other hand, solicit Elias's prayers for them, thus:

Dear brother, we entreat your prayers for ourselves, that the God of Israel may abide with us. Our fathers prevailed with God in prayer, and were remarkable for spiritual gifts; we are no more than grasshoppers in comparison to them. But it is a consolation to us that the sword and arms they so skilfully used, are in our hands: may the Lord enable us to handle them.

A friend, calling on Elias, expressed a hope that the complaint in his foot would soon be removed. 'No', said he, 'it is death that is here at work.' Then his wife observed that such expressions disheartened her greatly. To which he replied, that 'the kindness of the Lord was very great towards them, in sending death to work in the foot, the most distant part from the seat of life; the union between us will be thus gradually dissolving, and I shall be slowly removed home.'

My friend the Rev H. Griffith, of Llandrygarn, Anglesey, who was in the habit of seeing Elias in his illness, favoured me with the following account of the happy state of his mind, a few days before he expired:

Bodlondeb 4 June 1841

The state of Elias's mind is very comfortable, and at times even ecstatic. One night when in great pain, he felt so happy, that he thought he was in heaven. But he does not like to say much on this head, lest he should appear to boast. His own expressions are: 'I am as happy as to the frame of my mind as a person can be under such pain as I suffer. There is *no* cloud intercepting between my soul and my God; those comforts I used to enjoy in the means of grace and in the ministry are still flowing freely into my soul: I think they are sometimes more strong and lively in their effects now than formerly.'

Elias seemed to be aware some months before his end, that his labour in the vineyard was about to terminate. He used to say that 'he did not receive from the Lord the communications for the ministry he used to have, but that he received greater comfort for himself as a sinner by reading the Bible and prayer, than he used to have before.'

Elias was confined to his chamber for almost three months. His illness, especially towards the end, was painful as well as lingering. He died peacefully at eleven o'clock on the evening of 8 June 1841, aged sixty-seven years and one month. The Rev H. Griffith, Llandrygarn, describes his funeral in the following words:

Bodlondeb 17 June 1841

Rev William Roberts, of Amlwch, preached an appropriate sermon the evening before the funeral at Llangefni chapel, to a very crowded congregation. His text was 2 *Kings* 2.11–14. He drew a fair comparison between our departed friend and the prophet Elijah, in reference to the ministry, life, and departure of each, and then brought forward several motives for encouragement under this afflictive dispensation.[1]

The following morning, 15th, we assembled at Fron by nine o'clock, to pay the last tribute of respect to the mortal remains of this most respected and highly gifted servant of God. When the coffin was brought down to the door, I read *Philippians* 1.18–24, and 27, and made a few remarks, and then concluded with a short prayer. Elias having in his life expressed a wish more than once of being interred near his most affectionate friend the Rev Richard Lloyd of Beaumaris, at Llan-faes; arrangements were accordingly made.

---

[1] Elijah is rendered *Elias* in the Welsh Bible, which imparted additional effect to the words in the 14th verse, 'Where is the Lord God of *Elias*?' The congregation was so absorbed in grief, that although they made efforts to sing, they were obliged to desist. Forsaken and disconsolate they 'hung', as it were, 'their harps upon the willows' and 'sat down and wept.' A beautiful, affecting tribute of Christian love!

Llan-faes churchyard is secluded and peaceful, a scene of natural romance and beauty, the site too of an ancient monastery of Franciscan friars, about a mile and a half from Beaumaris, and fourteen from Llangefni. The procession consisted of coaches, gigs, horsemen, footmen – an immense number of people. Along the road from Llangefni to Menai Bridge, the greatest marks of respect were paid. Between twelve and one o'clock, the procession made its appearance at Menai Bridge, where great numbers fell in with it. From thence to Beaumaris, crowds were continually falling in with the procession. By the time the cavalcade reached Beaumaris, the crowd was immense, and had the most solemn appearance. The procession was here a mile and a half in length, and considered to amount to 10,000 people!

It was truly gratifying to witness the great respect that was paid to departed worth. All the vessels in this port had their flags flying at midmast. As the immense concourse of people was passing through the main street of Beaumaris, the window blinds of all the houses were down, and all the shops were entirely closed, without distinction of grade, or difference either as to religion or politics. All, of every denomination, were anxious to testify their respect to the memory of this great man.

The procession proceeded onward through the town on its way to Llan-faes, the place of interment. On the Green, the choir of the Calvinistic Chapel, Bangor, drew up on either side of the road, singing a funeral hymn while the assemblage passed through. After reaching the Church, the services were solemnly read by the Rev H. Griffith, assisted by the resident minister. After the ceremony was over, the people returned to Beaumaris, where a funeral sermon was preached at the Calvinistic Methodist Chapel by the Rev John Foulkes, of Abergele, from *Hebrews* 13.7, the Rev D. Roberts, of Bangor, having commenced the service by reading and prayer.

It would be a most difficult task to assign with anything like precision the number of persons in the procession, as thousands were continually dropping out, and fresh groups falling in at every cross road and hamlet by which it passed. It was a most interesting spectacle to witness numbers of aged females appearing at different points of the route, whose tears plainly indicated the great pleasure and benefit they often had received under the eloquent and powerful preaching of Elias.

The following are observations of the Rev Thomas Phillips, agent of the Bible Society, made on the departure of Elias, as he visited his dwelling and other places, in the autumn of 1841. 'In my last journey, I saw the *place* where the good and great man Elias was born, the *chapel* where he preached his first sermon, and the *house* where he drew his last breath. The sight of these places, especially of the latter, gave rise to a train of reflections, most salutary in their effects at the time, and calculated under the divine blessing to produce an abiding impression on the mind. I felt conscious of unusual solemnity in approaching the late dwelling of our departed friend! Recollections of former visits, with all their circumstances of pleasure and profit, crowded upon my mind – his person, manner, piety, sermons, speeches, and especially the awful solemn ordination charge which I received from his eloquent lips, were now *present*; – not indeed as realities, but reminiscences. The sombre appearance of everything within and without – leafless trees, fading flowers, darkened windows, and mourning habiliments; all these "outward and visible signs", while they deepened the feeling of solemnity already awakened, furnished sad evidence that a great change had indeed taken place. Entering *Fron* under these circumstances, was like approaching a body deprived of its vital animating principle. It was the same house, but the chief object of attraction had disappeared! He is dead! "He shall return no more to his house, neither shall his place know him any more!" '

The following is the Epitaph that is placed over Elias's remains; it was written by the Rev T. Phillips, at the request of Mrs Elias:

IN THIS SACRED SPOT
are deposited, at his own request,
the remains of

THE REVEREND JOHN ELIAS

late of Llangefni in this county,
who, during the long period of forty-seven years,
laboured with singular diligence and success,
as a minister of the Gospel,
in connection with the Calvinistic Methodists.
He was a Christian of the highest order,
an 'Israelite indeed in whom was no guile.'
In the several relations of life,
he was upright, friendly, and affectionate.
Endowed with extraordinary graces and gifts,
he became, among his own countrymen,
the most attractive preacher of his day.
Institutions aiming at the promotion of religious
or charitable objects,
found in him a powerful advocate.
But his highest distinction was
the holy influence diffused by his character and spirit,
wherever he came.
Zealous for truth in doctrine, and purity in life,
he fought 'the good fight of faith,'
seeking not his own honour, but the good of souls,
and resting all his hope on the cross of Christ;
in this hope
he finally triumphed over death,
and slept in Jesus,
on the eighth day of June, 1841;
in the sixty-eighth year of his age.

Letters

To Mrs Elizabeth Elias – his first wife

HOLYWELL AND LIVERPOOL ASSOCIATIONS –
DEATH OF PERCEVAL – A RIGHT SPIRIT

Liverpool 16 June 1812

It is with much pleasure I send you a few lines, to inform you that, through the tender mercy of God, I arrived here last night well and comfortable. I had a prosperous and delightful journey, nothing of an unpleasant nature occurring. I was pretty comfortable also as to spiritual things, and the frame of my mind; I had great support in the work notwithstanding my unworthiness. I have a new and additional cause to say that the Lord is good and gracious; yea, I know by experience that he is good to the ungrateful and evil.

We had comfortable opportunities in preaching at Holywell during the Association; though there were but few weak instruments, yet the Lord was gracious to us for the sake of his great name. Mr Charles did not come there; and Mr T. Jones, of Denbigh, could not preach in the street on account of his infirmity: consequently, John Roberts and myself were obliged to preach three times, each twice in the street, and once in the chapel. The people appeared more sober and serious than on any former opportunities. We arrived here yesterday; and had a meeting at Pall Mall Chapel in the evening; William Jones of Llanrwst, and myself, preached to an immense congregation as usual, there was no diminution in the attendance, notwithstanding the difficulty of the times. We expect Mr Charles here on Monday; Wm Roberts, of Amlwch, is not come yet. However if we should be favoured with the Lord's gracious presence, it will be well whoever the instruments may be: we have *his* promise – and he abideth *faithful*.

It is likely you have seen by this time the account of the horrible murder of the Honourable Mr Perceval, the Prime Minister,[1] the most shocking news I ever heard. Every Christian should be distressed at such a deed. There is a loud call from God to us in this as well as other painful circumstances these days. Oh! for wisdom to hear and consider the rod, and who appointed it. This town and the adjacent country are, through the mercy of God, very quiet at present; and the disturbance at Manchester and the neighbourhood has ceased. The Lord may in his great goodness restore peace to this kingdom again, for the sake of his great name.

My dear, I hope that your spirit is under the discipline and protection of the Lord, that your soul is supported with calmness, notwithstanding all your trials and troubles, and that you are always enabled to cast all your cares upon him that careth for you, and to taste the peace that cometh by faith, and abundantly enjoy the influence and comfort of a meek and quiet spirit, which is in the sight of God of great price. Meekness, humility, and content-ment are material parts of Christ's image. And to be like him is our greatest privilege and happiness. Don't be cast down; these inestimable excellencies are to be obtained freely from God, being treasured up in Christ for such poor creatures as we are. I have great pleasure in pleading for you and the dear children before the throne of grace, and am much enabled to give myself and you, and all my concerns *entirely*, into the Lord's hands. He has been merciful to us, and I don't think that he will leave us for his great name's sake, though we deserve being forsaken for ever. The Lord is very pitiful and of tender mercy; and we are experimentally acquainted with him that said, 'I will never leave thee nor forsake thee.' This promise is a *sufficient* inheritance for me and my family, as long as I live. Oh! that we were enabled to live, without wandering, on this delightful inheritance. Losing sight of God and his promise is a great cause of our spiritual poverty.

---

[1] On the 11 May 1812 Spencer Perceval, Prime Minister from 1809, was shot in the lobby of the House of Commons by a man who bore a private grudge against him. Perceval was a strong Protestant.

Cardigan 1814

I avail myself of an opportunity of sending you a few lines, to testify of the goodness of God towards me, preserving me in my journey, affording me good health, and giving success. I have no time to write much, and the few moments I have, I snatch by stealth as it were. I know you will be glad even of a few lines. We want room for the hearers, they are so very numerous. Last night we were favoured with the market-house at Newcastle,[1] as the chapel is too small. I was obliged this evening to preach in the window of a large chapel, which was quite full: and there were as many at least standing outside. Not only are the congregations very large, but the Lord in mercy blesses the Word preached to them, crowning the opportunities with his gracious presence. An unspeakable privilege for such an insignificant thing!

Llanfair Caereinion[2]

The Lord has been very gracious to us, in this cold weather. The congregations are very large everywhere. The Lord, to my great surprise, does not leave us. I preached in a field adjoining this place, and we were favoured with the Divine presence.

To his daughter, Phœbe Elias

I. MAY MEETINGS

London 16 May 1819

There is a great stir in this large city, these weeks, but not a tumultuous, rebellious stir, not any insurrection, persecution, or blood shedding, no; it is a religious and holy commotion, it is about the dissemination of the Word of God, and the propagation of the Gospel of Christ through the *whole* world.

Last Sabbath day I preached a missionary sermon, in the Welsh

---

[1] Newcastle Emlyn, nine miles East of Cardigan.
[2] Eight miles west of Welshpool, Montgomeryshire.

language, in Albion Chapel, which belongs to the Scotch Church. The chapel was full of Welsh people, and we collected £30 9s for the London Missionary Society; a large collection from the poor Welsh.

I was last Tuesday at the annual meeting of the Church Missionary Society, in Freemasons' Hall. The place was crowded to an excess. There were a great many very respectable ladies; the place was so full, that many of them almost fainted away. But nevertheless, they were so anxious to hear the good news about the success of the Gospel in foreign parts, that they stopped there all the time, though the meeting lasted many hours. I sat there six hours; and I was very much delighted indeed, seeing so many of the clergy so zealous in that good cause. Lord Gambier[1] was in the chair.

Yesterday, I was at the glorious anniversary of the British and Foreign Bible Society. We had a very full, interesting, and delightful meeting. A very respectable gentleman came from Paris to the Bible Society meeting, and presented the New Testament in the Turkish language, into which he had translated it. He could not address the meeting in English: but he had a letter from the society, which the Rev D. Wilson[2] read in English, which together with the presentation of the New Testament in the Turkish language, had a wonderful effect on the meeting. I could not help shedding tears of joy, in viewing the heavenly gift prepared for the dark and deluded Turkish nation, by a gentleman of a people that were lately our enemies!!! Several young noblemen, some of them about the age of thy brother, spoke wonderfully on the occasion. Oh, how pleasant the sight, to see young men of rank, wealth, and talents, consecrating themselves and their ability, in the bloom of youth, to the best of causes! A minister from Ireland, one of the Wesleyan Connexion, presented £1500, being one-half of a legacy bequeathed by a lady to the British and Foreign Bible Society. The female character rises to a very high degree by their liberality and co-operation with the Bible Society. There are at present many hundreds of young ladies of great

[1] Baron (James) Gambier of naval fame.
[2] A London Anglican minister, afterwards Bishop of Calcutta.

respectability, education, and fortune, going from house to house among the poor, to enquire whether they have Bibles in their cottages, and to solicit their penny-a-week subscription to the Bible Society. They look upon their work as a great honour and privilege, and so it is; to do good, to do something for the Lord, and for the benefit of our fellow-creatures, is our duty and our honour. Trusting in Christ alone for justification, forgiveness, acceptance with God, and eternal salvation; and living in this evil world by the rule of God's Word to the glory of his name, is the only way to obtain happiness and honour.

My dear daughter, I often pray to the God of all grace that he may enable thee to trust in Christ alone for salvation, and that he may keep thee from all temptations, from the world, the flesh, and the devil, and keep thee in his house all the days of thy life, for thy benefit and his glory. Oh! take the Word of God always for thy rule, in all things and at all times; a rule for thy passions, temper, and conduct. This is the way to honour, happiness and glory. Beware of a haughty and fretful temper. Study to be of a humble, mild, kind, modest, and loving disposition; the ornament of a meek and quiet spirit, which in the sight of God, is of a great price. It is a better ornament than all the jewels and costly apparel in the world. It is a Court fashion, and after this manner all the nobility of the highest Court are adorned themselves. And the Prince himself wore this noble garment. It is to be had *gratis*, without money. It is the King's gift. And there is a messenger sent from the Court to teach us how to wear it.

My dear Phœbe, do all in thy power to honour and please thy mother; that is your duty, and will be your honour and happiness; you shall be happy in her happiness. The Lord will reward them that obey and honour their parents. He hath promised, and he is faithful to fulfil his promises. I feel many anxious cares for thee and thy brother. I pray that God would take possession of your hearts now, in the days of youth, and keep you from the snares and temptations that destroy thousands of your age. I am sometimes satisfied he will hear me.

2. ON TEMPORAL AND SPIRITUAL PRESERVATION – ATTENDING THE LORD'S TABLE

London 22 May 1821

It affordeth me much pleasure to find, that thou dost acknowledge the goodness of the Lord towards thee, and confess thy rebellion against him. The Lord's temporal mercies have been very great towards thee, especially in preserving thy life when attacked by various diseases and great debility. I hope this divine mercy manifested so remarkably for thy temporal life was with a view to thy eternal salvation. The goodness of the Lord was truly remarkable in preserving thee from many foolish and insidious paths of the flesh, into which many youths are decoyed, and ruined in them! Oh what a mercy it is that thou hast been preserved from the ways of the destroyer. I have no doubt but that God will reward thee in this world; for it is said, that 'in keeping his commandments there is great reward.' The consideration of being kept steady and serious when young will afford thee consolation and cause of thankfulness when old, if spared so long, and render even thy dying bed easier and more comfortable. I know not how to praise the Lord sufficiently for preserving thee. I think that if thou hadst trod the paths of the youths in our country, it would have brought me to the grave. I humbly hope that he that hath hitherto preserved thee from deceitful paths and all evils will do so to the end. He is able and willing, trust wholly in him: avoid giddy acquaintance: 'follow righteousness with those that call on the Lord.'

I am very glad to find that thou hast great pleasure in hearing sermons, and attending the *private Society*, considering it a privilege to be there, praying to the Lord to keep thee there all the days of thy life. I sincerely trust he will grant that favour. But hast thou not a desire to devote thyself to the Lord for ever, and subscribing *with thy hand* unto the Lord, saying, 'I am the Lord's'? *Isaiah* 44.3–5. And art thou not ready to say, as the Hebrew servant, putting his ear to the door of his master, 'I love my master, I love his work and family, I will abide here for ever?' And art thou not desirous, my dear Phœbe, to take hold of the covenant thyself, by receiving the Lord's supper, the seal of the covenant? Do you feel no desire to commemorate the death of our Lord Jesus Christ on the cross for poor sinners?

3. SIGN OF GRACE – ATTENDANCE ON THE MINISTRY

Llandeilo Fawr 10 May 1822

I am not sorry to hear thee, dear Phœbe, also complaining of the hardness of thy heart; it is a mercy we feel our obduracy, and a sign that the Lord begins removing it away. Oh continue looking to him in the means of grace, watching daily at his gates, waiting at the posts of his doors (*Proverbs* 8.34)! Oh surrender thyself to the Lord! he will receive thee. It would afford me great pleasure, my dear child, to see thee disposed and enabled to draw near the Lord's table, publicly devoting thyself to him and his service all the days of thy life; I hope thou shalt be in the house of the Lord for ever.

You cannot form an idea of the crowds that attend the ministry everywhere; yea, many of the higher ranks, and of the clergy also. I had a pleasant journey through Pembrokeshire. Mrs Bowen of Llwyn-gwair, and her son, were present at many of the opportunities. I slept on Saturday night at the house of a magistrate, and dined the next day with two justices of the peace. I preached twice on a Sunday in a waggon, in a field near Carmarthen. I have indeed greater need of receiving abundance of blessings from above than any individual. I earnestly entreat all my brethren to pray for me.

4. TEMPTATIONS

London 15 April 1823

Thou complainest in thy letter, my dear Phœbe, of Satan's temptations: it is no wonder he harasses thee; he cannot be quiet, he is always sinning; and he has great enmity towards those that seek to follow Christ. I am very glad thou art acquainted with his devices and temptations, and perceivest his nets. It is a vain thing to spread a net before every winged fowl. If it should be thrown in the sight of the bird, he will take to his wings and fly away. So if the Christian should see Satan's nets, he will take the wing of faith, and fly to Christ for protection and strength. That is the time of greatest danger, when Satan is able to hide his nets, so that the soul is not able to see them. He puts some false colours on them, shewing them to be fair, beautiful, and innocent. Beware of them; and go on thy knees, under all temptations, oppositions of all enemies, and trials; go to the throne of grace, and to the Bible, for weapons: a shield may be obtained, the shield of faith. Oh take it, and buckle it on; with this thou canst 'quench the fiery darts of the evil one.' Be strong in the Lord; cast thy burden upon him; yea, give thyself to him, he will preserve thee either from temptations or in them.

Spread all these peculiar cases of temptation, oppression, and woe, before the Lord in prayer, as Hezekiah did those blasphemous letters that came from Sennacherib; he will hear and also deliver thee. Some temptations are of a peculiar nature, and it is better to make them known to some friends, but not to all, for all are not able to sympathize with us; and all cannot keep a secret and hide the sins of each other. If thou shouldest reveal thy complaints to man, seek for the most spiritual, godly, and wise. And as to thy general complaints and circumstances, and thy experience, however dark and low – mention them to the church. Thou mayest by that means have great support, strength, and succour. Thou mayest relate much to thy mother: and thy father would be glad to go under thy burden, and to give every advice and direction in his power. Thou mayest be sure he will keep the communications, and will take thy complaints before the throne of grace.

I am sorry thy mother is poorly and coughing; request her to take *calomel pills* in the morning. She must not go to the shop that day. She will afterwards take Griffin's Tincture Asthmatica.

'I intend going this evening,' says Elias in another letter to his daughter, 'to hear the clergyman that was a missionary in the

Mediterranean, Egypt, and the land of Canaan, the Rev Mr
Jowett.' May the Lord grant his blessing upon the Word! I was last
week in two excellent royal yachts, made for George III and
George IV. I never saw such excellent and beautiful things before.
The chambers within were all made of mahogany, and beautified
with gold; the chairs were covered with crimson silk; I also saw
their beds, and was by their writing desks, where they used to
write. I saw what this world can give to men. I returned from
thence, saying, 'Vanity of vanities. all is vanity.' I hope thou con-
tinuest faithful with the Sunday school at Bethesda, and that thou
enjoyest the means of grace; the great King has engaged to be in
his walks. The Lord will reward thee for thy kindness to thy
mother.

To Phœbe and John, his children, after the death of his first wife[1]

1. THE WORD OF GOD THE ONLY TRUE DIRECTORY FOR LIFE AND HAPPINESS

London 28 April 1829

My beloved children – There is no greater worldly joy to me than
that you should be comfortable and happy. I hope you are so; and
that you endeavour to render each other comfortable by aiding
one another, at least bearing and forbearing with each other. Let
your eye be on the Word of God as your rule in all things, accepting no other to think, aim, speak, or act by. Pray for the Spirit of
God to enlighten you, and teach you to understand the Word of
God, and enable you to walk by it. Never judge anything innocent,
in temper or in conduct, of which the Word of God disapproves.
Every duty is clearly pointed out in the Bible, and every sin is

---

[1] As his children were of age, and capable of managing the shop, he gave it up
to them after the death of his first wife. She died on 2 April 1829.

fully specified in the same book. If you will humbly and diligently attend to the holy Scriptures, looking by faith to Jesus, you shall be rectified and delivered from evil. Thus saith the Psalmist, 'Wherewith shall a young man cleanse his way? By taking heed thereto according to thy word.' *Psalm* 119.9. Indeed the only sure means for attaining holiness, is the rule of God's Word – the way of pleasantness, and the path of peace. And they that walk according to this rule, 'Peace be upon them, and upon the Israel of God.' Now I must conclude, as much business of a religious nature calls me. I received yesterday information of the departure of three preachers, R. Jones, of Ty Bwlcyn, John Humphreys, and Peter Roberts. 'The righteous are taken away and does any one lay it to heart?'

2. ELIAS'S INTENDED SECOND MARRIAGE[1]

Liverpool 24 December 1829

I received, my dear children, your letter. I am much gratified and affected by your kindness. I intended saying all to you on that delicate subject sometime ago. My thoughts were never more sober and serious than in this affair; and never was I more in the fear of God. I shall not hurt you in anything: indeed I should prefer going to poverty myself, rather than doing such a base thing. I shall return home soon, as I said, and settle and secure everything for you, before I change my situation in life. The alteration will not make any change in my relationship to you; it will not cool my affections towards you, nor lessen my care for you. I experience great kindness from friends and others here. I have scarcely an hour's time for anything, having to preach every night, and being engaged tomorrow all day in religious exercises, preaching in the morning, administering the Lord's supper in the afternoon, and preaching again in the evening. I go on Monday to preach at Wrexham.

[1] To Lady Bulkeley, the widow of Sir John Bulkeley. See p. 162.

To his daughter Phœbe after her marriage –
Mrs Williams

1. INSTRUCTIONS TO HER IN HER NEW SITUATION

Fron 15 March 1831

I received your kind letter, which affords me much pleasure in informing me of your arrival at Machynlleth in good health, and that you are comfortable. Your welfare, temporal and eternal, is as near my heart as ever. All true happiness, as you know, proceeds from the favour and pleasure of the Lord; there is no real felicity, but such as flows from peace and communion with him. Now, I hope as you are entering upon a new state of life, and settling in a strange neighbourhood, that an ardent desire to obtain daily peace with God through faith in Christ, and to enjoy much communion with him, will be deeply rooted in your mind, and be a leading object in your thoughts. Pray much to be favoured with his guidance, and his help, to enable you to live to his glory in all things; and if so, you shall be truly happy. Pray much that you may be taught of God, to live becomingly as a *wife*, a *neighbour*, and a *member* of a Christian church.

1: *As a Wife*

Let us pray that you may be like the holy women of old; a woman possessing godliness, and all her behaviour becoming such a profession; decent, chaste, a keeper at home, good, that the Word of God be not blasphemed. It is necessary to a becoming deportment as a wife that you should live godly, discreetly, and be of a meek temper.

1 To live godly – Have your eyes on the Lord in all your ways, and strive to walk in all well pleasing before him: be frequent at the throne of grace, not trusting to your own understanding, nor relying on your own strength, but in the grace that is in Christ Jesus. A godly life sweetens the marriage state, and is a great ornament to this holy condition. 'Godliness is profitable for all things.' It is the greatest ornament of a woman.

2 Live discreetly – A wife cannot conduct herself as such in an estim-
able manner without discretion. Many events take place in a family
which render discretion in a wife towards her husband and family
absolutely necessary for their mutual comfort. Abigail's discretion
was of greater value to Nabal than all his wealth. It is possible to ward
off many evils, troubles, and sorrows, by discretion, and in the same
way to increase and multiply family comforts.

3 Live meekly – 'A meek and quiet spirit in the sight of God is of great
price.' It is valuable also in a family and neighbourhood, and comely
in the sight of men. It is a source of much happiness in the marriage
state. It strengthens the knot which love has tied, and confirms the
union which fellowship and friendly intercourse have formed, and
adds sweetness to the marriage relation, and to the communion
connected with it; it renders cares and troubles easier to be borne. A
meek disposition is considered as peculiarly congenial with the
character of the sex. The want of it strips a female of much of her
comeliness. The power of godliness in the soul nourishes this amiable
disposition. These things confer honour on the married woman; and
give a right to call her godly, holy, and a virtuous woman; a woman
that is an ornament to religion, a crown to her husband, a source of
comfort to her family, and a pattern to her neighbours. Let 'the wife
see that she reverences her husband', by obedience and submission
as far as is agreeable to the Word of God.

II: *As a neighbour*

In order to live becomingly and exemplarily as a neighbour, it is
necessary to be humble, to abstain from pride – a proud heart,
proud eyes, and every proud demeanour. Close your ears against
what others may say of you; and bridle your tongue from speaking
disrespectfully or contemptuously of any. Beware of meddling
with other people's matters and beware of setting your mind on
high things; condescend to men of low degree. Be kind to all,
merciful and meek; not despising or condemning any, having a
clearer perception of your own defects than of the faults of others.[1]

---

[1] Elias thus speaks, on the same subject, in another letter, 'I always think it
unprofitable and unbecoming in a wife to go into her neighbour's house without
sufficient reason; spending time in what they call visits in Anglesey, and parties
among the respectable people, is very trifling and worthless. It is but seldom that
such meetings are conducted in a religious manner. You may enjoy a few bosom
friends; but let your chief delight be always in the means of grace, and in your

III: *As a member of a Christian church*

Strive to act without giving offence to Jews or Gentiles, or to the Church of God. Be humble, watchful, and peaceable, and kindly affectioned to all the brotherhood, endeavouring to follow the Lamb in all things. See that the whole of your deportment be to the honour of the Gospel, walking in wisdom towards those that are without, kind and condescending towards every brother and sister, even the poorest in the congregation. Take delight in the conversation of the elder women, those that are most remarkable for their grace, deepest in experience, highest in godliness. Endeavour to make thy home in the church at Machynlleth, and beware of finding fault if all things should not be conducted in the same way there as at Bethesda. Endeavour, as you have been removed there in the course of providence, to reconcile yourself to the change, otherwise your spirit may suffer much injury. Remember me kindly to your husband; my wife desires to be kindly remembered to you both.

2. REVIVAL OF RELIGION

Fron 10 February 1832

The news I have to communicate now is delightful and heart-cheering, especially in these evil and perilous times, and when so much bad news comes from every part of the world. I am very happy to inform you that there is a very great revival at Nebo, near Amlwch; more than fifty have been already added to the church there, in a short time. The most ungodly in the neighbourhood have been alarmed and soberised. The pillars of the kingdom of Satan have been thrown down and shattered, not by the pestilence, but through the Gospel. Now, instead of the laughter and

---

own home. There is a promise that the Lord 'will bless the habitation of the just.' And it is said, that the voice of rejoicing and salvation is in the tabernacle of the righteous. Take care that you live together in harmony, peace and holiness, that your prayers may not be hindered. *Proverbs* 3.33; *Psalms* 112; 118.15; 1 *Corinthians* 11. 3.'

idle talk in the corners of the chapel, the sighing of the penitent, the groans of the convinced, are heard; yea, most earnest prayers and hearty thanksgivings ascend to heaven. O! most delightful change. O! may it enhance and spread throughout all the Principality. The glorious work of grace in converting sinners is going on in other places; souls were added to the church at Parc, Gors-lwyd and Pen-gorffwysfa,[1] and many were received to the society at Bethesda, and some at Llanfechell. Great rejoicing took place one night at W. Parry's premises at Llanfechell, when Mr W. Roberts of Llannerch-y-medd, was preaching there: W. Morris and Ellen, formerly of the old shop, as well as others, entered[2] the church. Very powerful revivals are carried on in several parts of Cærnarvonshire, such as Llanystumdwy, Brynengan, and other places! It will be a wonderful thing if Wales should be favoured with such gracious operations as these, instead of the awful judgments that afflict many countries these days!

Oh may we long more earnestly and ardently for the gracious visitations of the Lord to our country and neighbourhoods, but especially to our own souls. I hope, my dear Phœbe, that you my dear child, are not destitute of these delightful visits of heaven these days. May the Lord *speak* to your precious soul as you read his holy Word, and as you hear the preaching of the Gospel; and may you draw near to him as a Father, through the blood of Christ; yea, may you come boldly to the throne of grace, to receive grace and mercy to help you in the time of need: *help in need* as wanted, according to circumstances and necessities, and *in time*, that is quite enough; no more is required. It is most profitable to take every trial and burden unto the Lord, to set before him all your complaints, and to cast all your care upon him, for he careth in a very kind and tender manner for us. We may safely entrust him with the concerns of our bodies and souls, our temporal and eternal interests. He is very kind and pitiful, and ready to hear different cases of distress; able to bear all our burdens, to relieve all our wants, and wise to lead us through the intricate wilderness, and guide us safely to the end of the journey.

[1] These places are all in the extreme north of Anglesey.
[2] Joined.

3. AFFLICTIONS SANCTIFIED

Fron 8 February 1833

Every storm that drives us nearer to God, is good and profitable. But worldly prosperity and ease are of great injury to the mind, if we should become estranged thereby from our God. We shall, relying and depending on Christ as poor sinners, have *strength* to fulfil every duty, to bear every cross, to endure every affliction, and to be thankful for it. I shall be glad to know that you have received great *benefit* from all troubles, that you have grace to glorify God in them, and that you are purified in the furnace of affliction. The time of trouble is but short. Our greatest concerns ought to be for grace to live godly in the world: we shall be called out of it very soon.

4. SUPPORT UNDER AFFLICTION

Fron 8 August 1834

I am glad that you are now in a more comfortable situation.[1] I rejoice that you are enabled to look up to the great *Governor* of the world; he is good and wise; he will not forsake those that trust in him. His dominion is over all and every event. There is nothing difficult for him to perform. I am moreover glad that you have pleasure in reading the Bible. It is the tree that sweetens, under God's blessing, the bitter waters of Marah. The consolation had in the Scriptures, is far superior to any other; there is a well of joy that never fails like others. Strive to look up to Christ by perusing the Bible, in hearing sermons, and in prayer; and run, as the chief of sinners, to him.

5. PHŒBE AS A WELSH TEACHER

Fron 8 August 1835

I am glad you have been with Lady Emma;[2] she is a very pious

---

[1] His daughter had removed to London.
[2] She had accepted the situation of a Welsh teacher to the daughter of Lady Emma Pennant.

lady; but she is afflicted now: I hope if you should continue going
thither, that you will have much wisdom to conduct yourself
with humility and due respect towards her and the young family.
If Lady Emma should be disposed to converse with you on
religious subjects, let her have the precedence always; you may
say a word now and then with great reverence and godly fear. If
you should continue to attend her, you may, by degrees, say a
little more, in case she gives encouragement. Beware of saying
any thing that has a tendency to extol party; but may it be your
aim to *exalt* Christ.

6. DEPARTURE OF FRIENDS BY DEATH

Fron 30 April 1836

Many of my old friends have been removed this year out of the
world. Mrs Hughes of Bangor, Mr Roberts (Tanner), Mr G.
Owen, of Holyhead; and Mrs Griffiths of Penybont, Llangefni.
There were good evidences in their deaths as well as lives, that
their religion was sound, and that consequently death is gain. It
is *most delightful* to be ready to depart, our affections being set
upon things above, and our conversation in heaven. What a happy
frame of mind! Thus we shall go through the world more comfortably. Being enabled to live more godly, following Christ more
closely, and aiming more at the glory of God in all things, is most
necessary and valuable, deserving our chief attention and labour.

I have not much to say of the success of religion in this country.
The experiences of Christians are rather low and poor, and the
churches are lethargic and dead! Yet there is nothing outwardly
that is uncomfortable and reproachful: nay, there is union and
brotherhood among us.

I am glad to find that you continue going to Miss Pennant, and
that Lady Emma Pennant gets better. I think she may be called,
as John named some one in his time, 'the elect lady.'

If you should see J. Jones, the bookseller, tell him that I am
disappointed today, as I have been many Saturdays before, in
not receiving the 'Record' newspaper. It is a greater disappoint-

ment on a Saturday than any other day, as I want to see it before
I go from home on my journey to preach.

7. ON THE BIRTH OF A CHILD

18 November 1836

I am very thankful to the Lord for his goodness to you. Though
it is said that 'a woman, when she is delivered of a child, remem-
bereth no more the anguish, for joy that a man is born into the
world,' yet I hope you will not forget to praise the Lord for his
great mercy and wonderful kindness towards you in your late
critical and dangerous situation. May it be your chief aim from
henceforth to live to him that delivered you.

You are now in a new state of life, and fresh duties will attend
it: you are now a *mother*. It is a state of great importance and care,
and very weighty duties belong to it, but God can give ability to
fulfil them. The greatest of *all* its concerns is, that you should
bring up your offspring to the Lord: dedicate him often to him,
even now when he does not understand advice or instruction: and
if he should be spared to understand instruction, and to gain
knowledge, may you early train him up in the Lord's ways, and
teach him to praise him from his infancy. God has been praised
by 'young ones sucking the breast.' *Psalm* 8.2. May he be a
Nazarite from the beginning! Never give him spirits in meat,
drink, or physic. There are now thousands of Nazarites in Wales,
willingly, and to their advanced age. When I have an opportunity,
I will send a present to my grandchild.

8. ON THE BIRTH OF ANOTHER CHILD

Fron 11 August 1838

It is good news that you have again had a great deliverance. I hope
you perceive the hand of the Lord in the case, and that your soul
magnifies and blesses him for his great kindness. We are too apt to
forget the goodness of the Lord to us in difficulties, after deliver-

ance out of them, and to be ungrateful for great mercies. The best way to shew a thankful spirit for such remarkable deliverance is by living in a more holy manner to the Lord; and considering our life when it is spared, as his *peculiar* property, and ourselves under new and strong obligations to him. So you are after this deliverance. It is my earnest prayer that you may have *much* grace to train up the children to the Lord. They are, remember, to live for ever! It is not of so much signification by what means they may be removed hence. Short is life, near is death; but an endless eternity is before them! There is only one way to happiness, that is through Christ. Pray for them; and when they come to understand, tell them early of divine things. God has heard the prayers of mothers for their children before now.

To his son, John Elias

1. TEMPER AND CONDUCT

Llanfechell 1819

I am very glad that thy associates are respectable and Christian-like young men. It is wise, my son, to select young men of sense and piety for thy companions, and to prefer conversing with such, rather than with vain and foolish youths.

Take great care of thy *temper*; learn to be master of it now in thy youthful days; yea, if some laugh at thee, or despise thee, or offend thee, receive it mildly, and take care that thou dost not suffer thy self to be under the dominion of an angry, surly, and revengeful temper. It is not manly, much less Christian-like – nay, it is Satan-like. Therefore, my dear son, beware of this temper; it is a disgrace to the human nature; it is a great defect in the moral character of man, to say that he is of a rash, angry, and revengeful temper.

Be always ready to forgive every evil deed thy fellow-creatures may do against thee. An unforgiving temper is mean, it does not become such a creature as man. When we consider the aggravations and the number of our sins against God, the offences of our fellow-creatures against us will seem small, and unworthy of being re-collected; yea, they will appear light and trivial. Our God forgiveth graciously without any merit in the transgressor. To say that this way of forgiving is very *difficult*, and contrary to our natural temper, is very poor excuse; and a very great shame to us, it should appear that our nature is so contrary to that of God. It is a poor excuse to plead that we cannot act against our natural temper; there is strength enough to be had in Christ, and we need only to apply to him; he is ready to deliver us.

2. SATAN'S DEVICES AND TEMPTATIONS

Llanfechell 18 March 1820

He that is a great debtor and yet weak and poor, is happy to pay a little at a time; he shews good will even in that way. So I am circumstanced; I confess that I am much in your debt, having received two letters since I wrote last, and have no time to write now. I fully intended devoting last night for this purpose, but a letter came unexpectedly from the secretary of the London Missionary Society. Today is Saturday, when I am much engaged.

I hope you are coming to a more settled and happy state of mind, on Scripture grounds. You stand in need of knowing more of Satan's devices. He oftentimes appears as an angel of light, sometimes shewing the greatness and number of our sins; but his end is not to lead the offender to see the evil of them, to hate and forsake them, but to cause him to despair, and to hinder him from going to the Saviour! And if Satan can prevent the sinner from going to the fountain, he will rejoice, for he knows that nothing else can cleanse him. At another time, he endeavours to appear as if very anxious for Christ's glory; he tells the sinner that it is not in Christ's power to receive such a sinner, that his heart should be more broken, and his repentance more deep and evident. But this proceeds from no regard in Satan to Christ's glory, but from his cunning craftiness to prevent, if possible, the poor soul from going to Christ.

Sometimes he appears as if he hated hypocrisy, and greatly desired that the afflicted sinner should possess *real* religion, when in fact his aim is to induce the person to give up religion altogether, under the pretence of the fear of hypocrisy. At other times he assumes the appearance of one that cared much for the name of the Lord, and the honour of religion! 'You are,' suggests Satan to the fearful sinner, 'too weak to stand before such enemies; there is not strength enough in thee to withstand them long. You will some day fall into the hands of the enemy, and you shall be buried in one of the graves of lust. It is better for thee,' adds Satan, 'to stop to have more strength before you start for the warfare, otherwise you will be wounded and slain.'

The enemy of souls uses these and similar devices to prevent, if possible, the soul from going to Christ. Yea, he uses many of the scriptures for that end. If he ventured to say to Christ, 'It is written,' how much bolder we may expect he will confront us? But we want strength and help to say, 'It is written,' in return to Satan, to take the sword out of his hand to fight with him therewith. Whatever comes to our mind to dishearten and to hinder us, is not from the good Spirit. The Bible is altogether in favour of the sinner and gives him every encouragement to go on, as he is, to Christ. If any scripture should dishearten him, no doubt but that it is Satan's interpretation of it that causes that; Christ does 'not break the bruised reed.' The Father is represented as running to meet the prodigal son yet afar off. Grace is but a tender blade in its commencement; God is careful of it, and kind and tender towards it in all his dealings; he will keep it alive and make it grow.

Trouble not yourself much about the master of hypocrites, but rather be earnest for the truth, and say to thy accuser, 'I do not intend dissembling or being a hypocrite; the wise builder did not attend much to observe the marks of him that erected his house on the sand, but he was continually digging for the rock.' Do not continue much in fears of turning back, but rather press on through all difficulties. It is not well for soldiers on the field of battle to fear they shall be killed by every shot they hear; but rather to be faithful to their sovereign, using their arms, trying to overcome their enemies, and expecting victory.

It is not well for mariners to gaze in a dreadful storm, on the swelling billows, thinking that every wave they see will plunge them to the deep, and put an end to them. It is far better to be alive, as they are in such cases, and doing their duty with the helm and sails, and to lift up their hearts in prayer unto God, who governs the wind and the waves, and expect to arrive soon at the much-desired-for haven. As to the warfare of the Christian, none are destroyed that look unto their Captain, depend on him, and follow him. And there is no shipwreck in the Christian navigation, when they sail according to the directions of the Pilot; he not only can, but actually does, in great kindness, govern and rule the sea. You say that 'in your fears, you do not love Christ, but rather despair'; cry unto God then for help to love him better. Do not trouble your mind respecting the profession you have made of him, however poor, but rather pray that you may be faithful to him till death.

3. AFTER BEING AT THE LORD'S TABLE

Llanfechell 1 April 1820

We thank thee much for thy kindness in offering to come home to help us in the shop. That is the right way: 'Thy days shall be long in the land.' However a kind providence has so ordered it, for thy continuance at school to finish thy education: thy sister being able to give thy mother very good assistance at present.

I am glad that thou didst venture to approach the Lord's table, which is an unspeakable privilege. But I was sorry to find that thy mind continued to be so confused and distressed. Doubtless Satan had a hand in disturbing thee. The accuser of the brethren has no respect for the death of Christ; nor does he care how inconsiderate and heedless men come to that holy commemoration. Yea, thousands of Satan's children approach the Lord's table, while living at ease in the most open sins, but he never disquiets them. He is *enraged* at thee, and seeks to entangle and hinder thee. Do not attend to his suggestions; and do not regard thy frame and feelings so much. There is no particular kind of feeling indispensably necessary in order to become a worthy communicant. The disciples of Christ were not in so desirable a frame when they communicated in the night the holy supper was ordained. Alas, they slept before a few hours elapsed, and that while their Lord was praying and sweating great drops of blood! Indeed, were I to regard my feelings, I should be frequently obliged to rise up from the table and depart. Remember that it is not a small privilege to make a solemn and serious remembrance of Christ's death, even if thou wert obliged to attend at the table for years, previous to that desirable frame of mind. I have been there destitute of such feelings, yet can testify that it was good to be at the ordinance. Therefore, 'rest in the Lord and wait patiently for him: cast thy burdens on him, and thy thoughts shall be established.' *Psalm* 37.7; 55.22. *Proverbs* 16.3. Make no rash and hasty resolutions. Thou mayest say to thy accusers that thou wast doing thy duty in commemorating Christ's death, however hard thy heart might be.

4. PRAYING IN PUBLIC

18 October 1821

I cannot give a decided and full answer to your letter about engaging in prayer before ministers; for I am not certain what is the *mind* of the Lord in the business. Of this I am sure, that caution and deliberation are good in all such cases: it is the same caution as is required before one commences a building or engages in a battle. I do not think that it is better for you always to refuse going to prayer on such occasions, when you are requested. But I wish you would be slow and cautious, considering who asks you to engage in such an important concern, and what might be his motive in so doing. Many a one may request you thus to commence the public service from some carnal curiosity, to see what talents you may have.

Moreover, consider well and carefully what is your own motive in such a great undertaking, especially when you feel some desires and propensity for it. Be very careful that you have no end in view for such a holy work, but to glorify the Lord. Besides, be assured

that if you engage in such a public part of the service of God, it
will be necessary for you to be more *watchful* and circumspect in
all your conduct and conversation, such as becometh the Gospel of
Christ; the more public we may be engaged in his service, the
greater will be the dishonour we shall bring upon his cause if we
should be inconsistent. If any one takes the place and work of an
elder, he should have the spirit and conduct of such a person.

You should watch against inconsiderate, hasty dispositions and
tempers, and against an unsteady fluctuating mind, and discon-
tentment with your situation in life. And you should be particularly
guarded that you be not entangled with youthful lusts, and that
you be not too anxious and forward, and hasty in thinking to enter
upon a new state. It would be proper to make that a subject of
prayer before God in private for a whole twelve month, before
you say much of it to any individual: that plan was very useful to
me. I went even for a year before the throne of grace in that respect,
before I opened my mouth to any person about it.

It would afford me great pleasure to see you increasing in your
talents, and becoming more useful in the vineyard of God, and
going on from one situation to another in it. But I should be glad,
at the same time, to see you more deliberate, casting the account
previously; it is most desirable that your mind should become
more steady and quiet, and more full of evangelical *graces*. All
these things are to be had by applying to God. Think of these
things, and the Lord give you a good understanding.

5. THE ROMAN CATHOLIC QUESTION

London 26 April 1825

The Lord kindly continues his support to me; and the Word is
attended with some effect. Two females entered the society this
week; and there is some stir in the church also; the prayer-
meetings are multiplying.

You have seen in the newspaper that there is a great probability
that the Papists will gain their point! There are twenty-seven

more votes this time in favour of the second reading of the Bill![1]
But who knows from whence deliverance may yet come; it is not
even now too late with God. Israel were delivered though the day
of their destruction was appointed, and the letters and powers for
that end were sealed with the king's seal! And Mordecai was
saved, notwithstanding the gallows were made ready for him.
Let us confide in our Lord for ever!

The Duke of York made a remarkable speech yesterday evening,
in the House of Lords, against the Papists. I was last night in the
House of Commons till near midnight, yet they had not finished
when I left: there was a great debate on the Roman Catholic
question. Some want all the poor ignorant Papists to have the
power of voting for a member of parliament. The greatest zeal I
ever witnessed, was manifested on both sides of the house: I had
some grounds to hope they shall yet be confounded. Those on the
side of the Catholics were unable to argue together on the subject.
Brougham[2] went on with such a zeal, and became so warm and
passionate that the Speaker was obliged to desire him twice to
desist; and *Plunket*,[3] one of the greatest orators in favour of the
Papists, told Brougham that there was no sense in his speech, that
he had been excited and confused by too much zeal, and that he
did more harm than good to the cause, by trying to plead for it.
There was such vehemence and excitement in the house, sometimes this side, and sometimes that, that it was fearful to be there.

I was today in a very different place, in a church hearing *Mc
Neile*, a clergyman from Ireland; it was delightful: he preached a
very excellent sermon on *Isaiah* 59.19. It was a sermon for the
Hibernian Society, and it was suitable for the circumstances of
the times. He said some remarkable things of Satan, the great
enemy, raising up and employing instruments against the Church
of God ever since the fall of man – that the Papists have been his
chief agents for a long time. Then he dwelt on their false religion,
their deceitfulness, and their wrath in Ireland, especially their *anger*

[1] A Catholic Relief Bill introduced by Sir Francis Burdett, MP. for Westminster.
[2] Henry Brougham, famous Whig politician.
[3] William C. Plunket was attorney-general for Ireland.

Crymllwyn Bach. Elias' birthplace.

The Parish Church, Aber-erch, where Elias was baptized and where he attended with his grandfather.

Ynys-y-Pandy where Elias worked as a weaver.

Hendre Howel, where Elias became a member of the Society.

'Bala and the Lake from Tomen y Bala', by J. Warwick Smith.

A view of the Menai Straits.

Llanfechell: the right-hand house in the row, now modernised, was the home and shop of John and Elizabeth Elias.

Calvinistic Association Meeting at Bala, 1820,
when Elias was one of the preachers.

Old Chapel, Llangefni.

A modern representation of Elias' preaching.

Y Fron, Llangefni, the home of Elias in his later years.

A service in Caernarvonshire in 1910, which illustrates how the tradition of open-air preaching which commenced in the earlier revivals continued into the present century.

A sketch map of North Wales

against the truth, against the Bible Society, against schools on Bible instructions, and preaching the Gospel, and every good on right principles. Then he shewed, to the great joy of the believer, that the Spirit of the Lord was promised to put him to flight. I have no time to add. You ask for a long letter, but you do not know how much work your poor father hath to do. I was this week much engaged in a committee of the Bible Society; it was very large, some of them persons of very high rank. I also met the directors of the London Missionary Society another day; they were both very good meetings: and we had delightful news from abroad.

6. TRUST IN GOD

London 7 April 1830

We have been here a week:[1] and we have had delightful opportunities in the house of God: I was much supported in preaching the Gospel, and that to very great congregations. We know not what the fruit will be, O! may it be great. All things are very quiet and peaceable amongst us. The Governor of the world can, in his mercy, cause this peace and calmness to continue.

My son, it is my earnest wish that you should be comfortable, having your thoughts *quiet*; and beware lest anything that occurs should be the means of intercepting your communion with God, and marring your soul's spiritual welfare. Strive to confide in the Lord as to your temporal and eternal concerns, and thereby enjoy calmness and peace. Beware of being over-anxious and careful, and thereby impeding yourself. The Lord is able to support and direct you in all your concerns, and throughout your pilgrimage. Cast all your burdens and cares upon him; yea, pour your heart before him in prayer: 'Call upon him in the time of trouble, and he will hear thee, and thou shalt glorify him.' Beware of entertaining *hard* thoughts of God in anything. Take care you do not think that he is unwilling to hear you, or to do that which is best for you. He is infinitely wise to see what is most profitable for you.

---

[1] His second wife to whom he was married in February, 1830, was with him in London.

He is most rich, possessing all things; he is almighty, able to do all things; and he is most gracious and ready to bestow gifts upon the most unworthy; and those that put their trust in him shall want no manner of thing that is good. He has been most merciful to us as a family, and shewed compassion to us in many difficulties and changes, as you know. It would be most base and unbecoming in us to be slow in confiding in him ever hereafter, for he continues faithful and unchangeable.

With regard to thy single state, commit thyself in that circumstance also to the Lord; he is incomparable; he gives helps meet to those that wait on him. A good wife is a gift from the Lord, and the best earthly gift. Beware of trusting in thy own understanding, or depending on thy own strength. Entrust all the affair *honestly* to thy heavenly Father; he will bring it to pass for thy benefit and comfort, and his own glory. If you could succeed in obtaining a wife with great property; happiness, you know, is not necessarily connected therewith. Godliness, wisdom, sobriety, cheerfulness, concord of minds, agreement in views, are infinitely better. A moderate portion of worldly goods, together with the above qualities, constitute a great treasure. We are poor, if without these excellences, though united to the richest families in the land. Be very considerate and watchful in this very important business. I do not mean that you should spend much time over it; but view and weigh the matter with a sober mind, yea, consider most carefully everything before hand. I repeat it, you cannot fail by giving yourself and concerns into your heavenly Father's hand; none was ever disappointed, who did so, and you will succeed if you will act in this manner.

7. WISE AND USEFUL DIRECTIONS CONCERNING MARRIAGE

London 12 May 1831

Strive against a hasty spirit, lest you should be injured and wounded thereby. Perhaps the Lord may *complain* that you never do solemnly and impartially ask his counsel and direction in

search of a wife. He has in his family many that are most excellent;
and he may be pleased to bestow one upon you, for your great
benefit and comfort: would it not then be most desirable to apply
to him in this respect?

It is the Lord's *province* to guide your mind in the choice of a
partner: if I were to point out any individual to you, and the
connection turn out unpleasant afterwards, how uncomfortable I
should be. But when you are disposed to think of any person, I
shall be happy and ready to give you my opinion and advice. The
common way of the Supreme Governor of all events, is to direct
the mind of a man to the person he means to give him. But when
a man is inclined towards an individual, it is his duty to enquire
whether she is suitable for him according to the Word of the
Lord. If the Word is against her, it is not the Lord that disposeth
the mind towards her. I am glad you have been able to be prudent
in a certain affair. I hope you will continue to be kind to the
individual and his family; the Gospel teaches us to be tender-
hearted, patient, and forgiving: we shall never be losers by following its directions. Beware of saying a single word derogatory of
him. A disturbed state of mind is very injurious. It is very difficult
to see or do anything aright then. Trusting in the Lord calms the
mind. *Proverbs* 16.3. *Psalm* 37.3–7.

The restless agitating spirit that is in the world has injured the
minds of the people greatly. I do not know what will become of us.
You shall see the account of the meetings in the 'Record' newspaper.

Thy mother and Mrs Watkins have been to the King's Palace;
they were even in the chamber next to his Majesty,[1] yet notwithstanding that, they did not see him. There are many that are like
them, I mean in a spiritual sense.

8. THE CHOICE OF A WIFE

Liverpool 10 August 1831

A man should, before he sets his mind and affections on a female,
consider whether there are things in her conducive to his religious

[1] King William IV.

interest and happiness. He should think whether it is probable that he can live in a peaceable and comfortable manner with her in reference to worldly and religious things. And he ought to know whether the person he chooses is religious, sensible, sedate, and regular in her conduct; and whether she is of the same views as himself in doctrine, discipline, and religious habits and manners. There cannot be concord, comfort, and peace without these essential qualities. How can there be agreement, consolation, and felicity, if one should greatly love what the other much dislikes.

As to worldly things, they are *secondary*; yet it is prudent and consistent with religion and godliness for a Christian to seek one like himself with regard to worldly things. It would be improper, and not in the least religious, for you to choose one that has nothing, as the Lord has in his providence blessed you with some property; more added to it, would make your situation more comfortable, especially if you should have a family. It is but reasonable that each of the parents should contribute somewhat towards bringing up the children. Yet worldly considerations should not preponderate in the choice of a wife. Suppose two females were under a man's consideration, one possessing a moderate portion, being religious, fair, wise, sedate, proper in her conduct, and having tolerable education – the other having much larger property, but inferior to the first in person, wisdom, temper, conduct, and manners. If a man should fix upon the latter, notwithstanding all the personal and religious excellences of the other, I should not consider him wise in his choice, nor in the way to *increase* his comfort and happiness. The gifts and virtues of the first excel so much, that the riches even of an earthly kingdom would not out-weigh them, if the scales were in the hands of a wise and good man. It is of the utmost importance to have and enjoy everything in the favour and blessing of God. Be sure to have his presence in all your ways through the wilderness; our path will be safe, if the *pillar* of divine favour go before us. Be careful you do not get indifferent towards some old religious people in your neighbourhood; but shew that you love and regard them more and more. 'Follow righteousness, faith, charity, peace with them that call on the Lord out of a pure mind;' 2 *Timothy* 2.22. Let the godly be your companions.

Grievous news: there is a war between King Leopold and the Dutch – 50,000 French soldiers, and an English fleet, are gone to Belgium to assist him![1]

9. EMPRESS OF RUSSIA AND THE BIBLE

Fron 8 February 1832

I saw the wonderful information, by reading the *Evangelical Magazine*, this evening, that the Empress of Russia has given 100 roubles to purchase Bibles for eleven Sunday schools in England. Two Bibles for each school for two children that would commit to memory and repeat the 3rd and 4th chapters of the Gospel according to St John. These words will be printed in the Bible: 'The gift of the Empress of Russia.' This is the first instance ever heard of an Empress contributing towards a Sunday school. This is but a beginning. The way it took place is this; an English Lady is with the Empress in the Russian Palace; a godly minister, who knew the lady, wrote to her to solicit her charity for Sunday schools: and somehow or other, the Empress saw the letter, and she was disposed to contribute to the cause as above stated! Your mother would not let me go to rest this evening, without communicating this to you, in order, she says, to reconcile you to the Russians; you will be reconciled doubtless to the Empress without delay: perhaps the Emperor[2] will send his gift also.

10. GOD'S WILL CONSULTED ABOUT MARRIAGE

Fron 13 November 1832

My Son – You acknowledge that God governs all things and every individual, and that his will shall be done. Then you may *perceive*

---

[1] In 1831 Belgium was claiming to be independent of Holland. The two had been united by the powers in 1815.

[2] Nicholas I had married Princess Charlotte Louise, daughter of Frederick William III of Prussia.

that your attempts in the affair of a wife, are not according to his will; otherwise you would have succeeded before now. And if our motives and endeavours in this business are contrary to the mind of the Lord, it must be a kindness in him to entangle and hinder you in it; you shall perceive that in time. We may say of some, had they been impeded and stopped to enter the marriage state, they would have been far better off now. Perhaps the Lord deals as a kind father towards you in preventing you to have your own desires. Think not that it will be better if your state of life should be changed: don't *mistake* things, my son. Ask God to give you a pious, prudent wife for a help meet; and know that your daily bread depends on him also. Oh! pray earnestly and humbly that God may forgive your mistakes hitherto in this respect, lest those errors should be suffered to become like dark clouds, and be the means of obscuring and confusing thy prospects hereafter.

To Lady Bulkeley

I. CONDOLING WITH HER ON BEING BEREAVED

Llanfechell 4 September 1819

My only object is to send you a few lines that may, under the blessing of him who is the Father of the fatherless, and the Judge of the widow, be useful in inducing you to consider the hand of God in your mournful situation. Your temporal loss may be subservient to your eternal gain. Your grief is not improper in a moderate degree; but if your sorrow grew to excess, you should refrain from it; for what cannot be remedied, must be submitted to with calmness, equanimity, and resignation of mind. When you muse on your great loss, remember then who gave him to you. The union was the Lord's doing, and that not in a very common path. And now in his own way and time he hath taken his own gift from you: and therefore the best way is to be *silent* and quiet, as the royal Psalmist was when he said, 'I was dumb and opened not my mouth, because thou didst it.' It was the Lord's will to take him from you, and to leave you for a while to travel alone towards the other world. He does all things according to infinite goodness and wisdom. He that took away your dear partner can support you under your severe trial, and can also make your loss up in his own good way. Remember, that though your dear husband is removed from you, Christ is *always* alive, and is better than any husband to them that believe in him. He is infinitely rich and immortal. Take hold of him as your never-dying and all-sufficient husband; then you shall never be desolate; you need not be solitary, the Word of God may be your companion, and the Holy Ghost your guide through the wilderness of this world to the heavenly city.

I hope the Lord will enable you to improve the death of one so near, as a *mirror* to see the vanity of this world and all that is in it. What a dream is mortal life! And what shadows are the objects of sense! All the glories of mortality will appear as *nothing* to our mind at the awful hour of death, when we must be separated from all creatures here below, and ushered into the borders of an immortal world. No human greatness will make any figure in the valley of death: every distinction vanishes then, except that of piety and virtue.

The consideration of death, especially our own, is a very fit subject for our meditation. It is a wonder and pity that death is so seldom the matter of our meditation and conversation. Men in general prefer to converse upon any subject rather than death! A lady of high rank and great learning used the following similitude to shew the *unreasonableness* of neglecting conversation about death: 'Were any number of persons,' she said, 'intending to embark for a distant unknown country, of whom some might be called tomorrow, and all must be called soon, would they not, whenever they met as friends and fellow travellers, be enquiring among themselves how each was provided for the journey, what account each had heard of the place, the terms of reception – what interest and hopes each secured – what treasure remitted –

---

¹ This lady became his wife about eleven years afterwards!

what protection ensured? And would they not excite each other
to dispatch what was yet possible to be done, and what might
tomorrow be irretrievably too late?

2. THE RIGHT SOURCE FOR HAPPINESS
     AND SUPPORT

Llanfechell 2 March 1824 [?]

I cannot but sympathize when I consider your weak state of
health in a strange place. It is true that affliction is not pleasant;
but it may, under God's blessing, prove useful. Our *lives* are in
God's hands, and at his disposal: as he is infinitely wise and good,
he never sends maladies upon us without some wise end in view
– that he might speak to us on the bed or in the room of affliction.
We are apt to be too carnal and earthly-minded to hear his voice in
ease and prosperity; the objects of sense and th·ngs of flesh and
blood engross too much of one's mind, therefore the bitterest
afflictions are needful and good, when blessed by God, as *means* to
bring our minds to the divine Word, to consider our ways and
condition before him, and our own latter end. Indeed we cannot
be too careful and impartial in self-examination, because our
eternal all depends upon having right understanding between us
and God in time.

I know that you are not a stranger to the consideration of your
fallen state, and the depravity and sinfulness of your heart by
nature; and perhaps you are sometimes tempted to despondency
and despair on that account. There is *nothing* in the Bible that has
any tendency to bring a convinced sinner to despair, no, not a
single word. And we need not draw a veil over the sinfulness of
our sins, in order to have ease and comfort. Ah! no, for there is in
the Gospel of Christ *every* thing we stand in need of, held out
freely to such sinners as we are. There is an all-sufficient Saviour,
perfect righteousness, full forgiveness and complete salvation, and
all free without money and without price. And we, poor, guilty,
and lost sinners, are invited, as we are, to be partakers of this great
salvation.

The only way to be interested in this wonderful salvation, is to believe the testimony of God respecting his Son. O, let me entreat you to come to Jesus, to believe on him, and to accept of him, the great and precious Redeemer. O, give yourself up to him, depend on him, and look up to him; and there your soul shall have a resting-place in all your trials through life, and in death itself. O, beware of unbelief and despondency; and say not, 'My sins have been too great, too numerous, or too aggravated to be forgiven.' O remember that 'the blood of Jesus Christ his son cleanseth from all sin,' and 'that he is able to save unto the uttermost all that come to God by him.' But if you should be disposed to doubt his willingness, surely a serious consideration of his gracious and pressing invitations is enough to satisfy you; attend to such words as these: 'If any man thirst, let him come unto me, and drink.' *John* 7.37. *Revelation* 21.6. If you are willing to accept the Saviour and salvation through him, as the chief of sinners, then all doubts and objections will vanish in a moment; you will be enabled, believing in Christ, to hate and oppose all sins, and to love and delight in all the ways of God, and to walk in them diligently, and then you will find that his ways are pleasant. Indeed you will be enabled to walk with God: Duties will be delightful, temptations will be overcome, and the sufferings of this present life will even work for your good. Yea, 'our light affliction, which is but for a moment, worketh for us a far more exceeding and eternal weight of glory.'

To the Rev W. Roberts[1]

I. ON BEING BEREAVED OF A CHILD

Fron 12 July 1838

I hope you both shall have much strength from above to bear under the trial that is so painful to flesh and blood. To be enabled

---

[1] A near relative of Elias.

to *view* the secret movements of the good and wise providence of God towards us, would afford great calmness and ease of mind. He does all things right, they cannot be better: and he can bring us to *see* that, and to reconcile us to his proceedings, though so disagreeable to our natural feelings. To lose dear infants, and to commit them to the dust, is most poignant bitterness. But some meet with more distressing circumstances in the conduct of those that are spared! Your little child was born for eternity; it is her dwelling, her home. The Lord has been pleased to remove her there, according to his eternal counsel, sooner than you expected. Who can say how great was his goodness in this act? She was taken out of the reach of many temptations, and out of many evils and sorrow. You have no need to be uncomfortable as to the state of the child; your heavenly Father took her to himself. It was very distressing to you and her mother to behold her affliction; it was becoming to mourn and to sympathize; but now, she being dead, arise and wash away your tears, and worship God. 2 *Samuel* 12.20. May the Lord give you help in the time of need, may he support and comfort you!

2. ON ANOTHER CHILD BEING REMOVED

Fron 17 August 1838

God who is wise and good has sent you once and again to drink of the bitter waters of Marah! Where you expected comfort, there you met with great anguish. 'Behold for peace I had great bitterness.' *Isaiah* 38.17. However, remember that it was the Pillar that lead you to Marah. The Lord who guided you there, has a tree that will sweeten those waters. Dear brother, I have thought much of you and Mrs R., and spread your cause before the throne of grace; but I can do no more; I cannot help or lessen your burden. I am afraid of grieving by trying to console you, making your wounds smart and bleed by endeavouring to heal them. He only that wounded you, can make you whole. I know that nothing can ease and comfort you under these painful circumstances, but observing the hand of the Lord, and remembering that '*he* did it.'

Psalm 39.9. He is excellent in all things. Who can improve or mend his work? Who can make that straight, which he hath made crooked? *Ecclesiastes* 7.13. What he doeth and why he doeth, you may not know now, but you shall know hereafter. *John* 13.7. It is a great thing to have the grace of God to support you, to make you resigned under his almighty hand, and to be *silent*. May you not be too much cast down and disheartened! The Lord took your offspring out of a very evil world, where many young ones meet with what is more distressing than death, more painful than that separation to pious parents. Moreover, God can support and make you happy without them, all your toilsome journey. Remember also that those infants were destined for eternity. Do not murmur because they have been removed to that world in the morning of their existence. When we consider eternity, the difference between twelve or twenty years, and seventy or eighty, is but as nothing! 'The Lord gave and the Lord hath taken away,' in his own time and way, 'bless the name of the Lord.' *Job* 1.21.

To a Sister-in-Law

REASONS FOR PEACE OF MIND UNDER BEREAVEMENT

1829

I take my pen to write a few lines to you, though I am much tired after the labours of yesterday. I can sympathize with you in your distressing and painful situation, into which the all-wise and good Disposer of all events was pleased to bring you. God is *infinitely* wise and gracious, he knows what is best for you. He has some wise end in this dispensation that is for your benefit, though bitter, very bitter indeed to flesh and blood; and you shall see this. He knows how to support and comfort you under this heavy affliction, and I doubt not but that he will do so. It is true your son was likely to be a comfort to you in your old age. But it

---

¹ Her son, a sailor, died at New Orleans.

pleased God to take him away, and to disappoint your expectations, and to place you under this affliction.

But all was God's doing, he cut the ties asunder which bound you to your dearest earthly object; he caused the fair flower reared by your tender hand, to wither! And now you are weeping over the wreck of your earthly hopes. But still remember, 'It is God's doing;' and he who hath done it is a God of love. This world, we know by sad experience, is a vale of tears, but our sorrow and sighing shall soon be over: adversity is but for a day – a night of affliction and weeping – an hour of temptation, a moment of mourning under our Father's rod; however it is 'light affliction.' But under all, we have a heavenly Father to go to, a throne of grace free and open; yea, a sympathizing Brother in the court above!

Dear sister, *endeavour* to look above; and you shall see a Father, Brother, and a Husband that shall never die! Jesus, dear Jesus, who once died for us, and is now on the right of God, pleading for us: He is and will be for ever better to you than ten sons, yea, than ten thousand. He will be with you in all your trouble and sorrow. God is unchangeable and abiding in his love and blessings. O think of eternal love and grace, eternal salvation, eternal inheritance, which passeth not away.

> *O child of sorrow, be it thine to know*
> *That Scripture only is the cure of woe:*
> *That field of promise, how it flings abroad*
> *Its perfumes o'er the Christian's thorny road!*
> *The soul reposing on assured relief,*
> *Feels herself happy amidst all her grief;*
> *Forgets her labour as she toils along,*
> *Weeps tears of joy, and bursts into a song.*

I wish you would consider *one* thing more, that Jesus hath the keys of death – that he is the Sovereign Arbiter of life and death! Death is the servant of God, and is at the command of Jesus. Death must have a commission under the broad seal of heaven before he can fling a dart. The precise time of death is the result of a wise and irrevocable decree. The place as well as the time of death is fixed; whether it takes place on sea or land, at home or abroad, the manner and the circumstances of death are determined. The different modes of departure out of this world are either permitted or appointed by him who is excellent in counsel. Therefore it is becoming all Christians to acknowledge the dominion of God, and to conduct themselves submissively under the loss of the dearest earthly friends. May you, dear sister, through the blessed Gospel, receive and enjoy much consolation at the throne of grace!

To Mr Thomas Owen, prisoner in France[1]

I. WISE COUNSELS

Llanfechell 9 November 1807

I have been thinking much of you in your present painful situation, far from your family and friends, and in a strange country. But when I consider that the Lord reigneth, then I am silent. He is infinitely good and wise, and he doth everything in the best way: but we are very blind and ignorant, and cannot often understand his purpose. Clouds and darkness are round about him; yet righteousness and judgment are the habitation of his throne. I hope you do acknowledge the Lord's hand in your affliction, and that you submit yourself under it, that you may be exalted in due time. I pray and hope that it may be for your good, and that you will come out of the furnace of affliction as gold purified in the fire: and then you will have to say as the Psalmist, 'It is good for me that I have been afflicted; before that, I went astray, but now I have kept thy word.' It is true you went astray before this heavy

---

[1] He was twelve years a prisoner of war there, and was greatly respected by all his fellow-prisoners. He was a moral man and much attached to the cause of religion. He had his liberty at last, returned home in a bad state of health, and died. Elias thought well of his spiritual state. He was married to a cousin of his wife.

trial: it is much better to be in a temporal prison in a foreign land, than to be in a backsliding state, and in captivity to lusts and Satan.

The Lord may sanctify your bodily captivity as means to liberate your soul from a spiritual one. The Lord hath blessed the affliction of the outward man before now, for the renewing of the inward. You are the prisoner of hope in every respect; therefore turn your face towards him that sitteth on the mercy-seat, in faith, repentance, and prayer. He will have mercy upon you, because he is merciful and gracious. Call on him in the day of adversity and he will hear and deliver you in his own good time. Jonah was a backslider, and the Lord put him in prison, into the fish's belly, a dark receptacle; in which he prayed unto the Lord his God: he said, 'Though I am cast out of thy sight, I will look again towards thy holy temple: that is, I looked towards thy temple before my backsliding many a time; but I have been thinking under thy correction, that I have forfeited that privilege for ever, and that I shall not see thy face nor thy temple any more; but now thou hast enabled my distressed soul to look again towards thy holy temple, though I am now in the belly of hell, yet from hence – from this depth of adversity, I will look towards thy temple. I remember thy gracious promise that whatsoever prayer or supplication is made by any man who is acquainted with the plague of his heart, towards thy mercy-seat, thou wilt hear in heaven, thy dwelling place, and forgive him, and do according to his wants.' That temple was a type of our blessed Mediator: look to him from where you are, and as you are, for he is mighty, and ready to save to the uttermost. He is the propitiation for our sins. *Isaiah* 53.6, 10. O look unto him whom you have pierced with your sins, and turn to God through him; he will receive you graciously, heal your backsliding, and love you freely. He will renew the manifestations of his love to you, and then you may say, 'I sat under his shadow with great delight, and his fruit was sweet to my taste.' His love is better than wine, and you may drink freely of it until you forget your trouble and adversity. Communion and fellowship with God in the Mediator will make the prison a heaven to your soul; and then you will cry out, 'Whom have I in heaven but thee? And there is none on earth that I desire besides thee! My flesh and my heart fail, but God is the strength of my heart and my portion for ever.' The Lord is near us everywhere, and you may enjoy communion with him. 'Come boldly unto the throne of grace, that you may receive mercy, and grace to help you in the time of need.'

2. GOOD CONSIDERATIONS

8 December 1809

Our Lord can comfort you where you are; he is not in want of anything to help him to administer comfort to his people. He can do it without any worldly help; yea, he can do it when every earthly thing opposes it. He can turn a captivity, a prison, death-bed, yea death itself, into a comfortable situation for his own people. His fellowship is the best comfort in this world, and in heaven also. I have been thinking of a few things that may be useful for you to meditate upon in your captivity.

Think much of your own *vileness* and sinfulness by nature, and then you will see that you deserve the worst things here and hereafter. Consider God's *goodness* in that he chastised you less than your iniquity deserved. And consider the *wisdom* and equity of God in that he hath done everything so well, so that it cannot be better. Consider the *shortness* of time and the approach of eternity. Everything will be over with us here below very soon, and we shall be in an eternal world before long: our crosses and troubles are but for a moment. Think much of *salvation* by Jesus Christ. It is a preparation for eternity – a free, a full salvation, every way suitable for the chief of sinners. Consider the *person* of the God-man, Jesus Christ: he is white and ruddy, the chief among ten thousand; yea, more excellent than all men and angels, he is altogether lovely. Think of the *fulness*, freeness, and meetness of that salvation which Christ hath wrought out. Here is righteousness for a guilty sinner, a fountain opened for sin and uncleanness; in short, life eternal for a lost sinner. Therefore look, look unto him, believe and trust in him.

To the Church of God in London[1]

I. GREAT CARE FOR SOULS – PWLLHELI
   ASSOCIATION

Llanfechell 8 October 1817

I have been much distressed for you in your present destitute circumstances; and was for a time apprehensive that I should not meet with a suitable preacher willing to come to you at this time. At length we prevailed on J. Humphreys of Caerwys to visit you; I believe that he will answer the purpose. He grows in the esteem of the people, and is well received in Wales: he preaches well, and is irreproachable as to his life and conversation: he is moreover of a quiet and peaceable disposition. All we can do is to desire and pray that the Lord would employ and bless him among you, and edify you through him, and make you a comfort to each other.

We had a comfortable Association at Pwllheli. We encouraged all the churches in North Wales to draw near to God in deep humiliation, and to entreat him to favour his people again with a spiritual revival, producing powerful and deep impressions on the souls of the people. It was resolved that all the churches, on a certain hour of a given day, should offer up their prayers unto God for the out-pouring of the Spirit. It was shewn that judgment comes upon the land in consequence of open notorious sins, such as adultery, drunkenness, Sabbath-breaking, swearing, covetousness, oppression, pride – but yet, at the same time, that there is danger lest the church should participate in those sins, by not maintaining discipline, suffering such evils in their families, being remiss in opposing them in their neighbourhood, and by not being grieved and sorry on account of the transgressions which they cannot prevent. Much was said against going on with the work of the Lord in an indifferent, dry, and unholy manner. Much was also said with a view to maintain the bond of union in all the churches, and for that end to be self-denying, and forbearing and forgiving in our disposition.

---

[1] A society of Christians belonging to the Welsh Calvinistic Methodists.

2. NEW CHAPEL – WATCHFULNESS AND PRAYER

Llanfechell 8 August 1822

I have no objection to be named as a trustee for the chapel with those good men whom you have mentioned. O brethren, be watchful against the devices and inroads of Satan. I do not remember the erection of many chapels, but that the great enemy would, some way or another, endeavour to bring in confusion, and so injure the great work. I was reminded thereby of Israel building the second temple; sometimes their adversaries would offer to join them in the building, at another time they would attempt to impede them in the great work. (*Ezra* 4.) Satan is not pleased to see Christ enlarging the place of his tabernacle. He will endeavour to hurt the good cause some way or other: wherefore, brethren, be sober and watch unto prayer. Take care that self is not allowed to take share in the business: let every one beware of *shewing* self in words or actions. Let it be the *aim* of all to do the work as unto the Lord, and not to man. Let brotherly love continue among you; avoid everything that has a tendency to cool love, to create disputes, contentions, and hatred. In all your meetings with respect to the chapel, let your conversation be quiet, kind, and guarded; and let all, should there be any disagreement, endeavour to excel in all long-suffering and patience: all may come unto the same mind in time by the exercise of kindness. Now, whilst you are building, is the time of collecting. It would be well if you had many such collectors as Mr Edwards, City-road. I hope that the Lord, whose is the work, will dispose the hearts of the rich English folks to aid you. He that inclined the minds of the poor Israelites in the wilderness to contribute towards the tabernacle so freely and abundantly that it was necessary to stop them, and afterwards induced them to bring in their presents so munificently towards the erecting of the costly temple of Solomon, may influence the hearts of men to contribute enough towards the building of your place of worship. The gold and the silver are the Lord's, as also the hearts of the people. Pray much for the Lord's countenance on the work, and his favour on you in carrying on the cause; otherwise the new chapel will answer very little purpose. If the Lord should become displeased and hide his face from you, the chapel would soon be three times too large. His good will and pleasure with us is the cause why our chapels are too small. (O, abide with us, blessed Lord! otherwise we shall soon see many of our large and excellent chapels empty.) O may there never be a cause to apply the term *Ichabod* to your new chapel! But may the gracious presence of the Lord always fill it! Hold prayer meetings for the purpose. The Lord favours us generally in this Island (Anglesey) with the very gracious influences of his Holy Spirit. I may indeed say that his operations are so effectual on the people, that everywhere the blind see, the deaf hear, and the dead arise!

3. REVIVAL OF RELIGION

Llanfechell 26 October 1822

I am going to Dolgelley Association today. I am very glad to hear that you go on so comfortably with the new chapel. I hope all things will continue pleasant till it is finished; and that the Lord will shew his approbation of the work, pouring his Holy Spirit on the means of grace, blessing the preaching of the Gospel for the salvation of many sinners.

The revival goes on very delightfully in this island. The kindness of the Lord towards us is wonderful. His visits and the convictions under the Word are truly powerful. Very wild and hardened sinners are alarmed and converted; multitudes are made willing in the day of Christ's power. I have had the privilege of receiving hundreds into church-communion. I received one hundred at once in a certain place; in another place fifty, in another thirty, and in another thirty, and many in several other places. Besides, other ministers have received a great many into the church. This is the Lord's doing, and it is marvellous in our eyes. Indeed the church in our country is ready to cry out in wonder, asking, 'Who begat these? and from whence came these?' Let not my brethren in London be discouraged; God is the same with you.

4. CHURCH DISCIPLINE

Llanfechell 9 October 1823

It gives me great pleasure that I have succeeded in persuading Mr
R. Lloyd of Beaumaris to come to you. I hope that his visit will be
beneficial and blessed to many of the hearers. I am happy to find
that some fresh members have been received into the church; but
it grieves me that you are under the necessity of turning some out.

We had comfortable services at Beaumaris Association, except-
ing the unpleasantness of being exposed to stormy weather when
preaching in the open air. The most notable subjects under our
consideration in the church meetings were discipline and instruction in doctrines. It was observed that preachers and elders ought
to labour more in teaching the people, and in maintaining discipline; it was on the last point we chiefly dwelt. It was feared that
great ignorance prevailed among us as to the nature and end of
church-discipline. It was apprehended that some understand no
more by it than turning a member out of the church, and that those
thus expelled were under discipline; which idea is very incorrect.
Discipline is carried on *within* the church; and as to those turned
out of her, they are not now under her government. To be under
discipline, is to be under instruction and teaching; it is, in fact,
teaching. Then these few points respecting discipline as teaching
were observed; that –

1 The great Teacher is Christ; he teaches by his Word and Spirit. He
  is a meek, wise, and patient teacher; his example is perfect.

2 The school is the visible church in this world. 'All thy children shall
  be taught of God.' *Isaiah* 54.13. In him they have a shepherd to guide
  and to lead them in the right way.

3 The Bible is the book of the school. The things to be learned are
  those of the Bible. They learn in order to know, to experience, and to
  practise them. So their education consists in doctrine, experience,
  and conversation.

4 The under-teachers or monitors in the Christian institution are the
  officers of the church. These are to keep their eyes on the great
  Teacher, as well as on those who are pupils. They are to follow his

example themselves, and set it before the people, saying, 'Be followers of us as we are of Christ.'

We observed these three things respecting this school:

1 Who and what sort of persons are to be received into the school of Christ? It is not every description of people that are received into a respectable seat of learning in this world: the terms of the establishment are published, and such as approve of those stipulations are admitted. The candidates must be sensible that they need instruction, and be willing to receive it in a submissive obedient manner, heartily consenting to all the rules of the school, and conducting themselves peaceably towards their fellow-students, as well as respectfully towards those that are out of the establishment.

2 How are the officers to treat them after receiving them in? They are to teach them all things appertaining to their salvation, all spiritual knowledge, all the counsel of God; and how to demean themselves in all things towards all, towards God and man always, warning men of all their perils and dangers – 'Warn the righteous man that he sin not' – exhorting and advising them, lest any should be hardened through the deceitfulness of sin – watching and looking after them – encouraging and persuading them to love and every good work – governing those under their authority in the Lord – insisting upon obedience not in words only, but also in deed – exercising a just discrimination of character, giving to all what is due and proper; comforting the feeble-minded, supporting the weak, rebuking the froward.

3 Turning out of the school, or church, when there is need. This is the last thing we are to resort to, when all other means have been unsuccessful, such as warning, advising, rebuking. Those must be expelled that have been guilty of some shameful public sin; and those that obstinately continue in their sin, disregarding reproofs and rebukes; and those that cause strife, agitation, and confusion – 'Mark them which cause division and offences, and avoid them.' They are not allowed to remain in the Connexion; and those that disturb the church are to be cut off – not suffering the leaven to remain long, lest the whole be leavened and injured. The surgeon, after using all means in vain to prevent mortification in any part, has immediate recourse to amputation, that the body may be saved. Should strifes

or discords arise in any church, they should, if possible, be immediately extinguished; and if two persons or more at variance cannot be reconciled, they should all be turned out very soon, lest their disagreement should produce party spirit in the church.

Dear brethren, I wish you most heartily much of the Lord's presence. Avoid everything that may tend to quench or grieve the Spirit, and cause the Lord to hide himself from you. Cherish brotherly love, and shun everything that leads to contention. Be diligent to keep the unity of the Spirit in the bond of peace. And the God of peace be with you. Amen.

My kind love to the preachers, elders, and all the church; the children and teachers, especially those in the society.

5. THE OBSERVANCE OF THE SABBATH

Llanfechell 22 June 1827

This is the first opportunity for writing to you I could avail myself of since I left London. The Lord was very merciful to me in my journey through Glamorganshire, and all my way till my return home; my labour was great, preaching often in the open air; my body became feeble and faint. But the thought of having the privilege of addressing thousands of my fellow-creatures on the concerns of their souls relieved me, and rendered the work more easy, and even made it appear as nothing. I arrived at home from Bala Association by eleven o'clock on Thursday night. I was under the necessity of going to the Amlwch Quarterly Meeting the next Sabbath day. We had very profitable services there. John Davies of Nantglyn, preached on *Isaiah* 43.19–21; Morris Roberts, on *Zechariah* 13.1; Henry Rees, on 1 *John* 1.7; Michael Roberts on *Philippians* 1.21; John Jones on *Isaiah* 53.5; James Hughes on *Mark* 13.37; and the unworthy writer of this on 1 *John* 2.16. The Spirit of the Lord accompanied the Word in a powerful way to the hearts of the people. You would be reminded of the Lord's work in former times, by seeing the gracious effects on the hearers.

The subject we had chiefly under consideration in our private meeting was that of the fourth commandment, the keeping the Sabbath-day holy. We had commenced our observations on it at Bala Association, and followed them up at Amlwch. Four things were considered:

1 That the commandment is moral, that it is unchangeable and abiding, being of the *same* nature as the other commandments. It was shewn that ignorance of, or inattention to, this truth is often the cause of negligence and indifference in observing the Sabbath. The morality of the commandment was proved in many ways, such as these: that there are ten commandments in the moral law; if the fourth should not be moral, there would be only nine commandments! It was observed that it is likely that this precept respecting the Sabbath was the first that was given to man in Eden; and that it was given to the father of the human race before the fall; and consequently must belong to the whole family of man always. And it appeared to us that the command-ment is proper, useful, and reasonable in its nature. We observed that it is most reasonable that man should worship God; that a sociable creature should worship him in a public, social, and congre-gational manner; that consequently a specific time for it must have been appointed, and none could have been so proper to fix the time as the Creator of man. It was also observed, that the seventh part of man's time was very suitable, being not too great a portion; that God had published it out of the midst of the fire, like the other nine; that we never heard that God ever wrote anything except the moral law, which he inscribed with his own finger on the table twice. It was also noticed, that Christ, in his answer, included in the great com-mand all that was on the first table. The change of the day of rest under the Gospel proves nothing against the moral nature of the command – the first day is now the holy rest – 'Remember to keep holy the seventh day.'

2 We made some observations on the word *remember*; that it is in no other commandment but this; the others are expressed as the first, 'thou shalt not have other gods but me'. But here, 'remember the Sabbath day'. The word 'remember' signifies the antiquity of the command, alluding to the first appointment of the worship of God on earth, as if he had said, 'Remember how God sanctified it'. The word 'remember' intimates (2) its constant and abiding nature. It

signifies (3) that there is great necessity for this rule; and (4) the word reminds us of it before it comes, that we should prepare for it beforehand, and welcome it. It means also (5) that we should remember the day in all its hours, to act properly all the Sabbath day. We are also taught (6) that we should remember it after it has gone by, to meditate on what was done in it.

3 We made some remarks on what is *required* in this commandment, to sanctify it. To set the day apart to God, as separate from all the other days; to give the whole of it to God, to consecrate the whole of it for his holy service. It is not a carnal or animal rest for man; it is a day to worship God with the soul and body, in private, in the family, and congregation – a day to remember the work of God in creating, governing, and saving – to remember the resurrection of Christ, having finished the work of redemption. It is a day to worship God in Christ; yea, looking to him in that day, delighting, rejoicing, and resting in Christ. It is a Sabbath for the soul. Our meditation, conversation, and conduct should be as becometh the sanctity of the Sabbath; viewing it as delightful and glorious.

4 We made some observations on what is *forbidden* in this commandment; not only things that are sinful at all times, but also some things that are lawful, yea, necessary as duties at other times, such as all worldly employment as could be accomplished before or after the Sabbath. It also forbids any further gratifications and indulgences in sleep, eating, and drinking, than such as are necessary for the support of nature, and making us fit for the service of God.

It was also observed, that the conduct and manner of people on the Sabbath discover and manifest how the matter stands between their souls and God; that those that dishonour the Sabbath are enemies to God; and that those, on the other hand, that truly regard and keep the Sabbath, make it manifest that the Lord is their God, that he sanctifies and makes them ready for the everlasting Sabbath. If we should be in a proper frame of mind on the Sabbath, we should be prepared for the exercises of prayer and praise, and hearing sermons.

The great cause in your church is very near my heart. O that I may hear that it greatly prospers among you! My great grief is that I was not more useful among you when there.

6. ANXIETY FOR THE SUCCESS OF THE GOSPEL

Llanfechell 28 March 1828

I feel anxious to send you a few lines, observing that Easter and
the yearly meetings are drawing nigh, remembering that I had the
privilege of being with you at each Easter of the last three years. I
should be happy to hear that the Lord has rent the heavens, and
descended among the Welsh in Jewin-street,[1] and that the mountains have melted before him. May the preaching in your Association this year, be in 'manifestation of the Spirit, and with much
power'! May the weapons of the warfare be powerful through God
to the pulling down of *strong holds*! The castles there are strong,
and stand up yet against the Lord and his Christ! Satan, the strong
man armed, stands up against the Gospel, and keeps his possession
of sinners! Ignorance, thoughtlessness, carnality, worldly-
mindedness, and legal spirit, are like strong castles, and it is by
these that Satan, the world, and sin keep possession of men, and
stand up against the success of the Gospel.

Ministers of the Gospel are the soldiers employed by Christ,
the King of glory, to fight against those powerful enemies, and to
attack the strong fortifications. The Gospel succeeds by no carnal
weapon; it is by no earthly sword, neither by any human learning,
gifts, or reasons that the castles are to be cast down, and men to
be taken out of the possession of these enemies. The Word of God
is the sword, the bow and arrow in this warfare. And it is through
God that the weapons are strong, effectual, and successful to cast
down the towers, and to deliver men out of the power and possession of their strong enemies. It is by the secret and powerful
operations of the Spirit.

Satan is not afraid of the soldiers, though they are armed, or of
the knowledge or gifts of any preacher; but he is afraid of the
presence of God, the leader of the true army. As the Philistines
cried out, 'Woe to us, God is come to the camp', so a cry would be
made in hell, and a great alarm in the regiment of Satan, if God
should be pleased to appear among you at the Association. 'The
weapons are strong through God' only. The sermons are powerful

[1] London E.C.1.

when he speaks and manifests himself: the Word goeth forth
with power. Then the castles – thoughtlessness, unbelief, carnal
reasons, love to empty pleasures – will come down, as the
strongholds of Jericho formerly. And sinners that are kept in
bondage by sin and Satan will come out of their prisons – 'the
snare is broken.'

O that God would manifest himself among the hundreds that
hear the Word there, who have hitherto lived in their sins and in
the possession of Satan! Dear friends, are you free from the blood
of the ungodly multitude that hear the Word in your chapel?
Do you pray as often and as earnestly as you should for the presence
of the Lord in your assemblies, that he would own and bless his
Word? Let every one in the church examine himself, and see
whether there be anything in him that grieves the Spirit, and
causes God to withdraw far away from his people? May you that
grow old in age and profession take care that you do not wax
rusty and stiff in your experiences, living in a backsliding spirit,
strangers to communion with God, unconcerned about divine
things, and indisposed to glorify him! It is very painful that any
that profess that they are going to heaven, and as they think draw
near the much-desired haven, should become more worldly-
minded, and as they approach the confines of the world of spirits,
should become more carnal! O strive that you may in your old age
'bring forth fruit, and be fat and flourishing,' *Psalm* 92.14! Oh!
young people, take care that ye be not light and trifling in your
religion, spending the morning of your age, the summer of your
life, without the power of religion and the fellowship of God. O
strive that ye may experience the peace and joy that are in true
religion, and enjoy the feast of the Gospel! If you should but
have these blessings, you would not feel any disposition to taste
the poor enjoyments of worldly people, and you will not be
buried in the graves of lust and sin. Let every one of you be
laborious in the vineyard of the Lord, according to his state and
situation, during the period of his life. Let each examine himself,
Is there anything I may do for God that is not attempted? If so,
let his hand lay hold of it immediately, for there is no work nor
device in the grave.

Teachers of the Sunday School, is there anything more that
ye may do? Is there no room for you to be more spiritual in your
conversation with those that are under your care? Could you not
say a few words respecting the evil of sin, the miserable state of
a person without Christ, the dreadful situation of those that die
in their sins? then of the glory of Christ, and the great privileges of
those that believe in him? Leave off every conversation that tends
to excite curiosity, or leads to pedantry or self-conceit. Let all
your conversation tend to the salvation of souls, to their sanctification and consolation. Remember the little children, for few
parents bring up their children as Christians ought to do. Have
compassion on the rising generation, and give them a religious
education in the nurture and admonition of the Lord, until their
parents be awakened to a sense of their duty. O that they may be
soon aroused before their death cometh! May the glory of the
Lord appear among you all! and when you draw nigh to God,
remember me, the poorest of your brethren, and your servant for
Christ.

7. GROWTH IN GRACE, ASSURANCE, PRESUMPTION

Llanfechell 31 January 1829

I send you these few lines in hope that your souls prosper, increasing daily in the knowledge of God in Christ, and true holiness. I
know that you enjoy many spiritual privileges and precious
advantages, for which you should be grateful to the Lord. I am
glad that you faithfully and diligently attend the means of grace,
and that union and brotherly love continue among you. But, O
my friends, we need to grow more and more in grace, experimental knowledge, and every spiritual and evangelical virtue!

Be very thankful to the Lord for what he hath already done for
your souls, for inclining you to hear the Gospel and to receive the
benefits resulting from it, enabling you to forsake your sinful ways
and ungodly companions; turning your faces towards Zion,
disposing his people to give you a place among them, and keeping
you there until now, when so many have turned back, or have

been cast out of the church. But you that have been enabled to cleave to the Lord's house, ye 'are all alive this day!' Is not this wonderful? And should you not be very thankful?

Still, there is much danger from indifference and 'ease in Zion.' The outward concerns of the church are now so calm, that even 'the house on the sand' may stand; and while the 'mid-night cry' is not heard, the foolish virgins may be found with the wise; and while they all slumber and sleep, it is difficult to distinguish between them. But, my dear friends, this is the time for us to examine and prove ourselves, and to labour to ascertain what we *are*, and what we *have*. As there are some that build without a rock for their foundation, and as there are virgins without oil in their vessels with their lamps, is there no danger lest we should be such? Should we not therefore frequently try ourselves by the Word of God, and see what we are, and what is our state, not in the opinion of men, but in the sight of God? Are there not many who proceed at a *venture* in their religion, not knowing or caring to know their real state before God? What is the religion of such? Nothing more than a feeble hope that it will be well with them in the end! Is not such a course dangerous? And is it not great loss to ourselves? If our religion is not genuine, is it not a great calamity to us to be ignorant of it, when we may obtain the truth? It will be a terrible thing to make this discovery in death and at the last judgment! To find ourselves without a rock while the house is falling! – without oil in our lamps, and the door shut against us!

On the other hand, is it not very distressing, if we have true religion, that we should be so insensible of it as to deprive ourselves of much of that calmness, comfort, joy unspeakable, pious confidence in filial nearness to God, sacred delight in meditating upon him, and implicit confidence in him, warm love towards him, and a lively zeal for him, with which true religion is accompanied? If assured of our interest in Christ, we should be more thankful to God, more courageous in facing our enemies, and more submissive under the cross; we should then be able to look forward to death with less terror, to judgment and eternity with greater pleasure. My dear friends, I will make so free with you as to exhort you to examine yourselves seriously and impartially in the following

things: I desire that each may do so, as if he or she were mentioned by name, and sought to obtain thorough satisfaction to
their own mind respecting this all-important subject: let each one
ask himself,

1 Have I been brought to see and consider the greatness and infinite
   purity of God, before whom I am at all times, and to whom my heart
   and ways are exposed?

2 Have I seen that I am a responsible creature, bound to give an
   account of my thoughts, words, and actions? and that his holy law is
   a perfect rule for my soul and body, both in private and in public?

3 Have I believed that I fell awfully in Adam? Have I seen myself an
   enemy to God, and full of sin against him? Have I seen that 'sin is
   exceeding sinful', and that I deserve the wrath of God to all eternity
   on its account, and that hell might have been most justly my abode for
   ever?

4 Have I seen that my own righteousness is nothing better than filthy
   rags, my own doings full of imperfections, so that I have nothing by
   which to merit the favour of God, forgiveness of sins and salvation?

5 Have I discovered the value of Christ as a Saviour to lost sinners?
   Have I been enabled to flee unto him, like the man-slayer to the city
   of refuge? Am I satisfied with what he did and suffered? And am I
   assisted to take hold of him, and to make use of him, as he is made
   known in the Gospel? Have I tasted that the Lord is gracious? Is he
   precious to my soul, and is he in my estimation altogether lovely?
   Are his mercies sweet to my taste, like the goodly fruit of a tree?
   Have I given my soul into his hands to be preserved unto that day?

6 Does my soul desire to know him more, and to love him better, to
   enjoy more of his fellowship, and to be more conformable to his
   image?

7 Do I feel *grieved* on the account of the plague of my own heart, and
   the corruption of my nature, though I may have given myself for
   ever into the hands of Christ, and though I am persuaded he is able
   to keep me, and consequently satisfied as to my own safety? And do
   I long to be free from sin, that every grace may be more lively and
   strong in me, and that I may answer some useful purpose in the
   world to the glory of God?

8 Do I thirst for more intercourse with God in the means of grace? and do I find the ordinances empty without his presence?

9 Is his cause near my heart? Am I anxious to witness greater success attending the preaching of Christ crucified, and to see a greater number of sinners converted and saved?

My dear friends, if you find yourselves defective in these things, go, go immediately, where they are to be obtained. Go as needy, guilty, and lost, to Jesus, the blessed Saviour. 'He receiveth sinners,' and is able to save to the uttermost, supplying every want from his own fulness, and that freely. Go with boldness, go with confidence to the throne of grace, a most suitable place for a sinner who has neither merit nor goodness in himself. Go there full of misery to receive mercy, completely unworthy, to receive grace; go at all times to receive 'grace to help in the time of need.' Is there any want that cannot be supplied by mercy and grace? O set a great value on the throne of grace! approach it frequently in private in your own personal case. That God may visit his church among you, cause his face to shine upon you, strengthen your grace, and increase your number, is my desire and prayer.

8. THE SAVING INFLUENCES OF THE HOLY SPIRIT

Llanfechell 24 September 1829

I should have written to you long ago, had I not been exceedingly engaged in the great work, ever since I had the pleasure of being with you. I have visited every chapel in this Island,[1] forty in number, preaching and keeping societies at the same time, encouraging and urging the people to pay off the debt on their chapels; I had moreover to preach in different places on the Sabbath day; so I had no time to write even to my dearest friends.

We had a very excellent and precious Association at Pwllheli. Several of the brethren from South Wales were there, and preached very well; John Evans, of New Inn,[2] W. Morris, M. Howells, D.

[1] Anglesey.
[2] Probably the New Inn of North Carmarthenshire.

Evans, and D. Naylor. We had a most delightful meeting in private; it was respecting the operations of the Spirit, especially his work in convincing and regenerating sinners, and uniting them to Christ.

1 Respecting *Conviction*. We observed that none can convince a sinner, no, not even by gifts and learning though ever so great: it is entirely the work of the Spirit of God. Conviction consists in enlightening, teaching, and manifesting; in other words, bringing to light, shewing openly what was hid before; making sin to appear very sinful; exhibiting sin in the heart, the corrupt nature of man; shewing the demerit and punishment of sin, and that our sins are numberless and incalculable; making it evident that our state is ruined and hopeless as to anything man can do; bringing the sinner not only to assent to this view of the matter, but also to perceive that such really is his painful condition. He clearly sees that he has no ground to stand upon; his legal hopes expire, he is thoroughly awakened out of his thoughtless and indifferent frame of mind, he is brought to cry out for his life, 'Save Lord, I perish'. O what need is there of this spirit of conviction in our preaching! The Holy Ghost continues convincing the believer whilst in this world. There is great need of this work in the church.

2 Respecting *Regeneration*. This is also the work of the Spirit of God; it is called, being *born* of the Spirit. He implants a new principle or nature in the soul of man; it is creating a new nature in all the parts and powers of the soul. It is not a notion in the head, or words on the lips, but a nature in the heart. Though the old nature is not cast out, yet it is brought down from the throne of the heart, and the new nature is placed there to reign; a light in the understanding, and obedience to God and Christ in the will, a right judgment in the conscience; a right ordering of the affections, and their delight in divine spiritual and holy objects, a retaining of them in the memory; keeping the affections and desires in due subordination. Hence follows the bitter and constant warfare of grace and corruption in the heart.

3 Respecting our *union* with the Lord. The soul is now united by the Spirit to Christ. We cannot say that either of these operations of the Spirit is before or after the other. There is no one, who is not regenerated, in Christ; nor any in Christ before he is born again. The

regenerated is alive, and there is no spiritual life but in Christ: in him is the fountain, yea, the beginning of the life and strength of the Christian.

I must conclude, I have no time. We enlarged greatly on the above subjects: they are much needed in the country. O that God would be pleased to pour his Holy Spirit from on high! I am very sorry that I have not more time to write to you; it was exceedingly difficult to obtain this little interval for writing the above. I salute the church in the most affectionate manner. My very kind regards to Mrs Jones, Mrs Davies, the Preachers– Hughes, Williams, Lewis, and Cleaton; to Mr Jones, Rosemary- lane, and his household; all the Elders; the Sunday School, the Society of the Young; Hughes, Hyso-street, and many more if I could recollect their names; also, those that are engaged in collect- ing money to pay the debt of the chapel. May the Lord be with all in his grace and mercy! I remain, through grace, your affec- tionate brother and servant.

9. LAMENTING THE DEAD STATE OF THE CHURCH

Fron 28 June 1831

Oh, my dear friends, be not content to live far from God! Oh, seek his face, seek him with *all* your heart! *Deuteronomy* 4.29. Is it not evident we do not seek him thus with the whole soul? If we sought him so, no doubt we should find him. Do we daily make use of Christ by faith? And pray, looking earnestly unto Jesus, for salvation? There is no acceptance of our prayers, but only through him; and we cannot pray successfully but under the guidance of the Spirit. Oh, let us pray for the spirit of grace and supplication!

It is a dark night on the Church, the depth of winter, when she is sleepy and ready to die, and the Lord is hiding his face in the ordinances, and when only a few are crying out for his appearance, and those scarcely audible in their call! It is still more awful, if while they are asleep they should think themselves awake, and imagine that they see the sun at midnight. Yet such are the circumstances of the Church generally. Yea, the darkness of night,

I say, is upon her, and she is slumbering, having lost the presence of her Lord, and so unhappy as not to know the loss she has sustained!

To Mrs Jones and Mrs Davies, London

1. DESIRES FOR PROSPERITY IN THE CHURCH

Llanfechell 30 January 1829

Dear Sisters, – I am thankful to you for your kind letter; in this you excel the brethren, like Deborah and Jael in former days. I have not received a letter from London this long time. I was longing to hear of your welfare. Your letter gave me great joy; I was glad to find that things were in a lively and comfortable state among you. I am, however, very sorry to learn that so few have entered the church during the last two years. It is painful that the church is so barren. What has become of all the excellent sermons that were delivered in your pulpit all that time? If none are born again among you, is there any growth in the children that are already in the house? Do they feed upon the bread of life, and gain strength?

Notwithstanding appearances, let us not despair or be disheartened. Perhaps some of the good seed cast into the ground is not devoured up by the birds, or scorched by the heat, or choked by the thorns, but may yet appear and bear fruit. God is ever living, almighty, and infinitely merciful, and he can of these stones raise up children unto Abraham, and make a barren church a joyful mother of children. It is a great blessing to be enabled to remain in the Lord's house. A delightful morning, a glorious day, will yet surely come. The dawn is to be seen over the hills, in the faithful promises. Let us believe, expect, pray, and labour.

Dear sisters, I pray that you both may have much of the Lord's countenance and fellowship: and may you enjoy every personal and family blessing, and a continuance of his mercy to be faithful in your situation with the great work! It is my earnest desire that you may have much spiritual support for your souls in the means of grace, especially in private prayer and hearing sermons. Use the time you may have together in praying and conversing about the things of the Gospel. Let your love for each other, and mutual fellowship, be godly and spiritual. May your conversation be like iron sharpening iron, animating each other to love unfeigned and good works. Trust in the Lord for ever; he can and will keep you. Your situation is important, one the wife of an elder, and the other an housekeeper and mother to ministers – high places! Pray that you may shine in them.

I have neither room nor time to enlarge. I am almost always from home; I am going out again next week to the monthly meeting at Mold, to open a chapel near Wrexham, and from thence to Liverpool, and thence to Denbigh, and homewards in March.

2. SPIRITUAL DECLENSIONS–THE SABBATH

Llanfechell 3 August 1837

Dear Sisters – I am sorry to perceive by your letter that none come now to the church as members. Who can refrain crying out, 'I have laboured in vain, I have spent my strength for nought and in vain.' *Isaiah* 49.4. I am still more distressed at hearing that some go out of the church. O foolish creatures, selling the church of God for the empty toys and pleasures of the world and flesh! Each of them will, alas, cry out one day, 'How foolish was I, and without understanding'! But the loss of such is not after all a loss to the church. 'They were not of us; they went out from us, that they might be made manifest that they were not all of us.' 1 *John* 2.19. Perhaps the church, if divested of more of those hypocrites that press on her skirts like a heavy load, would move on more light and lively towards home. The iniquities of the visible Church have separated between her and God, and her sins have hid his face from her. *Isaiah* 59.2. Yet let us remember, to our no small comfort, 'the Lord's hand is not shortened that it cannot save; neither is his ear heavy, that it cannot hear.' *Isaiah* 59.1. Our prayers grow cold and insipid, there is very little earnestness and importunity in them. And very few warm and anxious prayers are offered up for ministers: if God does not give plentifully to them, they are empty, and can afford nothing to others. O that the Church was awakened to pray! there is abundance in the storehouse of grace, there is fulness in the promises.

We continue to converse in our meetings, and in the churches, on keeping the Sabbath more holy, and we have room to think that the Lord is pleased with it. We are persuaded now, that our manner in spending the Sabbath, especially as to our spirits and words, is very displeasing to the Lord: and if the frame of our minds and conduct is offensive to God on the particular day we have to wait on him, how can we expect to have his favour, his assistance, and to see him working among us? We examine every one in the churches as to his manner of spending the Sabbath; we ask him two things in particular: 1. Does he call the Sabbath a delight? 2. In what sense is it a delight to him? We have remarkable answers from many. But the most part are lamenting on account of the state of their hearts on the Sabbath. We are in hopes that the attempt will be blessed for the revival of our churches. If private prayers were more frequent and earnest, and the conversations more religious and spiritual on the Sabbath, the public ministry would be more effectual, and more blessings would be communicated. There is great need to see more of the effects of sermons on the members of churches. How can we expect to see much of the powerful effects of the Gospel on the *world*, when so little of its sacred influences are visible on the Church? When the doctrines of grace are not powerful enough to awaken those that sleep, how can it be expected that those that are *dead* can hear it and live? Let us earnestly pray that the Lord's voice may sound in the ministry, and that in so powerful a manner that those that sleep may awake, and the dead be raised up.

Dear sisters, you may by prayers do much towards the success of the great cause. The throne of grace is open for you, and the prayers of women are as acceptable as those of the most popular ministers, in the name of the great Mediator. If you would walk with God and please him, be often at the throne of grace, seeking for guidance and strength. May your conversation with each other as you live in the same house, be religious, spiritual, and profitable;

let it be chiefly respecting God and the Bible, yourselves, and the other world! As you are now dear friends together, watch and pray that no enemy may succeed to damp your mutual love or to bring in suspicions. Encourage and stir up each other to love and to good works: teach, support, and comfort each other; 'Bear each other's burdens.' Be of the same mind, and think the same thing in *the Lord*. And the God of peace be with your souls!

The Church of God in Liverpool
Mr John Roberts

I. PROVIDING A 'SUPPLY'

Fron 24 January, 1832

I am truly sorry I have been so long unable to write to you, and to inform you of a 'supply'. A young man in this country is coming to Liverpool next month; his name is W. Jones; he preaches well, and is very acceptable; powerful effects sometimes follow his ministry. He means to stop a month or two in your town to learn navigation. Don't praise him, especially before his face, for he is but young. On the other hand, don't look cross or stern upon him, despising his youth, that he may not be discouraged, but pray for him.

I have no time, I am sorry to say, to write on the greatest point – preaching and pains with the work. Give yourself constantly unto the Lord, that he may use you as he pleases. Pray that you may be entirely for him as the *man of God*, without self-seeking or self-preaching. He can very well teach, support, and employ you. Depend upon him.

2. CONGRATULATIONS ON THE BIRTH
OF A SON

Fron 15 November 1832

Your letter gave me no small pleasure, not only in hearing that you are better, but also on account of the Lord's goodness to you as a family, in the deliverance of Mrs Roberts, and the birth of a son. May you both gratefully acknowledge that you have received a great gift from the Lord, more valuable than any earthly inheritance. No doubt the cause of thankfulness is hereby increased. Though your anxiety will be greater, yet you can commit all the care of your young child and yourself to him that conferred such a gift upon you. He said, by giving him to you, 'Nurse this child for me;' and so you may go as often as you please to him, and ask him, 'How wilt thou have me nurse this lad for thee?' He that commanded you to train him up for him, has everything necessary for that purpose, and enough of temporal and spiritual things besides for your son. Dedicate him to the Lord, that he may be his all the days of his life. I feel much obliged to you both for wishing me to baptize your son; but it is not likely I can, in any reasonable time, come to enjoy that pleasure. It is, however, of no importance what minister of Christ performs that office.

3. CHURCH DISCIPLINE – ELIAS ABUSED IN THE PRESS

Fron 1 April 1833

I do not know what to say respecting a certain case; however, it requires much caution. You cannot receive him back into the church without his making a clear public confession of his repentance for his first fault, 'receiving money for his vote;' and also for his obstinacy in rejecting reproof and correction; and for his contempt of church discipline, and moreover for spending the unrighteous wages, and so disabling himself to return it. I do not think that any one of his sins is unpardonable. But it is impossible to forgive them without repentance: and further he cannot be received into the church without an humble confession of his repentance, and sorrow that he is unable to return the evil reward. Yet be gentle and kind.[1]

---

[1] There had been a contested election for a Member of Parliament in a certain place, and the above individual, on returning to the society, had been excluded by reason of receiving a bribe from one of the candidates. It may be truly said

My letter in the 'Record' newspaper has made some noise. It was inserted in the Bangor and Caernarvon newspapers without my consent. I was abused in a Carmarthen newspaper, and vilified in a pamphlet at Caernarvon. But I am not sorry for what I did. I am not the worse for being beaten about. I received several letters of the opposite nature, commending what I had done: one was from an M.A. at Oxford, a stranger to me, saying that the Calvinistic Methodist Connexion is the most upright and pure denomination in the world; also wishing that they were at Oxford. But I take no notice of what is said by either side. My conscience is clear as to what I have done.

I wish you may be strengthened in your health, and have much support in the great work. I perceive that I want more sobriety and spirituality in every opportunity to preach to the people. I see myself failing in awakening attention and thoughtfulness in the hearers. There is a great heedlessness in many; and others regard nothing but the man and the point! Alas, there are but few that feel the efficacy and perceive the excellency of the truth! O that we were enabled to preach the Word until the people felt!

4. LAMENTATIONS OVER THE STATE OF THE CHURCH

From 2 November 1833

The evening of my life is now far advanced; it would afford me great pleasure to be enabled to do yet a little more, before the night cometh when none can work. I fear, dear brother, that it is night on the Church both in England and Wales, and that both preachers and hearers are very great strangers to particular visits from the Lord! And what is still worse, they are unconcerned

---

that with regard to discipline, Elias was a Moses and a Phinehas in fervent zeal for the glory of God and in opposition to sin. Yet when he saw any signs of repentance and a likelihood of reformation, he was a spiritual physician, and very ready to 'restore such an one in the spirit of meekness.' He feared much lest discipline should ever be lowered in the Connexion. Thus the care of all the societies was a heavy burden upon his mind; and it is thought that this aggravated his bodily disorder in his last days.

about them! If we were examined as to when we experienced things under sermons, which we were certain could not be produced by words proceeding only from the pre-meditation, memory, and gifts of the preacher, should we not be almost silent? If we should be asked of the seasons when we were in great and powerful wrestlings in private prayer for those things, should we not be ashamed to confess that our prayers have been quite the reverse? O how cold, slack, and feeble! If it were asked our hearers, if it were enquired in the church, when did they feel under the ministry, things they know that the gifts, manner, delivery, voice, or eloquence of man could not produce, would not the greater part be silent, being ignorant of such a thing? Are these not signs that God is hiding his face, and none arising to lay hold of him! 'O that thou wouldest rend the heavens; that thou wouldest come down, that the mountains might flow down at thy presence.' *Isaiah* 64.1.

5. 'THE PREACHER': A PERIODICAL

Fron 17 December 1835

I did intend looking carefully over the manuscript you sent me, but time failed me; I have, as they say, too many irons in the fire. I am obliged to return them as they were, since the messenger is waiting. As to my sermon on *Colossians* 1.16, I shall have no objection for you to print it, in case you write it over again, and change some words that might not be deemed quite proper. I can entrust the whole to you confidently. I put in some words by way of introduction, and a few for the purpose of filling up, and others I altered. I have but very little time. I commit another sermon to your care, that on *Matthew* 17.5. I think the manuscript pretty correct. However, I could not go through it carefully. I am sorry the *Preacher* is not better distributed among us. The travelling booksellers are not sufficiently careful in collecting the money for the books. We want faithful, laborious booksellers to traverse the country. Some hundreds could be disposed of in that case. I dare not speak a word in the monthly meetings respecting the books.

The elders have been so much disappointed by distributors of books, who leave them under the burden. I am sorry you sustain loss as well as trouble with the *Preacher*. It is a pity you are not encouraged to go on without any loss. The books are very useful, and those that read them like them much. I hope you may yet find some way to go on more successfully in the work. The labour is enough without the loss. Some notes you took out of my sermons I will confidently entrust unto your care for publication, without my seeing them. I am publishing a small tract on the temperance society, by way of conversation; it is in the press.

6. DEEP INTEREST IN THE AFFAIRS OF THE CHURCH

Fron November 1836

It affords me much pleasure to hear that Mr Rees is likely to reside at Liverpool. It is to be hoped you will have him as a gift from the Lord in his good providence; and that you as a church seek him from God. I trust you perceive that he is but a conduit pipe, that he cannot be of any use but in the degree in which the true and living water is conveyed through him. There is no one in our Connexion whom I should be so glad to see going to Liverpool as Mr Rees, yet no implicit confidence should be put in us ministers. I hope you are all of the same mind. There is not much dependence on the zeal of some. They will extol one person and make him a king to-day, but they will to-morrow cry, 'Away with him.'

I have no time to look over old sermons, I am in hopes of having new ones; I do nothing as I should, but I am not idle. As to the sermon on 2 *Corinthians* 4.7, I have looked over the manuscript, it is tolerably large and correct. I have been very busy the last weeks in trying to write a small tract, 'A persuasive to the Welsh to encourage the observance of the Sabbath, by sending petitions to Parliament.' I have endeavoured to show that it is the duty and privilege of temporal rulers to protect Christianity and morality. It is now in the Bangor printing press. I am very glad to find that the old dear chapels, where many souls have been saved, are now disencumbered from debt – places where the Lord of hosts was seen 'with his train filling the temple'; 'this is the Lord's doing.' I am happy to hear of the success of the Protestant Association. I hope that its members will soon fill all the offices in the town.

7. GREAT CONCERN FOR SOULS –
   WISE DIRECTIONS

Fron 18 November 1836

No doubt but that afflictions are necessary, and that our heavenly Father has a wise end in view in sending them. They are administered by gentle measures. He restrains the wind of affliction in a kind and compassionate manner. O how sweet is the word, 'But he for our profit, that we might be partakers of his holiness'! As this is the end, who would not exclaim, Welcome crosses, afflictions, troubles, and chastisements!

As to the trouble of your mind in respect of your ministry and eternal state, it is right it should be so, and it is awful that any preach the Gospel without experiencing such troubles and trials. We ought to consider our accountableness to God as to the work of the ministry, and our manner in it, and our state of mind, our situation as sinners before God, each for himself. Our office, work, gifts, or manner of fulfilling our engagements, bear no relation to our state before God. It is true that our poor, carnal, cold formal manner in the work is a great sin, and we should grieve on account of it. I have constantly some cause of shame and sorrow in my ministry. I know not how it is that some seem to take pride in their manner of preaching! Though my deficiencies and failings in the great work increase my grief very much, yet by trying as a guilty sinner to go to the throne of grace, and to lift up my eye to Christ who offered an atonement for sin, I see the way to the pardon of all my iniquities, even the sins of my holy things. I cannot approach the throne of grace as a preacher or a godly man, but as a lost sinner, and as one that hath sinned grievously as a Christian and a minister. I can testify that to draw near God in that way is good for me. Let us pray, when accused that we do not taste or know the things we preach, for a more enlarged experience, but let us not be discouraged. We can never say too much of Christ and his treasures of grace, by way of commending him and salvation to others. Therefore, brother, let us pray that we may become better acquainted with divine things ourselves, and speak better of them to others. But after all, we must rest as lost sinners on Christ and his sacrifice.

8. INVITATION TO PRAYER – DANGERS

Fron 1 January 1838

We held a prayer-meeting at nine o'clock this morning, supplicating the throne of grace for the out-pouring of the Spirit; as we were invited to do by the Rev J. H. Stewart of Liverpool. Oh that every true Christian were really awakened to call upon God for his blessing! There is a great need of it. What will become of us this year? There are many dangers: but alas, only few consider them! God can deliver us. Awful clouds overhang Britiain: where are the believing importunate persons in prayer? Let Christians look up; from thence deliverance may come. It is very dark and gloomy below. Men of this age think, alas, they can do all things – some to preach and some to govern the country – without God! But without him I can do nothing.

9. DIRECTIONS IN TRYING CIRCUMSTANCES

Fron 14 May 1839

I am glad you are disposed to return good for evil. Such conduct will be comfortable to your conscience, and honourable to your profession and office. Such disagreeable circumstances are not strange to many. Let us go to the Word of God for directions, and to the throne of grace for strength; so we shall live to the glory of God and our own comfort. The storms will pass by presently. We shall land, out of the tempestuous ocean, in the much-desired haven. Oh may the Pilot be with us in the vessel, and manage the helm, which we should gladly give him! Let us not trust in our own understanding, neither let us be governed by our own inclinations.

Two brother ministers in this country have been appointed to come to you for a while. O seek for the divine blessing to attend their preaching! If the Lord does not favour you with his presence, it will be but poor work, whoever comes. But if he that descended on the day of Pentecost in his mighty operations should come amongst you, the preaching will be remarkable whoever the ministers may be, and will not soon be forgotten. O that God would be pleased to manifest himself! We are too carnal and selfish; there is too much of the man in all we do. But God must come to view, in his excellency and glory, before the cause of religion is revived among us. Some good men were lamenting the deadness of Christianity before the days of Whitefield, and using strong and excellent reasons against infidelity, yet nothing availed. The spiritual sleep was increasing, and infidelity was gaining ground, until God appeared through the fiery ministry of that great man. Oh, there is as much need of his manifestation now as ever!

I have been about a week at Beaumaris, and was three times in the warm bath. I have cause to be thankful that I am much better. I now begin to hope I shall be able to attend Bala Association. I have not missed one there these forty-six years. I preached the last three Sunday evenings. Though I am somewhat restored in my bodily health, yet I feel a want of quickening and restoring as to the spirit of the ministry. Preaching appears to me as something new. I have as much need of teaching and strengthening as the first time. It is my great desire, if spared a little longer, to be made more spiritual than ever.

10. DANGERS TO THE FOLD APPREHENDED

Fron 30 May 1839

I feel very strong desire to attend Bala Association this year. I feel that I am poorly and nervous; yet the Lord may support me, and enable me to fill up some gap there, to prevent certain evil things coming in. The times are evil! The watchmen are not very alert and observant. The multitudes of enemies that surround the castle walls bear deceitful colours; not many of the watchmen know them! They are for opening the gates to many a hostile regiment! O let it never be said of the Welsh Calvinistic Methodists, 'Their watchmen are blind'!

To Mr John Jones, a Preacher at Liverpool

ON THE DEATH OF MR HUGHES,
A FELLOW-LABOURER

Llanfechell 29 November 1828

I am truly sorry that I did not write to you sooner; but it was not the want of love, or indifference to your painful situation that prevented me, but the multiplicity of circumstances and calls in the great work, and frequent absence from home. And indeed, I know not, being so filled with amazement and grief, what to write. The loss of many in Liverpool is very great by the departure of Mr Hughes: I feel greatly for his widow and children and the church. But I imagine that your loss is very great in some respects. You have been deprived of a careful father in Christ, a kind brother, and a diligent and faithful fellow-labourer; and you are left as it were alone, to lead a very large army: but we should remember that it is the Lord that wrought this, who does all things in infinite wisdom and goodness.

I know, dear brother, that your thoughts are very low, sorrowful, and perplexed, as you were before much dejected on account of the greatness of the work, and your imperfections and weakness in it. Now as a much heavier burden rests upon your weak shoulder, no doubt you feel it very much, and perhaps, sometimes, fear sinking under it, and that you may not be able to go on. But remember, brother, that if God sees fit to increase the burden, he can strengthen the shoulder. He can make your grace stronger, and multiply your gifts, and increase your comfort in his work; he can give you wisdom and strength necessary to feed and to succour the church in all her various trials.

In thinking of you, the words of the Lord to Joshua after the departure of Moses came unto my mind; which are the following: 'As I was with Moses, so I shall be with thee; I will not fail thee, nor forsake thee.' St Paul used this expression for the consolation of all believers, in his day. *Hebrews* 13.5. And you may apply it to yourself, as your special comfort, in your present trying situation. The Lord said to Joshua three times, 'Be thou strong and of good courage; for unto this people shalt thou divide for an inheritance the land which I swore unto their fathers to give them. Be thou strong and very courageous, that thou mayest observe to do according to all the law, that thou mayest prosper.' Again, 'Be strong and of good courage; be not afraid, neither be thou dismayed: for the Lord thy God is with thee, whithersoever thou goest.' *Joshua* 1.6–10. O my dear friend, apply these most comfortable words to thyself: 'Be strong' – to lead the Israel of God, with your eye upon the covenant and oath of God! 'Be strong' – to observe and keep the Word of God, as a Christian and a preacher, let it not depart out of your mouth; meditate on it day and night. Then you will prosper in your ways. To grieve the Spirit and to lose the gracious countenance of his God, is the chief danger of a preacher. 'Be strong,' – believing in the promise of God to be with you, then who can be against you to any purpose? Who can frustrate your success? He has supported many weak ones whose strength failed them. The weak brother that writes to you now, is an experimental proof of that. Rest on God: be submissive and calm; work and be not discouraged. Though you have lost a father and a brother in the church, our heavenly Father is still alive: our elder and best Brother liveth for ever; yes, holding the stars in his right hand. He will ever keep them from falling, and preserve them in their brightness: and even you and I, if kept in his hand, shall stand and shine. Besides you have, my friend, many brethren in Wales, who are ready to assist with their prayers and counsels. I will not enlarge. I desire that you will receive the above lines as a token of brotherly love and Christian care for you: and please to read the following lines to the church:

Dear Brethren in Christ – 'Grace and peace be multiplied unto you.' I have thought much of you; and have prayed and felt much for you, ever since I heard of the death of my dear brother and fellow-labourer, and faithful servant in Christ, your most devoted minister in Christ, the late Rev J. Hughes. I know that your grief and sorrow after him are very great, and that you consider yourselves as children bereaved of their father. Though itinerant and stated brethren that officiate among you are very laborious and faithful, yet his place and office are no doubt observed by you as unsupplied and empty. The sorrow of none, perhaps, is greater than that of your minister and elders, who labour constantly among you. Dear friends, your grief and sorrow are meet and becoming; yet there is danger lest you should fall into discouragement and let your hands hang down in the work. Our dear brother, though so faithful, was but a servant of the Owner of the work; an instrument in his hand, though so useful; a shepherd under the great Shepherd, though so careful. The Lord of the vineyard is still alive. The good Shepherd yet careth for his sheep, yea, he is still among them, though the day be cloudy and dark. He will never leave them. 'None shall be able to pluck them out of his hand.' He will stand and feed them by such hand as he thinks proper. His eye is ever on them, and his arm always underneath them. He will preserve them day and night, lest any should hurt them.

But I would not have you to be indifferent to the providential dispensation, and the voice of God towards you, in the very afflictive circumstance that occurred to you. I should be happy to advise you in the words of the Apostle, 'Remember him who had the rule over you, who spoke unto you the word of God; whose faith follow, considering the end of his conversation.' Remember him, and think of his holy life, and his consistent walk; his sound evangelical sermons; his wise, serious, and weighty counsels; his peaceable and kind spirit; his endeavour, skill and authority to preserve peace in the church: though dead, he yet speaketh. Do not forget him: hearken, 'follow his faith;' adhere to the doctrine of faith which he believed, experienced, and preached; which he preserved firmly, and continued holding forth triumphantly, which also supported him in the painful struggles of death. Observe and closely follow his example, living by faith. It is not a dead and fruitless faith he had, but a living principle, faith receiving strength out of the fulness of Christ, to live godly in the world. Follow the weighty counsels and useful rules he often gave you in the church. There is not a church in Liverpool that enjoyed such provisions and superintendence as yours. I hope their good effects will not terminate in this age.

Consider the end of his life; he held on his way; he increased in strength; he overcame in the battle; he triumphed to the end: he kept the faith spotless, kept his garments uncontaminated; he held his crown untarnished; he finished his course victoriously; he reached the goal; he had an abundant entrance into the eternal kingdom of his Lord. Such was the end of his life and conversation. His religion answered the best purposes in life and in death, administering profit and comfort to himself, benefit to others, and bringing glory to God. Remember and consider his counsels and exhortations; strive for experiences similar to his; walk in his paths, and seek for strength from above.

Though he has fled from you to the peaceful habitation, the world of perfection, where there is no sinning and no woe, to receive the crown of life from the righteous Judge, yet, Jesus Christ is the same. The earthen vessel from which you had the precious treasure is broken, but the treasure remains the same; it was not lost by breaking the vessel. Some other vessel shall be provided to convey the treasure to you. The pipe through which the waters of life flowed clearly to you, for a long period, is broken by death, but the waters never fail; they will run to you again through some other pipe; you shall not perish through thirst in this evil parched wilderness. Jesus yet cries out, 'If any one thirsts, let him come unto me and drink, and take of the waters of life freely.' O make use of them!

Dear friends, allow a poor brother that loves you much to give you some further advice in your present mournful circumstances.

1 Pray for more of the Lord's gracious presence among you, and a
more copious out-pouring of the Holy Spirit upon you. Jesus Christ
promised his Spirit to comfort his disciples after his departure from
them; and he doubtless can comfort his church upon the loss of a
faithful minister.

2 Resolve one with another that all of you in person, family and church,
will strive to walk in the paths you were taught, and earnestly
encouraged to pursue, by the brother that is fallen asleep in Christ.

3 Persevere and labour to preserve church union among you. 'Let
brotherly love continue among you, endeavour to keep the unity of
the Spirit in the bond of peace.' Let each resolve, by the help of
God's grace, that nothing on his part, either in judgment, words, or
conduct, shall be the means of disturbing the peace of the church, or
weakening her union. Christ did not pray so earnestly for anything,
neither did he seek anything so frequently in his last prayer, as the
union of his people, that they might be one. The Apostles, in their
letters to the churches, earnestly exhorted them to maintain brotherly
love and union, to be of 'the same mind, of the same judgment,'
agreeing together, thinking the same thing, and having the same love
together; and thus they taught them that this is the way to obtain
edification and consolation and the presence of God. He is the God of
love and peace. And he dwells where these excellences reign. The
union of the church is the true minister's fulness of joy; 'Fulfil my
joy by thinking the same thing.' It will be easy to be peaceable if we
have grace to be humble and self-denying. The contentious and
quarrelsome loves himself more than Christ and his church. He
would, for the sake of name and opinion, destroy, as far as his
influence goes, the church for which Christ died! I think better
things of you.

4 Pray much for growth in spiritual, experimental, and evangelical
religion, and for spiritual taste, that you may love the Gospel for its
sound doctrines, and not on account of the gifts or delivery of any
minister. And endeavour to come to hear the Word as the hungry
man comes to the table, to satisfy his craving appetite; not as the
glutton at the end of the feast, undecided out of what dish he may
eat, but like the little children, desiring the sincere milk of the Word.

5 Let every member of the church be careful as to their expressions,
that their conversation be always seasoned with grace, tending to

administer grace to the hearer. Real grace governs the tongue: the professor whose tongue is ungovernable, deceives himself. The tongue has injured flourishing churches often. Let us use our tongue for the glory of God.

6 Let the churches be very careful as to their young ones. Let them feed the kids near the Shepherd's tents. Take care of the lambs that belong to Christ's fold. The good Shepherd bears them in his bosom. And the church officers who love Christ are commanded to feed them. One of the signs of the foolish and false shepherds is this, 'Neither shall seek the young one.' *Zechariah* 11.16. O brethren! care for the young, for out of them God will raise up for you priests and Levites. Some of them will be princes in all your land presently. Now I conclude – but say to the elders (as Israel did to Joshua, in chapter 1.17, 18), Pray for me also.

To the Rev Henry Rees

ZEAL FOR THE CAUSE OF GOD,
AND USEFUL HINTS

Fron 2 March 1838

I am sorry I cannot visit your parts now, according to the desire of friends. I have arranged my time for weeks, if spared. I am almost every day engaged in preaching the Word in this island: and that is the reason I have been so long in answering your letter. I have been wonderfully supported as to my health; yet, though I travel so much, I am far from being strong and well. I pray I may have grace to employ what health I have in the service and for the glory of him that gives and supports it. I am glad to find that the zeal of teetotallers continues with you. The cause of total abstinence prospers with us also; and some of its members join our church. I was last week in many of the Teetotal Abstinence Meetings, and it was good to be there.

Dear brother, my mind is constantly grieved that the divine light and power, once known and felt, do not accompany the ministry in these days! Neither the Total Abstinence Society, though so good, nor any other consideration of the kind, can give ease to my troubled mind in this respect. I fear that there are many among us who see the need of nothing more than what we now have. When prayer is made in behalf of the ministry, all that is asked is that the minister may be enabled to *speak freely*. This is granted, and many desire no more! There is danger in our being in such a state. Few consider the ministry of the Gospel as a means to a high end, and a means only. The best preacher is but an instrument, and the best sermons but means; they will not answer the end, except God himself will work through them. Alas, how few consider that Paul and Apollos are nothing, and that it is God that does the whole work!

I hear that unsound and slight thoughts of the work of the Holy Spirit are entertained by many in these days, and that he is grieved thereby. I heard a man this week assert in a speech that 'Influences are inseparably connected with all truths, so that if the truth be set forth sufficiently clear, accompanied with strong reasons and earnest persuasions it will prevail with all.' If so, nothing more is wanted but that we be strong and eloquent speakers, persuasive, impressive, and clever; and we shall then overcome the world! Is there not here a want of perceiving the corruption, obstinacy, and spiritual deadness of man, and the consequent necessity of the Almighty Spirit to enlighten and overcome him?

We do not yet dare to speak in terms like these just mentioned, but is not our conduct too like those who think so? O that the day would dawn! O that God would manifest himself! O that the Holy Ghost were on some occasional opportunity so poured under the ministry of some of God's servants, until there should appear an evident difference between his work and everything human, and between the divine ordinances in and through which he works, and those ordinances wherein he hides his face and leaves men to themselves!

My mind has also been grieved in hearing of your trouble in the church, as you have stated. And glad am I to find things are likely to terminate better than you feared. May the Lord appear among you, may his glory descend, may the 'cloud and fire be upon the tabernacle,' that the authors of discord may be terrified! May the divine defence be upon you! I was sorry to find that any thing in this affair had operated on your mind in a way of discouragement and dejection. I am very sensible of similar effects in various circumstances connected with the ministerial work; but as soon as I have emerged out of the storm, I have been compelled to blame myself frequently, and to attribute my perplexity and dejection to the weakness of my grace, and want of near and frequent communion with the Lord. Therefore, my dear friend, take courage and be strong; draw near to the throne of grace, for 'grace and mercy in the time of need.' Commit the cause of the church in all its dangers to him, whose she is, that he may govern the minds and tongues of all. Do not cherish the wavering that is in your mind respecting your stay at Liverpool. The field, it is true, is very extensive for you to cultivate, and you also feeble; but you are in an advantageous position to seek to do good: and though you cannot of yourself do anything, yet the Lord can make use of you as an instrument. You say 'you are not a sufficient preacher.' But where is the man to succeed you? Who is sufficient? If some one would say, 'I am sufficient', it might be said to such a one, 'Thou art weighed in the balance and found wanting.' Therefore, if no one can be found a sufficient preacher, it matters not whether you or another be at the post. Remain quiet until a sufficient preacher be found to succeed you. Be still, brother, till some clear proof appears that providence removes you. My prayer is, 'O that the Lord would make me useful somewhere!' Since he can, I will wait on him.

To the Rev Robert Jones, Ty Bwlcyn

9 March 1801

My dear brother, rather father in the Gospel – Our churches stand in great need of divine support and help. The world as such is as well as can be expected; but the church is not so! I fear from the present approach of the church to the world, that we come nearer to the world than they do to us! I fear that much of that arises from the decay of discipline; and I think that much of that decay proceeds from not watching and ruling our own spirits. We weaken ourselves exceedingly by improper indulgences, and consequently we cannot rebuke them in others, as they are in us as well.

To Mr Daniel Jones,[1] a preacher at Liverpool

ON TRYING CIRCUMSTANCES

Llanfechell 16 October 1812

I am very sorry for your great troubles. To sympathize with you is easy for me, but to make the storm subside is impossible. However, there is One, I am happy to say, who can do that unspeakable kindness; though he appears sometimes sleeping when his disciples are overwhelmed with the greatest waves, which makes them think that he is regardless of their misery and ruin; yet he is with them, even then in the vessel; and he will arise in his own time, and will say to the tempestuous storms, 'Be still'; and to the furious waves, 'Be calm.' The change in these elements will be as if laughing with joy, as the Greek word signifies. The raging sea will subside and laugh in its beauty and gladness.

So, brother, whatever storms of affliction may overtake you, yet if you have Christ with you in the vessel, it will come to land safe. There will be no shipwreck; he can manage and over-rule the storm. I myself know much of fears, depressions, tossings within, but it was useless to make my complaint known to any one. It was well for me many a time to draw near to God; I know he delivered me for the *sake* of his great name, which ground only I had to plead before him. This consideration was always on my mind,

---

[1] The son of the Rev Robert Jones of the preceding letter.

when I attempted praying in respect of my worldly circumstances, that it was not wealth nor honour, nor ease and pleasure, that I wanted; nor was it poverty itself I feared; but failing to pay my way, and to do justice to men, thereby giving cause to the enemies of God to *blaspheme* his holy name and Word. This I greatly dreaded. The Lord, out of great kindness, has hitherto preserved me from those evils; and I hope he will henceforth keep me to the end. If he should thus favour me, his name shall be praised for ever. This is my desire for you also; and my advice to you is, 'Commit thy ways to him, and put thy trust in him for ever.' The dark tempestuous night will not continue long. Infinite love and kindness dwell in the person that rules the storms. 'He will restrain his strong tempestuous wind in the day of his east wind.'

To the Church of God in America

I. THE MINISTRY – THE CHURCHES

Llanfechell 24 November 1826

We are happy to hear of B. Davies's arrival among you. He may be the instrument of God's appointment for usefulness. He was active, useful, and exemplary in the Lord's vineyard in Monmouthshire. We have no objection that he should be ordained. It is customary that one minister or more should be present when a person is set apart for the ministry. There are many of the Presbyterian Church in the United States, and rather resembling us, not only in the faith, but also in discipline. I have a book called, *A Platform of Church Discipline, practised in the Churches of New England* by Cotton Mather, D.D. The church discipline set forth in that treatise is almost altogether agreeable with our views in that respect.[1] It would be almost desirable if you could obtain a minister from one of those churches to assist you in ordaining B. Davies.

[1] Elias was also pleased with (Archbishop) James Usher's plan of Church Government.

We hope the Lord will teach and lead you in the way you should go. It is of the greatest importance to be enabled to commence the cause, to establish a Welsh church in America that is likely to flourish for ages to come; profitable to the children and grand-children of those that exist now.

Take great care you are not formal and carnal in the worship of God. Be frequent and earnest in private prayers: one common cause of our poverty in public worship is our indifference in private prayer. Let preachers and hearers be truly sensible of their utter inability in the Lord's service; and be most anxious for his presence in every department of the work. Be very particular as to the persons you may receive into your small church; and keep strict discipline over your members, that there may be nothing in any of you to cause the Lord to hide his face from you. Be careful that every member maintains a full and regular family worship in his house, and also proper discipline. Be sure to bring up your offspring in a religious manner, training them up in the nurture and admonition of the Lord. The privileges of the church belong to them. O do not deprive them of the most valuable things possible! You will very soon go the way of all the earth, and leave your children in the wilderness of America. Would not the thought of their growing up an ignorant and an hardened race be most distressing? If they should preserve their language, living at the same time destitute of the power and excellency of religion, they may become ultimately very heathenish and ungodly! O labour with them in the best things, and pray much for them! Pray that they may see the cloud of the Lord's glory on his tabernacle among you, that they may desire to remain there all the days of their lives, to behold the fair beauty of the Lord. 'Let thy work, O Lord, appear unto thy servants, and thy glory unto their children.' *Psalm* 90.16.

If we are truly in Christ, united to him by faith, we shall be united to each other in him, in a union that the vastness of the extensive seas cannot impede, nor even stern death dissolve. It is 'unity of the faith, and of the knowledge of the Son of God.' And we shall be presently in the world above, one glorious body for ever.

The work of the Lord prospers in our country, and appears promising. Great multitudes hear the Word; Sunday schools are very encouraging. Some enter the Connexion in different parts of the country: two or three come in together sometimes. It is but seldom we hear of any backsliding or falling unto open presumptuous sins. Peace reigns in general through our churches. A remarkable union prevails in our monthly and quarterly meetings throughout Wales. I have the privilege of being a member of the Association now upwards of thirty years, and I never before witnessed such an endearing union, and such affectionate fondness for each other, as appear among us in all our meetings these years.

What we dwelt upon in our Associations lately, had a reference to practical religion. We exhorted each other, and all the churches, to strive together against the corruptions of the land, such as drunkenness, uncleanness, and other vices. We also stirred up each other to be more particular as to family religion, especially the great work of governing the household well, and keeping the children in due subordination and subjection. It was shewed that there is room to doubt our religion, if there are not good fruits of it in the family. We also encouraged each other to pray more earnestly and frequently for the outpouring of the Spirit. All our exertions in every branch of the work are in vain without the Spirit; he only makes the means of grace profitable and effectual. We made observations on prayer in general – the nature of private, family, and public prayer; on the manner we ought to pray; the things that should be in us praying, as great reverence of God's name, and humility before him by reason of our nothingness and sinfulness, the greatness and purity of God. We also pointed out the necessity of applying to the Mediator in prayer; and we alluded to the necessity of suitable words in prayer, especially when public. They should all be words of prayer, words uttered to the Highest – words not to exhort, not to preach, nor to reprove a fellow creature. Our words should be comprehensive, weighty, sober, and suitable; arising out of serious thinking and feeling of the heart; containing confession, petitions, and thanksgiving; our words should not be vain and numerous.

2. ON THE HELPING OF THE YOUNG
AND THE KEEPING OF THE SABBATH

Liverpool 7 September 1827

I am truly sorry that I have been so long in writing to you. My engagements prevented me. I was obliged to go to London soon after I received your last letter, and afterwards to Bristol, and from thence to an Association in Glamorganshire. In a word, I have had little leisure since. I am now at Liverpool; and so many things belonging to the great work here demand my attention, that I have but very little time to write to you, and I should not deem my letter worth sending to you, had I not an opportunity of forwarding the Confession of our Faith, in English, with it.

I am sorry we have not yet met with a minister to send over to you. Continue praying earnestly to the Lord of the harvest that he may send labourers into his vineyard. And let him have his own time and way for that purpose. He may raise up some useful preachers from among yourselves; or send some over the great ocean unto you. Nothing is impossible with him.

Present my kind salutation to the church; many of them I had never the pleasure of seeing in the flesh, and several of them I was happy to see many times, but I do not expect that joy again until the great day when we shall meet together before the seat of Christ. The good news respecting your faith, zeal, and order, gladdens my heart greatly. O labour and strive for a spiritual, evangelical, and godly frame and temper of mind! Warn each other kindly, freely, and honestly, to avoid resting on, and trusting to the form of godliness, but to labour for the power of it. Let the old professors pray, who perhaps saw better times, and experienced more lucid and powerful things formerly; let them pray, I say, for the renewal of the Holy Ghost, the reviving of the gifts of God in them, that their youth may be renewed like the eagle's, and that they may bring forth fruit in old age, and be fat and flourishing. *Psalm* 92.14.

Be diligent in your endeavours for the good of the rising generation; your labour will not be in vain. Persevere in bringing them to the Sunday school: and take care that every part of the work in the school be carried on in a serious manner, suitable to the holy day, and to the exalted ends of such education, the glory of God and the salvation of souls.

As to the society for seriously disposed young people, which you have mentioned, I have a good opinion of it. I think that a society of that nature, instructing and informing the young, may be very useful. You will take care that it be well and prudently governed. It is better to avoid carrying it on like an *experience society*. On the other hand, mind that the meeting be not of a trifling and disputing nature: but may solid instructions be communicated, teaching the young in doctrine and discipline and everything proper, also warning them of evil and corrupt habits of the age and the neighbourhood. Use holy pleasantness in teaching the young; try to shew them that the ways of wisdom are the ways of pleasantness, and all her paths peace; that the yoke of Christ is easy, and his service perfect freedom, and that there is great reward in keeping his commandments.

It would be very desirable for you to establish a meeting to teach *singing*. Such meetings have been very useful in some of our districts. Very vain and giddy youth were induced to attend to learn singing, and then became gradually fond of the means of grace, and several of them were at length converted, manifesting becoming conduct; some of them died happy, and went home joyful.

We spend a good part of our time now in our private religious meetings, at our Associations and in church-meetings, in conversation respecting the Sabbath. It was observed that a religious decline appeared in our manner of spending the Sabbath, especially in conversations before the preaching, and after it on the way home, and with our families.[1] We examine every person in our

[1] We endeavoured to strengthen our minds in the morality of the fourth commandment; that it is in its full force and strength under the evangelical dispensation, requiring us to keep a day of every seven holy to the Lord. This point was proved by several reasons, such as the establishment of it in the garden of Eden, and giving it to the father of the human race, not the father of some particular nation, but the head of all of us. The patriarchs were counting their years by sevens. The observance of the Sabbath was a commandment given to Israel before the law was given on Sinai. *Exodus* 16; then its delivery on Sinai out of the midst of the fire, its being placed in the midst of the ten commandments,

churches, asking them if they can call the Sabbath a delight. It is pointed out in what sense the Sabbath is a delight to believers. We have consequently a way to enter into conversation with them respecting the state of their minds, their family religion, and the government of their households. We believe that the religious state of persons or churches is very perceptible in the manner they keep the Sabbath. It is very painful to think that the manner of many observing the Sabbath shews that they have but little delight in Christ, and slender hope of heaven. So they have no inward ground for keeping the Sabbath properly; yea, by trying to be outwardly decent and consistent on the Sabbath, it becomes a burden to them.

Perhaps conversation on these things, in your little church meeting, would be profitable to you.

3. DEEP CONCERN FOR THE CAUSE OF GOD – INFLUENCES OF THE SPIRIT – THE TRUE GOSPEL IN PRACTICE

Liverpool 22 August 1831

I was very glad to find that the cause of Christ had prospered among you; and I hope that it will still go on, that the church will increase daily in number, and the members in grace. I read accounts of powerful revivals in some parts of the United States, and I hope that those remarkable visitations of heaven reach your congregations. A more copious out-pouring of the Spirit is

---

its being twice written by the finger of God. Isaiah shews the Lord's great esteem and care for this dispensation, by his introduction of it (56. 1—6). Christ comprehends this precept in the first and great commandment, in summing up the moral law, declaring that it was made for the benefit of man, especially for the good of his soul. Much was said on the expression, 'Remember,' to shew that we ought to remember the Sabbath before it comes, preparing for its arrival, – remembering that it is the Lord's day when it comes, that we may not act unbecoming of the great and holy day. We made some observations as to the frames and dispositions of mind suitable for the Sabbath, such as meditating on Christ and his work, his glorious resurrection, resting on Christ in his obedience and suffering, then delighting in conversations respecting the Saviour, and so calling the Sabbath a delight.

wanted to set all things in order. Errors in doctrine, licentiousness in conduct, deadness and formality in profession, will not stand before the strong influences of the Spirit. He leads us into all truths, he sanctifies the hearts and lives of Christians; he comforts and gives even strong consolation.

I am amazed, if these are powerful outpourings from above on the English in America as stated, that the doctrines of divines there are so confused and carnal. The truths of the Bible respecting the covenants, the fall of man, original sin, the suretyship of Christ, his substitution in the place of his people, the imputations of their sins to Christ and of his righteousness to them, are all darkened by those writers! I think that when the Spirit is more fully poured on people, those precious pillars of truth will be raised up out of their dusty holes; then the things of God shall be spoken in 'words taught by the Holy Ghost,' and the corrupt reasonings of men will be silenced by the strong light of divine truth. But do not mistake me, I do not say that all the ministers there are erroneous; I declare nothing but what I have read. May the Lord restore a pure lip to the ministers, and may the old paths be sought, where the road is good, and may we walk in it! There is no danger there. It is my earnest wish that my dear brethren, the Welsh, may be established in the truth, and taught and led by the Holy Ghost, and made wise unto salvation. It is not well that you should contend and dispute with any, but that you should be 'strong in the truth,' and experimentally acquainted with the divine taste and excellency of the truth in all its branches; that having 'drunk the old wine' you may not desire the new presently, but that you should say, The old is the best.

The truth is known by the following things:

1 Every branch of the Gospel doctrines is perfectly consistent with what is said in Scripture of all the perfections of God, his wisdom, omniscience, love, justice.

2 All parts of Gospel doctrines are quite consistent with each other; there is no need to conceal one truth in publishing another. The doctrines of the Gospel make up a complete entire glorious body.

3 All the doctrines of the Gospel inculcate holiness in heart and

conduct. It is 'a doctrine according to godliness.' Every branch of it is in concord with every commandment in the moral law; it is entirely on its side.

4 Every part of the doctrine of the Gospel is very clear, yea, all the things that belong to our peace are plain and clear to the weak; but darkness, confusion, and strange things are in a false doctrine.

O, dear brethren, pray much that you may know the truth experimentally, feel its power, and experience its holy effects, bringing man down to nothing, excluding boasting from him, exalting the love, grace, and wisdom of God in all things in our salvation! Behold the glory of God in Christ, in the doctrine of the Gospel, till you are changed more daily unto the image of Christ. This is the only glory of the believer – the image of Christ. May your conduct, in all things, be worthy of the Gospel of Christ! The Gospel of the grace of God teaches all effectually that believe and enjoy it, 'to live soberly, honestly, and godly in the world.' Believing the Gospel gives a disposition and strength for this. To live godly is not a burden, but a pleasure to such. God's commandments are light and joyful to them; his ways are those of pleasantness to them. Strive that pure and evangelical religion may be much on the increase among you in each person, family, and church. O may each carefully observe that nothing separates or darkens between his soul and God! Cherish a tender conscience, and a broken heart; avoid an indifferent spirit, a hard heart, and a sleepy conscience. Press on for more intimate fellowship with God in private; that will be strength to you in all public engagements.

O be careful that family religion is encouraged and supported among you! Be very particular on this head, if you wish that the kingdom of Christ should be extended and established among you and your children. I mean the worship, duties, and government of a family. Let family *worship* be maintained in a regular, particular, respectful, serious, and animated manner. Let family *duties* be properly attended to, every one in the family particularly observing his own duty. O how beautiful, and O how delightful, is that family wherein every one goeth on in the path of duty according to the Word of God! Family *government* should be maintained;

every head of a family should govern his own house in the fear of God, according to his Word. 'He will command his children,' and all under his care, 'to keep the ways of the Lord.' 'He will keep his children under subjection.' Rule over them in much love, tenderness, patience, and diligence. Be tender towards the family, but sharp against their sins; zealous and persevering for the Word and glory of God.

Let the *church* be particularly attended to; take care that church discipline be maintained in everything according to the Word of God. Examine minutely to see that the operations of the Spirit be in those you receive into the church. To admit those that have impenitent hearts, and have never been convinced of their lost state and the evil of sin, injures the church greatly. O be sure that those you receive among you are such as cannot live without Christ! he is the foundation, see that they build upon him only. Let not your chief endeavour be to enlarge your party, but to save sinners, and to bring them to Christ, aiming at having those into the church that shall be saved. Do not meddle with other denominations, neither try to seduce any of their people, and do not dispute with them; if they should disparage you, endure it: go on with your work quietly and peaceably. Endeavour that union and peace continue in the church, and brotherly love increase more and more; 'Let all things be done in love.' Yea, when there is need to chastise, let it be done in love and the spirit of meekness, being tender-hearted and forbearing towards each other, and for-giving each other when required. 'Bear ye one another's burdens.'

Avoid that readiness to blame and condemn each other; let every one be more sharp against every fault in himself than in others, desirous to take out the 'beam that is in his own eye first, before he goes to pull out the mote that is in his brother's eye.' Strive always at having profitable things to converse about in your church meetings. Let Christ, his person, offices, life, death, his intercession, the full free salvation he finished, the work of his Spirit in applying it to sinners, be the chief subjects of your conversation in the society. Strive in particular, brethren, for much of the Lord's countenance in the means and ordinances of grace, especially in the church. It is but a dark and dismal night everywhere that is destitute of the light of his countenance. His reconciled face in Christ is our delightful sun. So, when the children of this world are mad for earthly things, and cry out, 'Who will shew us any good?' but are disappointed everywhere, we shall be calm and call on the Lord most high in prayer often, saying, 'Lord, lift up the light of thy countenance upon us, and we shall be whole.'

O brethren, be not easy without his presence! I believe that some of you know the difference between the shining of his countenance and every other thing. I often fear that many are now in the churches that know no difference between the hiding and the shining of his countenance. O be not satisfied with any thing instead of him – fluency, or any gift in prayer, or preaching! His countenance pre-eminently excels all things as to light, strength, virtue, fruit and the consequences hereafter. It extracts the heart out of the creature, and draws the soul heavenward. It conveys the affections to the things where Christ sits, it causes the traffic of the soul to be in heaven, seeking a better country than any here below. They are made pilgrims here, their treasure and home being in the heavenly world. O brethren, let us cry earnestly that we may be made more heavenly continually! we shall be here but a short time. It will be dreadful to die, having our delight here below! Yea, very painful it will be to die, if the affections should not, before that time, be swallowed up with heavenly things. The children of this world are driven in death from home poor and wretched. But true Christians are then called home, yea, a full, good, and delightful home – to their Father, Husband, and best Friend – leaving the intricate, entangling desert of this trouble-some world! Brethren, where is our home? It is not likely that we shall meet here: shall we meet in the peaceable delightful habita-tions above, dwelling with God and the Lamb, without sin and misery for ever?

Now, brethren, I must finish. The God of peace be with you. May he make bare his arm, may many sinners there be saved, and may the cloud of God's glory be on your tabernacle! Give my very kind regards to all that know me – to the preachers, especially Messrs W. Thomas, D. Stephens, and M. Roberts. You shall

receive more news by Mr B. Davies. The Rothsay Castle was lost
last week, near Beaumaris! – ninety lost their lives, about twenty
escaped.[1]

4. MISSION TO AID THE CHURCH, REV H. REES[2]

Fron 12 September 1838

We shall hear again from Mr Rees; we should be very glad if he
would go to you. We have none, I think, that is so suitable as to
mind and other gifts. The Lord may make his path clear to visit
you. We should be sorry to send any to you that were not likely to
answer the end in view. We know, at the same time, that God must,
in his grace, work among you, to heal and make you active in his
work. The Lord has several instruments, some suitable to this
work, and some to another. It is my earnest desire and prayer
that he would incline the hearts of some suitable ministers to visit
you, to make their way clear, and to support and enable them to
come to you in 'the fulness of the blessing of the Gospel of Christ.'
Until then wait on the Lord; be not disheartened nor dismayed,
but be of good courage. Do not despise the faithful brethren that
preach to you now; the Lord can make them useful. May the
ministry revive and flourish there like Aaron's rod! May the
cloud of the Lord's glory descend and rest upon the tent where
they minister! There is no need for great gifts to defend the truth;
it is strong and will prevail. There is need of great parts and
fluency to support error, to clothe and cover it, but all is too little,
'the day will discover it.' Observe the erroneous; they form new
and philosophical expressions to support and advance their
cause; wise is their plan, for the Bible will not support their
doctrine. But the 'words taught by the Holy Ghost' are sufficient
to defend the doctrines of grace. Be careful that you be not
entangled with the vain and 'perverse disputations of men of

---

[1] The *Annual Register* (1831) gives a detailed account of the disaster. About
one hundred and fifty persons (mostly holiday makers) were on board: only
twenty-two escaped. The vessel (a Steam Packet) had sailed from Liverpool.
[2] This and the immediately following letters refer to a branch of the Welsh
Calvinistic Church in U.S.A. which required counsel and help.

corrupt mind,' and thereby lose fellowship with God. See that it be clear between you and heaven at the throne of grace. Pray to the Lord to arise and defend his own truth, and he will do so. Let two or three of you agree to pray for his presence; he will allow you the unspeakable favour.

5. THE REV H. REES ENCOURAGED TO UNDERTAKE A MISSION TO AMERICA

Fron 5 April 1839

I was very glad to receive a letter from you. I have been a prisoner for more than three months: but the Lord was very kind to me: the bodily affliction was light, and by measure. It was not indifferent as to my experience; there are some symptoms now that I shall recover a little again. It is my wish that the furnace may purify me, as the sons of Levi formerly, that I may offer unto the Lord an offering in righteousness; *Malachi* 3.3. All that I have to do now, is to endeavour to write a few lines now and then for the Spiritual Magazine, hoping they may be of use to some hereafter. I now try to meditate and write a little on the subject of *applying salvation* or partaking of the blessings of salvation.

Forgive me for being thus engaged with my own small concerns, at a season when you are almost overwhelmed by thinking of your great journey. I shall drop a few lines, as you particularly wish to hear from me; but only few, as I am still so unwell. I hope, however, to be able to write more at large before you start. I am glad, on some account, that Mrs Rees is rather disposed to stay at home, though I am not indifferent to the feelings of you both on the occasion; I think, however, that your trials will be less, on this plan: and I hope you shall meet again joyfully and comfortably, nothing unpleasant occurring during your separation. The children of this world leave their families and face dangers, for the sake of a few of the poor things of the world. How much more worthy is your journey and business in this undertaking! You go in the service of him who is the Owner and Governor of the wind, sea, life, and death. You shall 'dwell in the secret place of the

Most High, and abide under the shadow of the Almighty.' Who
can hurt you there? *Psalm* 91.1. Many of the Welsh went over to
America with a poor object in view. I do not know of any of our
countrymen going into that far distant land on the same business
as you. I know that there never were so many and earnest prayers
offered up to heaven for any Welshmen crossing the Atlantic, as
there will be for you; and I think they will not be in vain. Whitefield went over the Atlantic thirteen times. He not only had the
protection of the Highest, but also much of his presence, on the
long voyages. The Lord made use of him in the vessels for the
spiritual benefit of many. The voyages were longer and more
uncomfortable in those days: 101 years last November,[1] he sailed
the first time. They were long before they lost sight of Britain;
they were four months on sea. Yet I say they were comfortable,
conversing about little else on the voyage, than God, Christ, and
eternal things. You may now, brother, go to America, under the
protection of divine Providence, and preach there for months, and
also return home, in the time of Whitefield's first voyage.

As to the talk of war between Britain and the United States, it is
of no moment. I hope and think there will be no conflict between
the countries: although there may be some bickering and unpleasantness between the quarrelsome people in America and
Canada. But I trust the governments of the two countries will not
be so foolish as to go to war for the sake of a little, cold, fruitless
land. May God prevent such an event.[2] You will be far from the
State of Maine, where the disturbance is. The State of New York,
where you are going, is one of the most quiet in America. But you
may turn back at Ramsey, leaving the Lakes, if a quarrel should
arise before you return, which I trust will not. There is a way to
Ohio without going to the Lakes. Whitefield would not be
detained at all, though the sad news of the Spaniards having
entered Georgia, had reached him here. God will take care of, and
protect, the embassy of peace. I think much of Mrs Rees; the
Lord deals graciously with her, disposing her mind to stay at

[1] In fact the year 1737 had virtually ended before Whitefield went aboard ship.
[2] The dispute concerned the boundary between the New England State of
Maine and New Brunswick in Canada. It was amicably settled by the Ashburton
Treaty in 1842.

home. She has a favour never shewn to the wife of any preacher in our Connexion before – the privilege of giving her husband to a particular journey for the Lord and his cause. Many a wife in Liverpool gives up her husband to a greater and longer voyage for the sake of a little earthly gain, having not the privilege Mrs Rees has. My dear friend, I am very poorly and quite tired; I cannot write more. If I should continue to amend, I will write again before you sail.

To the Association at Denbigh

ON THE APPOINTMENT OF REV H. REES AND
MOSES PARRY FOR A MISSION TO AMERICA[1]

Fron 11 March 1839

Dear Brethren – I know that 'a man's way is not his own.' I was in hopes I should get better, and should be able to attend the meeting, and have the pleasure of being among you. I should be very glad to salute the dear brethren that are to be set apart for so great a journey for the cause of Christ; but it pleases the Lord to imprison me with a light affliction, that I cannot come. It is my desire to submit under his parental hand.

Dear brethren, I most heartily pray that the Lord would appear evidently among you in his infinite grace and mercy. There is a great need of a more distinct manifestation of God's gracious presence in our private meetings, especially of church officers. Our manner of proceeding with the great things of God's kingdom is too much in a common, light, and carnal way; and many are satisfied with it! There have been in former times such visits from the Lord in our religious meetings as are not known to us at present. And gracious manifestations and powerful influences have been promised in God's Word; but we are too indifferent and dead to pray earnestly for them! – *Isaiah* 64.1. A whole spirit, hard heart, worldly selfish prayers, are like mountains between many of the professors and God! His manifestations in his power and grace would melt these away. The manner of our preaching, praying, singing, and hearing, would be greatly changed, were we favoured with these gracious visits; the shadow of death would be exchanged for the shining of clear light, and the cold winter for the warmth of summer. I do not think, dear brethren, that these manifestations are more needed in Denbighshire than in Anglesey.

As to the departure of the brethren, I have heard that they intend delaying their journey till May; if so, I may yet have the pleasure of seeing them before they go. I often think of them with great concern: no doubt but that very sober, weighty, and serious thoughts on the subject of their mission occupy their minds. They are impressed that God calls them to this great undertaking by the voice of the brethren, and they consequently obey. I am persuaded of the necessity of sending missionaries to America, and of the suitableness of the brethren that have been selected for the purpose. But I fear that but few of us that send them feel the weight of the business in hand as we ought. The churches, preachers, and elders, in quarterly and monthly meetings, are too light and trifling with a cause so important as this and the like – such as the admission of preachers and ministers to the exercise of their sacred offices!

In former days, when the Lord was very near, and his Spirit poured plentifully on the church, and his officers full of the Holy Ghost, they were very serious; fasting and praying when they ordained church-officers or sent ministers to some particular places, or were engaged in some particular work. So it was at Antioch. When they were serving the Lord and fasting, the Holy Ghost said, 'Separate Barnabas and Saul for me.' Though the Holy Spirit named both, yet in setting them apart, they again fasted and prayed, commending them to the grace of God for the great work before them. *Acts* 13.1–3, 14.26. Those two eminent men entered cheerfully upon their great and dangerous journeys, being sent by the brethren, commended to the protection and favour of God; the Holy Ghost guiding them, and taking the lead as it were, in the whole transaction. They accomplished the labour appointed them, and returned praising God. *Acts* 14.27. Would to God we also were of the same spirit and manner in

sending these dear brethren – commending them to the grace of
God! To be in his favour and protection is enough for our comfort
and safety, either at sea or on land. I cannot enlarge – to write even
this much, was labour and pain to me; I am very poorly; but I am
considered as improving in health. Forgive my freedom and
imperfection.

The message of Messrs Rees and Parry
to the American brethren, in 1839,
on their return to Wales

We thought of giving you a word of advice, through your valuable
magazine ('Cyfaill'), before taking our leave of you. But we judged
it would be far better for us to let two letters which we received
from Mr Elias, appear in it, than to send any thing of our own.[1]
Though the letters were written to us and the brethren, at a
Quarterly Meeting (Association) in Denbighshire, yet the nature
and spirit of their contents are such as may be useful to all the
churches. They were composed by one of the most spiritual and
faithful ministers that ever appeared in Wales, and then when in
his old age and the prisoner of Jesus Christ by bodily afflictions for
several weeks. They are a true and correct transcript of the weighty
spiritual and humble manner of this eminent minister of Christ,
at the close of his most useful career. He is with us in his old age,
as Moses was with Israel, engaged with all his might in the most
earnest manner in all our Quarterly Meetings, encouraging and
exhorting us to cleave to the Lord in our spirit and life, and main-
tenance of the pure doctrines. And many of us, by thinking that
the time of his departure is at hand, are ready and disposed to
exclaim, 'Stay, O Elias, stay, we cannot just now do without
thee.' Such men are not always to be had: Christ calls for them;
he purchased them at such a dear rate. The crown of righteousness
awaits them that fought the good fight of faith so well. And
heaven also draws to itself out of this world everything that is pure

[1] One of those two letters is the preceding.

and agreeable to its nature, leaving behind the wood, hay, and stubble for the devouring fire of the last day. May the Lord make the letters useful to you! It is not likely any of you will ever see or hear their author again.

Elias's Letter to the Church in America in 1840

ON THE TRUTH OF GOD AND THE LOVE OF IT

Fron 5 March 1840

I am very glad that your zeal for the doctrines of grace continues: to love the truth is much superior to and better than loving the gifts and fluency of the preacher. The reading of one New Testament in some town in France lately, was the means of bringing a hundred Papists and infidels to hear sound doctrine regularly, to which they had been utter strangers. The signs of true conversion appear in thirty-five of them. The mind and view of this age with regard to preaching gifts are incorrect. Some may have powers to preach in an eloquent manner, but knowing at the same time but little about preaching the Gospel. However, the talent to preach is an ability to set forth clearly the doctrines of grace, and as near and as much as possible in God's own words, 'The words that are taught by the Gospel;' the preacher speaking to the people, understanding, believing, and experiencing the truth himself, and very anxious that the people themselves should be brought to understand, believe, and enjoy the truth themselves. Real ministers are taught and enabled by the Spirit to 'speak as it were the words of God, in the manifestation and power of the Spirit.' The Gospel is a message from heaven, and faithful preachers are ambassadors of God. But there is a disposition in this age to view preaching and hearing the Gospel in a worldly manner. Some preachers are seeking respect and honour; and hearers are looking for something to amuse them, and not their own profit and God's glory.

I have been lately thinking of proper dispositions towards the Word of God, by hearing and reading it. I thought much of the words in *Ephesians* 4.20, 21; that is, learning Christ, *hearing him, taught by him, as the truth is in him.* Notwithstanding all that is said of learning in this age, there is room to fear that but few learn this exalted doctrine, the truth respecting Jesus; outwardly by his ministers preaching his Word, and inwardly by his Spirit engrafting it; learning respecting Christ's merits, till we come to apply them to ourselves; learning obedience to him, till we are made like him; looking to his glory till we are changed into his image; learning to put off the old man, and putting on the new man; to deny ungodliness and worldly lusts; to live soberly, righteously, and godly; to look for that blessed hope and the glorious appearing of our Saviour; yea, so learning of Christ himself by his Holy Spirit. When we are thus taught the truth as it is in Jesus, it will be experienced and loved. It is a rare and strange thing to many to receive the truth in the love of it. 1 *John* 2.20, 27; *Matthew* 11.29; 2 *Corinthians* 3.8; *Titus* 2.12, 13; 2 *Thessalonians* 2.10, 11.

I will take the liberty, brethren, to make a few observations on the important subject of *receiving the love of the truth.*

Christians *love the truth* because it is more precious than gold, better than food, sweeter than the honeycomb; it is the truth of God; those that love God, love his Word, because they had life by it. *Psalm* 119.92, 93. Also because they enjoyed a delightful feast in it. But, alas, the greater part of the people read and hear the Word, and discuss it in a cold, unsavoury, ineffectual, and unfruitful manner.

1 Those that have *not* received the love of the truth are in a miserable and dangerous state. They do not believe the truth nor obey it. They are open to all sorts of errors, to believe a lie, and to turn from the truth to falsehood, vanity, and fables. 2 *Timothy* 4.4. Some have turned to Judaism, heathenism, Mahometanism, and Romanism. Some turn now to Infidelity and Popery, and many kinds of errors. Some are ignorant of the truth, without love to it and life by it. Those are satisfied with unrighteousness. Erroneous judgments and conduct are quite agreeable to them, yea, such unreasonable subjects as

infidelity and Romanism. They were given up by God to believe a lie! Strong delusions, and awful mistakes! These are lost persons, and likely to remain in that state, loving darkness. *John* 3.19. There are none, in their natural state, that love God and the truth. Alas, they are ready to argue against it, and to turn their ears from it to fables!

2 It is an unspeakable privilege to receive the love of the truth; it is received as grace and favour: none naturally possess or deserve it. If so received, there is no room to boast. Their eyes were opened to see the truth, and their hearts to believe and obey it. *John* 8.32; *Romans* 6.17. Those that know and believe the truth love it. The truth of God is most delightful and desirable to all the godly. *Psalm* 119.47, 167; *Psalm* 103; 1 *Peter* 2.1, 2. They had life and nourishment and support in all their afflictions through and by the Word. *Psalm* 119.93. *John* 6.68; *Isaiah* 1.18. They shall not be deceived nor lost. It is said, 'They would deceive the very elect, if possible:' but it is not possible; they have the anointing, the unction; the Spirit leads them into all truth; they know the voice of the good Shepherd; they will not follow strangers; neither can Papists, infidels, Socinians, nor any other erroneous and dangerous persons deceive them. They shall not be lost but saved. They delight in the words of eternal life. They have received the reconciliation – Christ as represented and testified – they have 'passed from death unto life.' 'They *have* life.' To receive the love of the truth is of unspeakable importance.

We may draw the following inferences from this statement: that it is a cause of grief that so many read and hear the truth, and yet do not love it. They love not the law as the rule of life. *Romans* 8. They love not the Gospel as the testimony of God respecting his Son, and of the way for sinners to have life. *John* 5.40; *Romans* 10.16. They will not have Christ to rule over them. They will not submit to his sceptre. The appearance of many hearing the Word, and their manner of living, prove that they do not love the truth. *Psalm* 2.1–4. *Luke* 19.27. The ears of many are itching, and most desirous for a certain talk, for some strange and new things, 'like children, tossed to and fro, carried about with every wind of doctrine.' It is evident then they never received the love of truth. Those that possess it, will not exchange it for anything else. The old is the best. *Ephesians* 4.14; *Luke* 5.39.

3 Let us *examine* ourselves, whether we have received the love of the

truth. Do we love the doctrines of the Gospel in all its branches, not thinking that it places man too low and wretched under the fall in Adam, nor exalting too high the sovereign grace of God in the salvation of man? Can we say to Christ, though others are offended at his doctrine and leave him, 'Where shall we go, for thou hast the words of eternal life?' Some called Christ's doctrine hard sayings, and others the words of eternal life. The true disciples had received the love of the truth. Can each of us say, 'The doctrine of the Gospel is the form of sound words. I will never forget them, for with them thou hast quickened me. I saw in them the way of obtaining life, and I was favoured with it'. *Psalm* 119.63. *James* 1.18. 1 *Peter* 1.23. *Isaiah* 38.16; 64.5. Can each of us say, 'I should have perished in many a tribulation and affliction, had not thy truth been my support and delight?' If this is our experience we cannot but love the truth; it is our life and comfort; we cannot turn to any other. *Psalm* 119.92. *Romans* 15.4.

4 There is a *safe ground* for those that receive the love of the truth – to rejoice. It was entirely by grace, for naturally they hated it like others. It was by sovereign grace they were brought to receive it as the Word of God, and love it as such. 1 *Thessalonians* 2.13; *Ephesians* 4.21. God began in them a good work, with an intention to finish it. *Philippians* 1.6. They shall be kept from being deceived, and from believing a lie. They know the voice of the good Shepherd; they will not follow strangers. The Holy Ghost is their guide. *Matthew* 24.24. *Revelation* 13.8. *John* 10.4, 5. 16.3. 1 *John* 2.20, 27. They shall be saved; for none shall be destroyed that love the truth. They keep the Word of God, he also will preserve them in the hour of temptation. They bought the truth, and they will not sell it for anything the world may offer, yea, not even for their own lives! *Revelation* 3.10.

5 I shall now conclude with a word of *advice*, which I should be glad of communicating to every Welshman in America. Be not satisfied with reading and hearing the truth, nor with arguing in its behalf, and even professing it. See whether you love it; be not satisfied without that. Beware that you love not some idle talk, some enticing words, some amusing conversation, or some things that please the carnal mind, instead of the divine truth, the everlasting Gospel. Take care that you do not delight in the gifts or manner of the preacher instead of the truth. You, whose conscience testifies that you have not received the love of the truth, be not content without this. Neither

being grounded in the principles of the Gospel, nor the frequent hearing of sermons, nor professing religion, can keep you from improper conduct, false opinions, and everlasting destruction. You that have received the love of the truth, greatly admire the grace of God, magnify your privilege, and be very thankful.

Remember, we have the truth fully; it deserves being received; none by nature receive it in love. However, all that shall be saved, shall be brought to love the truth and receive it. Read 1 *Timothy* 1.15. *Jeremiah* 17.23. *John* 12.48. *Romans* 8.7. *Deuteronomy* 33.3. *Acts* 2.41. 1 *Thessalonians* 2.13. *Psalm* 119.48, 92, 127, 163.

To Mrs Jones of Wrexham[1]

1. ON THE DEATH OF HER HUSBAND –
GREAT LOSS TO HERSELF AND THE CHURCH
THEREBY – THE ALL-SUFFICIENCY OF GOD

Llanfechell 27 February 1805

I received, on my way from Shrewsbury to Llangollen, the melancholy intelligence of Mr Jones's death: my mind was filled with surprise, concern, and grief. In this painful feeling I thought how sorrowful and distressed must the surrounding country, and especially the churches, be. But alas, how much greater must be your sorrow and grief, your loss being necessarily far greater than that of any other person! With many others I have lost a faithful brother, one much endeared to the church; the little flock at Wrexham an excellent leader, diligent in their cause, careful and watchful over them; he was indeed a vigilant guardian. Alas *Adwy* and *Rhos* also; they have lost one that cared much for their

---

[1] These five letters of Mr Elias to Mrs Jones, were no doubt read with great pleasure to many members in the church, and were under God, very useful; for the influence of female friends extends far. Mrs Jones was wonderfully enabled to supply the place of her husband in the path of usefulness; and she was remarkably kind and gentle in leading on the tender flock by her experimental conversation and Christian example. She and her husband were also great friends of those eminent servants of God, Thomas Charles of Bala and David Jones of Llan-gan.

souls, one that was always endeavouring to procure ministers to preach the glad tidings of salvation to them; and who shall be found capable of succeeding him? But you have lost a beloved brother in the Lord, a faithful and kind husband, yea, a father in the church, and a father of your children, one that was careful for your soul as well as body, one who not only provided for his family, but was particular with respect to its religious duties! It is not a small matter to have a friend who loves to present the cause of his family before God.

I have been, by meditating on your great affliction, induced to write these lines. I know not how to console you. Nothing sublunary, I am aware, can comfort you; but there are comforts which the world knows nothing of, that are sufficient and adapted to support and comfort distressed souls in all their troubles. The Lord calls himself the 'God of all consolation.' Yes, he supports his people in all their afflictions. God is an omnipotent, all-sufficient Comforter, no sorrow is too great for him to heal; 'his consolation no one can take away.' The Holy Spirit is in his office the Comforter of the Church. The disciples, when they were cast down with sorrow at the departure of Christ, were consoled by him. If then he was able to comfort them at the loss of their spiritual Bridegroom, it is certain he can console you at the departure of your natural husband. He can reveal to you the hidden things of God, so as to make you rejoice in the midst of sorrow. He can shed abroad the love of God in your heart, and show his pre-eminent plan of salvation, so as to make you easy in your distress. Yes, he can make you experience and enjoy the divine and infinite merits of the blood of Christ, so that the storm shall become a calm. He can lift up your mind above earthly things, to the contemplation and enjoyment of heavenly things: so that every loss shall be made up to you, and more than compensated. God himself is sufficient to supply the room of every creature. Therefore when he takes away any of his creatures from us, he must not be considered as going us any wrong; inasmuch as he can do more than fill up the vacancy. Perhaps the consideration of two or three things may be of service to you in your present circumstances, however painful they are:

1 Consider that the *hand of the Lord* was exercised in your distressing
and bitter visitation. David considered this till he became dumb
before God. This made Aaron hold his peace; and this caused Eli
to say, 'It is the Lord, let him do what seemeth him good.' The
consideration of this made Job say, 'The Lord hath taken away,
blessed be his name.' *Psalm* 39.9. *Leviticus* 10.3. 1 *Samuel* 3.18.
Job 1.21. It is too difficult for flesh and blood to say from the heart,
'Blessed be the Lord,' when he taketh away. But he giveth power to
his people to say so unfeignedly, *yea*, when he taketh the most
beloved objects away from them. There can be no doubt that the
hand of the Lord was in the visitation that befell you. Yes, it was the
Lord's doing: 'the number of men's months are with him;' 'the
keys of death are with him.' *Revelation* 1.18. Thus we see that pain
and sickness are his ministers. Inasmuch then as the hand of God
was in your bereavement, it is dangerous to say ought against it.

2 Consider also the *character* of this God; He is a just God; and
'approveth not to subvert a man in his cause.' *Lamentations* 3.36.
'God is love,' and 'hath loved you with an everlasting love.' Therefore he will surely do whatsoever is best for you. He loves you
infinitely more than you love yourself: he is wise and knows what is
best for you, infinitely better than you do yourself. That therefore
which hath befallen you was for your good. He gives us the bitterest
draughts with the same love he does the sweetest. Yes, the very love
that influenced him in giving his only begotten Son to die for you,
and calling you by his grace, and incorporating you into his church,
disposed him in depriving you of your husband, though you may not
in your present distress recognize his love and goodness in the act.
But when the storm hath ceased, you will clearly understand his
purpose; and therefore, though 'clouds and darkness are round
about him,' yet 'righteousness and judgment are the habitation of his
throne.' *Psalm* 97.2. You may therefore rest assured that he doeth
all things well, though we do not perceive how they are so. O for help
to bow with thankfulness to him!

3 Consider the *vanity* of things temporal. If there was anything sublunary to rest upon, it would be a faithful and a godly husband; but
the things that are seen, yea, the best of them, are temporal, but the
things that are not seen are eternal. Endless thanks for the things
that are not seen; the true Christian hath blessings above the sun,
that will never come to an end. He is united to one that will never

die; and our sainted brethren there will never leave us, and we shall
enjoy each other in the Lord; and every thing which now mars our
fellowship shall be done away. Oh, welcome blessed state!

4 Consider that many godly people have been *calm* under heavier
affliction; Aaron's children died under the divine displeasure; yet
'he held his peace.' Eli's sons died under the judgment of the Lord;
yet he said, 'Let him do what seemeth him good!' All Job's children
died at once; yet 'he blessed God.' But as for you, your husband
finished his course in the church of God; he died, clothed in garments
of righteousness, with his crown on his head; the Lord took him
away in his love, from his labour in the vineyard, to rest; from the
warfare, to enjoy peace; from the field of battle, to the dividing of the
spoil; to sing victory over every enemy through the blood of the
Lamb; yea, from corruption to perfect purity, without spot or
wrinkle, or any such thing. He took him from a world where Satan
dwells, to a state where he and his temptations and accusations never
enter. It will be a subject of great wonder to see such as we are, there;
yet it is likely we shall be! He is gone from a world where many a
dark cloud intervenes between us and our God, to a country where
no veil shall ever prevent us seeing him! O happy change! O perfect
deliverance!

5 Further, dear sister, I have only to recommend to you the words of
David, 'I shall go to him, but he shall not return to me.' We ourselves
have but a small part of our race unfinished; we are hastening speedily
after our brethren. We shall meet them soon in the heavenly Jerusalem; every wave carries us to the desired haven, every day hurries
us to eternity! O that we may walk more with God while here! O
that we might live in closer union and fellowship with the Bridegroom, of whom we shall never be deprived! Though death tears
asunder natural ties, yet such is the union between the believer and
Christ, that death shall never dissolve it. Christ, our Bridegroom,
hath suffered death instead of his spouse; he kept his hold of her
even in the death of the cross! Bitter as its pangs were, yet he did
not give up his people even then. Therefore if he did maintain his
possession of them then while he himself was overcoming death,
how much more will he adhere to them while they are undergoing
death themselves, he having swallowed up death in victory! If he
kept close to them in death with its sting, how much more will he do
so in death robbed of its sting? 'O trust in the Lord always, for in

the Lord Jehovah is everlasting strength.' O commit your burden to him, and 'your thoughts shall be established.' Put all your trust in him, for he careth for you. God, in his holy habitation, is a father of the fatherless, and defendeth the cause of the widow. Therefore never say in your present distress, 'I have no one henceforth to care for me.' He is an almighty, all-sufficient God in all circumstances; 'He is a sun and a shield,' a sun to dispense every good thing, and a shield to protect us from all evil.

2. INWARD DEPRAVITY AND ITS WORKING

London 13 January 1806

No doubt the corruption and spiritual diseases of your heart, the members that are on earth, the body of death, must trouble you greatly, and give you much pain. And the body of death is a source of constant grief to us; who shall deliver us? Oh! the sad tendency which is in us to depart from God, and to turn away from spiritual and eternal things! How prone are we to go, in our affections and meditations, after carnal, perishing, and earthly things! Oh, how dark and blind is our *understanding* as regards God, Christ, his Gospel, and his glorious salvation for wretched and lost sinners! Oh, how obstinate and stubborn is our *will*! how unwilling we are to receive Christ, even on the Father's testimony, and the exhibition of him in the Gospel as a full and free deliverer! Oh, how reluctant is our will to submit to the authority of the Word, and the way of God in his providence and grace! Though we often say, 'Thy will be done on earth, as it is in heaven,' yet we are far from being in submission to his will.

The state of our *affections* is also a source of great grief to us. O how cold are they towards God and Christ and holiness, so that all our duties and services are very lifeless and frigid! Alas, how cold are our prayers, our preaching, hearing, and praising! Really, sister, I am quite ashamed to be cold and indifferent towards One that is so worthy to be loved as God is; and so dead in a work that is so deserving of our utmost zeal and activity, as the work of God! I am, sometimes, surprised that God has not cast me away, spewing me out of his mouth. But, alas, how lively

are my affections towards things that are below, yea, also things
that are forbidden and sinful!

As to my *conscience*, the state of it in general gives me often no
small pain and trouble. It is often very sleepy; when it should raise
a loud outcry against sin, it actually sleeps until we *fall* into the
power and vortex of temptation. On the contrary, instead of being
calm and peaceable through the virtue of the blood of Christ, it is
awakened by any accusations, and becomes often alarmingly
tumultuous and agitating, so that it is very difficult to endure it,
until we have a view of the sacrifice of Christ again.

And as to the *memory*, it is very corrupt, sinful, causing me great
sorrow, trouble, and discouragement. Alas, how many most
valuable and excellent things do we lose through the unfaithfulness
of our memories! We often lose, through the treachery of the
memory, the grandest truths, more precious than much fine gold.
Many most friendly communications, many a most delightful
message did our Heavenly Father and the spiritual Head send us,
in the means of grace and the preaching of the Word; but this
treacherous faculty lets them afterwards slip entirely. O what
glorious discoveries we have had of Christ, delightful experiences
of the efficacy of his salvation, and sweet enjoyment of his
presence! But these most valuable gifts have been many a time
lost after they were possessed!

The temptations of Satan also cause great affliction and trouble.
He goes about and spies where there may be any breaches in the
walls of the fortress, that he may come in to us to hurt and injure
us; yea, he seeks nothing less than to devour us, to sift us as
wheat, and nothing will satisfy him but having us off the threshing
floor, even to perdition. And had it not been for him that overcame the grand enemy on Calvary, and who intercedes for his
people that their faith fail not, we should have been utterly
destroyed ere now. The world, with its nets and snares, also
occasions great uneasiness and trouble to us; but Jesus 'overcame
the world – be of good cheer.'

Thanks be to God that in the midst of all our lamentations we
have sufficient ground, however poor we may be, to take courage;
yea, and consolation also. God was mindful of us before we were

born; he ordained a full salvation for us before the foundation of
the world. He contrived a glorious and just way to forgive us all
our sins, and to wash us thoroughly from all our iniquities. The
Son of God assumed our nature in a pure state, and became our
surety. As sure as our sins were imputed to him, and as certainly
as he died for our transgressions, and purchased us to purify us,
so surely he will have all our corruptions and iniquities subdued,
and in due time destroyed! He would have his church 'without
spot or wrinkle, holy and blameless;' therefore, dear sister, be not
discouraged; there is greater power opposed to our corruptions,
than that which is for them. The purpose of the Father, the blood
of the Son, and all the operations of the Holy Ghost, are engaged
for the dethronement and destruction of all our sins! O let us
attentively view the glorious plan of the eternal Trinity; the
amazing work of the Mediator from his birth to his resurrection,
and his work of continual intercession, for us in heaven; together
with the inexhaustible fulness of the gracious promises! Here is
ground for exultation in the midst of trouble, and for lifting up
your head from under the feet of all your enemies. Be not disheartened even in the sharpest conflicts; our life is at present hid;
no arrow or shaft shall reach it. We shall presently have most
complete victory; and then we shall lay down our arms for ever,
and leave all our enemies behind! Will it not be wonderful to
find ourselves thus victorious?

The work is great here: preaching every evening; four sermons
on Sunday, and three societies in the week to attend to; yet I
am not tired of the work; the Lord is very good and gracious to
me in his service. He does not altogether hide his face from me.
I wish you much of his presence in your labour of love.

3. SOURCE OF ALL BLESSINGS AND CONSOLATIONS – SALVATION APPLIED BY THE SPIRIT

London 22 October 1806

I snatch a few minutes to write to you as soon as possible. I arrived
at my journey's end tolerably comfortable. I had better company
on the way than I expected, though I was obliged to conclude they

were not pious persons. They treated me very kindly, but they were not my brethren. The occasion led me to think more firmly that the people of God were my friends. I commenced my labour on the Sabbath, though I was much tired, and very fearful that I should be forsaken by the Lord. But he, in his infinite goodness and compassion, passed by my unworthiness, and favoured me with a measure of his presence. The work appears very delightful, a great multitude attend the preaching of the Word, and there are signs that God is working on many of them. But alas, my distance from God is great; this is my constant grief. I am very fearful lest I should prove to be a cloud without water; and that the Lord's vineyard should be disappointed in me; that when it is dry and thirsting for rain, it should find me nothing but a dry, useless cloud! Indeed great shame belongs to us for being so barren and useless in the church of God. His patience is wonderful in sparing such as I am without turning me out of my stewardship. I have no place to flee to for my life, but to the sacrifice of Christ. Yet a person who is a sinner by nature and practice, yea, the chief of sinners, can approach the just and holy God through the infinite sacrifice of Christ. Even a cold and unprofitable preacher, who is worthy of the deepest place in the bottomless pit, can apply in this way for a full pardon! This is the refuge, this the place where I expect to have life and a perfect remedy for my diseases.

I doubt not but that you have seen and known much of your own spiritual maladies and miseries, so that you sigh and grieve much on account of it, and cry out, 'Who will deliver me from the body of this death?' Yea, I think that you are often cast down and discouraged by looking at the corruption and plague of your heart, and fear often that you have not real religion, that you are not one of the children of God, and that your profession will end in death. Perhaps you are apt to say, 'It is true that this is my state, but what shall I do in such a case?' I answer, try much for a fresh view of free salvation. Think:

1 That it is perfectly free: it was in infinite grace that God loved and chose those that shall be saved. It was not by foreseeing any goodness or excellency in them more than in others: no, it was done through foreseeing all their evil.

2 Think that whilst we were yet without strength, sinners, yea, ungodly, that Christ in due time died for us, with a perfect knowledge of
all our sins, and bore the load of all our transgressions, and the curse
of them, and punishment justly due to us for them. Oh, then, when
assailed by all your accusers, look to *Calvary*, and behold by faith
the most extraordinary surety dying on the cross, the 'Prince of Life,'
the 'Lord of glory!', the 'Son of God,' nailed there on the cross, and
enduring all the curses of the holy law, and the infinite weight and
sharp edge of the sword of justice, fully awakened against him for
the countless sins of his church, his bride! By suffering for all her
sins, he endured all the wrath due to her, and paid all the mighty
debt, and conquered all her enemies. By looking on him through
faith, doubts and fears flee away, accusations are silenced, and the
soul obtains peace and rest. Even the greatest sinner is induced to
venture on him when he is enabled to behold him by faith. All vain
and painful reasonings then come to an end; the person sees that he
is really a sinner; that Christ is truly a Saviour; that the testimony of
the Father respecting him, is a divine truth; and that consequently
he can, whether a true Christian or not, turn to him as the deliverer
of the chief of sinners.

3 Think of the work of the Holy Ghost, calling and following those
that shall be saved, as altogether a work of grace. It is not calling
those that were already virtuous, prepared, and disposed to be godly
and pious. O no! You and I are witnesses of this. He opens the eyes
of the blind, subduing the disobedient, making them willing in the
day of his power; yea, he even raises up the spiritually dead. It is
entirely the work of the Holy Ghost to apply to us the free and gracious
salvation, planned by the Father in eternity, and executed by the
Son in time. Praised be God for a *free* salvation! Nothing of ours is
wanted to complete it. Moreover, all the visits of the Spirit are also
entirely of grace. It is not on account of our worthiness he visits us
at any time. O no! we do not ever deserve any such favour, not even
in prayer on our knees, nor in reading the Bible, nor under sermons,
nor any where. We indeed sin against such visits and manifestations
after being favoured with them; we grieve the Comforter, lose the
joy of salvation, and walk sorrowful all the day long; even fearing
that we shall see no more of the Lord's goodness again. But, O
infinite mercy! he visits us again out of free grace entirely as before.
He stands firm to his engagements and promises, saying, 'I will not
leave thee nor forsake thee.' I will visit you again, and your hearts

shall rejoice. He follows after his people out of infinite grace, and supports them in every trial, having his eye on all their ways, seeing their souls in troubles, restoring their minds, healing their backslidings, forgiving their transgressions, and healing also their infirmities. O keep your eye steadfast on this salvation! it is sure to lift up your soul from under all oppression. Put your trust in the Lord, and be at rest in him. Commit your ways to him, and your thoughts shall be established. Draw near to God in all your trials for guidance and support; he is a present help in trouble. Call not yourself destitute, for God in Christ is your unchangeable, incomparable husband. Much of his communion will gladden your heart in every tribulation. Be very thankful to him for the place you have in his house, and for the employments in it at Wrexham. I hope that the dayspring from on high is about to visit the church. It is a privilege to abide in the house by night. It will not be so for ever. It will be said shortly, in reference to the state of the church, 'there shall no night be there.'

4. THE CHRISTIAN'S SAFETY – SATAN'S DEVICES

Llanfechell February 1808

It is in vain for you to expect rest from enemies till death; yet you may be sure of sufficient strength to meet them. God gives us the victory through our Lord Jesus Christ. Your adversary, the devil, goes about seeking whom he may devour, but he is confined in a chain by the Lion of the tribe of Judah; he is not allowed to devour his sheep: indeed, none can pluck them out of his hand. There is no promise that we shall be without temptations, but there is a promise that 'with the temptation he will make a way of escape.' Our great High Priest can succour those that are tempted; he is always ready to do that unspeakable favour. To be near to Christ is our greatest strength in the midst of all our enemies. It is likely that the serpent deceived Eve in the absence of her husband. It is certain that when we are far off from Christ our enemies triumph over us: when we are near to him and enjoy his fellowship, we are more than conquerors through him that loved us.

25 January 1809

I was glad you were engaged in the Lord's work, notwithstanding all your enemies, fears, and disappointments. You say you fear greatly when you hear of the falls of others, thinking that you shall also fall one day yourself. It was not by fearing to sin that others fell into it, but by being careless and trusting in their own strength. The Lord left them to themselves, and consequently they fell. I know that you are in great danger, your heart being corrupt, the old man being alive and very strong; and by feeling him so strong you often fear that he is not on the cross. The evil spirit is a very malignant, cunning, and strong enemy. He is very alert and active in endeavouring to hinder and entangle you on your journey, sometimes by spreading his nets and temptations before you, embellishing them with the most captivating colours, the most enticing to flesh; putting a thick veil over their evil nature, the danger of falling into them, their dreadful consequences, the most poignant anguish.

Satan, I expect, tries to conceal all these things from the poor sinner when tempting him! The deceitfulness of our enemies is more dangerous to us than their strength: 'The serpent beguiled Eve through his subtlety;' 2 *Corinthians* 11.4. If he deceived her that was perfect, without sin, how much easier it is for him to beguile us! Our danger of being entangled is vastly greater. The very work of Satan is to deceive the nations. *Revelation* 20.8. And also, we have a 'heart that is deceitful above all things, and desperately wicked!' And there is great danger lest 'any of us should be hardened through the deceitfulness of sin.' *Jeremiah* 17.9. *Ephesians* 4.22. *Hebrews* 3.33. Sin and Satan promise a great deal; they fulfil very badly! Promising pleasure, but causing sorrow; honour, but bringing reproach; profit, but entailing loss; they promise freedom from punishment, but alas, they lead to dreadful misery! But our God, notwithstanding the cunning craftiness of Satan and our own wicked hearts, can make the simple wise, and enable them to perceive the evil afar off, to run into the strong tower, the name of the Lord, there to take shelter, and there they are perfectly safe. No castle equal to this! Yea, Christ in his offices delivers the souls of his people from deceit; their lives are most precious in his sight. Our Jesus is infinitely wise and able to make the artful counsel of our enemy foolishness, and rescue his simple ones out of his nets.

It is your business to watch and pray. Hearing of the falls of others should not discourage but cause you to watch and pray more, and also to praise God more. It is wonderful that we are the persons that hear of the falls of others, and have warnings thereby, instead of others hearing of our falls, and being warned at our cost! I have seen many in such a situation as yours, losing their steadfastness and slipping into sin, to the no small temporal and spiritual disadvantage and distress of themselves and families, yea, to the grief of the church and great reproach to the cause of Christ and his Gospel. I have known some who were carried under disgrace and sorrow to their graves, by reason of such miscarriages. But the Lord hath hitherto preserved you in a wonderful manner for the comfort of yourself and children, and the brethren, and for the honour of religion and the Gospel of Christ: and I trust he will preserve you to the end. Keep always in mind the greatness of your privilege, having a place and influence in the house of God, and engaged with his great work. Abigail saw it a great honour for her to wash the feet of David's servants. How much greater is it to be a support to the cause and servants of Jesus Christ! Though you do not perceive great success at present attending the cause of God, yet it is sure to prosper. If you should not see the prosperity in your days, some of your children are sure to see it at Wrexham and the country round. It is now sowing in tears, it will soon be reaping in joy. It is a privilege to be with the work.

5. GUIDING AND SUPPORTING PRINCIPLES
IN TIME OF AFFLICTION

London 28 January 1811

I am sorry I have delayed so long writing to you. When I received your letter at Caernarvon Association, I was on my way to South

Wales. After my return home I had but little rest ere I commenced my journey to London. I have thought much of you, and of your trials in respect of your brother, and of your apprehensions under it. But I hope this, with other things, shall work together for your good. It is well to remember that our Lord's dominion is over all persons, over their lives, faculties, and all their circumstances; and that we have lost all right to every blessing temporal and spiritual, so that it is perfectly just in God to take away what gift he may think fit, from whomsoever he pleases. None has a right to ask him 'What doest thou?' The Lord has a greater right in, and claim to, our relations as his creatures, than we have in them as our kindred. Therefore it is our duty, and it becomes us, to hold our peace, like Aaron, before him, and to say like Eli, 'It is the Lord, let him do what seemeth him good.'

It is a great thing to pray from the heart, 'Let thy kingdom come; let thy will be done on earth, as it is in heaven.' It is easy to say so with our lips when we have all things to enjoy according to our wishes. But it is a great matter to be able to say so when things come upon us contrary to our wishes. We are very prone to murmur at God's method of dealing with us, and to quarrel with second causes, thinking our case would have been better, and we had been differently circumstanced, had it been some other way. We do not consider that in so doing we rebel against God, and oppose his just government and wise providence. He is infinitely wise and good, and carries on all his operations in perfect wisdom, equity, and goodness. Nothing can be made better than God has done it. Who can make that straight which he hath made crooked? None ever can. If all the saints and angels were to attempt it, their efforts would be all in vain. 'He shutteth, and no man openeth.'

But I hope you have such a high opinion of the Lord Jehovah, and the goodness of his providence, management, and dominion, that you humble yourself under his mighty hand. Labour and pray much, dear sister, for a more extensive knowledge of Jesus Christ every day, and of the full salvation that is in him for miserable, perishing sinners. Meditate on the infinite wonders of the Mediator's person, until the pleasant and bitter things of this world become as nothing in your mind. O how insignificant were all the treasures of Egypt in Moses' esteem when he saw the glory of Christ! The reproach of Christ appeared to him much better and preferable to the greatest riches of that kingdom. Many suffered joyfully the spoiling of their goods, in the contemplation of his inestimable treasures, durable riches, better and unfading glory and pleasure in heaven; which, in the end, will be their own property. All earthly blessings are only borrowed, and must soon be recalled. But the riches laid up in Christ are our own, and we shall possess and enjoy them for ever and ever. Not one that has an interest in Christ, having received him through faith, will ever become poor. Also, the painful crosses and bitter trials of this world are as nothing when we view the glory of Christ's person and the fulness of salvation. Then we see all afflictions short, light, and very useful, 'working for us a far more exceeding and eternal weight of glory.' We overcome the world in its frowns, its troubles, crosses, and afflictions, as well as in its deceitful smiles, by believing in the Son of God, whether those afflictions have regard to our health, families, prosperity, relations, friends, or reputation. Beholding the glory of him who for our sake became poor, despising the shame and enduring the cross, will make us easy and truly contented.

Distance from Christ is our weakness at all times and in every circumstance, but nearness to him is our strength. While we do not live by faith on him, and continue in his fellowship, we are withered and fruitless branches, for without him we can do nothing. We have no strength to face one enemy; neither wisdom nor power to resist the temptations of Satan and the flesh, when we are far from him; though it is true he hath secretly upheld us many a time when we did not enjoy the light of his countenance, nor were sensible we had strength from him in the hour of danger. Yea, we often feared that we were becoming a prey to our foes, and that they would have cause to blaspheme on our account. Yet, we were supported, we know not how, by the invisible power of an Almighty hand. We are alive this day, and may set up a monument, and call it *Ebenezer*, because hitherto the Lord hath supported and helped us.

But though we have been graciously and secretly supported by
the Lord, when our spirits and thoughts were very far away from
him, yet this ought not to make us careless and slothful, or willing
to remain any longer at this great distance from God. For it is a
very common thing for the Lord to permit his people to fall and
suffer greatly, when they are satisfied to live without his presence
and at a distance from him. Suppose we happened to sleep among
thieves and robbers, but escaped being robbed and ruined, we
know not how; should we on that account go willingly again into
the same company? Or rather should we not feel truly thankful for
such a great deliverance, and watch against the danger in
future? The Lord has wonderfully preserved us, though very often
lukewarm in religion, and living far from him, and going even to
the paths of the destroyer, where many have been robbed and
destroyed; yea, where we ourselves have suffered great losses;
but we are yet alive! O let us not presumptuously remain any
longer in this far country, in slumber and absence from the Lord
Jesus! 'Return unto thy rest, O my soul.' Christ is the person who
is an hiding place from the wind, and a covert from the tempest
and rain. O that we may sit under his shadow; we are too feeble
and light to stand ourselves in the storm. It is delightful to have
his shelter, a shelter perfectly strong and safe to protect us in the
greatest hurricane that ever was, or shall be. Such weak ones as
we are will arrive at home under his kind protection. May you,
dear sister, enjoy that protection till death.

To Miss Rogers, afterwards Mrs Davies
Of Carnachen-wen, near Tre-fin, Pembrokeshire

1. HUMAN DEPRAVITY, LAMENTATIONS
OVER IT – THE FEAR OF GOD

Llanfechell 15 April 1802

I am sorry I have been so long in fulfilling my promise to you:
being absent very often from home, I am exceedingly engaged
when at home. But I fear to think of my labour in the Lord's vine-

yard as too much. However, I know not, after thus beginning a letter, what subject is the most suitable to take in hand. No doubt you expect some information and a few observations from me. As to worldly news, it is of little profit; and I know you do not desire it. The discoveries I make in myself, though small in degree, are painful. There is an ocean of sin and misery in me, which, if truly seen by me at any time, has been perceived imperfectly; yea, such inexpressible depths of corruption in each of the faculties of my soul, that I can scarcely form any conception of the lamentable state of one of them.

There is such ignorance in my *understanding* respecting the things of God that I comprehend but very little of them. 'I am as a beast before God, and I have not the understanding of a man!' *Psalm* 73.22. *Proverbs* 30.2. When I attempt to acquire human knowledge and study some temporal subject, Satan and other enemies do not hinder me from dwelling on, and entering into, them. But alas, when I approach godly and spiritual things, my understanding is so dull, weak, and confused! Yea, moreover, Satan, the flesh, and the world are, as it were, in concert, active in disturbing me in this work, and preventing me from going on with it; sometimes by drawing my attention to natural objects; at other times by filling my mind with such ideas respecting the subjects under consideration as to prevent my understanding them rightly; and sometimes by inducing me to imagine that I comprehend them, in order that thereby I may be prevented from praying and labouring for spiritual understanding and wisdom from above.

My *affections* are very apt to run after improper objects, and are engaged too much and improperly on lawful subjects: but alas they are cold, confused, and dead with regard to heavenly and spiritual things suitable for life, death, and eternity! Yea, my affections are enticed by vanity from the living and true God, who is all-sufficient and possessing in himself everything that is delightful!

My *will* is very obstinate, stubborn, and unyielding towards the things of God, and very much disposed to have the rule and dominion, instead of bowing to the Lord's will; and even to murmur and complain when his will is accomplished in some of his dispensations!

My *conscience* is sleepy and hard, yea, and very dishonest with regard to the Lord's things! Alas, too apt to tolerate evil, without even speaking against it! The efficacy of Jesus' blood on it is scarcely perceptible.

My *memory* is also full of corruption. It is remarkable how little of good things it retains, and how much of vain thoughts. Far too much!

Alas, an ocean of deadly corruption moves over all my religious performances! Yea, my meditations on spiritual subjects, my prayers and praise, and my sermons, yea, all my holy things are made vile and distressing thereby. It is most astonishing that the Lord permits me to approach him with such odious sacrifices! Never was there any poison so obnoxious and contrary to man's nature, as my corruptions to God's mind and in his sight.! The *evils* that distress me mostly in the *worship* of God are:

1 Losing sight of *God* in his greatness and purity as the object of my adoration; and consequently all my worship is an empty name, without any object and to no purpose. It is easy to pray in a careless manner if God is not properly viewed. It is easy to preach or hear the Word of God as an empty human declamation, if God is not present. In that case, all the work will be 'the sacrifice of fools.'

2 Losing sight of *myself* as insignificant and ruined; of my great wants; of myself as a creature; and trying to be as God! – of myself as a sinner, but attempting to be some kind of saint, vain, wretched, proud, and selfish! Then my religious performances are somewhat like Cain's sacrifice or the prayer of the Pharisee, or the religion of the Laodiceans. *Revelation* 3.14–22. What a poor miserable state!

3 Losing sight of the great *Mediator*; my need of him; his preciousness, and the glory of his person, and the value of his offices! It is too terrible a thing for me, a guilty sinner, to approach the holy God, but through the Mediator. By attempting to do so, I disparage and slight all the purposes of God. I despise the eternal decree, covenant, and plan of redemption; all the promises of God; the incarnation of the eternal Word, his life and death, his resurrection, ascension, and intercession! It is impossible to receive anything from God but through the Mediator. This is the reason why we are so uncomfortable in the enjoyment of the means of grace, the Mediator is so little valued by us.

4 Being so indifferent as to the influences of the *Holy Ghost* in the work, to aid me in prayer, to seek the mind of God, and to understand it. None but he can teach us to frame such prayers as will be acceptable in heaven, and none but he can make the Word effectual on earth. To be indifferent as to his influences is then a most grievous sin.

Such a hell of misery I am! and such wretchedness remains in me, even under the means of grace, before the pure God! And I am fully persuaded that it is necessary to have some ocean, some treasure, some riches of grace that are unspeakable, in order to save, cleanse, heal, and purify such as I am! I am hell! I deserve the fire of hell for ever; yea, if there are degrees of punishment in hell, as there doubtless are, the deepest and hottest place there is my just desert by nature! I deserve such a hell daily even as a professor! But, notwithstanding all this, Christ anointed and appointed from eternity to save such a one, is sufficient, all-sufficient. I am happy to think that my salvation depends on the good will of the Three-in-One. I rejoice often, though with trembling, to think that God hath foreseen all my maladies and evils, even when covenanting to save me; yea, *then* it was agreed to give a sufficient sacrifice for all my vile transgressions; then it was planned to deliver me from all wretchedness and corruptions. And it depends on the engagement of the Trinity to make me perfectly holy ere long!

It seems evident that the effects of election, the covenant of grace, full redemption, and intercession, are now visible in you. Have you not been called, and others left? Why have you a taste and relish for the Gospel of peace, the tidings respecting the sacrifice of the cross, when others of your rank and station take pleasure in foolish vanities? And why were you preserved, when some fellow-professors, stronger in faith than you, as you thought, fell into sin? The gracious covenant, the perfect redemption, and all-prevailing intercession above, were, and are, the causes of this your salvation: then never doubt his great and glorious promises; trust entirely in him, abide under his protection for ever and ever. Grace be with you. Amen.

2. SPIRITUAL DECLENSIONS – THE
FEAR OF GOD – GROWTH IN GRACE

Shrewsbury 16 February 1805

I was glad to receive a letter from you, though you complain of bad news. This world consists of a great mixture of things; we cannot therefore expect good news always; and praised be God, all is not bad which we hear. There is much room to fear that the bad tidings of many falls will be heard, because many have been received into the Church without evident signs and proofs that a gracious change ever took place in them. It is therefore to be feared that some event will soon shew them to the world in their true colours.

The children of God themselves have become very lethargic and unguarded, and have grieved and provoked the Lord greatly, therefore they are weak and unstable under temptations. When I consider the slumbering state of the Church, I wonder that so few shameful falls occur. The infinite goodness of God hath preserved us hitherto, though we were very often deficient in the duty of watchfulness. No doubt it was for his name's sake he led us through many and great dangers, and 'he will guide us till death.' I think, as you have mentioned, that the Lord permits some to fall into open sins, by way of punishment for trifling with secret sins. O that we may hate sin yet more, because it is sin and so odious. If we detest one sin because it is an offence against God, we hate every sin on the same ground; for all sins are alike in their nature against a holy God.

I often apprehend that at the present time the *true* fear of God is scarce amongst us. The fear of the Lord is a most valuable treasure in the Church: the *dread* of sin is in its very nature, and a renunciation of it is sure to follow it always. 'The fear of the Lord is clean.' Those that truly fear God, do not allow themselves the things that others are pleased to indulge in. 'But so did not I,' said Nehemiah, 'because of the fear of God.' (Chapter 5.15.) And the true Christian cannot live as the hypocrite, on account of God's fear in his heart. He fears grieving and offending him, and bringing reproach on his name and cause here in the world. Besides, the

man that truly fears the Lord not only takes care that his conduct
is becoming before men, but also that his spirit should be in a
suitable frame before God. He is not only anxious to fulfil outward
duties, but also that his soul should act properly in them. The
corruption of his heart distresses him more than all the infirmities
of his life; for when his conduct is tolerably fair, the depravity of
his soul is then the same; yea, it is with him wherever he goes;
and there is no hope of full deliverance till death. This corruption
grieves the Christian in two ways:

1 Its inclinations to sinful actions. It is true the merciful Lord keeps
   believers all their lives from falling into them; yet inclinations to
   them are a continual source of grief and uneasiness to Christians,
   and they cannot be perfectly happy and comfortable until their sinful
   inclinations are entirely destroyed. Praised be God for preventing
   our evil inclinations from breaking out into deeds, and thanks be to
   him for implanting in us a nature and dispositions that are contrary
   to them! And indeed those holy inclinations which oppose corruption
   bear through the infinite mercy the sway now, and they shall have full
   possession of the soul presently. Thanked be the Lord, the morning is
   drawing near when we shall be free from all corruptions for ever, and
   come forth as conquerors into the mansions of bliss! Welcome,
   delightful morning!

2 The sinful attitude, frame, and disposition of our souls towards God
   is a constant cause of sorrow to us. Our sinful, narrow, or hard
   thoughts of God; a cold heart towards him; inability of abiding in
   his fellowship, are very painful. O that we had more free and elevated
   thoughts of God, and more warm and tender affections towards
   him! And O that our spirits would cleave more to him in every
   condition, and would abide longer in communion with him! O
   that we had more of his holy, lovely image on us in the world! We
   shall have it perfect before long.

   The way to obtain these inestimable mercies is by communion
and intercourse with the blessed Mediator. Saving virtues and
effects come from him to the poor soul that obtains a believing
view of him. If the woman that had the issue of blood was healed
in her body by touching the hem of his garment, how much more
shall a poor soul be saved and healed through embracing the

Saviour by faith! O what influences go out of him to such! There is an unfathomable ocean of all grace, virtue, and glory in him. Even the angels of heaven never saw the utmost of them. Yea, saints and angels never can have an insight into the whole of these mysteries. Even a view of Christ has already turned death back. There is no condemnation to those that are in Christ Jesus. The sight of him will at once make us perfectly whole. He can keep you from falling and present you faultless before the throne. To be faultless! O! infinite wonder! sinful dust faultless! Will it not be wonderful, dear sister, that such as we who are, as it were, oceans of corruption, should become altogether pure! Doubtless he that loved us and washed us should have the praise for ever.

3. REVIVALS – SUCCESS OF THE GOSPEL – SAFETY OF THE CHRISTIAN

London 29 October 1806

It gave me great pleasure to find that religion is undergoing a revival in your country. I have been expecting this delightful intelligence sometime from Pembrokeshire, knowing that many in your country are longing for it.[1] The Lord does not excite this longing in his children without intending to visit them. Be very thankful to him for the least manifestation of his favour to you. Give him no rest, day nor night; more is to be communicated from him, and more to be done in your country. He is never tired or weary in hearing prayers. The most agreeable and delightful prayers in his estimation are those for the success of his own work. The cry, the petition, 'Let thy kingdom come,' is sweet music in the divine ears, when sent up without hypocrisy, and by the influence of his own Spirit. Read the last chapters of the prophet Isaiah, the 72nd Psalm, with many other portions of the holy Scriptures, containing wonderful promises of the success

---

[1] Two ministers, H. Davies, and D. Griffiths of Nevern, had laboured in the vineyard of the Lord with great success in that county.

of Christ's kingdom. You will doubtless peruse them with a degree of delight and confidence, and also anxiety that the day may soon dawn. All that we have witnessed is but the dawn of a brighter day.

Dear sister, we ought to consider it a favour that we have been brought to love the prosperity of God's work. We were born thorough enemies to it; yea as great enemies as bloody Mary and Bonner, and other persecutors. It was as great a work to make us love him, as even Saul of Tarsus! But we can now say that we truly love him, and that the success of his cause is the joy of our hearts. Though we cannot say that we are of any use in the work, yet we say that we love it, and grieve that we are so unprofitable. Indeed it is wonderful that we have not before this period been left to become a reproach to the cause of God. When I think of the thousand temptations that have already attacked us, and of the ocean of corruption that is in our hearts, and of the evil world we live in, of the weakness of our grace, and especially of our distance from God, often I greatly wonder that such poor creatures as we, are in a spiritual sense still alive! The goodness of God alone is the real cause. O that we were more thankful to him! and O that we were enabled in every respect to place more implicit confidence in the Lord.

It will not signify much to us, how we may be circumstanced, if we have Christ with us. His absence is the greatest trouble believers meet with in the world. But he never hides his face from them without thereby doing them good. It is our safety, whatever storm overtakes us, to look to Jesus. If for instance, the guilt of our sins take such hold of us that we cannot look up, let us view Jesus as our great High Priest over the house of God. A believing view of his all-sufficiency, sacrifice, and grace, will make the storm subside. Beholding him as the just, acceptable, and successful Intercessor with the Father, will produce peace that passeth all understanding, and joy unspeakable. If we see our great ignorance, and the intricacy of the paths in which we are travelling, looking unto Jesus, the great Prophet and Shepherd, will also support and quicken us. He makes fools wise, and leads the blind.

To Mrs Foulkes of Machynlleth[1]

1. TRYING CIRCUMSTANCES

Llandrindod 22 July 1809

I think the waters do me some good; and I expect that my health will be restored in some degree, for some good end I hope: for I had rather receive help to be useful as I am, than have even good health to be idle. I am afraid that the portion of my life that is past was but little employed for the glory of God.

I have thought much of you and your family since I saw you. I long to hear how your son is.[2] I trust our gracious Lord has either removed your trial, or else that he gives you the necessary aid to bear up under it. Always remember that the Lord reigns, and that our health and senses and property and all that we have are under his control and government. It is true 'that clouds and darkness often surround his seat; yet righteousness and judgment are the habitation of his throne.' *Psalm* 97.2. He does all things well, though we do not perceive what may be his aim in them: but we shall see in his own time what was his mind in all his dispensations. We should endeavour to believe, in all trying cases, that it is his own glory, and our profit and sanctification, that God has in view in all his treatment of us. It is said that it is 'for our profit he corrects us, that we may be partakers of his holiness.' *Hebrews* 12.11. He makes all things work together for our good. We are very apt to think, with Manoah, that he is going to kill us even when he comes to do us some great good; and we are ready to say with Jacob, 'All this is against me:' yea, when all things are turning out favourable to us.

Dear sister, beware of entertaining hard thoughts of God in your trials. Aaron was silent when the Lord destroyed his two sons: and Eli, when informed by Samuel of most awful threaten-

---

[1] The benefit of these compositions we may suppose, was not confined to Mrs Foulkes and her family circle, but also conveyed to the religious society with which she was so closely united; being a society held chiefly for relating experience, and aiding each other in spiritual things. Mrs Foulkes was an excellent character, very benevolent, and useful.

[2] He suffered from mental derangement which led, subsequently, to his death.

ings, yet submitted, saying, 'It is the Lord.' Job blessed God
even when his ten children were killed. The case of each of them
was more distressing than yours. David, when in trouble, said,
'I was dumb, I opened not my mouth, because thou didst it.'
Ezekiel was very resigned and quiet when the Lord 'took away
the desire of his eyes with a stroke.' The God that helped him is
still the same, and his years have no end. These men had no
strength in themselves; they received strength from the Lord as
they wanted it. He is as full of compassion and readiness to assist
us now as others before us. Send your prayers and sighs up to
him.

Don't think of second causes; have an eye neither to man nor
to the devil; look beyond all to God alone. See and observe the
hand of the Lord in the visitation you experience, till you are easy.
Also consider that the Lord is able to restore your son, in his own
good time; I hope this will be the case.

Perhaps this storm that has overtaken you prevents some other
from assailing you that would be far worse. The Lord sometimes
sends one trial as a means to keep back another that would be more
distressing. He suffers one temptation to afflict his children, that
it may be the means of saving them from one that is more painful;
as the 'thorn in the flesh, the messenger of Satan,' was given
to buffet St Paul, that he might not be 'exalted above measure.'
The Lord had rather that the messenger of Satan should buffet
Paul, than he be puffed up with his thoughts. And Paul himself,
no doubt, preferred this, when he perceived the end of the Lord
in it. So, perhaps, the affliction that hath befallen you and your
family is intended to prevent some evils that would be more
overwhelming. I cannot say what they are, but God sees the
evil afar off, and secures his people in a refuge before the storm
comes. You shall hereafter see the end the Lord had in view, far
better than I can tell you. And I have no doubt but that you shall
have cause to praise the Lord for this distressing visitation. May
'patience have its perfect work.' 'Humble yourself under the
almighty hand of God, that you may be exalted in due time.'
Dear sister, all the storms will pass by soon. It is only 'for a night
that sorrow cometh.' But be assured that many a subject for

praise and singing shall be obtained in the valley of humiliation; yea, these trials shall be matters of joy and praise for ever. A view of Christ's glory and unspeakable riches of grace often causes the believer to forget his trouble. May your soul be enabled to see and delight itself in view of these.

2. GOD'S PRESENCE – THE PLEADINGS OF PRAYER

Llanfechell 8 September 1809

I am sorry to find that your storms continue. But God is infinitely more careful of you than I can be, and it is easy for him to make the storms calm whenever he likes. Yea, he will do so in the right time, when he thinks it best; yea, he will do it early, though he seems to delay. It is early in his wise judgment, though it may be late in your opinion. He acts with judgment, therefore wait upon him patiently. 'Joy cometh in the morning.' I trust you will find that this painful visitation is for your profit in the end, though, for the present, it is unpleasant. Thoughts of peace and not of injury are those which he entertains towards you, though he uses rather sharp means to prove you. Yet you shall clearly see that this kind of treatment was necessary, and that it was the best. Beg of him to be with you in the fire and water, as he promises. Even the centre of the burning furnace is a good place, if he that was the fourth with the young men in the plain of Dura be there. Yea, it will be delightful to be on the waves of the sea and in the howling wilderness, yea, the swellings of Jordan, if he be with us. His presence is sufficient to make the most miserable place a heavenly rest.

The Lord has many ways to answer the prayer of his people. When Paul prayed many times for the removal of the thorn in his flesh, the answer was, 'My grace is sufficient for thee.' Indeed it was enough. So when Moses entreated the Lord to take away the fiery serpents; the removal of them was not the answer, but the direction given him to make a brazen serpent. Then do not conclude that the Lord does not hear you, nor your friends, in reference to your son's case, because he is not immediately restored. God has his own time, as well as way, to answer the prayers of his people. He is sometimes pleased to keep them long at his door, before he grants their requests. Christ gave the devils their desire immediately when they asked leave to enter into the swine. But the woman of Canaan had to cry after him before she was answered; he delighted to hear her voice. Therefore, my dear sister, be not weary in crying at the throne of grace. A faithful prayer shall not be made in vain; and it shall not return empty. If what you wish is not bestowed, yet help to wait and resignation to the Lord's will shall be granted, yea, acquiescence in his treatment as it is. O endeavour to surrender your son to the Lord: he has a higher claim to him than you have; it was he that gave him to you: and he hath sustained his life hitherto, and he will soon take him out of this world, from all his relatives, to himself. Therefore it is but right that he should do as he pleases with his own.

3. GOD'S SOVEREIGNTY, GREATNESS, JUSTICE, GOODNESS, AND LOVE

Llanfechell 18 September 1813

I hope you are nearly come to land out of the great storm on your mind. The Lord that rules the storms can make a calm in your breast, yea, in the time when the tempest and waves are the most furious and boisterous. He sits upon the floods, and rides upon the wings of the wind. Not a breeze shall blow, not a wave arise, without his command or permission. High sentiments and confiding thoughts of him are the most suitable means to make the mind calm and quiet in fiery trials.

May we entertain just thoughts of his *greatness;* that he is infinitely great in his essence and attributes, sovereignty and dominion; that he is the owner and Lord of all persons and things; that he has a full right to do as he pleases with his own; and that it is not proper for any to ask him what he is doing, or why he does this or that. He gives no account of any of his matters. He is above being called to give reason for his doings to any. He is the owner, supporter, and ruler of all men and things; therefore it is proper that he should do as he pleases. The claim we have to persons is but borrowed. It is he alone that has a real and unalterable right to them. The claim that we have to a husband, wife, parents, children, brothers, sisters, health, good name, possessions, or any worldly comfort, is but a loan, which he is pleased to favour us with for some time. Therefore we should be silent when he thinks good to take them away from us. And whatever messenger he is pleased to employ to call for them and remove them, we should not murmur.

The consideration of God's *justice* and *equity* in all his works and ways is an excellent means to silence us under every trial, though bitter to flesh and blood. Though God is the sovereign Lord of all, yet he treats all in every respect according to infinite justice. 'Righteousness and judgment are the habitation of his throne, yea, when clouds and darkness are round him.' We may be certain that he will act rightly when he works in darkness in our sight. 'His judgments are strong mountains.' The Judge of all the earth shall do right. 'He does not think it right to do wrong to a man in his cause.' 'Righteous art thou, O Lord, when I plead with thee.' *Jeremiah* 12.1. Whatever we may plead, he can prove his treatment just and proper. Perceiving and considering his justice will make us silent in the most trying circumstances.

Considering the *wisdom* of God, in all his works and ways is a remarkable means to make us quiet and resigned. Yea, when we cannot see the end and propriety of things, yet believing that the infinitely wise God ordered them so, is enough to make us calm and easy, being persuaded that he has some wise end in them, though our eyes are so dull that we cannot perceive them. It is impossible that any thing should be better than as it has been ordained by him. The time and manner of doing all things have been ordered by him in his infinite wisdom, though our corrupt nature is ready to plead that it would have been better if this or the other thing had occurred in some other time and manner. But this is our folly! We shall soon see that everything is arranged in its due place and in the wisest manner.

The consideration of God's goodness is necessary to make us easy under the painful and intricate changes of providence. It is a pure golden head that is under the locks that are dishevelled and black as the raven. All the entangled locks are altogether in their proper places, their root being in the golden head. Good and gracious is the Lord. He is an ocean of inexhaustible goodness; he can do nothing but good. There is much more good in his most afflictive dispensations than can ever be related. But we need spiritual understanding to perceive his goodness in many of his proceedings, especially those that are unpleasant to our nature. But the Lord will cause 'all things to work together for good to them that love him,' and they shall clearly see their benefit some day. Then they shall 'sing of mercy and judgment,' of corrections and of the furnaces of affliction.

But if the storm be so strong and overwhelming that the mind cannot have leisure to meditate on the above great subjects, endeavour to divert the thoughts from the painful circumstances of providence to the wonderful and glorious plan of salvation. That is an endless ocean of most joyful wonders at all times. There is an endless and unceasing fulness of every blessing that may be needful for us. We shall see there that God loves sinners in an infinite manner, so that he gave his own Son to undertake their cause, to assume their nature, to bear their sins, punishment and curse, to make an atonement for them, and to do justice to them; to open a way to God, and to ordain means, and make those effectual in rendering them fit for heaven, to be with God for ever, to intercede for them till they are brought home. Here is an ocean of wisdom that causes us to forget all our troubles, and enables us to live above them, and to count them as nothing in comparison of the glory we shall receive by their means.

To Mrs Lloyd of Beaumaris

TO SYMPATHIZE WITH HER ON THE DEATH
OF HER HUSBAND

Afflicted and sorrowful Sister – It came to my mind to write
a few lines to you, by thinking of your trouble and distress, and
by wishing to know how you are. I am aware, indeed, you are
sorrowful, but I hope your mind is supported under this trial by
kind visits from the Lord. Some sorrow and heaviness are continually occurring to us whilst we are in this world. It would be but
folly for us to expect much happiness in our time: it is but for a
short time that things that are seen endure. Friends for a time
are even our most beloved relatives. Many of our best friends
leave us at brief intervals as we travel together through this evil
world; and we ourselves shall very shortly leave our fellow-
travellers. What else but this can sojourners expect? It is better
not to think too much of those who have left us, but to proceed
and set our mind on the journey's end, and expect meeting them
there in our Father s house. This will be far better.

It is far better for our brethren who have arrived at home;
they were more ripe and fit for glory than ourselves. If the mind
must be with them, let it run to them in their glorious state. But
let not our meditations be occupied too much on them in the way
they were with us here below; neither let our thoughts be too
much with them in the grave; but let them fly upwards to those
dear friends in company with Christ in blissful abodes above.
Much benefit will accrue to us by ascending there in our meditations.

There is nothing but a vacancy in the situations and states they
occupied in the world; and there is no work nor praise in the
grave. But there is fulness of joy in the presence of God, where they
are now, yea, where the spirits of just men are made perfect.
There is no benefit by conversing in our thoughts with them as
here. There is much gain many ways by ascending upwards in
our meditations on them above. We may, by thinking of them
there, meet with Jesus, the Brother, the Bridegroom, the best
Friend.

Fellowship with God in Christ will sweeten all the bitter waters of Marah. We shall be reconciled in that sweet communion with all the dispensations of his providence. However painful to flesh and blood some of them are, we shall perceive that he does all things well.

Having a frequent view of God by faith, giving up his only begotten Son to die for us, we shall feel composed; yea, he bruised his Son for our sins! He did not spare him, that he might deliver us from going down to the pit. O what wonders! Let us frequently meditate on these astonishing transactions, and we shall be content that he may deal with us as he pleases, and take away what he likes. And did he indeed give infinitely more to us than all things he may take away from us! And does he take nothing from us but what he gave![1] I pray that you may be strengthened in weakness by his grace; his grace is sufficient for you. It is well with the destitute and fatherless who have God for their Father, and for the solitary widows, who have Christ for their Friend and Bridegroom. May he support and comfort you.

Your brother and servant in Christ.

To Mrs Roberts of Caernarvon[2]

DIRECTIONS TO HER ON A DYING BED

Fron 27 September 1833

I take the liberty to address you in your present affliction. I was sorry, indeed, to hear of your precarious state of health; I can, in a measure, sympathize with you, but I cannot support you,

---

[1] There was a son of this happy pair, who was likely to be very useful in the church of God, possessing great piety and talents, but he was removed by God in his mysterious providence to another world, in his youthful days, which was an additional grief to his widowed mother. Elias had great regard for him also, and gave a brief but pleasing account of him, by way of a preface to a little work in Welsh, called *The Remains of the Young Friend*. He hastened his death by being kind beyond his strength to the property and persons of the deceased who were thrown upon the shores of Beaumaris from the wreck of the Rothsay Castle. (See *pp* 272 and 388.)

[2] Wife of W. Roberts, surgeon.

nor give you any relief in body or mind. But I know who is the
Lord over every disease, distemper, and affliction. The commencement, continuance, and end of every disorder are entirely under
his control. His dispensations are all infinitely wise and good.
'He doth not afflict nor grieve the children of men willingly.'
He sees some necessity for all our troubles, and he can over-rule
all bitter circumstances, and make them work together for our
good. He can bless our bodily pains and troubles for our eternal
good, for turning our minds from the perishable things of time
and sense to objects that are eternal and imperishable. He knows
what is best for us. In troubles like yours, deep very often calleth
unto deep, deep affliction calleth unto deep reflection, to great
fears and distress of mind. The conscience is awakened to accuse
us of innumerable sins: and Satan is sometimes permitted to tell
us that our transgressions cannot be forgiven. But what saith the
Scripture, the unerring Word of God? 'Whosoever believeth in
him, shall receive remission of sins;' 'Him that cometh to me,'
saith the dear Jesus, 'I will in no wise cast out,' *Acts* 10.43. *John*
6.37. It is useless to deny our sins, or to try to extenuate them, or
endeavour to make excuses for them. But let our accusers bring
our innumerable sins against us, we flee as lost sinners to the
blood of the Lamb of God, 'which taketh away the sin of the
world.' Let us go as the chief of sinners; and let us beware of the
flattery of many, who will endeavour to comfort us by telling us
that we are better than many. No, no, we know better than that,
and we cannot be comforted on that ground. But as the chief of
sinners we are invited to trust in Christ for salvation. He never
refused any sinner. O, dear Mrs R., trust in him, for in him there
is a free and full salvation.

Let us think much about entering eternity. It is a most foolish
way many have to comfort each other in distress, endeavouring
to persuade the mournful to put away every thought respecting
eternity, in order to have quietude: a very poor way of comforting
immortal creatures! My dear friend, we need not forget eternity
in order to be comfortable; but we may look at things which are
eternal, till we feel our afflictions light. *2 Corinthians* 4.17, 18.
There is a strong consolation prepared for him who flees for

refuge, to lay hold on Christ. *Hebrews* 6.18. Consolation in Christ is the best, is the strongest, if we were to live here a thousand years; and we need not look for another in death or to eternity.

Now I must conclude; I am too poorly to write much (as you may see by my hand-writing), and perhaps it is much too long for you, in your weak state of health, to read, or to hear it read by another. I know my humble letter is full of imperfections. I did not aim at any elegant diction, but I wish to drop some word for your support or comfort in trouble. I think often of you at the throne of grace. I am anxious to hear how you are; perhaps Mr Roberts will kindly drop me a line.

To W. Roberts, surgeon, at Caernarvon

SYMPATHIZING WITH HIM ON THE DEATH
OF HIS WIFE

Fron 22 November 1833

I never wrote to you in such circumstances before; and doubt the propriety of writing to you at present, as it is perhaps too difficult for you to be able to read anything. I know you cannot find support or comfort in anything this world can afford. But let me entreat you most kindly to look above. There is a friend indeed, the Friend of sinners, who can sympathize with you; yea, more than that, he can support and comfort you. You may consider in your grief and sorrow that the disease and death of your dear consort were sent by God in his own way and time, and that no human skill was sufficient to cure the disease, nor to prevent death doing his work. May you be able to say as David did, 'I became dumb, and opened not my mouth, for it was thy doing'! *Psalm* 39.9. There is another and stronger comfort – your loss is her great gain. We have the strongest ground to hope, that to her to die was gain, because as far as we can see, she trusted entirely in Christ for all her salvation. He is a rock. No hope builded on him shall nor can be disappointed. Now, your sorrow, though the cause is great, yet must not be as the sorrow of the world, for they have no hope. O rather bless God for his great mercy and kindness to her!

My dear sir, I cannot write any more; it is too much for my poor frame.

To Rev Ebenezer Richard[1]

MINISTERIAL TRIALS AND SYMPATHY

Llandrindod 16 September 1808

The waters are beneficial to me, and I am likely to get stronger. Please to tell Major Bowen that I feel much obliged to him for his care for me, and that I send my very kind regards to him and Mrs Bowen.

Dear Brother, I wish you much of the Lord's gracious presence in the great work of the ministry everywhere. I perceive much of my own corruption and unfitness for the Lord's work. I find my spirit rather far from him and too unconcerned for man's salvation. I am constrained to exclaim, by considering the magnitude of the work, 'Who is sufficient for these things?' But as the Lord hath been pleased to take such humble instruments into his hands, and to put the Gospel treasure in earthen vessels 'that the excellency of the power may be of God, and not of us,' there is no reason to be discouraged on account of our great infirmities and unsuitableness. But we should endeavour to surrender ourselves to him; and though weakness itself, yet that weakness, in his hands, shall be 'stronger than men.'

Satan has two remarkable temptations, in order to confuse and hinder ministers in their work. He often endeavours to prevent them from seeing the greatness and spirituality of the work, that they may be careless and unconcerned in it, and consequently become proud and conceited, imagining that they are eminent persons. I think it is impossible for a man to become high-minded as he views the magnitude of the work. If we see its

[1] He was minister at Tregaron, Cardiganshire, and the father of the famous Henry Richard M.P. (born 1812).

vastness, transcendency, and responsibility, we see ourselves
very poor creatures in it, and in a very unbecoming frame for its
performance. The other temptation is, to dishearten us when we
perceive the magnitude of the work in some measure, and to
cause despair, preventing us from perceiving God on our side,
and the precious promises that administer help in the work.
But God can, notwithstanding these and numerous other temptations, support us for his own glory, and the good of his Church.
Let us therefore, brother, confide in the grace that is in Christ
Jesus, not only to enable us to maintain our place as Christians,
but also as ministers. Jesus received gifts, not only for the
rebellious, but also for the work of the ministry. O that we might
receive more of them continually! O that we might be in his
hands, and be of some use and for his glory, the short time we
shall be here! The grace and peace of God in Christ be with you!
Amen.

5 January 1836

I find in a letter I received to-day from my daughter, that you are
very poorly, which distressed me much. Though I know that every
affliction and infirmity is under the government of God, and that
he is you Father, yet I cannot help being sorry for you and your
beloved wife, as you have been overtaken by illness far from home.
No doubt it is a consolation that your sons are with you, and the
best medical help at hand; and that your heavenly Father is as
near to you in London as at Tregaron. I know that he will do all
things for you in the best manner; his goodness is infinite; and
his wisdom is such, that he cannot fail to accomplish the best end.

It oftentimes occurs that we cannot perceive at present what is
his meaning; but we shall know hereafter. We may, nevertheless,
have grace now to believe that his treatment is good, even when
it is painful. Our heavenly Father knoweth what is best for us.
Our bodies are earthly vessels; it is a wonder that they have not
before now been broken. As the Lord has thought proper that
we should, as vessels, carry his treasure, he will take care of us,
however frail we may be. Our tabernacles consist of dissolving

elements. The execution[1] has been in our houses now these many
years; and we know not the hour in which death may be commissioned to perform his fatal work; but we know in whom we
have believed, and that he is able to keep that which is committed
unto him. Not only will he receive our spirits, but also regard
whatever is dear to us. We may safely commit to his care all that
we leave behind at death. We may comfortably leave our orphans
with him; 'he will keep them alive; and our widows may trust
in him.' His great cause amongst us, that is very near our hearts,
we can calmly leave with him. Though we should rejoice to see the
day dawning more on the Church, and the ark on the shoulders of
more spiritual men before we are called home, yet the will of the
Lord must and shall be done.

Dear brother, I earnestly pray that the Lord would restore
you,[2] that you may be a long time useful in his vineyard, though
my mind ran to the time of our separation; it will however
come soon.

To a clergyman

1. DR HAWKER – ELECTION – HOW TO
PREACH THE GOSPEL

Llanfechell 24 December 1824

Though I am not of the same mind as Dr H.[3] as to some things,
yet I think he was a good and a useful man; but he might have
been much more so, if he had never entertained some of those
views which he held. I suppose that those who would preach
Christ to none but the elect are of the same views as Dr H. I
think that the sound doctrine that is generally called Calvinism is
much misrepresented: the Hyper-Calvinists give occasion to
the doctrine called *Antinomianism*.

I do not know how those that deny the *total* corruption of the

---

[1] The work of dissolution.

[2] He died a little more than a year later.

[3] Dr Robert Hawker (1753–1827), one of the most popular preachers of his
day. He was Vicar of Charles, Plymouth. In doctrine he was a High Calvinist.

human nature, and that salvation as to its plan, its performance, its application, is of grace only, can be considered as faithful ministers. On the other hand, I cannot understand how those that are against calling, inviting, persuading, and compelling sinners to come to Christ, can be said to preach the Gospel. I believe that declining to preach the Gospel to every creature is contrary to the Word of God, and inconsistent with sound doctrine. Is it not very different from the manner that the Prophets and the Patriarchs used to preach? the manner that Christ and his disciples used to teach? If God ordained the preaching of the Gospel as the means of *saving* some, then we should preach the Gospel to the lost. If faith cometh by hearing the Word of God, should we not preach the things that are to be believed to the unbeliever? If unbelief of the Gospel is a sin, is not believing it a duty? How can it be a duty of some to believe what is not the duty of ministers to preach? Should we not shew to our hearers their need of Christ, and even invite them under a sense of their wants?

I do not mean to say, that the whole should be directed to the Physician, or the guiltless to the sacrifice, or the clean to the fountain. It is incumbent on preachers to shew the people their misery and their utter ruin; and then, consequently, to exhibit Christ as a Saviour to the lost, and that whosoever believeth in him shall not perish. When we preach generally that Christ is a Saviour to the lost, and persuade every one that seeth his lost state to flee to him, we do it not under the idea that they are elected or redeemed, but as ruined; *thus* they are to go to him who is preached a Saviour to the lost, and fleeing to him as such is a sign that they are elected and redeemed. No one ever saw before he believed in Christ that he was elected or redeemed. So there is no need of preaching general redemption as a ground to call lost sinners to Christ; and there is no need of preaching that man can of himself believe the Gospel, as a ground to encourage ruined sinners to believe in Christ. Not the ability of fallen man is the rule or measure of his duty, or the ground for the justice of God to require it. The inability of man is no excuse for his disobedience. His sin, his enmity, are his inability. He ought to be ashamed on the account of them. I do not understand that the inability of any one to believe has been a hindrance to him feeling it, to believe in Christ; for there is strength for the helpless always ready, and faith is the gift of God.

But notwithstanding this, faith is the duty of man. It is the natural duty of man as a reasonable creature to believe the testimony of God respecting his Son. It was in his grace that God ordained that that which was the duty of man as a reasonable, accountable creature, should be an instrument, medium, or means of obtaining the life that is in Christ for sinners. So, brother, by preaching to the people, shewing them that they are sinners, and likewise their misery as such, endeavour to exhibit the suitableness and glory of Christ as a Saviour for such sinners; and invite, in a very strong and pressing manner, lost sinners as such; the weary and heavy-laden, the hungry and thirsty, to escape to him and to believe in him. Shew that he rejects none that come, and that none shall perish that believe. Yet beware preaching the feelings of their lost state, hunger or thirst, as terms of their accepting, or as things to gain their acceptance with Christ, or to merit their reception; this is altogether of grace.

Forgive me that I make so free, and write so much. I am in no wise suitable to give any information: I need to be instructed by you. Yet I have, at your desire, stated my opinion.

In answer to your question respecting my own feelings and the frame of my mind after preaching, I have to observe that they are very changeable and various. But I have had occasions to be thankful at times for what is called a hard and dark opportunity, as it caused me to pray and watch more, and to be more humble. It was after such sermons I have had the greatest proof and certainty of my being sent by God, as I have received in them several times such divine ideas as were not in my possession before. O brother, I have nothing to boast of: I am a greater sinner than anyone that has never been in a pulpit; yet a sinner that expects to be saved through grace, and by the salvation I endeavour to preach.

There is no vileness you lament of, that I am not well acquainted with, to my shame and sorrow: and as to pride, there is no room for it. I don't see I have anything to boast of; but on the contrary,

I have much to be ashamed of, by reason of preaching in such a dark, carnal, cold, sleepy manner. The greatest loss I feel, is that of the Spirit, and earnestness of secret prayer. It is bad and poor in the study, dark and embarrassing in the sermon owing to this. I want to go there oftener, and be more anxious before preaching.

2. SYMPATHY – SPIRIT OF PRAYER – WORLDLY AND CHRISTIAN COMPANY – DEATH – PREACHING

Llanfechell 30 December 1824

I am sorry to find, by reading your letter, that you are so distressed and cast down. I think you ought to withstand your present depression of mind, and take courage; pray and use every means to overcome it. It seems that the great enemy, Satan, seeing his advantage, is much bent upon trying to lead your mind to over-depression, in order to render you uncomfortable to your own self, and unprofitable in your ministry. Pray much to the Lord to support you with his free Spirit, and to help you again with the joy of his salvation.

You ask how we may regain the spirit of prayer after it is lost? It is by praying and waiting for the Lord in his ways and ordinances, yea, looking for him patiently. 'If the vision should tarry, yet wait for it, it will surely come.' Go to the Lord in private prayer, though there should be no desire; and tell your complaint to him, though your experiences are uncomfortable, and you are not favoured with the joyful frame and feelings you used to enjoy. Though we 'walk in darkness without light,' yet it is our privilege and profit to 'trust in the name of the Lord.' But we must always remember to ask for the Spirit, and every grace, in the name of Christ, the Mediator, depending on his sacrifice and infinite atonement, leaving it to the Lord to answer us in his own way and time.

Moreover we ought, when we have lost the spirit of prayer or some other gifts, to examine ourselves as to how that came to pass and what was the cause of such a calamity. Did we abuse the pleasure and the delightful enjoyment we experienced in prayer? Have we substituted our prayers instead of Christ? Or have we gone into some false way, and thereby grieved the Holy Spirit, who teaches and disposes us to pray, helps our infirmities, and intercedes for us, by producing unutterable groans in us. When we have gone from the Lord's ways, may we pray and endeavour immediately to be restored to the right path!

Next, as to a minister withdrawing from the company of worldly people as much as he can, I think there is danger on both sides. It is improper and unprofitable on the one hand, for a minister of the Gospel to be in the company of the world in their corrupt feasts, vain amusements, or any bad customs they may have. Yea, it is unprofitable for him to spend much time in going from house to house, though it be attended with no bad practice. Our time is short enough for the important work on our hands. Yet a minister should be ready to visit the sick and afflicted. Besides he should not be unsociable, nor appear uncomfortable; but he should 'be kind to all, apt to teach, patient.' His cheerful manner should recommend the religion of Christ, that 'her ways are ways of pleasantness.' He should shew a readiness to associate with them in every proper and useful pursuit, yet making it appear that our work is great, and that our time is short, so that we cannot spend it in vain. A minister of Christ should be the happiest of all men; and his manner and example should exhibit not only holiness and Christianity in bright colours, but also his happiness, delight, and enjoyment. He should be like a good mother with her children, who, in nursing and training them up, meets with many troubles and trials, yet she endeavours to be cheerful with them, yea, she gives the breast to her child with singing, though she was shedding tears most profusely a little before.

Besides, associating with Christians is a great advantage, profit, and refreshment to a minister. Fellowship in things appertaining to religion is an ordinance of God, and it should be used as such. I think you may injure your health, and spirit too, by being too much alone; doubtless depression of the mind is, in some measure, engendered thereby. Is there no friend in your parish or neighbourhood with whom you might profitably converse for an hour now and then? Yea, though he should not excel as a spiritual man, yet if he should be a moral and a sensible person, his conversation for an hour or two sometimes might be profitable: and you may impart some expressions or communications on eternal things that might be of greater benefit to him. I recollect reading of Mr M. Poole,[1] when he was much engaged in writing his *Synopsis*, he would generally go in the evening to a gentleman's house, in the neighbourhood, and conversing cheerfully with him, he would return to his studies, revived in mind and body; but he would say before parting, 'Let us have something respecting Christ before we separate.' Excuse me for dwelling so long on this subject; my regard and care for you, lest you should be overcome by this temptation, induced me to say so much. If you should give way to lowness of mind and discouragement, your health will be damaged, and your ministry will not be so useful. An ill report will be given to the religion of Christ, by affording an occasion to its enemies to say that it deprives persons of comfort and happiness, making its professors dejected, melancholy, and useless.

In respect of your mother's departure, I understand that the enemy of your comfort and usefulness takes occasion from that circumstance to trouble and injure you. I acknowledge that moderate grief and sorrow after your dear mother is natural, reasonable, proper, and Christian. But there is harm and great sin in immoderate grief; it is sorrowing 'like others that have no hope;' grieving after those that died in the Lord as others for whom there is no hope that they died happy. As you have the strongest ground to believe that your mother died godly, you may rejoice, for death was her gain. She had a long life in this world, you could not expect her continuance much longer. The wearisome days had overtaken her; she could have no natural comfort and enjoyment on earth much more. Her sojourning here below came to an end; do not grieve because she arrived at home. Her labour was ended; be content that she is gone to the delightful

[1] Matthew Poole, 17th-century Puritan divine, his 5-vol. Synopsis was compiled between 1666 and 1676.

rest. The warfare is over, she obtained the victory, and she sings now for it; and therefore you have greater cause to rejoice than to be dissatisfied.

As to your trouble and sorrow that you could not spend some time last year with your mother according to your promise, I see no cause for it; because it was not for want of love and regard for her that you did not visit her, but on account of an unsurmountable difficulty. Therefore it is clear that you were hindered by Providence in going there. You should be easy, lest you should be found fighting with God's plan, and fretting because you had not that which he did not intend for you. O brother, be resigned: and know that it is Satan that takes advantages from these occasions to injure you. This trouble of yours can answer no good end; and therefore your grief in this respect cannot come from God. He does not send thoughts into the minds of his people, without intending a wise and a good end thereby. If you should meet with the following books, I would recommend you to read them: *The Mute Christian under the Smarting Rod* by T. Brooks;[1] and *Token for Mourners* by Flavel.[2]

In reference to what you said in regard to the manner of preaching, I am sure that extempore preaching is better, and more likely to prove successful, than reading your sermons. That which is delivered from the pulpit extemporaneously appears in general to the hearers more weighty, and the minister looks more for help from God in that way. It is wonderful that preachers, yea, renowned preachers, like to read their sermons, when learned men of every other profession – lawyers, senators – deliver their orations and speeches extemporaneously. However, I see no objection against your reading your sermon once on the Sabbath, that you may gain some in your parish, and avoid causing any prejudice or hindrance to some of your parishioners.

---

[1] First published in 1659; one of the most famous works of this Puritan divine.
[2] First published in 1674 (in Vol. 5 of Flavels' Works, Banner of Truth edition 1968).

3. ON BAPTISM

Llanfechell 15 August 1825

You would readily make allowance for me, if you knew how I am circumstanced. I am often from home on preaching excursions. And when I am allowed to be at home for a short time, I am much engaged. About forty churches belonging to our Connexion in this island, expect me to visit them. I have besides so many different cases of conscience and discipline from several congregations to attend to and to give my opinion upon, which require much consideration and close attention. I have to correspond with my brethren in several counties; and besides I am obliged to make preparations for the pulpit; and I have but slender qualifications for the work! These matters fill my mind often, so that I know not what to write to my dearest friends.

Now let us turn to the subject of baptism, which you have mentioned. It was once my intention of writing a treatise on the Abrahamic covenant, which I look upon as the great foundation of Infant Baptism. That covenant was a revelation and dispensation of the covenant of grace; it was confirmed by God in Christ. And the law, or the Sinai dispensation, could not disannul it. Christ came according to that covenant, and died under the curse of the law, that the blessings of the covenant might come on the Gentiles by faith. In that covenant, God took Abraham and his seed, to be his people, and gave himself to them to be their God. He took into his fold the infant seed of his people, that they might be his visible people, or members of his visible Church. He appointed an ordinance, circumcision, as a means not only of receiving them into the Church, but also of sealing that privilege to them.

As to what you said that the covenant was made from eternity, between the adorable Persons in the Holy Trinity, concerning the salvation of sinners of mankind, it is all true. But you know that the several dispensations of that covenant are each frequently called a covenant in the Word of God. And he is said to make a covenant with his people. 'I will make,' saith he, 'a new covenant with the house of *Israel*.' *Jeremiah* 31.31. *Hebrews* 8.8. *Ezekiel* 20.27.

Therefore that expression, 'to enter into covenant in baptism,' is not so improper as you might imagine. The infant seed of God's visible or professed people are in covenant, having a right of membership in the visible Church; they have therefore a right to baptism as a seal of the covenant, or the Gospel dispensation. Circumcision was a seal of the Abrahamic covenant, and may be called *the covenant*. As the Gospel is another dispensation of the covenant of grace, and baptism the seal of it, we may view the infant in that ordinance as entering into the bond of the new covenant, as a member in the visible Church of Christ.

As to the nature of baptism, you know that it is one of the two ordinances we commonly call the *sacraments*. This word was used by the Romans to signify their military *oath*, but is applied by Christians to signify that which is sacred, and also solemn engagement to be the Lord's, as a true soldier of Christ. There is in a sacrament a visible and sensible sign, and representation of the blessings of the covenant of grace. And by using the sign according to God's appointment, the benefits of the covenant are held forth and sealed to believers. The outward sign in baptism – water and the application of it – represents those blessings of salvation, the blood and Spirit of Christ. The baptized child stands in need of these, and cannot be saved without regeneration, sanctification, and justification. Baptism rightly used may be a means of confirming the faith of the believing parent, that those blessings necessary for the salvation of his child are to be had of God. Therefore he is to pray in the behalf of his child.

Concerning the other questions, whether baptism lays any obligation on the baptized child, I think that baptized children are under an indispensable obligation to perform the duties which are incumbent on those who are given up to God in that ordinance. The Christian parent has a right – a reasonable, scriptural, covenant right – to give up his child in baptism to God, to be for ever his. He is most glad to do this, because of his love to God, and his affection to his child; and therefore his baptized child is bound to be the Lord's for ever. It is unknown to Christian parents whether their children will give up themselves to the Lord when they grow up to manhood: nevertheless, the obligation will be in force, as soon as they are capable of doing good and evil. Therefore it is plain that the parent may give up his child to God, and put him under an obligation to him, which is good because it is just, being founded on God's right to the obedience of the child. And the parent ought, as soon as the child is able to understand such things, to charge it upon him as his duty and privilege to be the Lord's.

There is no new obligation laid on the baptized, the obligation being natural and reasonable, though increased by an additional tie. It is a strong engagement and a sweet encouragement to do our duty, to believe God's testimony, to obey his commandments, to worship and serve him all our days. As God took the baptized under his name and into his visible Church, he is consequently under a strong and additional obligation to serve him. It is true that faith and repentance are the gifts of God, but the ground of our obligation to do a thing, is not our ability to do it. We are obliged and bound, as reasonable creatures, to obey our Creator; and our inability, which is moral and sinful, not natural, cannot be an excuse for our disobedience. There is a provision of grace in the covenant, and revealed in the Gospel, as sufficient for all wants. We are, as has been said, under obligations to do the duties required, so are we encouraged by our baptism (which is the seal of the covenant) to seek the grace which is necessary to enable us to perform the duty. I am of the same opinion as yourself, that some make too much, and some too little, of baptism. Those that look upon baptism only as an old custom, or some ancient ceremony, to be used in giving a name to the child, do certainly make too little of it. Those on the other hand that view baptism as regeneration, attended with forgiveness of sins, making it the essence of Christianity, make too much of it.[1] My dear brother, let us pray more and more for the teaching and guidance of the Spirit of God, that we may see everything as it is in his light. If you do not understand my English, I will write my next letter in Welsh.

[1] It is evident from the works of the Reformers that compiled the Prayer-book, that they did not consider that spiritual regeneration always attended baptism. See Cranmer's Defence, Book 4 Chap 7, p 439. Latimer, Parker Soc., Vol 1, pp 202, 470. Hooper, Parker. Soc., pp 74. Jewel on Baptism, pp 263, 297.

4. UNFRUITFULNESS – DEATH – MARRIAGE

Llanfechell 14 December 1826

I have but little time, and less ability, to dwell profitably on the several important subjects in your letter.

As to your complaint of unfruitfulness in your life, I have to observe, that it is very true that we have great cause to complain and to be ashamed of our unfruitfulness. Yet there is danger lest we should despond and become less active by looking at our unfruitfulness. Let us be ashamed and lament our unprofitableness, and let us be very earnest for forgiveness, and let us praise the Lord for sparing us, but let us not be discouraged. May we be strong in the Lord, giving up ourselves to him, to be instructed, strengthened, and used as he pleases.! He may teach even those that are so dull, strengthen those that are so weak, and use as instruments such as are in themselves so unsuitable. May we be ready to perform the humblest service for him with pleasure, counting it perfect freedom! And if he should think fit to let us die without knowing that we have been of any use to him in our day, yet that would be no decisive proof that such is the case. The Lord makes use of some, and conceals that circumstance from them. Be not discontented because you need greater gifts, and better health, thinking if you should have those blessings you would be more useful. Your heavenly Father knows what is best for you. Give yourself up to him as you are, and say often at the throne of grace, 'Behold me, send me.' The point of greatest importance, is that 'the live coal from the altar' should be applied to our hearts and lips, as it was to Isaiah's, that we might be warm in our hearts and truly zealous for glorifying God and saving souls.

As to the other subject, being ready to *die;* I might say that those that are in Christ are always in a state ready to depart: but they may be often in a frame of mind that is very unsuitable for death. Then in order to be in a proper state and frame, we must be living by faith, and resting always on what Christ our Mediator did and suffered; and we should be always under the sanctifying influences of the Holy Ghost, mortifying our carnal and worldly lusts, and raising up our affections and setting them on things above, 'where Christ sitteth.' We ought to be more accustomed to heavenly things in our meditations. And we should possess a greater assurance of hope, knowing that 'we have a house not made with hands,' and that we shall be with Christ, which is far better, when this tabernacle of clay is dissolved. Oh, brother, let us strive for these things.

As to the idea of changing your situation in life, I know not what to say. It is easier for you to judge of the necessity of such a step than another. An experienced brother might give you much direction as to the choice of a partner, if you should think that it is your duty to marry. You should primarily seek one possessed of godliness. It would be deplorable, indeed, to bind a minister of the Gospel to live together with one that is ungodly. You should next seek for one that possesses a suitable temper – sedateness, and caution, being sensible and discreet. One about the middle age would be the most suitable for you; an aged person could not afford you much comfort. And you that are a little advanced in age could not be of much comfort to one that is very young. As to property, it should be of the lowest consideration; yet, marrying one that is of a low family and uneducated would certainly lower you before your parishioners. May the Lord direct you and give you a wife, then you will be right. 'A good wife is a gift from the Lord.'

5. LOVE TO GOD – OBEDIENCE – JUSTIFICATION

Llanfechell 6 March 1828

I will now endeavour to answer your questions. Is our *love* to God merely on account of his own excellences, without any reference to ourselves? God is, undoubtedly, worthy of our love, as he is good, yea, goodness itself. There is nothing in God which is not worthy of our most perfect love. Therefore it is our duty to love him with all our heart, mind, and strength. But at the same time, everything in God has a relation to the welfare of those that love him. It is true our love to God ought not to be mixed with any self-love; yet the consideration of his goodness, and the experience of his grace, cannot fail to influence our love to him more and more.

Is it our *duty* to do what is commanded, without divine assistance? The granting or withholding such assistance has nothing to do with the consideration of our duty; whatever God commands, it is our duty to do whether we can or not. God required nothing of us that was unreasonable or impossible for us to do in the state we were in before the fall of Adam. And though our condition is changed by the fall, yet God was under no obligation to change or abrogate his law on that account. Our inability to do anything that God requireth of us is altogether a sinful inability. Divine assistance is not necessary to make obedience to God's commandments to be our duty. To give that assistance to a sinful creature is an act of sovereign grace. Surely we are warranted by the Word of God to call sinners to repent and believe, and to invite the heavy-laden sinner to come to Christ.

As for *justification*, and whether the pardon of sins to come is included in it – I do not like the expression; it savours something of an antinomian spirit. When God imputes to a believing sinner the perfect righteousness of Christ, he is cleared from all sins before the throne of God, and is brought to such a condition that no sin to come can damn him; but the law of God brings no sin to come against the sinner at his conviction. There are several excellent treatises, in English, on the subject; I published one in Welsh on it, which I suppose you have seen.

6. RELIGION AND POLITICS – DANIEL ROWLAND – THOMAS CHARLES – AFFLICTION – SELF-DENIAL – GRIFFITH JONES

Fron 8 April 1835

You enquire about the state of religion in Wales. As for the externals of religion in our Connexion there is nothing uncomfortable. Our Sunday Schools are well attended, and our hearers are numerous; professors are increasing, unity and peace prevail in our Associations. But as for spiritual religion, I am afraid it is at a low ebb in most of our congregations.

However, our Connexiton is kept wonderfully free from the political mania that is too general in the country, and also among some professors in Wales. The vitals of religion are eaten up by that demon, wherever it prevails. I hope the Lord will keep our Connexion in the same peaceable and loyal paths our fathers trod before us.

As for a new edition of the Rev D. Rowland's Sermons and Memoir,[1] nothing can be more acceptable. Materials must be scarce; and you must take care you do not lose by the publication. Our countrymen buy but few books. As for printing a volume of Mr Charles' Letters,[2] that also would be most acceptable. Whatever proceeded from him is excellent. But I think you will not be able to meet with many of his letters in Wales; he had opportunities of communing with his friends personally here. You may find out some of his old correspondents in England.

7 April 1839

It pleased the all-wise God to confine me to my house the greater part of this year, under a mild but lingering illness. I am still rather weak and unable to do much. The Lord was good indeed to me, under the slight affliction with which he was pleased to visit me. He kindly kept me resigned under his good hand: and he granted me great pleasure in meditating on his gracious and wonderful way of salvation. The truths I had the privilege of preaching to others were great supports and consolations to my soul in affliction. I do not wish, if it is the will of God to spare me a little longer, to preach any other doctrines; but I do earnestly wish and pray to be enabled by the Spirit of God, to preach these blessed truths with more clearness, plainness, and spirituality.

To witness the effects of the Holy Ghost powerfully working through the Gospel ministry would afford me the greatest gratification. It cannot be too deeply impressed on our mind, that

[1] Daniel Rowland of Llangeitho (Cardiganshire) 1713–90.

[2] Thomas Charles of Bala (Merionethshire), 1755–1814. Very many letters of Thomas Charles are to be found in the 3-vol. *Life of Thomas Charles* by D. E. Jenkins, Denbigh, 1908.

the most eminent ministers are but instruments, and the most excellent preaching but means, and that the Holy Spirit only can do the work. Surely we are nothing, and are unable to do anything.

As to conversing with our hearers concerning sermons, it may be useful. But to tell my experience freely, I have no high opinion of my mode of delivering the truth. I often perceive my deficiency in preaching so much that I am greatly humbled. Any talk about my discourses could not remove my painful sense of imperfection in preaching. It is, at the same time, an encouragement to find that the Lord condescends to employ me as an instrument to call the attention of some of my hearers to some portion of his holy Word. If any of them mention, in course of conversation, some truths they heard, we may take advantage to press them further on their attention, without taking any notice of what they might have said about our sermons.

As for the anecdote respecting the Rev G. Jones,[1] I have no authentic account of it. Mr Williams of Pant-y-celyn, mentions something in his elegy about the great man's preaching before Queen Anne. The Elegy was translated into English by the Rev E. Harris, Vicar of Llandysilio, near Narberth. I am sorry people are so slow in taking Mr G. Jones's Works. I have recommended them in two monthly meetings in this country.

I feel anxious, if it should please God to give me health and spare me a little longer, to have more grace and godly zeal, to do something for the glory of his great name. I think it is not worth a wish to live for any other purpose. I desire to give myself up entirely into his gracious hands.

7. ILLNESS – DISTURBANCE – REVIVAL –
MILLENNIUM – MINISTERS

Fron 19 February 1840

I am not near well. I was obliged to stop at home the last two Sabbaths. But I know I am in good and faithful hands; the Lord

---

[1] Griffith Jones of Llanddowror (Carmarthenshire) (1683–1761). The Elegy states: 'Clywodd hithau rym ei ddoniau Freiniol ardderchocaf Anne.'

knows what is best for me. It is my desire that I may be enabled to do more for his glory while I am here below. I wish, yea, I long, to see the arm of the Lord made bare again, doing wonders through the ministry of the Gospel in this country. How glad I was to see an account of the revival at Kilsyth[1] and in the East Indies. I think we ought to pray more earnestly for a revival in England and Wales.

I am sorry to find that infidels swarm in your towns and populous places in England. Alas, we cannot boast of the morality, quietness, and peaceable disposition of the Welsh lately, especially in some parts. The disturbance at Newport[2] will be a lasting stain on our character. Welshmen, alas, condemned for high treason! I was so anxious to know how our friends, the Calvinistic Methodists, conducted themselves in that part of the country at the time, that I wrote there to enquire; and I had the satisfaction to find that their conduct was proper and Christian-like.

Though Wales, through the mercy of God, has been hitherto kept from infidelity, especially North Wales (few professing themselves to be infidels), at the same time I cannot but fear that thousands of our countrymen are godless, 'without God in the world.' Ministers of the Gospel, I think, are too sleepy and careless in the midst of all this evil; and many good Christians are living too far from the Lord! What shall we do? Our enemies are awake and very active. Let us pray more in faith for the appearance of our Lord in his grace, and for the outpouring of his Spirit according to his promise. The work of God will be revived, and sleepy people will be awakened. Then these infidels and unbelievers shall, according to Scripture language, fall on their faces, and willingly acknowledge the power and divine influence of the Word.

As for the subject you mentioned, the millennium, I have no time to say anything upon it. I do not expect to live till then: Indeed I do not expect to see Christ with my bodily eyes till the last day. However, I think the term *personal reign* is used in a

---

[1] Stirlingshire, Scotland.
[2] Newport, Monmouthshire, the scene of a Chartist riot in November 1839 in which twenty-four Chartists lost their lives.

very improper way; for who denies the personal reign? Christ is personally a King, and he does and shall reign personally. But we have no foundation to expect that his human nature shall be visible to the inhabitants of the earth till the last day.

11 January 1841

I received your kind letter to-day. I am sorry I cannot do more than acknowledge the receipt of it. I have been for the last fortnight very indifferent, being unable to go from home. I went lately to a monthly meeting held at Caernarvon; I took cold, and am ever since poorly.

I am sorry you imagine that you trouble me with your letters; that is far from being the case; I am very glad to receive them, though I am not able to answer them. You cannot conceive how great my labour and anxiety are. My parish is much larger than your two; and I am but a poor workman.

The ministers of the Gospel are under great necessity of being experimentally acquainted with the work of the Holy Ghost. We are weak and blind; we are not able to understand or do anything in the great work we are engaged in. If St Paul was not sufficient to think anything of himself, much less are we able. If he needed the Spirit to teach and to enable him to give utterance to the truth, how much more do we! It is true, ministers have a special interest in the promises of the Holy Ghost that Christ gave, though each individual believer has also a vital interest in them. It is the Spirit that leads the ministers of the Gospel into all truth; that reveals the things of Christ to them, bringing all things to their remembrance. It is he that gives them an effectual and saving experience of the truth; yea, he makes manifest the deep things of Christ. 1 *Corinthians* 2.9, 10. It is the Spirit that gives light and power to speak. The *manifestation* and *power* are needed by us. O that we might have more of the communion and fellowship of the Holy Ghost! Let us pray more for it, and may we sincerely shun those things that grieve him: and may we not be content to go on with the great work without him! And let us never imagine that we can do anything in our own strength.

11 February 1841

I am a prisoner at home since the beginning of January. There are some pains and swelling in my leg and foot; I cannot move without pain. I know that it is good, ordered by infinite wisdom. I can write but little.

It is evident that sermons in our day are very defective as to the *light* and *power*, the life and effects, that attended them formerly. The cause, no doubt, is this, that the Lord has withdrawn himself, in some degree, from us, the preachers, and has withheld from us the powerful operations of his Spirit! We, alas, were the cause of this. Perhaps there are many ministers among us that never were sent by the Lord, and many, alas, content to go through the work without the Spirit's influences; and thus grieving the Holy Ghost by this indifference to his operations, willing to go on without him! There are too many preachers who do not experience the power and relish of the truth themselves. They view preaching as a human object, as that of elocution, or some art or science.

I do not think that many of those powerful preachers, who were owned much by the Lord in Wales formerly, thought highly of their own ministerial powers. They had a very humble opinion of themselves, and used to go into the pulpit as poor, needy, and trembling creatures; their dependence for everything was on the Lord. They were very anxious that the people should be benefited and eternally saved. Before these spiritual blessings can be regained, we must see and know their value and excellency, and perceive that we lost them through our own fault and neglect. We must repent, confess our sins, and seek forgiveness. We should request our brethren in the ministry, and hearers, to unite with us in prayer to God for the Spirit. We ought to renounce everything in us, or amongst us, that we think gives any occasion to the Lord to hide his face from us.

I must conclude; if you knew my pain, you would excuse me and all deficiencies.

Essays

1 Thoughts on the Bible

It is a high privilege to have God's Word, and to have it written in our own language. The Israel of God in former days acknowledged it as an inestimable favour: 'He sheweth his word unto Jacob, his statutes and his judgments unto Israel. He hath not dealt so with any nation: and as for his judgments, they have not known them.' *Psalm* 147.19, 20. It is impossible, according to God's general method, for men to know him as the God of salvation, but by his Word. Though 'the heavens declare the glory of God, and the firmament sheweth his handiwork,' yet it is his 'law that converteth the soul, and maketh wise the simple.' Though 'his eternal power and Godhead are clearly seen in the works of creation, that even the Gentiles are without excuse,' yet there is no account of a Mediator, nor a salvation for the sinner, any where but in the Word: 'The mystery which hath been hid from ages and generations, even the hidden wisdom, which God ordained before the world unto our glory,' is made manifest in the Word. *Psalm* 19.1, 7, 8. *Colossians* 1.26. 1 *Corinthians* 2.7. All the counsels of God, and, as it were, his heart, are made manifest here; and treasures come to light that were never seen in the works of creation.

It is likely that even angels did not know of any way to save a sinner, till God revealed his gracious purpose and method in the promise (*Genesis* 3.15). We may suppose that Satan imagined that, if he could bring a man to fall into sin, he would be in chains of darkness as fast as himself, and that there could be no way or hope of deliverance. Adam doubtless did not know of any way wherein to expect salvation: and he had nothing else to do, but to endeavour to depart, as far as possible, and to flee from the God he had sinned against. The holy angels, it is likely, could not but expect the destruction of man with the angels that fell. But God in his promise revealed his counsel, and the plan he ever had in his mind, for the salvation of the sinner, to the joy of angels, and the disappointment and terror of the hellish host; and this promise, and the fulfilment of it, are before us in the Word. The way that was revealed has been accomplished, and 'consecrated through the veil;' and all this has been made so manifest that even children and the plainest people can read in the Bible the hidden and glorious counsel the Holy Trinity had from eternity, in reference to fallen man. Yes, and also read of the sure fulfilment of this counsel, in the mission and incarnation of the Son, his active and passive obedience; also, the sending of the Holy Ghost, and his work in calling, regenerating, and sanctifying; in leading, comforting, and sealing; yea, completely glorifying true believers in the end. In a word, all that God is in his perfections and his works, is clearly seen in the Word. It makes manifest what was in eternity, and what should be in time, and shall be in eternity, when time is no more. It is immeasurable, like God himself. There will be nothing in time, or in judgment, or eternity itself, but according to this.

From these things I infer that it is our *duty* to read and search the Scriptures. There is a particular command for this. Moses, after warning the people to keep the law in their hearts, exhorts them to use means for that end. 'Thou shalt,' he says, 'talk of them when thou sittest in thine house, and when thou walkest by the way, and when thou liest down, and when thou risest up. Thou shalt bind them for a sign upon thine hand, and they shall be as frontlets between thine eyes.' *Deuteronomy* 6.7, 8. Again, it is commanded thus, 'Thou shalt read this law before all Israel in their hearing. Gather the people together, men and women and children, and thy stranger that is within thy gates, that they may hear and that they may learn.' *Deuteronomy* 31.11, 12. The women and children were not summoned on other occasions, even on their particular feasts. This shews the necessity there is for people of all degrees to read, hear, and meditate on the Word of God. 'Give attendance to reading; meditate upon these things; search the Scriptures!' 1 *Timothy* 4.13, 15. *John* 5.39.

Besides, as the Word of God is given us in our own language, it is evident that it is our duty to read and search it carefully. The publishing of an Act of Parliament is a sufficient command to read it. It is not necessary for a person, when he writes to a friend, to use many arguments to induce him to read it. The sending of the letter proves that the man expects his friend to read it, and understand his mind. But Oh! shall the Act of the highest court that ever existed, the Law-book of the eternal Trinity, be neglected and left unread and unconsidered, though the King himself sent it to us, even to our country and houses, in our own plain language? Yea, shall we manifest such contempt for an act or law the most just and fair, the most mild and profitable that any subjects ever heard of? Oh! shall the most glorious and excellent letter from a Being of the greatest love, yea love itself, be left unsearched, or not searched diligently, though it be full of the best news, yea, news most beneficial for eternity? Let us also remember that the Bible is a letter sent from a far country, yet gratuitous as to all its blessings, every expense and debt being paid by blood divine; a letter also addressed and directed to the sinner.

The *character* and examples of the godly shew that we ought to read and search the Scriptures. David, in the first Psalm, describes the blessed man, and sets him forth as one whose 'delight is in the law of the Lord, and who meditates in his law day and night.' It will be difficult, if our delight be in the law of the Lord, to prevent us from reading and meditating on it continually. 'Where your treasure is, there will your heart be also.' So if our treasure be in the Word, our heart will be with the Word also. And if our heart be there, it will be difficult to keep our eyes from being there. 'Mine eyes,' says David, 'prevent the night watches, that I might meditate in thy word.' It is said of the Jews in Berea, that 'they were more noble or generous than those in Thessalonica, in that they received the Word with all readiness of mind, and searched the Scriptures daily, whether those things were so.'

The wisdom that is from above is gentle, or generous. When God implants this supernatural wisdom in the soul, the man is made truly gentle and noble-minded. He is beautifully holy and serious; he is excellent in his conversation and walk. The Word of God is the rule of this delightful conduct. It is a disgraceful thing for a man of rank to act as a beggar and a mean man. Generally the children of this world differ much from each other in this respect. The children of God excel all. The treasures of learning that enable them to excel are gotten out of the Word of

God. The Bible is a complete treasure-house to the Lord's people. This is the Testament in which they have an inheritance superior to the world. This is the chamber in which their royal vestments are kept. This is the palace in which they enjoy their delicious feasts and delightful music. Yea, this is their flowery garden, and shadowy walks in the heat of the day. Therefore their life and support are in the Word. *Matthew* 6.21. *Psalm* 119.148. *Acts* 17.11. *James* 3.17. We shall adduce one example more, that of Christ in the synagogue of Nazareth. It is said, 'He stood up for to read.' The Eternal Word, the Wisdom of God, read the written Word, and rose up for that purpose out of respect to it. Surely then we who are weak and foolish ought to read and search it attentively, praying for the help of the Spirit to lead us into it, and to bring us into possession of its endless treasures. *Luke* 4.16.

It is our duty not only to read the Word, but also to *search* it *reverently* and *earnestly*. Many read it as the word of man, and not as a book of divine revelation. They therefore *run* over it, without searching for the pearls that are in it. The Gospel is 'the wisdom of God,' that is, in it does he chiefly shew his wisdom. In it are the 'treasures of wisdom,' in it are 'the mysteries of God the Father and Christ;' and this wisdom is to be 'sought as silver, and searched for as hid treasures.' *Proverbs* 2.4. People use diligence and labour to get silver, and search after hidden treasures, yea, they venture through much labour, and at the risk of their lives, into the dark bowels of the earth, to seek for them. As the precious ore is not generally to be found on the surface of the earth, they will dig into the greatest depth for it; so, the Bible is a precious mine, full of the most valuable treasures, much better than fine gold. The mystery and grace of the Gospel are so deep and precious that even the angels *desire* to look into them; 1 *Peter* 1.12. They behold such treasures in the mine of the Gospel, as they never witnessed anywhere besides. *Ephesians* 3.10. And the prophets formerly, though they were favoured with great revelations as to the state of kingdoms, yet enquired and searched diligently for that salvation that is fully manifested unto us in the Gospel. This is the field that contains the treasure that excels all other treasures, and he that finds it selleth all that he hath, and buyeth that field; labouring diligently in digging and searching for it. *Matthew* 13.44.

Christ commands us to search the Scriptures. The Jews read them constantly; but for want of searching them diligently, *so as* to be enlightened by them, they failed in obtaining the treasure that is in them. So now, many of us read a chapter frequently in the Bible, and are pretty well acquainted with its history, yet have never been enlightened as to the spirituality of the Word, and consequently remain destitute of the great treasure that is in it. I will again repeat the words of Christ: 'Search the Scriptures,' to have their testimony respecting your state by nature; search them respecting Christ, to see what he is in his person, and what he is to a sinner. Search them; indeed there are in them things suitable for your state, whoever you are. Compare them with each other, and earnestly pray for the Spirit to guide you into them. Bring your religion to them as unto a touch-stone. Doubtless, if it does not stand this test, it will not do so in the judgment. Search the Scriptures for the way you should walk in; and the weapons to withstand the world, the flesh, and the devil; and the promises to plead before God; and also for a ground of strong consolation in life and death.

Consider the *causes* why people, yea, many professors, read so little of the Bible, and seek so little about the mind of God in it. I will try to name some of them.

1 The *opposition* that is in corrupt nature to the things contained in the Scriptures. Though it is the unanimous opinion of all people that the Bible is a divine and an excellent book, yet there cannot be any congeniality between the souls of any and the Word of God, except such as have received the 'divine nature.' It is a painful and irksome thing to a man that is an enemy to God, loving sin and delighting in vanity, to read the Word of God, as it describes the nature and odiousness of his enmity, and condemns unsparingly his sin, and shews the vanity of the things that are highly thought of and loved by him, yea, alarms his conscience with thoughts of death, judgment, and eternity. And what is still more unpleasant is this, the Word shews the insufficiency of the righteousness he trusted in, and the folly of his hoping for heaven; and it exalts Christ as all in all, in whom he hath never seen any form or comeliness.

2 The next thing that hinders people from reading the Word of God is the want of the *influence* of the Spirit on their souls. When the Holy Ghost apprehends by means of the Word any person, there is a great change wrought in him; he receives it with all readiness of mind, and searches the Scriptures daily. When the Spirit regenerates a person by 'incorruptible seed, the word of God,' he soon 'as a new born babe, desires the sincere milk of the word that he may grow thereby.' 'I will never forget thy precepts,' says David, 'for with them thou hast quickened me.' Yea, whether the Spirit consoles or alarms a person by the Word, he is sure to cause him to attend to it closely. Therefore, if the word is silent to thee, God is so also; thy case is consequently awful.

3 *Pride*, or self-conceit, is another great hindrance in the way of many to read and examine God's Word. They think so much of their knowledge of the Scriptures and the great things of religion and godliness, that they imagine that it is not necessary for them to read and search the Word. These are like coasting sailors that are accustomed to sail near land, and scarcely ever lose sight of it. It is the opinion of such men that it is useless to take pains to learn and search into the art of navigation. They think they can steer the vessel wherever they like, without that trouble. So these men with regard to the Scriptures! But O! they are an unfathomable ocean; no man ever saw their extent, nor understood their depth! Yea, every subject in the Bible is like the sea; however deeply men, under the leadings of the Spirit, have dived into them, yet no person ever saw the bottom of them. Therefore let no one think that he understands enough of one of God's great things. I venture to say that you, however excellent, know but very little of things that are most necessary and relative to your salvation. Therefore proceed in the diligent search of the Word of God, crying with Agur, 'I have not the understanding of a man.' And pray that the Spirit 'that searcheth the deep things of God' may guide you. And trust not to your own understanding. *Proverbs* 30.2.

4 The next thing that hinders the reading of the Scriptures is the *remains* of the unchristian spirit, yet existing in the country, saying that 'ignorance is the mother of godliness,' when God says that 'men are destroyed for want of knowledge,' (*Hosea* 4.6), and that he despises all that depreciates knowledge. Let us observe, that the shepherds of God's sending are those that feed the flock with know-

ledge and understanding. And if God would not have his people full
of light, there would be no need for the ministers of the Gospel to
be candles. *Jeremiah* 3.15.

The Scriptures write 'Tekel' on the consciences of many; and this
prevents them reading the word carefully. *Daniel* 5.27. But O! there
is a day coming, when they shall be brought to a strait pass, like
Balaam; when the Word without a veil, and their consciences without
any lethargy, will meet thus in judgment!

5 Another thing which prevents even the children of God from reading
the Scriptures is *backsliding*. One of the first things we have an
account of in the restoration of the church, in the days of Josiah and
Nehemiah, is the reading of the law, that is, all the Word that was
written in those days. It appears by this, that the law was much
neglected when they were in a backsliding state. By meditating in the
Word and remaining in it, the growth is clear, 1 *Timothy* 4.15.
So, by neglecting the Word, declension is evident. It is clear that the
child in unwell when he is indifferent to the breast; so it is plain that
the Christian is not in spiritual health, that is, without a taste and
disposition for the Word of God, when he neglects to read and
digest it. This is the instrument that is useful for doctrine, 2 *Timothy*
3.16. And by this the Spirit will make millions perfect for ever! Let
every one say, 'May I be among them, partaking of the same operation, and thus finally of their eternal privilege!'

2 On the use of reason

Much is said about *reason* in these days. Some exalt it exceedingly.
They will put it on the throne to judge even the Revelation of
God, and they will submit the plan and counsel of God to its
decision! Others despise reason, as if it had no work to do in the
things of revelation and religion. However, I will endeavour to
make some observations respecting reason, shewing its proper
place and province in respect of the Scriptures.

Reason is a *faculty* or power in the soul to perceive and judge
things and to receive ideas; to compare things one with another;
to distinguish between good and evil, truth and falsehood; it is a
power of the soul to comprehend, to compare, to judge and draw
inferences and conclusions from sure, tried and known principles.

It examines one's own ideas of things, and judges whether they agree with the truth as generally received.

By reason is sometimes meant the *conclusion* and proofs that are legitimately drawn from evident and clear principles, according to established rules. Reason is not a rule to judge, but its employment is to judge according to rule. However, there is a false judgment as well as a correct one. Reason is sound and correct in its operations when a man is endowed by God with sufficient light to comprehend and to judge rightly of things as they are in truth, on solid principles according to a proper rule.

Incorrect reason is that of a corrupt man. It comprehends and judges erroneously, from false principles and wrong rules. 'His understanding is darkened, and his heart blinded;' his mind and conscience are defiled; his wisdom is foolishness. Such 'become vain in their imaginations; professing themselves to be wise, they become fools.' So a man should 'not trust in his own understanding.' 'For there is a way that seemeth right to a man, but the end thereof are the ways of death.' 'The natural man receiveth not, neither doth he know the things of the Spirit of God.' *Ephesians* 4.18. *Titus* 1.15. 1 *Corinthians* 2.19. *Proverbs* 3.5. So we can perceive clearly that natural reason is not qualified to be a guide in religious things. It is blinded and confused by sin, and led by imaginations and lusts to choose false principles, to draw erroneous inferences, and to make wrong conclusions from them. 'The carnal mind, or reasoning, is enmity against God.' *Romans* 8.7. So it is evident that natural reason is not fit to be a judge in religious things; and that it is not right to submit divine revelation, or any branch of the doctrines of Christ, to its test or decision.

Reason knows something of *natural* religion, yet it errs sometimes even in this respect. It may perceive there is a God, and that he must be infinitely powerful and wise; that man ought to fear and worship him. It may also understand that man is not what he ought to be. But natural reason knows nothing of *supernatural* religion, nor of the way to restore fallen and rebellious man to a state of reconciliation with God, and true happiness. Reason, even in its perfect state, could only form its conclusions from right principles. It had not then one principle to draw a sure conclusion from it as to the continuance of man's happiness, but the perpetuity of his holiness and obedience to the law of nature. Then reason could not, without a revelation from God, know any thing of a way to make the guilty happy. The reason of a corrupt man knows nothing of the happy state of man before his fall. He does not consider his miserable state under the fall, nor the way to restore him out of the miserable fall, nor his state after death. Yet reason, in this darkness, tries to form principles, and establish conclusions on them, but they are weak, vain, and false. Reason, when it thinks itself sufficient to judge religious things, and to shew the way to be happy, becomes a rebel. But in submitting itself to God and the divine revelation, it is serviceable, and sits at the feet of its all-wise Creator; without this it is vain and mad.

It is highly unreasonable to confide more in reason than in the revelation that was given by the author of reason. Men often boast of reason, and *misapply* it to deny some of the doctrines of the Gospel, and to form false opinions, and lastly to deny the inspiration of the Scriptures! Reason, in the opinion of some, is *stronger* than the Bible, and then they try to bring the Bible before the judgment-seat of reason, and make it submit to its decision, instead of bringing reason to obey the Word of God. There are some that are not willing to form and *regulate* their opinions by the Scriptures, and even declare that they cannot believe the things that are in the Bible, except they see that they are consistent with reason! So they deny the fundamental doctrines of the Gospel, such as those of the Trinity, the eternal covenant, the divinity of Christ, his appointment as a surety for sinners, his complete atonement, the imputation of his righteousness to those that believe in him, the irresistible work of the Holy Ghost in changing and bringing sinners to Christ! If we believe nothing but what is consistent with corrupt reason, we should soon reject the Gospel, for there are depths too great for the short measure of reason to fathom.

It coincides with the corrupt opinions and lusts in man, to be filled with prejudice against the truth. Had there not been things in the Gospel too deep for reason, there would be no need of the work of the Spirit to bring men to believe it, more than to understand sciences. If we believe nothing of the Divine revelation but what corrupt reason judges we should believe, we would conduct ourselves towards God as if he was less worthy to be credited than an honest man! If an upright man was to say, in speaking of something great and wonderful, 'I was an eye-witness of the things; take my word for the truth of it,' it would satisfy. But if some one was to observe to him, 'I must consider whether the thing you have stated is reasonable; if so, I will believe it; if not, I must reject it;' would not such behaviour be deemed disrespectful towards the man? If reason was the rule of faith, the Word of God would be in vain. Then faith would not be placed in the Divine revelation nor in God, if reason did not coincide with it. Such persons will not pay as much respect to God and his testimony as is given by children to their parents and teachers!

As the Bible is the Word of God, it requires an implicit confidence and reliance without any hesitation and doubting. God's testimony possesses sufficient clearness, so that our senses cannot do a more becoming work than to submit. The testimony of God is the foundation of the strongest certainty. His wisdom and truth are infinite. A little humility is enough to make us acknowledge that we are not proper judges of the plan and counsel of God; but his incomprehensible things are all true and just. The testimony of God in his Word respecting things past and to come, things spiritual, invisible, and supernatural, is above the comprehension of reason. There are some things even in natural religion that extend beyond the reach of reason. But as to things beyond nature, which are Divine, such as the Trinity, the decrees and counsel of God, the person of Christ, sovereign grace, the imputation of Christ's righteousness – they are far beyond the ken of reason. Though there are great mysteries in the Divine revelation, above reason, yet there is not one doctrine contrary to it. God is above man's comprehension, and many things in his testimony as to the plan of salvation are so. 1 *Corinthians* 2.9, 10.

It may be *proved* by reason that the Bible is the Word of God; that it is reasonable to believe it all. It is not the office of reason to enquire what is to be received, and whether something is to be rejected, but to receive it all as the Word of him that cannot lie. The ground or foundation of faith is the testimony of God, and not reason. We do not believe on the account of reasoning, but because God testifies. It is reasonable to believe him respecting things we cannot understand. Our reason and judgment should be governed by, or according to, the Divine revelation; 1 *John* 5.9. We should believe every truth. Though we cannot understand perhaps the consistency and connection which one truth has with another, yet we ought to believe them, and believe they agree and harmonize together, though we do not see that now. As the Word of God cannot but be true, so all the Divine revelation cannot but harmonize in all its parts. God sees the suitableness of things to each other when we do not. *Acts* 10.13, 14.

Some men endeavour to reason and dispute, that they may not believe what they do not wish to be true. They also strengthen themselves in false opinions by wrong reasoning. This is the principle of nature's philosophy. The natural man is desirous of forming some system after his own inclination, and asserting that reason is on his side; so that the strongest proofs against his inclination, are not received as truths by him.

Reason should submit to God who made it; and beware lest it should rise against him, or try to be a judge of his counsel or Word. *Job* 35.11. What has the man of the strongest mind but what he received of the Lord? And what is man that he should dispute with the Lord? 1 *Corinthians* 4.7. *Romans* 9.20.

Though reason is corrupted by the fall, yet it may be useful when properly employed *in religious things*. God calls on men to reason with him. *Isaiah* 1.18; 5. 3. *Luke* 12.5, 57. We may reason reverently with him in prayer; and he that believeth in Christ can give reason of the hope that is in him. It is reasonable to believe in God, obey him, and serve him. *Job* 32.7. 1 *Peter* 3.15. *Romans* 12.1. Reason can see by clear proofs that there is a God, and that the Bible is his Word, and that consequently it should be believed as to everything, without doubting. *Romans* 1.20. Reason may be used to understand *some words* in the Scriptures, their connection with each other, and their harmony. Yet there is danger of exalting corrupt reason to a seat that is too high, and employing it in a work and office that does not belong to it. It is not its property to judge Divine revelation, nor to understand all the parts of Gospel doctrine. There are things, even in natural religion, above the comprehension of reason; so, there is nothing in the Gospel that is contrary to sound reason, yet there are truths in it that reason cannot fathom and perceive. Though those truths are above reason, yet it is reasonable to believe them. Francis Bacon said well, when he made this observation: 'The Lord's authority is above our reason and will; we should deny ourselves and submit to him, yea, obey his law, though our will should be against it; and believe his Word, though reason should oppose it. If we only believed things according to our reason, it would be giving credit to the matter, and not to the author.' Divinity is stamped on the Word of God. This did not spring out of the light of nature or reason. *Isaiah* 8.20. 'To the Law and to the testimony; if they do not speak according to this word, it is because there is no light in them.'

Reason could never, without the Divine revelation, find out that God ever intended to forgive one transgression; and it is impossible, even to the strongest reason, apart from the Divine revelation, to perceive the wonderful and wise way God contrived to forgive sins, and to save sinners. Reason cannot, without divine light, comprehend evangelical principles as to their utility, glory, and great importance, nor have any apprehension of the sovereign grace and love of God towards sinners. Reason can never show man the way to be happy, nor support a sinner in a view of the glory and greatness of God, the strictness of the law, odiousness of sin, and in a view of death and judgment, and departure into the strange invisible world. But faith beholds in the Divine revelation the Gospel of Christ, the way to have the pardon of sin, to remove the guilt, and to be 'pure before the throne of God,' a way to restore us to the image of God, and make us fit to be with him for ever! Let us praise God more for the revelation of his will in his holy Word. Let us submit our proud reason to God's Word, and take his will in that Word respecting all things, as a sufficient determination of them. 'All the saints of God sit down at his feet, and every one receives of his word.' *Deuteronomy* 33.3. Let us pray for the Holy Ghost to lead us into all truth, and enable us to believe the testimony of God, honour his truth and authority. God does, by his Spirit, reveal to his people the things that eye hath not seen, nor ear heard. Let every imagination, and every high thing that exalteth itself against the knowledge of God, be cast down. 2 *Corinthians* 2.9, 10; 10.5.

3 On preaching the Gospel

Much at present is said about preaching the Gospel. It would not, therefore, be unprofitable for preachers and hearers to examine themselves, and see whether they understand what is the nature and end of preaching the Gospel. Not every one who is called a minister of the Gospel preaches it. What he delivers may not be the Gospel, though so called. It may not be good news to a sinner who sees his miserable state before God. Let us consider then—

1 What it is to preach the Gospel. It is to declare and publish *good tidings* respecting the way of saving sinners from their sins and the wrath of God, shewing that salvation springs out of the sovereign grace and love of God. *Luke* 21.10, 11. *Acts* 20.24. *John* 3.16. It is to preach *Christ*, in his person, offices, life, death, resurrection, ascension, and intercession. It is to 'preach Christ crucified.' 1 *Corinthians* 1.23. It is to preach the blessings that are to be received through Christ's merits, reconciliation, forgiveness, justification, sanctification, full salvation. It is to publish Christ as everything which a sinner needs. It is indeed 'the Gospel of our salvation.' 1 *Corinthians* 1.30; *Ephesians* 1.13. It is to invite lost sinners to Christ; to urge them to believe in him, to receive him, and to make use of him. *Acts* 10.36, 43; 16.31. *Romans* 3.22; 10.9, 10. It is only by the Gospel that the *Holy Ghost* works savingly on the souls of men. It is the ministration of the Spirit: he works powerfully by it. If we expect him to work on the souls of men, we must preach it purely and fully. *Galatians* 2.5. 2 *Corinthians* 3.8. 1 *Thessalonians* 1.5; 2.13. *Romans* 1.16.

2 Let us next consider who are to preach the Gospel. Doubtless those whom Christ hath *called* and sent for that purpose. He received gifts for men, and he gives shepherds and teachers to the church. The body of Christ is not made up by any but by those who are sent

by him. Those whom he sends to preach the Gospel have themselves been brought to *understand*, believe, and experience its truths. He does not send any persons to warn sinners of their danger and their ruin but such as have known their own miserable and lost state by nature, and the terrors of the Lord. 2 *Corinthians* 5.11. He does not send enemies as messengers of peace but those that are able to say, 'We have peace with God, who hath reconciled us to himself, and hath committed unto us the word of reconciliation.' *Romans* 5.1; 2 *Corinthians* 5.18, 19. He does not send any to commend and exalt Christ who are ignorant of his greatness and saving excellences, but such as have seen his glory in some degree, and have tasted that the Lord is gracious. *John* 1.14. 1 *Peter* 2.3. Those who are sent by God to preach the Gospel do not set forth themselves but *Christ*. They seek not their own glory, nor wish for the praise of men on account of their gifts, skill, and eloquence or anything else. *John* 7.18. 2 *Corinthians* 4.5. 1 *Thessalonians* 2.6. They are *examples* to the flock; they are patterns in soberness, godly sincerity, simplicity, humility, and self-denying and every holy virtue. 1 *Peter* 5.3. 1 *Thessalonians* 2.10. *Philippians* 4.8, 9; 2 *Corinthians* 6.6.

3 Let us next observe what are the ends of preaching the Gospel. It is to *exalt* and magnify the sovereign grace and love of God. The chief end he has in view in all his works is to glorify himself, and to glorify his grace in the salvation of men. Therefore we preach among the Gentiles the 'unsearchable riches of Christ,' shewing the wonders of divine love, the abundance of mercy, and the riches of grace. As it is the chief end of God to glorify his grace in man's salvation, it should be the end of those that preach the Gospel of peace to exalt the grace of God. They exalt and *glorify* Christ, preaching him, his cross, and death, shewing forth his excellences, and suitableness as a Mediator and Saviour of sinners. Christ will be exalted when the Holy Ghost works by the ministry of the Gospel. We cannot preach the Gospel, leaving the Saviour out of the question, or making him some secondary thing in the sermon. 2 *Corinthians* 4.4. *John* 16.14. Another end is *saving* sinners. It is called 'the Gospel of our salvation;' publishing salvation. It was intended as a means to save souls. When the Spirit works by it, the Gospel becomes the power of God unto salvation. 'God, by the foolishness of preaching, saves them that believe.' *Ephesians* 1.13. *Romans* 1.16. 1 *Corinthians* 1.21.

4 As it is one end of the Gospel to save souls, ministers should preach

in a very *sober* and *earnest* manner. They should shew their hearers that they are guilty, vile, and lost sinners. Then they should preach Christ as a complete and willing Saviour to such. They should invite lost sinners, sensible of their misery, to flee to him, and shew that none who believe in him shall be lost. They should also declare that it is a great sin and folly to reject Christ; that the Spirit overcomes the obstinacy of men, and makes them willing to believe in Christ. Ministers should also shew that faith works by love, produces obedience, and brings forth every good work.

There is, however, room to fear that not every speaker in the pulpit, though very fluent and respectable, preaches the Gospel; and that many who intend entering the ministry do not consider its nature and great importance. Many think that, if they can speak boldly and fluently on some religious subjects, they may then preach the Gospel, when perhaps they knew but little of it themselves. They may take pains to deliver their speeches well and in a manner acceptable to the people, without any sincere aim or desire to set forth the excellences of Christ, and the grace of God in the salvation of sinners.

Ministers should preach the Gospel in a clear, *intelligent* manner, in plain expressions, easily understood by the people; words taught by the Holy Ghost; speaking them as the words of God in the manifestation of the truth, and in the demonstration of the Spirit. If so, there will be no mixing it with philosophical reasoning and tales, or curious perplexing expressions, contrivance of the flesh or the wisdom of the world. 1 *Corinthians* 2.4, 13, 14; 2 *Corinthians* 4.2. They should preach it *experimentally*. It is true that none but God can teach them to preach in that way. It is possible to please the curious and the whole-hearted with a dry human harangue. But in order to 'speak a word in season to the weary' there will be need for the teaching which is from above. The speaker must be acquainted with the misery of man by the fall, and his conviction of sin, dying to the law, fleeing to Christ for life and acceptance, and also with the succour of grace and joy of the Holy Ghost; being able to speak to the people the things he has seen and experienced. *Isaiah* 54.13; 50.4.

Ministers should preach in a *practical* manner: indeed all the doctrines of the Gospel should be preached so. Things relating to man's salvation should be known and possessed, to benefit him. They never were intended to be discussed and argued as curious points. It is a useless work for a minister merely to please, though it be as a very lovely song of one that hath a pleasant voice, amusing his hearers without bringing them to believe and to act. But let us teach them to do everything which the Lord hath commanded, and exhort them to attend to duties on evangelical principles. *Ezekiel* 33.32. *Matthew* 28.19, 20. Ministers should preach in the way of *application,* speaking to the people, not only concerning them, but also questioning them in such a manner as this, 'Do you see your ruined state, and the value of the Gospel and its treasures? Do you believe the Word of God? Do you receive Christ? Have you experienced the virtues of the Gospel, and imbibed them? Do you bring forth good fruits to God, conducting yourself as becoming the Gospel of Christ'? *Titus* 2.10–12. *Romans* 7.4. *Galatians* 2.19. *Philippians* 1.27.

Ministers ought to distinguish their hearers, appropriating to each his own portion, thus 'rightly dividing the word of truth,' and separating the precious from the vile; giving their own share to believers, the ungodly, and hypocrites, yea, to the people of God in various circumstances and trials. Preachers should not address any of their hearers as reasonable creatures that are not very sinful. If so, they would be like men beating the air, addressing such persons as are not to be met with. But they should accost their hearers as fallen and lost sinners, totally corrupt, shewing them their misery and the way to escape. They may address other persons as those that had been lost, but now are found; that had been far off, but were made 'nigh by the blood of Christ;' yea, now as in Christ, having received the reconciliation, being born of God. They should show the great happiness of such, and their obligation to set forth the goodness of him that called them, and to walk as the children of light.

O that every preacher would consider the unspeakable greatness of his work! Then levity, frivolity, and pride would no more appear in them, and the conceit of being great personages would cease. They would exclaim, 'Who is sufficient?' None, we are sure, but those whose sufficiency is of God. O that God would be pleased to raise up powerful ministers, each like the 'angel that flew through the heavens, having the everlasting Gospel.'

5 There is a great necessity that the hearers should consider the nature and end of preaching the Gospel. Without this, they cannot understand how they should hear. It is to be feared that many have but poor ends in going to hear, and an unsuitable and unbecoming manner in hearing the Word. Though there are great deficiencies and

even wretchedness in ministers, yet, it is painful to say, 'the people love to have it so.' Many 'turn away their ears from the truth, and are turned unto fables.' Many delight in hearing carnal preachers that use 'enticing words, according to man's wisdom.' *Jeremiah* 5.31. 2 *Timothy* 4.4. 1 *John* 4.5. Many go to the house of God as matter of custom, hearing nothing to profit; others come to admire the talents and eloquence of the preacher. Others come from some carnal curiosity; expecting something new and extraordinary. Few come with a view to hear and know 'what the Lord says,' hearing the servant of the Most High declaring the message of his Lord to them. O that God would be pleased in mercy to draw near to us, pouring his Spirit upon us, that his Word may be preached, heard, and received as the Gospel of his grace, and experienced as the 'power of God unto salvation,' by many sinners!

Fron 5 February 1841

4 On the important subject of the ministry[1]

There is a great need that ministers should be careful as to the matter and manner of their sermon, and that the people should mind what and how they hear. There is great danger lest the preachers should be worldly and light, and the hearers should be carnal and indifferent.

The situation of ministers is awe-ful, and their office most responsible as to endless consequences. A poor insignificant man standing up to address multitudes of his fellow-creatures, as a messenger from God, to make known God's mind; yea, all his revealed will to man, and nothing else but this manifestation; yea, publishing it to men, who are creatures accountable to God, transgressors of his law, enemies to him every way, who are under condemnation already, and to be judged by him in the last day. This messenger is to tell these people, honestly and faithfully, their awful state before God, and also the way in which he has in his sovereign grace contrived to save such creatures. He is to call on them to repent of their dreadful rebellion, and to invite them to reconciliation with God. He is to make known

[1] Written in commendation of *Important Doctrines of the Gospel*, a work by Rev R. Williams of Liverpool.

to them the way to be reconciled; and he is to preach the Lord Jesus Christ, publishing his death, the doctrine of the cross. But he is not to preach with words taught by human wisdom, but by the Spirit of God. Indeed, he is to make known to his hearers all the counsel of God, and to teach Christians how to walk and please God. He should most earnestly seek wisdom and strength from the Lord to enable him to fulfil his ministry and to make it useful to his hearers. He is to remember always that he is nothing in himself.

There is a great defect in the manner of many preachers. It can scarcely be said that the Gospel is preached by them. Their sermons are very confused; they contain many expressions which are not taught by the Holy Ghost; and subjects are so clothed with new words, that it is difficult to know what is meant. Though these preachers may not be accused of saying what is false, yet, alas, they neglect stating weighty and necessary truths when opportunities offer. By omitting those important portions of truth in their natural connection, the Word is made subservient to subjects never intended. The hearers are led to deny the truth which the preacher leaves out of his sermons. Omitting any truth intentionally in a sermon leads to the denial of it. Indeed, there are several deficiencies in many ministers; some acknowledge and lament them. There is room to suspect that those defects are intentional in others. I will name some things I consider as deficiencies in preachers.

There is need of shewing more of the greatness, purity, and *justice* of God, and the purity and spirituality of his law. It is impossible, without this, to shew the great evil of sin, and the demerit of sinners in suffering eternal punishment for sin. The great depth of the *fall*, and the total depravity of man, and his awful misery, are not exhibited in many sermons in scriptural language. It is not plainly declared that all the human race are by nature, 'the children of wrath,' and that the 'sentence of condemnation' is passed on every one; that none can save himself; that no one deserves to be rescued, and that none will come to Christ to have life. There are but few ministers that fully show that salvation springs entirely out of the sovereign *grace* of God, and that grace shines illustriously in the plan, work, and application of salvation. Salvation, we know, is entirely, in every respect, for the praise of the glory of his grace. There is too much of some dark, human mixture in many a sermon, under the name of preaching Christ. He is not, alas, preached clearly and scripturally as a complete Saviour. The glory of his person, the appointment of him in the place of sinners, the performance of his mediatorial offices according to the covenant of redemption, the completeness of his atonement, the perfection of his righteousness, are not clearly set forth. The expressions respecting the imputation of Christ's righteousness to them that believe are often very dark, confused, and wretched.

Few ministers speak clearly of the necessity of the *Spirit's work* in order to save sinners, and of the nature of his operations on those that shall be saved. How seldom do we hear of dying to the law, in sermons, and of the necessity of being born again, and being partakers of the divine nature, and that man does nothing that is truly holy, except it proceeds from a pure principle! There is but little said respecting the necessity of being taught, led, and strengthened by the Holy Ghost in everything, and the need of his blessing the means of grace. Ministers should tremble for fear their hearers deceive themselves under their ministry, and lest their sermons should give them ease and strength in their delusions. It is a great thing for a minister to be 'free from the blood of all men' that have heard him. One thing necessary for this, is declaring 'all the counsel of God' revealed to us in his holy Word. And the way for a minister to 'save both himself and those that hear him' is by 'taking heed unto himself and unto the doctrine, and continuing in it.'

2 It is a matter of the greatest importance that people observe *what* and *how* they hear. Hearing the Word of God is an ordinance of his appointment for the reception of faith and life. *Isaiah* 55.3. *Romans* 10.17.

Hearers should consider *what* they hear, for there are false teachers, and diverse and strange doctrines. Therefore they ought to search the Scriptures daily, like the Bereans, and see whether those things are as the preacher says.

They should also observe *how* they hear, what is their end and frame of mind in hearing. There are several kinds of hearing that are not for the glory of God nor the benefit of the hearers; such as to hear for the sake of the gifts, eloquence, and fluency of the preacher, or to feed the desires of their own conceited curiosity, or for the sake of carnal gratification. But they ought to hear with reverence what the Lord saith, trembling at his Word, understanding and receiving it, believing his testimony, obeying his commandments, keeping and hiding his sayings in their hearts.

There is nothing more proper and becoming for a preacher and hearer, than to converse about the doctrines of the Gospel in an humble spirit, willing to be taught of God, taking his Word to settle every dispute.

Shun the idea of submitting the Word of God to the judgment and reason of corrupt man. Avoid asking about anything God says in his Word, saying, 'Is that reasonable, proper, or correct?' To know what the Lord says respecting everything is enough for us; all his words are solid truths: there is infinite wisdom and perfect consistency in them all.

Fron 16 January 1840

5 On hearing the Gospel

As the preaching of the Gospel is an ordinance of Christ, so the hearing of it is the duty of all that can attend. What is the use of preaching if none will hear? But it is necessary to 'take heed how we hear;' *Mark* 4.24. *Luke* 8.18. There never was, at any time, in any country, greater opportunity and liberty to hear the Word of God than there is in Wales at this time; yet hearing is hitherto unprofitable to thousands! *Hebrews* 4.2. Many after hearing offend God, and are likely to fall under his wrath. *Hebrews* 3.16, 17. But there is a great benefit to be obtained by hearing the Word of God; 'faith cometh by hearing;' *Romans* 10.17; yea, souls receive life thereby. *Isaiah* 55.3.

There are unprofitable hearers. Many go to a place of worship with unworthy motives, and in a very improper frame of mind. Many go from habit, without considering the purpose of preaching and hearing the Gospel; they hear unconcerned, and regardless of God and his Word. Some go, whose end in doing so is extremely vain and sinful – to see and to be seen – and because many others go! The conversation of many in going to, and returning from, a place of worship, is very frivolous and corrupt. It is respecting dress and fashion, neighbours and their failings, or concerning some other worldly or vain thing. Few converse about the Bible, Christ, the soul, and the eternal world. Such persons are not anxious for the blessing of God, neither do they pray for communion with him in the means of grace. Some in a place of worship will look about, and then they will fall asleep; they appear as if they needed nothing. They consequently leave without any benefit to their souls, or sorrow for their loss.

There is another sort of hearers who appear to be greater professors than the above. They will talk much about sermons and preachers in a very improper manner; they will make comparisons between them, extolling the one and slighting the other. These are often unfair judges; they generally judge according to their own taste and opinions, and not according to the Word. They do not understand what are the qualifications of a minister of God. It might be asked them, 'Are ye ripe in knowledge, judgment, and experience, to judge these things? Would it not be more proper in you to learn, than to become the judges of teachers?' Ask these persons concerning their own eternal affairs; they will appear blind and confused. Ask them, 'Do you know themselves? Is Christ in you, the hope of glory? Or else are ye reprobates?' If they cannot discern their own case, what suitability have they to judge the ambassadors of God? The scales of these men are not correct to weigh ministers, being their own opinions and tastes, and not the Word of God. No wonder then, if the most scriptural, experimental, and godly preachers are too light in their balances.

The proper *qualifications* in the opinions of those hearers are these – boldness, fluency, eloquence, excellency of speech, enticing words, human wisdom, and a pleasant voice. And the ministers that please them are such as do not speak very plainly of man's miserable state, nor press things too keenly on the conscience of man, nor say much of the total corruption of man by the fall, and his inability to save himself. Such ministers exalt but little of the sovereign grace of God; they speak but little of the Spirit's work in changing the sinner; and they do not state too minutely the signs of hypocrites, and false professors. Their manner of preaching accords with the carnal ideas of their hearers, to support their selfish confidence, touching slightly their pride, worldliness and carnal lusts. Then they are pleased with the preachers and with themselves likewise under them. Doubtless they will say that they receive benefit under their ministry, but they mistake gratification for profit, excitement of feeling for support, the satisfaction of

their taste for spiritual edification. Hearers of this kind are likely
to idolize the preachers they admire; they will depreciate other
preachers, in order to exalt these. They become angry with all
that doubt the excellences of these ministers. They speak more of
them than of Christ; of their views than of the Bible. They plead
that there is need of eloquence and talents to draw the attention
of the people. It is possible for a preacher to draw the mind of the
hearers by his gifts to himself and not to Christ. He may increase
professors for a *sect*, disciples for a preacher, natural religion
without the spirit; but neither gift nor eloquence, nothing but
'the preaching of the cross,' is 'the power of God,' to draw the
sinner to Christ. It is God only that gives benefit and blessing by
his own ordinances. 'God giveth the increase.'

Preachers, yea, those that are truly good and pious, are *too
light* in the scales of these hearers. They are not eloquent and
gifted enough; their sermons, they say, are too plain, clear, and
void of ornament. They imagine they speak too openly against
sin, and that they humble and degrade man too much, and that
they exalt free grace too highly, giving all the glory to God, in the
salvation of man. So many godly preachers who live near to God,
being often at the throne of grace, under great distress of mind
for man's salvation, and whose sermons are scriptural, and
administer 'the sincere milk of the word' are nevertheless depised
by these hearers, as their discourses are not adorned according
to their taste. A 'pearl of great price' is often found in a mean shell.
The food that is cooked in the plainest manner is the most
wholesome and gives the greatest nourishment. It is indeed easier
for these godly ministers to endure reproach than others, because
they seek not their own things nor 'preach themselves.' Yet none
are more distressed than they, because their communications are
despised, their Master slighted, and free salvation neglected.

There are other sorts of hearers that receive no benefit by
hearing. One kind is very numerous, and contains thousands of
our youths. They come to places of worship, but retain nothing
of what is heard. They have some pleasure in the sound of the
Gospel and gifts of the preachers. Christ sets forth four kinds of
hearers in the parable of the sower; one kind only received benefit.

However, this was not owing to his being under a gifted ministry. The seed and sower were the same; it was because he understood, received, and kept the Word. This is the gift of God.

Next we shall observe the *manner* in which we should receive the Gospel; or what end and state of mind in hearing tend to the glory of God and good of souls. The greatest gain has been obtained by hearing the Gospel; 'faith and everlasting life,' have come by hearing, as observed already. 'It pleased God by the foolishness of preaching to save them that believe.' 1 *Corinthians* 1.21. We should consider preaching and hearing the Gospel as divine ordinances, and we should use them with great soberness and reverence, 'keeping our foot,' being ready to hear' considering ourselves as 'present before God, to hear all things that are commanded by God', through his ministry. *Acts* 10.33. *Ecclesiastes* 5.1. We should not consider a preacher less or more than a *messenger* from God to us. If we view him *less* than such, we degrade the ministry of the Gospel, and represent it as a human and a mean thing. If we consider him more than such a one, as able to administer some benefit to us himself, then we place preaching above and superior to the *means* of grace, and cease to wait on God. As to imparting any spiritual benefit, one minister is not superior to another; neither is he that planteth anything, neither he that watereth. The benefit, the increase is from God. 1 *Corinthians* 3.6, 7. We ought to *pray* more before we go to hear the Gospel, and look up more to God when we do hear. It may be said to many that complain they receive nothing under sermons, 'Ye have not because ye ask not.' *James* 4.2. Much is said about having blessings under sermons. But if you should ask many what is meant by a blessing, they cannot answer; perhaps they imagine that it is some pleasure in hearing.

However there are hearers that receive real profit by hearing. They have found a treasure of immense value in the Gospel field. They have exercised faith in Christ whilst hearing. The preaching of the cross has been 'the power of God to their salvation.' As by hearing they had spiritual life, so by the same means they receive nourishment and support. 1 *Peter* 2.2. They have benefit by means of sermons, when they come to see more

of the *evil* of sin and the plague of their own hearts, until they hate
and detest themselves more as sinners, and humble themselves
more in the dust. Also, when they have a clear view of the *glory*
of Christ, and greater aid to make use of him, and more communion with him. Also, when they are *sanctified*; when some sin is
mortified, and the image of Christ is made more visible on and in
them; when they are brought to love God, his law and Gospel
more, and to be more obedient to him. And lastly, when they are
made more *spiritual* and heavenly, their affections being raised
above the things of the flesh and the world, and set upon those
that are heavenly.

This is the time they have blessings under sermons, and true
benefit, being fed with spiritual food. Then God shall have the
praise; they will speak but little of the preacher; they will forget
him in admiring his Master; they will forget the cleverness of
the sermon, by viewing the wonders of the Gospel. The excellence
of the preacher in the judgment of these pious hearers is that he
is a godly, sober, humble, self-denying, conscientious, and
zealous minister. His fluency and gifts are but secondary things
in their esteem. Those that are of God delight to hear those that
are of God. 1 *John* 4.5, 6.

Ye hearers, pray for the spirit of hearing, for hunger and thirst
after real benefit; in hearing, pray for your minister instead of
judging him. After all, ministers are but instruments; you must
have the blessing from God himself, through them. Pray for a
humble, broken, meek, obedient spirit to hear the Word of God.

Use the Bible often; go to the throne of grace often; pray that
the truth you hear may not be unprofitable to you. Thanks be to
God for the Gospel.

Fron April 1841

MISTAKEN VIEWS

Fron 1840

I have been surprised and grieved by observing so many young
people delighting, these days, in new and strange things and
expressions. I am obliged to fear that many profess the Gospel,

and that some preach it, without receiving 'the love of the truth' and the unction or 'anointing that teacheth all things,' and without knowing the power and relish of the truth. Having never drank of the old wine, they thirst for the new presently. They are led about with diverse and strange doctrines, their hearts being not strengthened with grace. They are like children tossed to and fro, and carried about with every wind of doctrine.

I met on my journey with a small book, the production of Abercrombie; it is called, *The Harmony of Christian Faith ana Character*.[1] The author, by dwelling on the knowledge of the truth, and the great danger of making mistakes in things of vast importance, shews that some err because of their indifference to know the truth; others, because they dislike and despise the truth. He saith that some profess they love the truth, but that they depart from it in consequence of vain conversation and disputation, having never made a sober, diligent search into the truth; and so they are deceived, and consequently they deceive others, taking up some opinions and ideas instead of the truth. Some leave the sober views of the truth, having a desire of being singular, and appearing wiser than others. Yet others aim at being more wise than even what has been written. They having an active, restless turn of mind and a lively imagination destitute of sound judgment, form light opinions. They dwell on one side of a subject, and that without labour, taking partial views and weak evidences for their imaginations and conclusions.

Many of these trust to their own understanding, trying to shew that their powers of mind are stronger than those of others; that they can think more clearly, deeply, and fully than their neighbours, and that they attain unto things that others cannot, imagining that they are a few of the enlightened ones of the world, and different from the multitude that are content to tread in the path of their fathers. So they despise those that think differently from themselves.

The way to shun errors and desires after strange things is by being truly humble, living under the influences of the Holy Ghost, tasting and loving the truth. The Spirit will give light, strength,

[1] By John Abercrombie an eminent physician of Edinburgh (died 1844).

and wisdom to keep true Christians in the middle path of truth. Being in his hands and under his guidance they would not err, though they were fools. I am one of those that see their need of being always led by the Spirit.

UNPROFITABLE CONVERSATION[1]

Fron 1839

The conversation of many respecting the death of Christ is often very unbecoming. It is that of persons that have no corresponding feeling, no brokenness of heart and humility. They converse about it in a dry, carnal, and presumptuous manner. They never talk about it as the only way a person ever saw to save his life, when pursued by the holy law, and condemned by the justice of God. It is in fact the conversation of persons possessing mere head knowledge of things, without any experience of them in their hearts. I hope I can speak of the death of Christ as effectual in my salvation.

6 On the moral inability of man

There is a disposition in some to confuse and darken by their carnal reasons and improper expressions, subjects that are clear and manifest in the Holy Scriptures. Some do this in order to shew that the state of man, by the fall, is better, and less miserable than it is set forth in the Bible, and to depreciate the wonders of grace in the plan of saving sinners; and others under the appearance of attempting to answer the objections of natural and errone-ous men against Gospel truths, – sometimes by using human reason (they say) to shew the consistency of one doctrine with another. There is much confusion respecting man's ability, or inability, though the Scriptures are clear on the subject. In order to shew the truth on this point, I will make some observations on what the Scripture states respecting man's weakness, in con-

[1] An extract from an article by John Elias in The Spiritual Magazine 1839 (translated from the Welsh).

sequence of sin, to spiritual and holy things, and then on the nature of his inability.

The Holy Scriptures plainly declare, that man, in his fallen state, is *weak*, or without strength for spiritual things, 'For when we were yet without strength, in due time Christ died for the ungodly.' *Romans* 5.6. So the Father viewed sinners, when he gave his Son and sent him to redeem them; so Christ considered men, by coming to live and die for them: and so the Holy Ghost finds them, when he calls sinners to Christ, and applies salvation to them. For what things are they then incapable? They can do many things as men; yet there are some things, and those of the greatest importance, yea, all the things that belong to their peace, which they cannot do.

They cannot be *subject* to the law of God. They cannot give that obedience which he requires, to *love* him with all their heart, and obey him at all times and in all things. So it is evident that they cannot please God, for none can please him without being subject to his law. *Romans* 8.7. 8. And as they cannot please God, they cannot be saved; for those that displease him, are under his wrath and indignation. *Romans* 8.3. *Psalm* 22.29; 7.11. Though God, in his infinite mercy, sent his Son to die for sinners, so that whosoever believeth in him shall not perish, yet none can go to Christ and believe in him and receive life. *John* 3.16. 1 *Timothy* 1.15. *John* 6.44. They cannot *understand* the Gospel, or the things of the Spirit; neither can they think correctly of the things of God, however correctly explained; the 'natural man cannot know them.' 1 *Corinthians* 2.14. 2 *Corinthians* 3.5. They can neither turn nor change themselves; neither believe nor repent. In a word, man, without Christ, can do nothing holy. He is as incapable of acting in a holy manner, as a body without soul is in a natural manner. *Jeremiah* 13.23. *Acts* 5.31. 26.18. *John* 5.25. 2 *Timothy* 2.25. *Ephesians* 1.19, 20. *Philippians* 1.29. *John* 15.5.

Man, under the fall, is as incapable of *applying* salvation to himself, as of planning and accomplishing it. There is as much need of the Spirit to apply salvation, as of the Mediator to work it out, though he became the Author of eternal salvation unto all them that obey him. *Hebrews* 5.9. Yet no one *will* or can obey him, except the Spirit, in his infinite and overcoming power, works in him. The grace of God appears as clear in turning man, giving faith and repentance to him, as in redeeming him on the cross. Man is not only incapable of, but *opposed* to, the application of salvation. He has no inclination to come to Christ, nor to live under his government. He is incapable and unwilling to be made willing and obedient. *John* 5.40. *Psalm* 81.11. *Matthew* 23.37. *Luke* 19.14, 27. We cannot shew man's miserable state without setting forth his inability to all spiritual things; for there is a great degree of man's misery in this. And we cannot, without this, exhibit the glorious plan of salvation by grace, especially the work of the Spirit in applying it. Though salvation is so free and complete, and so clearly set forth in the Gospel; and though it is preached in the most gifted, clear, and winning manner; and though the danger of neglecting it, and the misery of those that reject it, be set forth in a most lively and awakening way; yet, man will not, neither can he, of himself, receive or use it.

Now we will make a few observations on the *nature* of man's inability to holy and spiritual things. (There has been much said and written on this subject; and many obscure and improper words have often been used, as is too much the case in controversy. I do not understand that it is requisite that we should give a philosophical description of man's inability; there is no need of knowing or saying more on this subject, than the Scriptures make known. We do not want unscriptural expressions or delineations on this point, or words that belong to human arts and sciences, such as philosophy and metaphysics; the expressions of God are the best. Let us beware, on the one hand, lest we should, by dwelling on the inability of man, set him forth as a stone or wood, or unreasonable creature that is unaccountable to God for his conduct; and let us take care that we do not think that man's inability is any excuse for his disobedience, or that the fault of his inability is at all connected with God. Let us be cautious, on the other hand, lest by endeavouring to explain the nature of man's inability by human skill, we should lower the necessity of the Spirit's work in his infinite grace, to convince man of sin, to bring him to Christ, to change him, sanctify, lead, support, comfort, and qualify him for eternal glory. However we may make the following observations:

Though man fell awfully in Eden, by disobeying and breaking God's covenant, yet he did not cease to be man. He still has the essential properties of man though he fell – the body and all its members and senses, the soul and all its faculties. And as a reasonable creature, he is yet accountable to God for all his conduct. The Lord did not give up his right to require obedience from man, and man's obligations to obey God did not cease.

But when man broke the covenant he lost the peace of God, and he lost his holy image also, and in this he *lost* the principle and holy disposition, the root of good works, so that there is in no man under the fall, the nature, principle, or disposition to do any spiritual good. There is no principle, a holy operation, within him; so he is dead in sin. *Ephesians* 2.1. *Colossians* 2.13. Not only is man destitute of a nature, principle, and disposition to act in a holy manner, but 'his heart is fully set in him to *do* evil.' 'The carnal mind is enmity against God.' The soul is under the dominion of a nature and disposition that is sinful and hostile to God and every good. *Ecclesiastes* 8.11. *Jeremiah* 17.9. *Genesis* 6.5. *Romans* 8.7; 1.30.

The moral inability is not less because there is no want of natural ability, members, senses, or faculties in man. The need of a nature, principle, and disposition to act in a holy manner is as great an inability to it as if there was a want of members or faculties to operate in a natural manner. As the body cannot act without the soul, so the soul cannot do anything that is holy without the divine nature. 2 *Peter* 1.4. As the eye cannot behold any thing without the humour,[1] so the soul cannot act in a holy manner, though possessed of all the faculties, without a holy principle and disposition to do so. A spiritual life is as necessary to act in a holy manner, as natural life is for its actions. There is no spiritual life but in Christ. 'He is our life,' without him we can 'do nothing.' *Colossians* 3.4. *John* 15.5.

All the faculties of the soul of fallen man are unable to act in a

[1] The transparent fluid parts of the eye.

holy manner, the one as well as the other, and are entirely opposed to everything that is godly. The understanding is dark, it cannot perceive the things of God; the will is obstinate, so man will not come to Christ; the affections are earthly and carnal, the conscience is corrupt. 1 *Corinthians* 2.14. *John* 5.40. 2 *Timothy* 3.4. *Titus* 1.15. So a man must be regenerated, risen, yea created anew, in order to act and live in a holy manner. *John* 3.3. 2 *Corinthians* 5.17. *Ephesians* 2.1. Man has entirely lost all power to spiritual and divine things. It is not the ceasing of action to holy things, as it is with men in sleep; and it is not the absence of strength in some part, as with men in complaints; but the man is altogether without strength and inclination to perform holy things in a spiritual and godly manner. He is dead! He is unable to be willing, and unwilling to be able to do what is good. The godly man has experienced his inability to holy things. There is no need to say much to prove this to him. But the natural man does not feel his weakness, neither does he receive the things that the Spirit declares respecting him.

There is great danger to hear, read, and converse, in an unfeeling and unsuitable manner on the theme of human inability. There is a danger of mistaking, or drawing inferences from this doctrine, respecting man's weakness to holy things.

We ought to be on our guard, lest we think that man's inability makes him *excusable* in his sin, or in neglecting his duties and the great salvation. By his inability he does not become unaccountable to God. The Lord's authority to demand obedience from man, and man's obligations to obey his Maker, are the same. Our disobedience is not less sinful because we are naturally sinners; and our sins are not less aggravating on account of our strong inclination to sin; and our vileness is not less evil because of our strong opposition to be holy. Let us beware lest we imagine that it is not sinful for us to be sinners. We should also beware of the thought that, as man is unable to change his nature, he is therefore excusable in living in his sin. It is no excuse whatever to him, neither does it lessen his fault at all, for he delights in his sin, and hates to be kept from it. He does not like to live a godly life, nor to be made willing and able. He contends with his Maker, opposes his Spirit, and rejects his invitation. *Genesis* 6.3; *Acts* 7.51. *Proverbs* 1.24, 25.

We ought to take care, on the other hand, lest, by proving that it is not the lack of members, senses, or faculties that accounts for man's inability to act in a spiritual manner, we should set forth that weakness as something *small*, and that man may remove it by some endeavour of his own; or that ministers may overcome it by strong reasons, solemn, alarming threatenings, and winning, captivating invitations; and thereby disregard and lose sight of the truth respecting the Spirit's work in man's salvation. There is danger lest ministers and people should fail in observing the need of the Holy Ghost working by his grace and infinite strength in man's salvation. There is as much need of his applying it, as of the Son's accomplishing it, as already observed. There is room to fear that preachers and hearers grieve the Holy Spirit by losing sight of this; and are, consequently, left destitute of his powerful influences and operations, because they do not seriously consider, nor humbly acknowledge, the necessity of the Spirit working powerfully by the ministry of the Word for man's salvation.

We should always bear this in mind, that God, in his infinite wisdom and grace, did foresee the sinful weakness of man, as well as other things, in his miserable circumstances; and provided, in his plan of salvation, deliverance out of it. As he contrived a way to pay the debt of sinners, to remove their guilt; so he planned a way to quicken, create anew, dispose, and strengthen them, to every godly and holy work. 'It is God that worketh in you both to will and to do of his good pleasure;' 'working in you that which is well pleasing in his sight.' *Philippians* 2.13. *Hebrews* 13.21. So that the application of salvation is as entirely of God as its plan; it is all of God, and the glory altogether belongs to him for ever, and he shall have it from the redeemed most freely throughout eternity.[1]

Fron 18 April 1834

[1] We see that man's 'cannot,' is that man 'will' not, 'Ye will not come to me.' The wills of men are so perverse, that nothing less than the Holy Spirit's power will ever subdue and turn them. Their rejection of Christ is not merely their misfortune, but their 'sin'—that unbelief is a wilful rebellion against even the mercy of God; and as such deserves damnation.

7 On the obligations of man

It is my wish to see your monthly periodical continue answering
its name, *Treasury* of spiritual and useful things. The taste of
this age tends too much to carnal and useless things, and this
sickly desire is over-fed and pampered by the productions of the
press. I hope you will continue to keep every useless thing out
of the Treasury. It would be proper also to reject every light
and trifling question, or such as are worded in a dark, mysterious
manner, or such as may not have a clear answer from Scripture.
And we ought, in answering questions, to have the Word of God,
the analogy of faith, the edification of the readers, in view. I
should not like to wound the feelings of enquirers or respondents;
my design is to edify, and not to hurt. I saw, some time ago, a
question in a number of the Treasury, that appears to me strange
in a person that acknowledges the divine authority of the Bible,
namely, 'What is the ground of man's obligations to obey the
commandments of God, to believe his testimonies, and particularly to trust in Christ?' At least the querist has been unfortunate
in wording the question. It is possible to ask many things that it
would be sinful to try to answer, and there are other things that
a Christian is under no obligation to answer. But we may make
some observations on the things contained in the above question,
though not in the manner in which it is asked.

1 Respecting the duty or obligation of man to obey every commandment which God gave him. It is more proper to ask, Does God
   command such a thing?, rather than to acknowledge that he commands such a thing, and then to enquire what reason is there for
   man to obey him. The consideration of the infinite greatness of God,
   as our Creator, Owner, Governor, and Judge, shews that we are
   under the most just and strong obligations to obey him in all things.
   All God's commandments to us are 'holy, just, and good,' and it
   would be very presumptuous in us to ask, Is this duty which God
   requires of us, just, reasonable, and good? Or, Would it be profitable
   for us to obey? Under what obligations are we to obey? *Romans* 7.12.

   When we perceive that God commands any thing, we should
   understand that we are under obligation to obey, and that it is a
   privilege so to do, 'esteeming all his precepts concerning all things

to be right.' 'His commandments are not grievous.' *Psalms* 119.128.
1 *John* 5.3. If the power and majesty with which God hath endowed
earthly kings place their subjects under obligations to obey them in
all things according to God's Word; and if the situation of employers
imposes an obligation on their servants to obey them; if the relationship and station of parents require obedience from their offspring;
much more do the greatness and the transcendency of God place us
under the strongest obligations to honour and obey him; knowing
that since the Lord commands us in all things, we are bound to obey
him in them. It would be presumptuous rebellion in us to ask,
Should we, or why should we obey? As the infinite God has manifested his will in his commandments, as to the way and manner he
would have us conduct ourselves, it becomes us to obey all those
commandments that concern us, for they are those of our Creator,
Owner, Ruler, and Judge. The greatest benefit does indeed accrue to
us from obedience. But our own advantage should not be the first
motive of our conduct.

2 Respecting our obligations to believe the testimony of God on every
subject. It is sufficient to say, 'If we receive the witness of men, the
witness of God is greater.' 1 *John* 5.9. When we see that He testifies
about any thing, it is sinful to ask, Are we bound to believe it? Or
what is the cause of our obligation to believe his testimony? It is the
same as to ask, Is God faithful and true, and worthy to be believed?
Should man believe him that tells the truth at all times, yea, him that
cannot lie? Rather let us ask what ground have we to disbelieve him?
What reason have we not to believe firmly God's testimony respecting everything? Is it not the true and the faithful God that testifies?
'God is not a man that he should lie.' But he that does not believe his
testimony conducts himself towards God as if he were a liar. 1 *John*
5.10.

3 Respecting the ground of man's obligation to believe in Christ. The
views of many about believing in Christ are very obscure, confused,
and erroneous. Many talk about believing as if they had not considered that their eternal happiness depended on it. Faith in Christ is
as necessary and indispensable for salvation, according to God's
appointment, as was the sending of Christ into the world to live and
to die. As the Father did, in his infinite love, grace, and wisdom,
appoint and send his Son to be the only Saviour to lost sinners, so
also he planned, in his boundless grace and wisdom, that believing

in his Son, Jesus Christ, should be the means, way, or method for lost sinners to come into possession of Christ as their Saviour, and salvation and eternal life as their inheritance. *John* 3.15, 16. 1 *John* 5.10, 11, 12. The connection between faith in Christ and obtaining eternal life is so strong in God's plan, that it is certified in his Word, 'that whosoever believeth in him should not perish, but have eternal life.' Doubtless the moral law required man to believe God's testimony respecting every thing; but it was infinite grace to connect everlasting life with believing God's testimony respecting his Son. Some think that they must believe that they are the elect before they can believe in Christ; but this cannot be correct, for there is no testimony in the Bible for any unbeliever personally to conclude that he is one of them. Others think that believing they are godly and that they shall go to heaven is the faith which is required of them. That cannot be, for none are godly before they believe in Christ. It is presumptuous for any one to think that he shall be in heaven before he believes in the Son of God.

4 What is faith? The consideration of human faith may help us to judge what it is to believe in God and in his Son.

To believe a *man* is to consent, to give credence to his testimony, respecting things that are unseen by the hearer, in consideration or opinion of the knowledge, honesty, and faithfulness of the speaker. Believing the testimony of men produces effects according to (1) the nature of the things related and their relationship to the person that hears the narration, (2) the strength of the statement, (3) and the firmness of belief. Believing a testimony causes sometimes wonder and astonishment, sometimes dread and fear, at other times sadness and sorrow, and sometimes trust, hope, and joy.

Similarly believing *God* is to give credence to his testimony in his Word, considering his knowledge, authority, truth, and faithfulness. Faith does not intermeddle with anything but what is clear in the Divine Word.

Faith in *Christ* is believing the testimony of God respecting him, in his holy Word – his person, his end in coming into the world, his offices, his perfect obedience in his life and death, his full salvation, and the promise of everlasting life to all that believe in him. 1 *John* 5.9, 11. *Hebrews* 5.9. Those that thus believe respecting him, accept him as the Deliverer, flee to him, receive and trust in him, and make use of him in his offices. The whole soul acts in believing. Grace influences all the faculties. The *understanding* is enlightened to behold great glory in the Saviour, as the Word testifies respecting him; the *will* chooses him as the only Deliverer; the affections love him supremely; the conscience is made quiet in him. The whole soul trusts in him. 1 *Peter* 1.8. 2 *Timothy* 1.12.

5 The divine testimony in the Bible respecting Christ is a sufficient foundation for a sinner to believe in him. He is set forth in the testimony as altogether such a Deliverer as we stand in need of; a Saviour to such sinners as we are. Yea, we are described in the Scriptures better than if we were called personally by our names, and our places of habitation – 'Sinners,' the 'chief' of them, the 'ungodly', the 'lost.' It is testified that he is a Saviour to such.

There is the *strongest* foundation for those that hear the Gospel to believe it. It is lawful for a sinner, yea, he has a claim, to make use of Christ, by believing as to everything that is testified about him, that he is such to any sinner. The man is not required to search into the mysteries of election. It would have been a reproach on the clear testimony of God in his Word for the man to do so.

The man should not look for any excellency in himself as a ground to believe in Christ. The strong testimony of the true God shows his Son as a willing and full Deliverer to a sinner, yea, to the chief; having come to seek and to save the lost, dying for the *helpless*, the *ungodly*, yea, for *enemies*. He is set forth as a Deliverer to such as these, and the Gospel is preached to them; and not one of them that believe in him shall be lost. 1 *Timothy* 1.15. *John* 3.15, 16.

As the divine testimony is a foundation for faith, so the command to believe in Christ sets forth the *duty* of all to believe 'the testimony of God respecting his Son.' *John* 6.29. 1 *John* 3.23.

O that we could see how glorious is the plan of God's salvation in the Gospel, revealing his noble purposes and method of saving sinners by faith in Jesus Christ. Even the *law* or *statute* of God directs the sinner that hears the Gospel to believe his testimony respecting his Son, and his plan of saving sinners; and the Father, in his infinite grace, infallibly connects this faith in the said testimony with eternal salvation. So we perceive the safest foundations and the strongest obligations for those that hear the Gospel, to believe in Christ, and the firmest assurance that whosoever believeth shall not perish, but that every one that trusteth in him shall have eternal life.

Reader, do you believe? Or do you 'make God a liar?' 1 *John* 5.10.

Do you love death? *Proverbs* 8.36. And will you not come unto him
that you may have life? *John* 5.40. If you feel your inability to believe,
by reason of your corruption and rebellion, your hard thoughts of
God and your unbelief, yet draw near to the throne of grace, being
ashamed and grieved, and ask for the gift of faith, for the sake of
Jesus Christ. *Philippians* 1.29.

Though man ought to believe, yet he is so rebellious and corrupt
that he neither will nor can do anything of himself. *John* 6.44. Yet
God in his infinite grace gives faith, 'It is the gift of God.' *Ephesians*
2.8. O be not easy without it! 'Ask it of God, he giveth liberally and
upbraideth not.' *James* 1.5. That you may have faith, and believe till
you know what faith is; and that those who believe may increase in
it, is the desire of your servant.

Fron 10 April 1833

8 On government, and the sin of despising it

God is the sovereign ruler of all the world and every thing in it.
'His kingdom ruleth over all.' In his infinite wisdom and goodness
he appoints men to rule under him in this world, according to
his Word and for his glory. God's care for men and his kindness
towards them appears much in this. For fallen men would be
worse in their manner than the brute beasts, had they not been
under government. As there is a government, it follows that
some are appointed to rule and some to be governed by them.
I will endeavour, keeping my eye on the Scriptures, to make
observations on family, church, and national governments.

Family Government. The family is the oldest society in the
world. Other communities are derived from families. God ordained
family government, appointing the head of the family to rule it.
He commends Abraham for ruling his house: 'I know him, that
he will command his children and his household after him, and
they shall keep the way of the Lord.' *Genesis* 18.19. The word
'he will command' – signifies that he had authority, that he used
it, and did govern. And the expression 'they shall keep the way
of the Lord' – shews that it was for God he ruled. The fourth
commandment shows that the head of the family, father or mother,

has dominion over it, and the master over his servants: 'Thou, nor thy son, nor thy daughter, nor thy man servant, nor thy maid servant.' God published this authority on Mount Sinai, writing it with his own finger.

Family government is clearly set forth in the New Testament as belonging to the Church of Christ. No one is chosen as an officer in his church, except such 'as rules his house well, having his children in subjection.' 1 *Timothy* 3.4, 5, 12; *Titus* 1.6. Good family government and obedience to it, would cause a remarkable revival in the church, good order and great comfort in the country. This would be the case if more heads of families were children of Abraham.

Church Government. Though Christ is the King of his Church, yet he places men to rule under him in his visible Church. Ministers of the Word, elders, leaders, and officers of the Church, not only teach and feed the flock of God, but also rule it. 'Those which labour among you, and are over you in the Lord.' 'The elders that rule well.' The Church is requested to submit to and obey them: 'Remember them which have the rule over you – obey them – and submit yourselves.' But 'neither as being lords over God's heritage, but being examples to the flock.' 1 *Thessalonians* 5.12. 1 *Timothy* 5.17. *Hebrews* 13.7, 17. 1 *Peter* 5.3. These under-rulers are not to make new laws, but to govern according to those that Christ gave, and in his Spirit, and to his glory. Observe, hypocrites have been in the church in every age, who 'despise government,' being ready to rise up against officers in the Church. They are guilty of gain-saying like Core (*Jude* 11), and saying to the officers of the Church, 'Ye take too much upon you, seeing all the congregation are holy.' *Numbers* 16.3.

National Government. God governs the world by setting kings and rulers under him; 'He setteth up kings.' *Daniel* 2.21. 'By me, says Christ, 'kings reign.' *Proverbs* 8.16, 17. God has ordained kings and princes to rule over people; from him their authority comes. They that obey God respect them; and they that despise national government despise the appointment of God. The wisdom, justice, and goodness of God appear in his work of appointing government and rulers among men. National dominion is for the advantage and comfort of human society. Men without government would be worse in their lives, as observed before, than the wild creatures. Yea, 'as the fishes of the sea, as the creeping things, that have no ruler over them.' *Habakkuk* 1.14. The good name, chastity, property, and even lives of men, would not be safe without governors. To be without government is worse than being under oppressive rulers. Many subjects have benefit in several things under the dominion even of bad men. It is said of Nebuchadnezzar that he was 'like a tree, in which was meat for all,' and 'that all flesh was fed of it.' *Daniel* 4.12. Saul, the king of Israel, clothed the daughters of the land in scarlet. 2 *Samuel* 1.24. Not the best of kings was called, by Jeremiah, 'the breath of our nostrils.' *Lamentations* 4.20.

Though affairs were so bad and disorderly in Israel under oppressive governments, yet the greatest evils occurred when they had no rulers. Such idolatry, injustice, uncleanness, oppression, and cruelty were practised, as were unheard of before; and the reason given for such a state of things, is this: 'In those days there was no king in Israel, but every one did that which was right in his own eyes.' *Judges* 17.6; 18.1; 21.25. It is a great judgment on a country to be without a king or governors. So those that despise government, and speak against rulers, stand in opposition to their own happiness. Those that speak evil of rulers, generally in their heart condemn government; they hate the officer on the account of his office, the governor by reason of his authority. But O their madness! When government is lost, 'the child shall behave himself proudly against the ancient, and the base against the honourable.' *Isaiah* 3.5.

It is a great blessing to our nation that it is wisely and justly ordered (*o drefniad doeth a chyfiawn*) and that God has now for ages given us kings that are fatherly and tender towards their subjects. Every one that calls himself Christian ought to respect them in word and conduct, and not to despise them.

God shews in his Word what is our *duty* towards our governors. To *honour* and respect them: *Psalm* 82.1–6. To think and converse respectfully about them: 'Thou shalt not revile, nor curse the ruler of thy people.' 'Curse not the king, no, not in thought.'

Exodus 22.28. *Ecclesiastes* 10.20. To *pray* earnestly for them: in their peace and success is our peace. 'First of all, let supplications, prayers, intercessions, and giving of thanks be made, for kings and for all that are in authority.' 1 *Timothy* 2.1. *To pay* taxes to them willingly and readily, without murmuring. Christ himself and Peter paid tribute; and he commanded to render unto Cæsar the things that are Cæsar's. Without taxes, government cannot be supported. It is our advantage and comfort to contribute towards maintaining a good order of things, towards defending our property and lives. It is not the subjects that are to judge things – what tax is proper and just – this is the province of the rulers. They are accountable to the Sovereign Ruler of all. The subjects, however, if they should feel some burdens too heavy, may send their complaints, in respectful and humble petitions, to their governors. *Matthew* 17.27. 22.21. *Romans* 13.7.

It is easy to prove by various reasons that we ought to *submit* to our national rulers; to the king as supreme, or unto governors, as unto them that are sent by him. 1 *Peter* 2.13, 14. Government and rulers are *ordained* by God: 'The powers that be are ordained of God.' *Romans* 13.1. He placed them in their offices, and endowed them with authority. *Daniel* 2.21. So to withstand them is to oppose God. *Romans* 13.2. A ruler is for the *benefit* of the nation: 'He is the minister of God to thee for good.' *Romans* 13.3, 4. Their work is to preserve justice and order, therefore we should honour them. 'A king that sitteth in the throne of judgment scattereth away all evil with his eyes.' *Proverbs* 20.8.

A Christian king and a nation professing Christianity ought not only to defend all moral excellences, but also *protect* Christianity from all its enemies. The following reasons prove this:

Those that confess there is a God ought to acknowledge that we should believe, worship, obey and serve him. *Hebrews* 11.6. His worshippers should, in their various stations, *defend* his laws, worship, and honour. So should the Christian king in his high office, and he should not suffer God, Christ, nor the Scriptures to be vilified. There is a great difference between religious liberty, and liberty to blaspheme religion. The kings of Israel (the only people God had then) were to *take care* of his law and worship. The godly and celebrated kings from the beginning, such as David, Hezekiah, Jehoshaphat, and Josiah, were remarkable for this. *Deuteronomy* 17.18, 19. Though the typical worship of that time has been changed, yet the moral duty for rulers to defend the law and worship of God is not altered. *Deuteronomy* 16.18, 20.

This is a blessing to a nation and a privilege to a king. There is no opposition to this in the New Testament. The Gospel does not unloose men from any moral obligations. Whatever God ordained formerly, and did not withdraw under the Gospel, there is moral rectitude in it. National governors should therefore plead for all moral and religious good, and *restrain* as much as possible, all evils especially such as disturb the country, hurt the cause of Christ and his Church, and offend God. *Romans* 13.1–7. 1 *Timothy* 2.2. *Proverbs* 15.8, 16. The promises of God that relate to Gospel times prove this. It is *promised* that kings shall use all their influence and power to promote the cause of Christ and his Church, the right worship of God, and respect for the Gospel; no doubt, then, but that it is their duty to do so. *Isaiah* 1.26; 49.23; 60.3, 11, 17. *Revelation* 11.15.

Godly persons never despise government. Christ and his apostles taught Christians to honour it, and they are, in every age, directed by the Spirit through the Word, to obey. Satan always endeavours, by means of foes, to disparage believers, and to assert that they oppose national government, in order to induce rulers to hate and persecute them. *Esther* 3.8. *Daniel* 3.12. *Ezra* 4.13. *Acts* 17.7, 19, 26; 24.5. But there is no danger to government from the godly. Irreligion, ungodliness, antichrist, unfaithfulness, cause government to be reproached. Such opposers are the children of Belial, of Satan. 1 *Samuel* 10.27. 2 *Samuel* 20.1. Satan is the first opposer of government; he tempted man to resist it. *Genesis* 3.5. The unrighteous are those that despise government, and speak evil of dignities. 2 *Peter* 2.9, 10; *Jude* 4.8. Flee from such. When governors rule well and in the fear of God, and subjects honour, submit to, and obey them, there will be the best order and greatest comfort in families, churches, and country. When men obey the Gospel, they will also submit to their rulers and not take occasion from their faults to disobey them or to dishonour them; but they pray for them, that the Lord would teach them and protect them. So it is the wisdom of rulers to respect the Gospel and defend the godly. The kingdom of Christ does not destroy any earthly kingdom that is not against him, nor does Christianity weaken any government but that of sin.

Ungodly men, infidels, the irreligious, erroneous, in every age despise government. *Proverbs* 24.21. 2 *Peter* 1.9, 10. *Jude* 4.8. Rulers should take care that they do not countenance infidelity, antichrist, and ungodliness; for they are not only enemies to God and Christ's government, but also to the national. *Psalm* 2.3, 10, 11. God's goodness is great towards a nation when the governors are kind, and the subjects submissive and obedient to them. *Isaiah* 49.23. 2 *Chronicles* 31.2, 3. *Psalm* 144.2. 1 *Peter* 3.13; 5.5.

God poured the heaviest judgments on the despisers of government in this world, and eternal punishment is threatened on them. *Numbers* 16.30–34. 2 *Peter* 2.9, 10. *Jude* 7, 8, 11, 13. They could not withstand such threatenings if they believed the Word of God; they 'neither fear God nor respect man.' It is the sincere prayer of every Christian, 'let not my soul come into their secret.' It is the desire of the godly man to 'lead a quiet and peaceable life in all godliness and honesty.' He will honour the king, and pray for him.

Fron 4 December 1832

Other papers

1 Documents on the better observance of the Sabbath

Whenever the important subject, the better observance of the Sabbath, was on the eve of being brought forward in Parliament, Elias was most alert in exciting and leading his countrymen and friends to pour in their petitions; as we may perceive by the following note, written from Liverpool:

'Shall the Methodists in Anglesey be, this year, behind all in sending petitions to Parliament for the better observance of the Sabbath? They used to be the first in the good cause. If we wish to be reformers, here is an opportunity for us; the carrying of such a measure as this, would doubtless be great means of reformation. We must however take care that we do not, in any of our attempts at reforming, disturb and mar the institutions of God. Friends are awake and zealous here in sending petitions from the three chapels, and a great many names are attached to them. Let us have petitions from Anglesey also. W. B. Hughes, Esq, would present them and plead the cause. He gave his vote for the bill.'

Elias was for aiming first at reform in things of the highest and greatest importance, thinking that those of minor signification would follow. We may suppose that his request was soon attended to, and that the whole county was immediately alive to the cause. One of the petitions sent to Parliament by this Connection in Anglesey, drawn up, as it is supposed, by Elias, is the following:

To the Honourable the Commons, of the United Kingdom of Great Britain and Ireland, in Parliament assembled.

The humble petition of a religious denomination of Christians, commonly called the Calvinistic Methodists:

Humbly sheweth, that your petitioners acknowledge the Sabbath as a divine institution of perpetual obligation; and that they appreciate the liberty that they enjoy to keep the Sabbath, and to worship God on his holy day.

Your petitioners cannot but lament at the same time the dreadful profanation of the Lord's day by multitudes of every class of society, in following worldly business, unnecessary travelling or sailing, and keeping open places of amusement.

Your petitioners sincerely deplore the awful desecration of the Sabbath, because of the great dishonour done thereby to the Most High, and the guilt necessarily contracted by the violation of the Divine commandment.

Your petitioners truly believe that national guilt brings down national judgments, and that they may expect, on the other hand, that the favour and blessing of God follow endeavours to promote the honour of his name and his worship on his holy day.

Your petitioners are, therefore, truly anxious that those temptations which at present powerfully prevail, so as to deprive many of the poor of the privileges of the Sabbath, should, as far as possible, be removed; and that all classes be protected in its due observance.

Your petitioners approach your Honourable House with sincere respect and confidence, humbly and earnestly praying that you will be pleased to give the subject your most serious consideration, in order to the adoption of such measures, as to your wisdom may seem effectual to secure the religious observance of the Sabbath, – be a barrier against much crime, strength to the nation, a safeguard to its peace, and a pledge of its prosperity.

Your petitioners, as in duty bound, will ever pray that God may incline you by his grace, and direct you by his wisdom, as Christian legislators in this highly-favoured nation, to defend his institutions and worship, and the honour of his name; and thereby to be a terror to evil-doers, and protection to them that do good, being moral, religious, and peaceable, those who fear God and honour the king. May God bless all your consultations for the peace, security, and prosperity of this realm.

Elias was a wise man, and would use proper means to accomplish his end; and accordingly we find him exerting his influence to engage people of rank and authority in the community to send petitions to Parliament, for the better observance of the Lord's day. The following letter was addressed to the Mayor of a certain town in another county of North Wales:

Llanfechell 2 February 1826

I am very sorry that you could not go on with the petition, especially as there is such a stir everywhere on this important subject, and numerous meetings held in order to petition Parliament. There was an excellent meeting held at Derby, where the Duke of Devonshire and the Rev Mr Gisbourn delivered very excellent speeches on the occasion. A meeting for the county of Pembroke was held at Haverfordwest lately, when the Right Honourable Lord Cawdor was in the chair. They resolved in these meetings to petition both Houses of Parliament. I am very unwilling to lose the opportunity of sending our wishes to Parliament on this important subject. If there be an intention of dissolving soon, we shall see in a few days; but if there should not, I hope we shall go on with the petition.

However, if you, after consulting with other gentlemen, should find an objection to co-operate in this important cause, I beg you will inform me of it plainly, that we may proceed to petition Parliament as a Connexion; but I much prefer the other way, that is, that the gentlemen and clergy should take the lead in this good work.'

A letter of Elias, on the necessity of energetic measures for the defence of the Sabbath, which appeared in the Welsh Spiritual Treasury, is as follows:

Fron January 1834

In consequence of reading the last number of the Spiritual Treasury, on the encouragement of sending petitions to Parliament to pass an improved act for the better observance of the Sabbath, I thought there was a great necessity to arouse Christians everywhere in this very important business. It is evident that Sabbath-breaking is one of those sins that brings divine judgment on our land. Unless the laws and governors of a country oppose Sabbath desecrations, the evil becomes national, and calls for judgment on it. I am surprised that any Christian can think of denying the morality of the fourth commandment, or the continuance of the obligation to observe it. God spoke the commandment with his own mouth, and wrote it with his own finger, like the other nine commandments.

I also wonder that any Christian doubts the propriety of a Christian Parliament forming an act to prevent the public violation of the Sabbath, and to encourage the religious and decent observance of it. There is no doubt as to the necessity of laws against the breach of the sixth, seventh, and the eighth commandments. Should we not consider our rulers as fathers in the nation? If so, the fourth commandment itself requires them to endeavour to bring all the subjects of the crown to a due observance of the Sabbath.

I read in one of the papers of the society you mentioned, the following passage: 'It cannot be doubted that nations and kingdoms flourish or decay in accordance with the practice of piety, diligence, and temperance; or the prevalence of ungodliness, idleness, and intemperance. The Sabbath-day is an encouragement to the first, and a preventive to the last. So the observance or profanation of this holy day is like a weather-glass, shewing signs of the rise or fall of a nation. This is also applicable to particular persons. The Sabbath, like its Lord, is a rise or fall to many; there is neither rank, riches, learning, nor talents, that can save the transgressors or the despisers of the fourth commandment from condemnation, while the humblest disciple that uses its privileges is exalted to honour, immortality, and glory. The Sabbath is properly termed the queen of the other days; and we may say that faith, hope, and love are her companions and servants. The gates of her palace are open, she invites all her subjects to her presence, and bountifully offers to satisfy all their wants. The Sabbath continues the same, though the ceremonial law has been abolished. Various comparisons in their greatest abundance cannot set forth the full value of the Sabbath to nations, churches, subjects, or particular persons. It is the memorial of the creation of the world, and the remembrance of the resurrection of Christ. It is the ordinance of our God, and the court day of our King. It is the seal of the covenant, and sign of our profession, the castle of the kingdom, the feast of the Church, the shield of the commonwealth; it is an almoner to the poor, a refuge to the weary, a teacher to the child, a guardian to the youth, a comforter to the old, a touch-stone of obedience to the professor, a day of jubilee on earth, the forerunner and shadow of heaven.

Attacks are made on the kingdom of darkness from this stronghold and castle, on the confines of the Church. To surrender it would render the territory gained by the militant Church an irreclaimable wilderness. We ought therefore to defend it, as most valiant soldiers, who when in possession of their stronghold will strive for every inch of the land against those who attack them. If the truths of religion are valuable, then the day for teaching them is important. If religion is good to bridle, her commandments to guide, her promises to support, then the Sabbath is of great value. If the public worship of God is to be supported, his Word to be read and preached, the sacraments to be administered, Sunday schools to be maintained, then the Sabbath is very delightful and valuable. Let us bless God for this day, and pray more to him that he may pour out his Holy Spirit to work powerfully, by the means we use on the Sabbath, till infidelity and irreligion are made to blush and are put to flight.'

2 Papers showing the loyalty of Elias

The loyalty of Elias, and his friends, will appear from the following documents. That loyalty, we are happy to say, was very genuine and faithful. The constitution of England they greatly loved and admired; they sincerely desired its preservation, and earnestly prayed for the public welfare. The Calvinistic Methodists are always glad to avail themselves of opportunities for manifesting their attachment to the throne. An address of congratulation to William IV had been made by them, on some occasion, most likely on his accession to the throne. Sir W. B. Hughes had been very kind in forwarding it to the Marquis of Anglesey, to be presented to his Majesty. No doubt it was drawn up by Elias; and we are sorry it is not now to be met with. But a resolution for a vote of thanks to Sir W. B. Hughes, and the letter that accompanied it, written by Elias, are in my possession, and shall be here introduced.

Llanfechell 20 September 1821

At a meeting of the Calvinistic Methodists, held at the New Chapel, Llandegfaen, 27 August 1821, on the motion of one of the friends, and seconded by another, it was resolved unanimously,

1 That the warm and sincere thanks of this meeting, and Connexion represented by it, be given to Sir W. B. Hughes, Knight, for his condescending liberality, and exertions on their behalf, in using his influence with the Most Noble the Marquis of Anglesey, to gain the permission of his Majesty for the above-mentioned Connexion, to lay their address before his royal person.

2 That John Elias be requested to send the thanks of the meeting to Sir W. B. Hughes, Knight.

We perceive, by such a document as this, the great respect that simple-hearted Christians in the Principality manifest towards the higher powers, when occasions require. It reminds us of the regard and submission of subjects, in ancient times, as recorded in Scripture. Such is always the effect of religion. The following is Elias's letter to Sir W. B. Hughes, accompanying the above resolution.

Llanfechell 20 September 1821

I am truly sorry that the task of presenting to you the warm thanks of our Connexion in Anglesey, happened to fall into such unskilful hands. But though I cannot do this with a dexterous hand, I can, however, with a sincere heart. We were anxious for some opportunity to send our dutiful and loyal sentiments to his Majesty; but to appoint a deputation to present our address was too great an honour for persons of our class and circumstances to expect; and had not you favoured us, we never could enjoy the privilege. To your kind application, and condescending favour of the Most Noble the Marquis of Anglesey, we are indebted for the honour of being admitted to the royal presence. Sir, though we cannot repay, at the same time we cannot forget your condescending liberality and kindness. We most heartily wish you, and your honoured and highly respectable family, the best things of time and eternity. That you, and every one of your family, may be

blessed with every temporal and spiritual blessing, both is and shall
be the prayer of your sincere and most humble servant,

J. Elias

Elias favoured me, the last time I saw him, with a copy of an
address they had just sent to the Queen, on her providential
deliverance from the fatal design of the assassin, *Oxford*, which
was forwarded by the son of the gentleman that assisted them
before, W. B. Hughes, Esq, M.P. Elias's letter to him for the
favour of aiding them in that respect, is the following:

Fron 24 June 1840

Dear Sir: I take the liberty of troubling you with the following
lines. We resolved unanimously at our Annual Association, held
at Llan-erch-y-medd, 19 June 1840, to send a congratulatory address
to her Majesty, our beloved Queen, on her late preservation from
an atrocious attempt on her valuable life.[1] Though we are as a
Connexion, an obscure and unostentatious part of her Majesty's
subjects, yet, at the same time, we will not yield to any denomination of Christians in peaceableness and loyalty. And our loyalty
not only consists in attachment to her Majesty's person, but also
to the British constitution. We are at a loss to know how to present
our address to her Majesty. We take the liberty of applying to you,
thinking that you know the proper channel to convey it, being
persuaded of your kindness, and recollecting the interest that your
late kind father took to have our address presented to his late
Majesty, George IV, at Plas Newydd. We presume to send the
present address to you, leaving it to your wisdom to have it
presented in the way that you think most proper.'

THE ADDRESS

To the Queen's most excellent Majesty:

We, your most faithful and loyal subjects, ministers, preachers, and elders,
of a denomination of Protestant Christians, called Calvinistic Methodists,
at our Annual Association, held at Llanerch-y-medd, in the county of
Anglesey, 13 June 1870, resolved unanimously, humbly to address your

---

[1] On 10 June, Edward Oxford, a youth afterwards pronounced insane, fired
two shots at Queen Victoria as she was driving through the Green Park, London.
She was uninjured.

*Majesty on your late wonderful preservation. We beg leave to express to
your Majesty our heartfelt sorrow and Christian indignation at the late
cruel and atrocious attempt against your Majesty's sacred person, and the
person of his Royal Highness, your illustrious consort. We sincerely con-
gratulate your Majesty on your preservation from so great a danger, and
from such a diabolical attempt. We are truly sorry that any person was to
be found in your Majesty's dominion, so destitute of the fear of God, and so
unconcerned with regard to the happiness of the nation, as to be capable of
attempting such a cruel act against your Majesty's person. We acknowledge
the mercy of God in the happy deliverance of your Majesty; and we feel it
our bounden duty to be thankful to the Almighty for protecting your
Majesty, and your Royal Consort, in such imminent danger, when the cruel
assassin 'imagined a mischievous device, which he was not able to perform.'
We offer our earnest prayer to Almighty God, in the name of the Redeemer,
in our public and private assemblies, that he would, in his infinite goodness
and mercy, keep your Majesty from all evil, and protect you in all dangers,
and that he may preserve your valuable life, which is so precious to us, for a
very long period; and that he may continue to us, in peace and undisturbed,
the blessings and privileges which British Christians enjoy, under the paternal
government of your ancestors and forefathers of the House of Brunswick, of
blessed memory; and which we are so plentifully enjoying under your
Majesty's mild government.*

Signed for the Association: JOHN ELIAS *Moderator*

EBENEZER DAVIES *Secretary*

25 June 1840

3 Short account of the life and death of John Lloyd of Beaumaris

John Lloyd has already been mentioned in the footnote on page
311. John Elias wrote a brief account of his life in a Memoir
containing some of his essays, speeches, letters, and prayers.
The account runs as follows:

'*Fron* 17 November 1831

There are innumerable proofs of that truth, "man that is born
of a woman, is of few days." The days of the longest-lived, are
but few: "He fleeth as a shadow and continueth not." We must all
die, as sure as we were born. "It is appointed for men once to die."

This appointment is so firm that it cannot be avoided by any means. "There is no man that hath power over the spirit to retain it; neither hath he power in the day of death: and there is no discharge in that war." No man can retain his own spirit when God requires it; neither can the nearest relative or the dearest friend retain the spirit of his beloved one from departing out of the body to the world of spirits when death comes, commissioned from above to take him away. When death is commissioned, he will by no means turn back, nor lay his arms down, till he has finished his work. It is in vain to lift up weapons against him, or to bribe him to depart, before he has accomplished his intentions. The strongest cannot withstand him by might, nor the richest bribe him with wealth. He will not listen to the deepest sighs, nor attend to the overflowing tears of the dearest friends.

Though the time of our departure is unknown to us, yet it is perfectly known to God. "Is there not an appointed time for man upon earth?" "His days are determined; the number of his months are with thee; thou hast appointed his bounds, that he cannot pass." We may be assured we shall not be here long; but we do not know how soon we may be called away. The unhealthy may think that death has already worked in his tabernacle, and the old that he shall be here but a very little time. But the young is not sure that he shall be here long, neither can the healthy and the strong be secure, thinking that death is far off. The young and the strong die; the tender, beautiful flowers are cut down. Though they are green, like Jonah's gourd, and their friends begin to rejoice in their shadow, yet some worm is prepared, and it smites them, so that they soon wither away, to the no small disappointment and grief of those who delighted in them. Few advance into old age in comparison of those that die young. Why are youth so thoughtless about death? Why so indifferent about being useful in their short time, and prepared to die, whenever death may come? To be ready for death is no impediment to a useful and happy life: but a state of preparation for death is the best in every respect; and nothing can be more delightful on the face of the earth than a young person living a godly life.

Nor is it an uncomfortable thing to see a pious youth die; for

God shows a greater favour to such, in calling them so early from the scene of labour to rest, or from the field of blood to bear the palm of victory; in taking them out of the reach of many snares, temptations and sorrows, without defiling their garments with any thing in this wicked world. The godly that were taken young out of the world will not complain in the blissful abodes because they did not continue longer here below, but delightfully rejoice that they so soon escaped out of a sinful and miserable world.

The subject of this brief account was one that was highly favoured by the Lord. He was born of pious parents, and consecrated to God when an infant; he was brought up in the nurture and admonition of the Lord. The Holy Spirit began to work early on his mind, so that he was preserved from those corruptions which are disgraceful and destructive to many a youth. He had great delight in the privileges of the Church of God, and entertained exalted and reverential thoughts of the Mediator between God and man. He highly valued the throne of grace, and had often great delight in drawing near it. It might have been expected that the Lord had some employment for a long time for him in his church below: but he had not so intended. He meant to leave him a while on earth, that it might be seen who were his people, and what was his delight, and then to take him to himself out of the troubles of this evil world. He left him to open like a beautiful flower for a short time, drew the attention of many to him, and then transplanted him to a world where his beauty and excellency will shine unspeakably more throughout eternity.

This young man, John Lloyd, was the son of the Rev R. Lloyd, of Beaumaris, and Elizabeth his wife. He was born on 4 June 1808, and baptized on the 17th of the same month by the Rev Rowland Hill of London.

The providence of God tenderly watched over him when he was yet a little child. A cart was one time very near going over and killing him. But God alone took care of his life, so that the wheel only touched one of his feet. He was in great danger at another time, when a horse came and attempted to bite off his face, but one of the angels started forward, and moved his head out of the horse's reach, so that he touched but the top of his ear.

Particular notice was taken of him from eight to ten years old, especially in being strenuous, earnest, and persevering in private prayers. Many an expression was audible; and the name of Jesus was most generally heard, evidently viewed as One infinitely worthy as a Mediator between God and man. He had been in school with a pious old woman from three to nine years old; and was afterwards, for four years, under the care of the Rev H. D. Owen, in a free school at Beaumaris, learning Latin. He was then removed to Mr Hastings' School at Chester, where he remained for more than a twelve month, attending to Latin, with some Greek, and several other useful branches of education.

Some of the Sunday-school teachers invited him, as soon as he came home from school, to take a share in their delightful work. They were in the habit of reading a chapter, and of asking each other the meaning of verses as they went on. This, it was thought, was the first thing that was particularly blessed to him. He was near twenty years old when he first approached the Lord's table, though he was encouraged by his friends to do so many times before. He had, after full communion with the church and partaking of the holy sacrament, a more enlarged and clear idea of the person and glory of Christ, in his work and suitability as a Mediator to a poor and needy sinner like himself, than he ever had before. Many of his friends thought there was not much difference between him and them in conversation and fellowship; but they perceived, when they observed him in private prayer, that he excelled in fervour and perseverance.

He was not from a child altogether healthy. Afflictions occassionally overtook him all his lifetime. His last complaint was occasioned by the distressing sight of the bodies of the persons that perished in the wreck of the *Rothsay Castle*, near Puffin Island. It produced such an effect upon him, that there is no doubt but it occasioned his death. He said to his father, when his mind was low and depressed in this affliction, that he was afraid his sins were not forgiven, though he was a member of the church. His father argued with him, and shewed that he had no ground to think so. He testified that he rejoiced in thinking of the way God had to forgive, and the delight he had in the privilege of forgiveness:

and his mind was made easy, and satisfied to a great degree. Some little time after this, when with his medical uncle at Caernarvon, his sister asked him if his mind was comfortable as to the state of his soul. He replied, that he was easy in that respect, as the Lord had arranged and settled all things concerning him. His mother having asked him what he thought of Christ, he meekly replied, in a few words, that his union with him 'still continued.' He experienced very little trouble in all his last illness. He had some view beyond mortal ken the last night of his life. He fixed his eyes upwards very attentively, with a very pleasant and sweet smile; and he did so many times, till his last hour.

His soul departed ten minutes before nine o'clock on Sunday morning, 2 October, to his blessed Lord, in the heavenly Paradise, through the merits of our great High Priest, Jesus Christ, 'the friend that sticketh closer than a brother.' In a little time the vessel arrived at the much-desired haven, out of the reach of all storms, where he now enjoys most delightful rest and eternal security; of this there can be no doubt.'

4 On singing, from the preface to Richard Jones of Wern's Hymnbook[1]

Fron 2 October 1835

Dear Reader – Here is a portion that one of Christ's servants, now in heaven, has left thee. It may be a great inheritance, not only to thee, but also to the Welsh nation for ages. The author served his generation laboriously and faithfully during his life, and he left these godly songs as testamentary gifts for them to enjoy after him.

The work shews the disposition and habit of the author's mind, that he lived near to the Lord, and that his meditations were often engaged with spiritual and eternal things.

There are some excellences in poetry that exalt it in some

---

[1] Richard Jones was a useful minister in the Calvinistic Methodist Connexion, as well as a composer of hymns.

respect above prose composition. It is well adapted to set forth the flights of the mind in meditation, especially on things that engage the affections. Poetical compositions on substantial and useful subjects are profitable to the reader. They are likely to impress the mind and affections, and to cleave to, and remain in the memory. A great portion of the holy Scriptures was composed in a poetical form; which proves that it is proper to compose observations and meditations on parts of Scriptures in the same way, if we take care that they are according to the analogy of faith, and that their tendency is evangelical and godly.

Many of these hymns now presented to the reader are worthy to be sung in divine worship, both public and private. Though we have abundance of godly songs in our language already, yet there is plenty of room for these too. The subjects of praise are so numerous, and the circumstances and experiences of Christians are so various, that it is very desirable to have a variety of spiritual songs, containing words of praise suitable to various subjects and circumstances. This book contains hymns and songs on many subjects, and explanations of many parts of Holy Scripture; it suits the experience of the Christian, in various circumstances – afflictions, or deliverances. We find herein songs on various subjects – on God and his perfections; on creation, providence, and salvation; Christ in his person, offices, humiliation, and exaltation; the Holy Spirit in his work of applying salvation, his grace and gifts in his saints.

I hope that this book will, under the blessing of God, be of great benefit to the nation for generations to come; and that many will have joy and edification, and God the glory due to his name, by the singing of the excellent hymns contained in this volume. It is the particular duty of every Christian to sing praises to God. It is likely that there is more singing of psalms and hymns in our country in these days than ever there was before. But every one ought to examine himself whether he *praises God by singing*.

We ought to attend to three things in singing – the tune, the words, and the state of our minds. (1) The *tune*, and the proper manner of harmonious singing. In order to sing in unison, and with melody in a congregation, tunes, and a proper manner of managing the voice, ought to be acquired. We should, in order to sing the praises of God, choose those tunes which are the most suitable to cherish sober and devotional dispositions in the mind, and engage all the powers of the soul. The praise is not contained in the voice and tunes, yet both ought to be adapted to the service of God. (2) The *words* of praise; we cannot sing the praises of God in every kind of words. The expression employed to set forth love, reverence, and gratitude to God, which animate the soul, ought to be proper and suitable. The words we use in singing to God's glory, whether in the form of psalms, hymns, or spiritual songs, should be all according to the analogy of faith, agreeing fully with the Word of God; and those who sing the praises of God, ought, at least, to consider and understand the words they sing. (3) The *state of our minds* in singing – 'Singing with the spirit,' 'singing and making melody in your hearts to the Lord.' It is as necessary to sing *to* the glory *of God*, in spirit and truth, as in performing any other part of God's service.

It is evident that the respected author of these hymns lived much in meditation on the subjects of which he sang so delightfully, He is now in heaven, understanding and enjoying those things in a manner we cannot now fully apprehend. May those that read or sing these hymns be led to live more with their affections and meditations on spiritual things, and then they will not, in death, be separated from the subjects of their affections and meditations.

Let us think, in singing the words, of the things contained in them, and take care that the disposition of the mind be suitable to the tenor of the words, that the expressions may set forth the melody that is through grace in our hearts to the Lord.'

Observations on Elias's writings

There are two of Elias's Treatises that are rather large: one on the *Sabbath*, and the other on *Justification*. And there are three rather smaller, each the substance of a sermon. The subjects of them are these, The Evil of Hardening under the Gospel, The Advantages of the Yoke to the Young, The Death of faithful Ministers. The date of each is given; but they are arranged rather according to the importance of their subjects and the connection they bear to each other.

Not much of Elias's oratorical gifts are retained in these publications. Indeed scarcely anything of that kind appears in them. That amazing overwhelming power flowed rather in his *extemporaneous* effusions. These publications contain, in some measure, the mind of an Owen, the point of a Baxter, and the simplicity of a Burder. I shall only direct the attention of the reader to the matter contained in them, making a few observations at the same time. Analysis of this kind may prove acceptable, giving people some idea of Elias's works, and inducing them to read. Bacon says that such remarks may serve important purposes, forming an index and synopsis.

Notice shall be taken also of Elias's discourse on the death of *King George the Third*, and another on the departure of the *Duke of York*.

1 The Sabbath

Elias's treatise on the Lord's day was one of his first publications, it was published in the year 1809. Though not so closely written as that on Justification, yet it contains equal power of thought, spirit and imagination. I do not know of any book that sets forth the duty of keeping holy the Sabbath day in so particular a manner. And it is remarkable for its persuasiveness, earnestness, and zeal for the due observance of that holy day; in fact, the subject is handled in a masterly manner.

This treatise comprehends in a small compass, much matter, yea, all that is necessary to be said on the subject for the use and benefit of the people. The following are the particulars that are chiefly discussed in the book. The *morality* of the command for keeping the day holy, the *change* of the Sabbath under the Gospel dispensation, the *nature* of sanctifying, or keeping it holy, with various exhortations and directions for the due observance of the day. He properly observes 'that the *whole* day, and not a part of it, is to be kept holy.' He also shews 'that the *whole* man is required for that purpose.' Here he particularizes every faculty of the soul, and every member of the body, as under the imperative command of God, to sanctify the Sabbath. He *urges* the observance of the Sabbath on several accounts, as 'from regard to God, the Sovereign Lord of time and all things; from respect to the Son, who rose out of the grave on the first day of the week, having completed the work of redemption; also from regard to the Holy Ghost, who descended on the first day of the week, the day of Pentecost, in a wonderful manner, to perform remarkable works; and because the Sabbath is a pledge of the perfect rest that remaineth for the people of God.' He sharply reproves the sin of *purloining* the sacred hours of the Sabbath.

Then he makes a few inferences, shewing, among other things, 'That as Sabbath-breaking is a transgression of the moral law, it is impossible to forgive it but through the atonement of Christ, who suffered the curse that was upon us for breaking the fourth as well as the other commandments, and that the Holy Ghost writes this also on our hearts, enabling us to conform to it.'

After this he exhorts the reader 'to pray earnestly for divine help in the work of sanctifying the Sabbath, leading us to things suitable to keep it holy, and to secure blessings on the means of grace.' He shews that the Sabbath 'is then a delight, and that the employments peculiar to it are sweet.' 'God's judgments on Sabbathbreakers are mentioned.'

Elias most seriously addresses three manner of persons, on the subject of sanctifying the Sabbath – men in offices and respectable situations, then heads in churches and families. The following is a typical exhortation:

'Ministers of the Gospel and church officers, be examples to the flock in good works. Shew the nature and excellency of the commandment to the people privately and publicly; also the duty, privilege, and benefit of keeping it holy: and on the other hand, the sin, the evil, and sad consequences of transgressing it. Correct and rebuke those that pollute the Sabbath by words or acts, especially professors, who by worldly, carnal, or vain conversation, corrupt themselves and others, before and after sermons, and consequently provoke God to blast their opportunities; for thus they deprive themselves of benefit in the means. You cannot be faithful without this.'

'To you, the heads of families most particularly, these words were directed, "Thou, nor thy son, nor thy daughter, nor thy man-servant, nor thy maid-servant." O! do your utmost to give good examples to your families for the due observance of the Sabbath, teaching and directing them to keep that day holy, commanding them to finish their work in time on Saturday evening, and thus to avoid occasions of breaking it. Alas, many a father and mother have sharply reproved their children for doing them a trifling injury, even the loss of a penny; but never said a word to them about the evil of breaking the Sabbath! O parents and heads of families, suffer not your children and domestics to pollute that holy day.'

Then he adds, 'I think that a reformation or declension soon appears in a church, according as the Sabbath is observed. When there is a revival in it, and powerful influences of the Spirit on the minds of the people, it is easy to attend to the Sabbath, and

to call it a delight; yea, they keep it minutely and holily: it appears
to them too short for the work. On the other hand, when there is a
decline in the church, there is less attention to the service of God.
To worship him becomes at length a burden; there is no enjoyment
in reading the Word, in hearing it preached, or in meditating on
it; nor in praying to God, in singing his praises, or in conversing
upon spiritual subjects. People are destitute of matter in their
minds for meditation, in consequence of not keeping the Sabbath
holy. There are no subjects in any of their thoughts suitable for
the observance of that holy day; consequently they come forth in
worldly conversation respecting their neighbours, or the most
common outward things of religion. The tenderness or obduracy
of conscience, the spirituality or worldliness of professors, appear
in their manner of spending the Lord's day.'

2 Justification

Elias's treatise on this noble subject is his principal work; he
understood it well, both experimentally and theologically. Indeed
he grasped it in a comprehensive, masterly manner; it is however
not diffusive and perplexing. But it requires considerable attention
and thought in the perusal; and this may be the reason why it is
not so universally read. People are fond of something light and
frivolous; however, this treatise will prove to a patient careful
reader, a great and delightful feast. It is wonderful how he could
have time to read and write so much and so well, with his other
numerous and important engagements.

The book is divided into ten chapters. Elias dwells in the *first*
chapter 'on the different meanings of the term justification in
Scripture, in order to arrive at the right sense of the word, as to a
sinner's justification. That is a grand subject.'

The *second* chapter is taken up with shewing 'that God is to
be considered in connection with this doctrine as a *Ruler* and that
he proceeds by law.' Then the attributes of this Ruler are viewed.
It is *in* the character of a Judge or a Ruler that he justifies.

In the *third* chapter Elias dwells 'on the *rule* by which the proceedings of justification take place.' He shews 'the necessity of such a rule for man's conduct in the first place towards his Creator, and then towards his neighbour.' 'It is the same as that implanted in man's nature, and written on tables of stone on Sinai. The sum and substance in both is the same.' 'Its perfection consists in this, that nothing can be added to or taken away from it.' 'Here also the extensiveness and unchangeableness of it are set forth.' He shews that 'the notion of making the law *milder* would bring great dishonour on God's name, and prove injurious to us.'

In the *fourth* chapter, Elias shews 'man's state as a *transgressor* of the law.' 'He is under the law,' says he, 'as the covenant of works, and consequently is in a sinful and miserable state, is unable to obey it in the *least* degree, yea, man is *indisposed* to observe the law; and yet, wonderful to relate, he *would* seek justification by it. But such a righteousness will not do for the law, therefore it continues to curse the sinner.'

In the *fifth* chapter Elias clearly shews 'that justification is *entirely* of grace; its signification in Scripture is *free* favour.' Then he proves 'that when we consider the Scripture representations of man and God, we must see that justification is of *grace*.' Then Elias observes, 'that grace, or favour, in each person of the blessed Trinity, is the *cause* of man's justification, shewing *how* it disposes each person to work in a particular way to save man.' Then Elias shews 'that God's end in this great work was his own *glory*, and that all boasting on our part is excluded.' Then he observes that this plan is consistent with God's attributes and government.

In the *sixth* chapter Elias clearly shews 'that it is *only* the righteousness of Christ that justifies the sinner.' He makes it very evident 'that man has not the righteousness the law requires.' Then he dwells on the nature of Christ's righteousness, and variously exhibits him in a covenant for that end; and clearly shews in what Christ's righteousness consists. 'It was done by him as Surety and covenant Head. It pleased the Father.'

In the *seventh* chapter he shews 'that God justifies a sinner by the *imputation* of Christ's righteousness.' The meaning of the word 'imputation' and its nature are considered, and also relationship with Christ as the foundation of that imputation. The doctrine of imputation is carefully investigated; and the effects of this imputation are clearly set forth. Objections to the imputation of Christ's righteousness are answered.

In the *eighth* chapter he satisfactorily handles 'this important doctrine of justification by faith. He clearly shows that the *testimony* of God respecting his Son is the foundation of justifying faith. He minutely views this faith in its various acceptations in Scripture. He states 'that the possessor of this faith, is a poor, guilty sinner, and that the object of it is Christ obeying and dying for him.' The acts of justifying faith are noticed. A few words by way of application are added.

In the *ninth* chapter the *privileges* of the justified are set forth, particularly the following: Peace with God, access to him, peace of conscience, spiritual joy, good hope through grace, sanctified affliction, perseverance of the saints, enjoyment of God's love, a happy death.

In the *tenth* chapter Elias shews very clearly the connection there is between justification and sanctification, and proves that believers cannot live in sin; they are one with Christ, and receive grace from him, grace reigns in them; sin is crucified in them; they love God; they long to be like to him, and to live more to him.

3 On hardening under religious privileges

Jeremiah 7.26

Elias delivered a sermon on the above subject, the great evil of hardening under religious privileges, at Llanrwst Association, 28 December, 1827, which was made very useful, and was some time afterwards published.

The following is a sketch of the sermon, with a few remarks:

TEXT
Yet they hearkened not unto me, nor inclined their ear, but hardened their neck; they did worse than their fathers. *Jeremiah* 7.26.

There is in this sermon an instance of Elias's happy mode of making an introduction. Then he shews that we are very much like the disobedient people mentioned in the text, though enjoying greater privileges; and that it may be said of many of us 'yet they hearkened not, nor inclined their ear.' 'Where,' he asks, 'are such rebellious sinners to be met with as in this Gospel land? Where can we find those that worship *nothing,* but in a country where the only object of worship is so clearly set forth?' Then he divides his text, proposing to speak:

1. ON HARDNESS
2. THE GREAT EVIL OF IT

1. ON HARDNESS. – Elias makes three observations on it – the nature, the causes, the effects of it.

1 *Its nature*
He notices that hardening is a metaphorical expression, denoting 'what is impenetrable, stubborn, unyielding, unbending.' *Ezekiel* 11.19.

This hardness is mentioned sometimes in Scripture, as being in the heart, face, forehead, as well as neck.

'Much is implied,' he says, 'in a stiff-neck, or hardening their necks. Israel were often called a stiff-necked people. No other persons are called so in the Bible. This sin belongs only to a people enjoying the means of grace. It signifies that they continue obstinate and disobedient, notwithstanding warnings, exhortations, and rebukes, together with all God's goodness and mercies towards them. It is a metaphorical expression, used in reference to many things. The metaphor is perhaps taken from a man, whose neck is so stiff that he cannot turn to him who calls after him, to hear what he says or wants. Thus is a sinner regardless of God, he will not turn to hear what he says, any more than if his neck were stiff as iron.' *Isaiah* 48.4.

'Hardening the neck is often taken in Scripture for refusing to hear. It may also be applied to the manner of a child struggling under the rod of correction, and becoming more obstinate; or to a bond-servant hardening himself under the scourge, ready to speak as the drunkard in *Proverbs* 23.35. Are not many thus regardless, notwithstanding all reproofs? Or it may be taken from the unruly manner of an ox, refusing to bend his neck to the yoke. How many, in various ways, are thus yet hardening the neck, and in a manner saying they will not have Christ to reign over them, notwithstanding all his entreaties?'

2 *The causes of this hardness*
It is natural for such to harden, yet some things are observed as producing this effect, such as

The *deceitfulness* of sin. 'This is done,' he says, 'by blinding the mind, misleading the judgment, enslaving the will, and beguiling the affections. It hides from man what he should see. Sin represents itself as most delightful, suggesting that it is hard to forbid the enjoyment of it. It commences by drawing man away from God and good things, and beguiling him from the path of duty into the conception of sin.'

Spiritual pride is another cause. 'The proud is too high to hear what the Lord says. Independence is the natural disposition of man, as seen in his conduct.' The ways to obviate this is shown.

3 *The effects of this hardness*
These are set forth in a striking and clear manner, as

Refusing to hear the word humbly, obediently, constantly, and affectionately.

Being without *understanding*, or not considering the things of God, though possessing great advantages.

Unbelief. Hardness is set forth as the cause of unbelief. *Acts* 19.9.

Impenitence. Sinners are too hard to change their mind and ways; but continue in their evil proceedings.

Being without the *fear* of God.

Resisting the Holy Ghost; being resolved to follow their own ways.

Hardening the heart against their fellow-creatures when in distress. And

Becoming *harder* in the commission of sin, as Pharaoh did.

2. THE GREAT EVIL OF HARDENING

Elias observes, 'They are inattentive to the words and works of the Most High, by which they are called to believe, repent, obey, and reform. They forget, and even reject out of their minds some considerations that arrested their consciences; they cleave to some carnal objects, their will bring very obstinate. They do not dread the greatness of God, neither do they fear the thunders of his threatenings; they are not softened by the sweet accents of his promises, nor by the delightful exhibitions of his wonderful love and free grace.' Then he notices the conduct and manners of people in the means of grace, as evidences of the evil; also their living in the vilest sins. He then observes that this involves,

The *greatest* rebellion against God.
Despising the riches of his goodness.
Loving darkness rather than light.
Quenching the Spirit.
Becoming unfeeling under the rod.

'The Spirit,' says Elias, 'shews men the evil of sin, yet they love it, and live in it; he manifests their dangerous situation, but they endeavour to close their eyes, that they may not see it; he exhibits the glory of Christ, and they despise it. The Word is the sword of the Spirit, but they disparage it, trying to turn the edge and authority of it away from them. Ministers are instruments in the hand of the Spirit, but they disregard them, reject their message, and view them as enemies, because they tell them the truth from God. Is not resisting the Spirit a most vile and abominable sin?

Elias speaks most faithfully, by way of application, to several sorts of people. The sermon concludes with advice to young people, and a word of consolation to those whose hardness is a burden to them, exhortations to feel and pray for those that harden themselves, and encouragement to ministers.

4 The advantages of the yoke to young people
Lamentations 3.27

This is another very useful Treatise of Elias; it has been very much blessed by the Lord for the conversion of several young persons. It originated in a discourse preached by him, on *Lamentations* 3.27, in the year 1812. 'I was induced to preach on that text,' says he, 'by heart-felt sorrow on account of the multitude of young people who live according to their own lusts, and under the dominion of Satan, rejecting the yoke of Christ; behaving themselves

as if it were lawful for them to live ungodly while young; thinking
that it would be sufficient to live religiously for a few days, under
affliction and in old age. It grieved me to the heart to see the flower
of men's lives spent in the service of sin and Satan, death seizing
many of them under circumstances of the most dreadful disappointment.'

TEXT
It is good for a man that he bear the yoke in his youth.

The preacher introduces his subject by observing 'that
Jeremiah had been under the yoke of God's government from
his childhood; and that he here declares the goodness of that
wherein the greatest part of men see none. "It is good for a man
to bear the yoke." '

Then Elias takes notice of the literal sense of the word *yoke*.
He considers the term in a metaphorical sense, as often used in
Scripture, observing that 'we are also to understand by it the
government of the Lord Christ.' *Matthew* 11.28, 29.

1 *First*, that man, by nature, is not under the yoke. 'He is not subject to
the law of God.' Men do not love the discipline of Christ because
they are not allowed to use such expressions, and to keep such
company, as they please, to walk in the way they would, and to
follow the customs they like. It is pleasant to them to be without the
yoke, that they may act as they like, without anyone to call them to
account. But awful will their condition be in the end.

2 In the *second* place, 'God bringeth unruly sinners under the yoke of
Christ; and though they are stubborn, yet God makes them submissive and willing in the day of his power. He causes his sharp
arrows to stick in their hearts, so as to make them fall under him, and
say, "Lord, what wilt thou have me to do?" bowing their necks to
his yoke.'

3 *Thirdly*, 'it is a great privilege to be under the yoke to Christ. It is
good to bear it. It is good in itself; even the yoke of affliction is
profitable. It keeps us from evil things, and binds us to the best
things.' *Psalm* 119.71. 1 *John* 5.3. *Psalm* 1.1. *Titus* 2.12.

4 In the *fourth* place it is a peculiar privilege to bear the yoke in the
time of youth, which is the most acceptable to God.' *Psalm* 127.3.

1 *Corinthians* 7.14. *Ecclesiastes* 12.1. Here Elias gives cogent reasons – 'that it affords peculiar advantages, to be useful for God in the world – and uses "most strong persuasives to induce the young to depart from evil." *Romans* 6.21. "The memory of such pious youths is honoured," he observes, "in Scripture; examples of which we have in Joseph, Samuel, Josiah, Abijah, Shadrach, Meshach, and Abednego, Daniel and Timothy".'

Here Elias addresses three sorts of characters by way of application, namely, 'youths that have not as yet taken upon them the yoke of Christ; those whose youthful days are gone, given to sin and Satan; and those who had the unspeakable privilege of being brought under the yoke in their youth.' Here are very useful admonitions and warnings. *Proverbs* 5.11, 12.

5 A sermon on the death of faithful ministers
Delivered at Pwllheli Association in 1825

Elias first gives reasons for the sermon: – 'In consideration of the painful circumstances of the churches in Wales, in consequence of the departure of several useful ministers this year, and especially of two, the Revds Ebenezer Morris, and David Evans, who had frequently preached at our Associations, under the divine blessing very delightfully, so that thousands heard them with great pleasure and profit, I judge it right to make the following observations.' The text is *Joshua* 1.2, 'Moses my servant is dead; now therefore arise, go over this Jordan, thou and all this people, unto the land which I do give to them, even to the children of Israel.'

The preacher begins by observing, that the Church is often in great danger, but that it shall be preserved through the mercy of God. Then he observes that the words of the text contain a call upon Joshua to enter upon the office to which he was ordained. Then he briefly comments upon the text, noticing the occasion of this call, and makes pertinent observations on the honour Moses had of being the *servant* of God. He also portrays the calm and happy frame of mind in which he spent the last month of his earthly pilgrimage. *Deuteronomy* 18.15. He then speaks of the *effect* his departure might have on the Israelites.

Next he draws five doctrinal observations from the text:

1 *That true ministers of the Gospel are servants of God.* 'They are to be known by the pureness of their doctrines, holiness of their lives, the genuineness of their motives, self-denial, and zeal for the glory of God. They are all *fellow*-servants; all should be *equally* humble; by *love* serving one another. Let them not seek for greater honour than that of *filling* their places as servants to such a Master.'

2 *True ministers of the Gospel are servants of God in his house.* Here Elias makes a comparison between servants *in* and *out* of the house of God; showing how superior one is to the other; observing, 'What a great charge it is to watch over souls!'

3 *Faithful servants in the house of God are deserving of honour.* Elias states what constitutes a faithful servant, and the nature of his responsibility; then observes, that he shall be rewarded by his good and gracious Master.

4 *God's most faithful and renowned servants die.* Here Elias mentions several important reasons why God calls them home. He describes God's preservation of Moses through many dangers; and shows how when he had finished his work, he was called home when no danger was near. He mentions what effect the departure of ministers should have on congregations.

5 *Though faithful ministers die, yet shall not the work of God be stayed.* Here Elias says many excellent things to encourage the church.

He proceeds in the next place to notice several things as incentives to ministers and others to take courage and go on. Then he addresses young and aged ministers, and states what they should take care of. He gives most faithful exhortations to all ministers. The preacher then directs our attention to the events which occasioned the discourse.

'It pleased God, for some wise end, to remove from us by death several of his eminent and faithful servants this year, such as the Rev Ebenezer Morris, one who was renowned, valiant, faithful, and laborious in the work of his Lord, one of the first three in the army of our spiritual David; also the Rev D. Evans, who was diligent, useful, and very faithful in the cause of Christ. It might be said of them, they were 'lovely and pleasant in their lives, and in their death they were not divided.' They died at the post of honour; death tore them from the heart of the Church. Oh what a pang she then suffered! They went to die in their robes, as Aaron did on Mount Hor. Their cloaks were not thrown aside, till, like Elijah, they were in their chariot, speeding homewards. They died in their strength like Moses, without abatement of their natural force; and like him they left the camp to ascend Nebo, to die, exhorting and blessing the people.

Then Elias addressed himself to the thousands who greatly lamented the departure of their ministers: – 'We shall see them no more in the pulpits, whence, like the dulcet silver trumpets, they have published the Gospel of reconciliation. We shall see their faces no more in our large Associations, where they often have been clouds, full of water, pouring the refreshing showers on the parched land; and where their evangelical and heavenly messages, "as cold water to thirsty souls," have caused the multitudes who heard them "to go on their way rejoicing." We shall see them no more at our church-meetings, where they have been as faithful and wise stewards, whom the Lord made rulers over his household, to give them their portion of meat in due season.'

He afterwards spoke, in a very solemn way, to the multitudes who had heard them unprofitably: – 'O ye people, is it a light thing for you to remember the exhortations, the tears, and earnest pleadings of the ministers, who are now no more?' Their pain on your account is now over, but if ye continue to despise salvation until death, your anguish beyond the grave shall never terminate! Tremble, therefore, ye despisers of the Gospel, lest the Master of the house, being angry, should say that none of you shall taste of his supper.'

6 A sermon on the death of King George the Third

Who departed this life 29 January 1820 in the eighty-second year of his age, and the sixtieth of his reign

The text is the following, 'And he died, and was buried in one of the sepulchres of his fathers; and all Judah and Jerusalem mourned for Josiah,' 2 *Chronicles* 35.24, 25.

Elias commences by observing the character of a true patriot. He notices Josiah's excellences: then

1 *The honour and obedience due to Kings.* He briefly and strikingly illustrates the names and appellations given in Scripture to kings, denoting their dignity and usefulness; and saying, 'If God sets up kings, and governs the world by them, he would have us honour and obey them.'

2 *Grief on the removal of a good King.* Elias sets this forth strikingly by several ideas; then finishes by such an exclamation as this; 'O! cruel death, the fears of a whole nation cannot turn thee away.'

Then Elias advances to the next part of his subject, observing that in many things there never was a king in Britain equal to George the Third. He notices his sobriety and early religious inclination; his great humility and dependence on God for aid; his fatherly care of his subjects, as to their temporal and eternal concerns; his knowledge of the way of salvation; that the Gospel prospered, and that excellent societies were established in his day. Then he relates several striking anecdotes respecting the good king, such as the following: 'It seems that there was a good man employed on his Majesty's premises, of whom he took notice. As he went about one Monday morning, he missed this person; he found out upon inquiry that he had been dismissed because he refused to do some work on the Sunday, which, as was stated by the master, was a matter of necessity. "Send for him back immediately," said the king, "the man that refuses to work on the Lord's day, is the man for *me*, send for him." '

'His Majesty was accustomed to rise early every day, and to spend an hour in his chamber, reading the Word of God and praying. He was often seen at the death-bed of his daughter Amelia, a pious princess. He used to stand over her, with tears running down his venerable countenance, exhorting and saying, "Trust in Christ *alone* for salvation, venture on him entirely, my beloved daughter." '

'The testimony of the late excellent Princess Charlotte is to the same effect. She observed, with tears, that her grand-father used to say often to her, "That *nothing* would make a dying bed easy, but true faith in Christ, and being under the influence of the Holy Ghost." '

'He greatly valued evangelical ministry, and good sound authors. It is said that some godly minister, whose turn it was to preach before his Majesty, had taken in mistake one of the plain sermons he had prepared for his poor parishioners. After he had preached the sermon before his Majesty, he made an apology, saying, "that the sermon had been prepared for his humble parishioners, and that he had taken it in mistake instead of another he had intended for his Majesty." "Well," said the king, "whenever you come here again to preach, be sure to bring one of the sermons for your poor parishioners; that is the sort of sermon that suits me." '

'The work of Dr Fawcett[1] on *Anger*, came into the king's hands. It was greatly blessed to him. He sent word to the author, saying, "He should be most happy to grant him any favour in his power, as he had derived so much benefit from his excellent publication. It happened some time after this, that a son of a friend of Fawcett had been tried for forgery, and condemned for the crime; he then reminded his Majesty of his kind offer. The king immediately granted his request, to the astonishment of all, as no instance of the kind occurred before.

'He was in truth the father of all his people, and a strong opponent of all persecutions. It was said that he would, if necessary, live upon bread and water to maintain a good government, and even sacrifice his life, to protect it from evil.

'The cause of the Lord prospered, and his Gospel had wonderful success under his reign, not only in England, but also in

---

[1] John Fawcett (1740–1817), Baptist theologian. His essay on Anger was published in 1787.

foreign parts. The slave trade was abolished: the Sunday School Society was established then: also, those noble institutions, the Missionary and Bible Societies. By these societies is accomplished what his Majesty greatly wished, "That every child in his dominions should be able to read."

'It may, in some degree, be said of him as of Solomon, that all "that came into his heart to make in the house of the Lord, and in his own house, he prosperously effected." 2 *Chronicles* 7.11.'

7 A sermon on the death of Frederick, Duke of York[1]

5 *January* 1827

The text is, 'Know ye not that there is a prince and a great man fallen this day in Israel?' 2 *Samuel* 3.38.

After making a proper and suitable introduction, Elias divides the text into the following heads: 1. That we ought to acknowledge the authority of those in exalted places. 2. That a prince, or a great man, dies like other men. 3. That their death calls for consideration and grief. Then he clearly points out the duty of people in different ranks of life. The departure of men is introduced in a forcible manner, such as the following, 'The degrees that distinguish people here, are not recognized in the other world. Greatness and glory of another kind are there. Nothing of an earthly nature gives a title to distinction and happiness in the world of spirits. The way to honour there, is by being *in* Christ as a new creature.'

He then directs attention to one that is evermore super-excellent, 'There is a Prince that is worthy of our confidence, "the Prince of the kings of the earth," one that was dead, but is now alive for evermore – *Revelation* 1.18. There is enough in his promises to supply all our wants. His riches, power, and fulness are inexhaustible. The humblest soldier may approach him in every difficulty. He will save such in every battle.'

[1] The Duke had distinguished himself by a speech in the House of Lords against the Roman Catholics' claims. April, 1825. He was humane in the army.

Then he thus observes on human frailty, 'Men, yea, the youngest, strongest, the most healthy, and sprightly, are compared to the *grass* of the field; and their goodness and glory to the flower thereof. *Isaiah* 40.7. The grass is weak and insignificant, but the flower is more so, as grass lives after losing its flower; but when the grass withereth, the flower is sure to fall. So it is with some men after losing their riches and honour; but when man falls in death, all his worldly excellences fade and vanish away. Riches, honour, strength, beauty, genius, learning, greatness, are as the flower of the grass, though so beautiful and gay for a little while, though so attractive and renowned; yet so soon will it wither, and all its glory vanish. The deadly stroke of death will bring the strongest grass down, and will cause the most beautiful to fall and wither. As we are to live for ever, let us set our affections on things that will continue longer than the greatest glory of this world, even on "things that are above, where Christ sitteth at the right hand of God." "Lay up for yourselves treasures in heaven, where neither moth nor rust doth corrupt." '

Index